FAR IN THE WASTE SUDAN

FAR IN THE WASTE SUDAN

ON ASSIGNMENT IN AFRICA

NICHOLAS COGHLAN

McGILL-QUEEN'S UNIVERSITY PRESS · MONTREAL & KINGSTON · LONDON · ITHACA

© McGill-Queen's University Press 2005
ISBN 0-7735-2935-7

Legal deposit third quarter 2005
Bibliothèque nationale du Québec

Printed in Canada on acid-free paper that is 100% ancient forest free
(100% post-consumer recycled), processed chlorine free

McGill-Queen's acknowledges the support of the Canada Council
for the Arts for our publishing program. We also acknowledge the
financial support of the Government of Canada through the Book
Publishing Industry Development Program (BPIDP) for our publishing activities.

This book was written while the author was an employee of the
Department of Foreign Affairs Canada. The contents of the book
reflect his own personal views and do not necessarily represent positions of the Government of Canada. They are, moreover, observations
of a particular period in Sudan (2000–03) and may not necessarily be
an accurate portrayal of the situation today. The author regrets any
unintentional embarrassment or offense that any of the facts related
in this book may cause to the individuals concerned.

LIBRARY AND ARCHIVES CANADA CATALOGUING IN PUBLICATION

Coghlan, Nicholas, 1954–
Far in the waste Sudan : on assignment in Africa / Nicholas Coghlan
Includes index.
ISBN 0-7735-2935-7
1. Sudan – Politics and government – 1985–   2. Coghlan, Nicholas,
1954–   3. Sudan – History – 1956–   4. Diplomats – Sudan – Biography   5. Diplomats – Canada – Biography   6. Canada – Officials and
employees – Sudan – Biography   I. Title.
DT157.673.C63 2005   962.404'3   C2005-902796-7

Set in 10.5/13.5 Minion Pro with FF DIN
Book design, typesetting, and maps by zijn digital

CONTENTS

FAR IN THE WASTE SUDAN

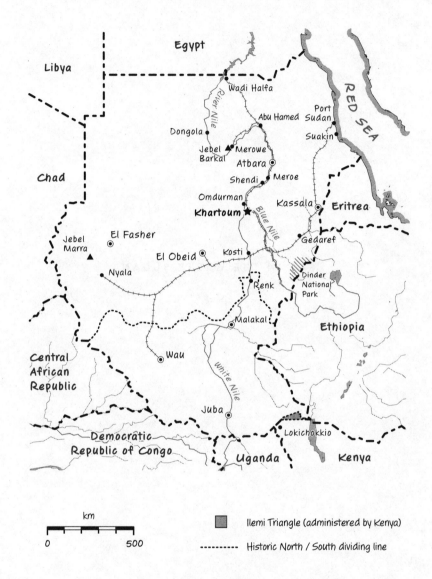

▨	Ilemi Triangle (administered by Kenya)
----------	Historic North / South dividing line

SUDAN

INTRODUCTION

SUDAN, THE LARGEST COUNTRY IN AFRICA, was known to Homer and Nero, but for centuries it was seen from Europe as little more than a desolate, empty hinterland of Egypt, even when Egypt was discreetly and unofficially folded into the British Empire in the late nineteenth century. Then, in 1881, a soft-spoken religious recluse called Muhammad Ahmad, who had for years lived on an island in the Nile 250 km to the south of today's Khartoum, declared himself a second prophet, or Mahdi. He called for a holy war against Sudan's decadent Egyptian masters and their Christian associates. By 1884 he had inflicted serious casualties on the British-commanded Egyptian garrison and controlled all of Northern Sudan except Khartoum itself. In London, Prime Minister Gladstone dithered over what to do, if anything, and was finally persuaded to send the country's latest hero – Charles Gordon – but only to evacuate the place. Gordon in turn delayed (rather inexplicably) and, in 1885, was spectacularly martyred by the Mahdi in Khartoum.

The Mahdi soon died, too – of typhus. He was succeeded by the Khalifa – but only in time for Britain to wreak its vengeance: in 1898 General Herbert Kitchener defeated the Khalifa's forces decisively outside Khartoum, and, the following year, Britain and Egypt signed a formal agreement by which they would rule Sudan jointly – the "condominium" of Sudan was thus born.

Britain was the senior, or at least the more effective, member of the partnership, but governing the Sudan – which ostensibly had little to offer in the way of natural resources or markets – was a thankless task, made no easier by the inexorable growth of political movements, which by the late 1940s had crystallized into two parties: the Umma, demanding complete independence for Sudan; and the Democratic Unionists, urging union with Egypt.

On the far side of a near-impenetrable swamp called the Sudd, Southern Sudan – ethnically, linguistically, and religiously having much more in common with southern Africa than the Middle East – was left pretty much to its own devices. Anthropology was then in its infancy, and a succession of learned white men travelled there to study the warlike Dinka, the Nuer, and a dozen smaller tribes, but the commissioners that were assigned to administer and police this vast territory made little impact. Using legal terminology that was also starting to be employed – at about the same time – to justify "separate development" in what is now South Africa, the British cordoned off Southern Sudan behind an east-west line that ran very approximately along the tenth parallel. Ostensibly, this was to protect the inhabitants of this region from the alien cultures of the North (and the line did coincide roughly with the extent of Islamic influence), but really it was an excuse that allowed the nabobs in Khartoum to neglect the South politically and economically.

By the mid 1950s, Britain had determined it was time to start quitting Africa; as one of the more troublesome and least productive colonies, Sudan was a good candidate to be the first to be abandoned. But barely had the official date for the handover of sovereignty – 1 January 1956 – been announced than Southern elements within the Sudanese Army concluded they were unlikely to get a fair deal from the new government and launched a rebellion.

Sudan's first period of civil war lasted from late 1955 until March 1972. The war varied in intensity and pace but was brought to an end with the Addis Ababa agreement of 1972, which ceded a degree of autonomy to the

South. Over the next ten years, this autonomy was gradually eroded – in part due to internal ethnic tensions within the South, above all between the Dinka and Nuer people – but the straw that broke the camel's back was President Nimeiri's introduction of sharia (customary Islamic) law to the entire country, including the animist and Christian South. War broke out once more in 1983; this time the rebels were grouped together principally as the Sudan People's Liberation Army (SPLA), under the American-educated Colonel John Garang.

In Canada, Sudan remained little known. There had always been a small but dedicated community of Canadian aid workers doing what they could to alleviate the perennial war- and drought-inflicted misery, and the country briefly grabbed headlines when the mastermind of a 1989 coup in Khartoum was assaulted by a bystander at Ottawa International Airport. But it was the arrival of a major Alberta-based oil company in Southern Sudan in the late 1990s and its role in bringing the first Sudanese oil to international markets that catapulted the country into the Canadian national consciousness and helped significantly to galvanize – or radical-ize – opinions throughout Europe and North America; Talisman Energy was accused by many of fanning the flames of Sudan's war and of helping an illegitimate and cruel regime maintain its hold on power.

It was in this context that Canadian Foreign Minister Lloyd Axwor-thy decided in early 2000 that the Canadian government needed an on-ground diplomatic presence in Sudan (which in formal terms would still be covered from our embassy in Addis Ababa, Ethiopia), so as to allow Ottawa to better understand and interpret the complex realities of the country. Although Canada by no means encouraged the ongoing presence of Talisman, the new office would also be available to provide consular support to the by-now sizeable Canadian expatriate population.

At the beginning of 2000, I was coming to the end of a three-year post-ing in Colombia, another country troubled by civil war and human rights abuses, and where oil was also a complicating factor. An earlier posting (1992–94) had seen me in Mexico at the time that country was convulsed by an indigenous uprising in Chiapas, with Canada coincidentally entering into the tripartite North American Free Trade Agreement (NAFTA) with Mexico and the USA. Although I spoke no Arabic, I did thus have some qualifications in reporting from conflictive locations where there was a Canadian stake, and I was accordingly chosen to be the first Canadian representative in Sudan, with the deliberately vague title of head of office (as opposed to ambassador or even chargé d'affaires). This is an account of the three years (2000–03) that I was privileged to spend in Khartoum.

This book is not a scholarly treatise on the origins of the current conflicts in Sudan, nor is it a polemic or critique of the present regime; it seeks neither to justify nor to criticize Canadian policy – nor to track methodically the various peace initiatives that were under way for the duration of my posting. Rather, it is meant as an impression – a series of snapshots at a particular moment in time – of an exceedingly complex country: it is at the same time home to the most hospitable people in Africa and to ruthless warlords and despots; it is beautiful but harsh and unforgiving; it has a colourful and romantic history familiar only to a now-diminishing coterie of aficionados of the late British Empire. I was lucky enough to meet with many of the key players in this period, from Talisman oil executives to Hassan al-Turabi and Sadiq al-Mahdi, and I have tried to let their words and deeds speak for themselves. Nevertheless, I could not ignore my own feelings; I was deeply affected by Sudan.

They say on the diplomatic circuit that you cry when you learn you have been posted to Sudan, but you cry harder when the time comes to leave. As I now go about business in one of the most beautiful, cosmopolitan, and inspiring cities in the world – Cape Town – scarcely a day goes by when I do not think with nostalgia of evenings sailing on Blue Nile, meetings with village chiefs in the baking desert villages of Northern Sudan, or flights on tiny United Nations aircraft deep into the heart of rebel territory in the lush South.

My memories are rendered even more poignant by – at the time I write this – almost daily coverage on the BBC and CNN of the horrors of Darfur, which were brewing when my wife and I made a memorable visit to the remote mountain ranges of the old desert kingdom in late 2001, but which we could not imagine would plumb such depths.

1

KHARTOUM

CLIMBING HIGH OVER THE PYRAMIDS OF GIZA, the plane soon finds the Nile and settles onto its course south. To the right the sun sinks over the western desert, and the golden brown sand turns first pink, then black. As we drone onwards, the pilot announces first Luxor, then Aswan and Abu Simbel. The names conjure up the 1920s: romance, comfortable decadence, and English tourists in white linen suits taking in the sights; the Winter Palace and the Old Cataract; Howard Carter and Agatha Christie.

Ninety minutes out of Cairo, we cross into Sudanese airspace. There are no more lights below, and the night is dark. We have left the Mediterranean, the Middle East familiar from almost every news bulletin for the past decade, and the Ancient Egypt about which everyone knows a little – we are now flying over Africa.

Khartoum. I remember the name from my English prep-school classrooms and the novels of G.A. Henty. 1885. The beleaguered Charles Gordon, soldier and man of God, the great hero of Empire, pitted against the evil, machiavellian Mahdi and his hordes of uncivilized dervishes, stoically awaits his fate in his desert fortress. The huge rescue expedition mounted by General Sir Garnet Wolseley labours its way up the Nile at a frustratingly slow pace, with the British public following its daily despatches with ever greater anxiety. The culmination of the adventure is operatic, as the Mahdi's fanatical dervishes storm the Residency and spear Gordon to death, while Wolseley is still two days away. Tennyson's eulogy echoes around the Empire:

> Warrior of God, man's friend, and tyrant's foe
> Now somewhere dead far in the waste Soudan,
> Thou livest in all hearts, for all men know
> This earth has never borne a nobler man.

And, finally, the long-coming but terrible revenge of Lord Kitchener, who thirteen years later – with his troops crying "Remember Gordon!" – obliterates the Mahdists at the battle of Omdurman; among the British ranks is one Winston Churchill. The thrilling saga was told indifferently in a 1960s Hollywood epic, with Charlton Heston as Gordon and Laurence Olivier as the Mahdi. *Khartoum*'s script was cheesy – Olivier, poorly made up in boot polish, had little to say other than "I am the Mahdi, the Expected One" – but the film had done nothing to diminish, to my ear, the resonance, mystique, and finality of the setting of this great drama: Khartoum.

AIRPORT ARRIVALS ALMOST INVARIABLY DISAPPOINT, but this one did not. I knew of course that Sudan was hot, but nothing had quite prepared me for the oven-like blast of air that met me on the stairway down from the plane (or for the heat from the steel handrail): it was 10 p.m. but the temperature was still above 40 degrees. People have reportedly been known to wilt at this moment and get back on board, without ever having set foot in Sudan, while a common misapprehension is that the jet engines must still be on, at too high a pitch and blowing their exhaust over the stairs. On the tarmac, a tall man in a long white robe, his head swathed in a white turban, inscrutable behind dark glasses (why? at this time of night?), held his hand out to me and said: "Welcome to Sudan, Mr Coghlan. I am Salih el Kronki, from the Foreign Ministry."

Khartoum airport, its runway aligned north/south with the prevailing winds and parallel to the Blue Nile, is only five minutes' drive from the centre of town. The airport authorities are lackadaisical, fatalistic, sometimes mysterious. Legend has it that one night they failed to switch on the approach lights for an incoming Boeing 707 cargo plane, operated by Aer Lingus; the pilot mistook the adjacent dark strip of the river for the runway and neatly put down his plane on the Manshiya Reach, where it obligingly floated long enough for the crew to clamber out then sank never to be seen again.

More seriously, three or four years ago, an incoming passenger plane arrived overhead at the same time as a haboub, one of the ephemeral but blinding sandstorms that may envelop the city for two or three hours at a time in summertime. Low on fuel and with the nearest alternative airport at least an hour away, the aircraft was heard by half the city, circling ever lower until it finally crashed in the slum quarter of Haj Youssuf; "It was the will of Allah."

Once, at 2 o'clock on a hot but dazzlingly clear blue afternoon, I went out to the airport to meet the incoming Ethiopian Airlines flight. "We have told them to go back to Addis," I was informed, "because the airport is closed." No-one could say why, and no-one even seemed curious.

Even more mysterious were events that took place here shortly after the attacks of 9/11. For years, parked among assorted dilapidated aircraft to the south of the terminal building, including an ancient DC-3, which years ago had flown the Falasha Jews out of Ethiopia, and an Aeroflot biplane, there had been a small executive aircraft that had once been used by a lieutenant of Osama bin-Laden to run guns. It had been seized by the Sudanese authorities. On 12 September, it "spontaneously" ignited and was burnt to a shell; none of the other aircraft was damaged. This was reported solemnly, unembroidered, in the press.

A few days later, a handful of people somnolently awaiting a delayed incoming flight from El Fasher were abruptly ushered out of the terminal, on the grounds that there had been a bomb threat. As they left, several looked over their shoulders; they later told reporters that they had seen twenty or thirty men "with long beards" being hustled aboard an unmarked grey-painted plane. The rumour spread that these were erstwhile al-Qaeda members who were being flown out at the behest of the USA (to Chad, supposedly), but the Americans vehemently denied it.

LIKE ALL SUB-SAHARAN AIRLINES, Sudan Airways was at the centre of many jokes and much black humour. Known as Inshallah Airways due to its fleet's punctuality and performance being subject less to human control than to the will of God, its motto was "We have six thousand years of history," a boast that inevitably attracted add-on comments like "and our planes are that old, too." Despite concerns regarding aircraft maintenance, Sudan Airways was said to be safe, at least, from terrorist attacks: in the first place, it was the airline most used by terrorists, who would never bite the hand that fed them; and, in the second, it was bombproof because no-one could ever forecast takeoff time within a margin of twelve hours.

Most of the aircraft used on internal flights were noisy and polluting Antonovs on charter from Russia or Ukraine and flown by Russian crews; I once sat by what was evidently meant to be the emergency exit, puzzling over a series of instructions in Cyrillic that appeared to explain how to use, in case of a crash, the thick hemp rope coiled under the seat in front of me. Flights would begin and end with long prayers, and the itinerary was always uncertain; even on international routes, such as London to Khartoum, the pilot might announce that Paris was being skipped tonight, on account of there being insufficient passenger interest, but a stop would be made in Cairo instead.

The airport itself was always clean but inhabited at night by legions of lean, generally tortoiseshell stray cats, who, under the bright fluorescent lights, would calmly clamber over the baggage carousels or through passport control. On arrival there was a Green customs channel and a Red channel, but, no matter where you stood, everyone was invariably searched, and thoroughly. Mainly, of course, they were looking for alcohol, which would righteously be poured down the sink in front of ashamed miscreant passengers, and anything looking remotely pornographic; a friend had his CD of the soundtrack of *The English Patient* confiscated, on account of its "unseemly" nature. Strangely, there were equally thorough searches going out, but no-one could ever tell me what they were looking for. Also strangely for the country's main airport, there were no arrival or departure boards: you had to observe critical masses forming at unmarked doorways and make enquiries.

For an international airport, there were very few international flights, and the majority left and arrived at the dead of night. Whereas fifteen years previously, British Airways, KLM, Air France, and Lufthansa had flown in, Lufthansa was now the only European leftover, and even it suspended services for a couple of months following 9/11. This was seen as symptomatic of the general decline of Khartoum from being a lively, vibrant, and worldly African capital in the late 1980s to its present plight as a sleepy and rather joyless backwater; "the fundamentalists" were generally blamed.

In the course of my three-year stay, I took Sudan Airways as little as possible; some embassies forbade their expatriate staff to use them and strongly counseled their nationals likewise. Concerns about aircraft safety were tragically confirmed when a Sudan Airways Boeing 737 crashed just after takeoff from Port Sudan on 8 July 2003; 115 passengers and crew were killed, and the cause was thought to be mechanical malfunction. Later it was suggested that the chief pilot had handed over controls to the novice copilot – "as a learning experience" – when one engine failed just after takeoff.

As long as my mission was in some way connected with development, I could normally get a ride on one of the flight of three light aircraft maintained by the United Nations' World Food Programme (WFP). Takeoff was always around 7:15 a.m., which meant getting to the domestic terminal at 6:30 a.m., just as the sun was rising over the far side of the runway, then checking in with the invariably surly Mustafa, WFP's flight dispatcher. The South African crews were always cheerier, and I soon got to know most of them. Tony, the senior pilot, had been flying in Sudan for at least seven or eight years, adeptly jumping from one company to the other, as contracts were renewed on an annual basis. They were all scrupulous about not drinking the night before flying but were nevertheless very active on the party circuit and very popular with the ladies (including, notoriously, the wife of a senior and well-known Western diplomat).

FOR OUR FIRST SEVEN WEEKS, my wife, Jenny, and I put up at the Khartoum Hilton, an ugly oblong Canadian-built block close to the confluence of the Blue and White Niles. The first odd thing we noticed about this Hilton – apart from there being no bar – was that, although it sported the Hilton logo on everything from the shampoo bottles to the teaspoons, Khartoum was not actually listed in the in-house magazine as a Hilton location. Because of comprehensive US economic sanctions, this and the Port Sudan Hilton had been hived off from Hilton International and parked in a Kuwaiti holding company. The second odd thing was the cost: USD $220 for a damp-smelling box-like room. The conventional explanation was that, due to the alcohol ban, the hotel had to make all its profit on the rooms, but most people thought it was more likely because there was almost no competition. The restaurant wasn't bad – it could probably claim to be the only Western-style restaurant in the city – but in our three years in Khartoum the menu never varied: Tuesday was Indian night, Wednesday Thai night, and so on. There were only two other hotels that could be said to be of a Western standard in all of Khartoum: the splendidly located but rather musty and reputedly infested Grand Holiday Villa on Nile Avenue and the Acropole.

Winston Churchill supposedly stayed once at the Grand, and it was a regular stop on the itinerary of Imperial Airways' flying boats, which, in the 1930s, would put passengers ashore within a few yards of its front portico. The Greek-run Acropole was located in a once-lively but now darkened and quiet area of downtown Khartoum, with no pool or garden. The rooms were frankly indifferent: shiny grey institutional paint, many with no windows, or windows that opened directly onto walls. But the ever-helpful George and his crew were legends in their time. No assignment or request was too much for them, as dozens of journalists, archaeologists, aid workers, and celebrities had found: pinned to the receptionist's wall was a glowing letter of praise from Bob Geldof, who stayed here in the 1980s at the time of one of Sudan's great famines. One feature that the management was unlikely to mention, but which would be joyfully if furtively pointed out by the cognoscenti, were some innocuous-looking indentations in the wall of the hotel annex: Abu Nidal terrorists once threw a grenade in here, killing several innocent diners.

The Acropole was also the only place in Khartoum where you could read a European newspaper. George paid small boys to befriend the Lufthansa cleaning crews, and three times a week they would ransack the incoming flights from Frankfurt for Herald Tribunes and Deutsche Zeitungs. Often, the copy you were reading might have coffee stains on it, or the crossword half complete.

Back at the Hilton, while workmen laboured at a snail's pace to ready our house in upmarket Amarat, we were soon racking up bills. This was a problem because no credit cards were accepted in Sudan, and most travellers' cheques were similarly rejected – especially those from American Express. I had known this and had alerted my employers to the fact but, of course, they had nevertheless still provided me with only American

Express cheques, and only an hour or so before leaving Canada. I would have to get by somehow.

The Mashreq Bank was delighted to take the cheques and open an account for us, but there was one drawback: it would take at least a month before the bank could clear them and thus allow us to draw any cash out again (this again due to sanctions). We counted up our meagre personal stache of US cash and decided to start stinting on the buffet. Even so, as the weeks went on, it became more and more of an ordeal to get past the front desk, where our attention would politely be drawn to a bill that after three weeks was in excess of USD $5,000.

AMARAT, THE QUARTER IN WHICH A HOUSE had been found for us, was also known as the New Extension and was widely and casually referred to as "the posh area of Khartoum." First impressions, though, were not positive. Although the quarter was laid out in a grid pattern in the 1950s, just before the British left, the then-asphalt roads had now either broken up completely or were buried in sand. In fact, where Street 29 (our street) met Middle Road, on a corner occupied by the Saudi Arabian Embassy, the sand was so deep and fine that you could easily get bogged down in it.

Men on donkeys would pad up and down at all hours, and large goats that apparently belonged to no-one would munch garbage, especially plastic bags, in front of our gate. In the morning, an entire industry would set up around the Saudi Arabian Embassy: there were men at tiny tables with typewriters, cables snaked down from overhead to power photocopiers, colourfully dressed tea ladies offered cups of hot chai, and, a few months after we arrived, a portable mosque was set up – all this to serve the hundreds of visa applicants that lined up every day, growing to thousands before the Haj season. This activity would spill all the way down to our end of the road, so that we had our own resident tea lady in front of the house for half of every working day.

Closer to the house, on the corner with Cemetery Road, there was a baker's where, at any hour of the day, you could buy ten miniature baguettes for fifty dinars (USD $0.20), and the Gaza Centre, a minimart that usually stocked milk and yogourt and where, for a few hours on 12 September 2001, posters of Osama bin-Laden appeared. Just around the corner and very convenient for the cemetery was the intriguingly named Mohammed Salah Idris Bleeding Centre. The length of Cemetery Road there were colourful fruit and vegetable stalls, in front of which the owners would sleep at night on their steel-framed string beds, wrapped in their white djellabiyas. Many of the buildings on Cemetery Road were only half-finished but nevertheless inhabited; it was said that if you lived in or owned an unfinished building you could thus avoid paying property tax.

Also on the sidewalk outside our high wall was a pair of ancient-looking amphorae in a specially designed metal framework. As good citizens, it was our duty to keep these full of water for passersby; this tradition, widely observed throughout Khartoum, seemed to me one of the more positive dimensions of day-to-day Islam.

Our large two-storey white house faced south (the favoured direction: the months when the sun was north of Khartoum were already unbearably hot, without what would have been the added agony of the sun shining in our front windows). As is typical, the rooms were large and high-ceilinged and there was absolutely no storage space at all; we had to have closets built in and resigned ourselves to using one room just to dump things in.

Also typically, the finishing was poor and few items of equipment ever worked reliably. There were upside-down door handles, and doors that didn't close or that left inch-wide gaps at their foot; there were burned-out lights in totally inaccessible locations and inexplicable wires hanging out of walls. It was a given that in summer the power would go off for eight or ten hours at a time (the explanation was always that the Roseires hydroelectric dam was either too full, or not full enough), which meant cranking up the giant generator hidden behind bushes by our front gate; but even this monster could not power everything, so that sometimes we would have to choose between having the fridge or the air-conditioning on. If the power went in the night, there was usually a sickening whirring as every piece of machinery in the house wound down, a pause, then a noise from the neighbourhood like a tank regiment warming up, as generator after generator was cranked up. Then the lights would come back on with temporarily blinding brightness. I gave up using the electric clock at my bedside, because every time the power went it would reset itself to 12:00. Another eventuality to be guarded against was that the cutoff valve on our rooftop water tank would periodically fail, and we would be woken in the middle of the night by the noise of water cascading down in a great curtain from the flat roof.

We had a beautiful garden, dominated by an enormous date palm. One evening I came back from the office to find Joseph, one of our three guards, gazing up into it. Upon close examination I could see a pair of legs hanging down. "It's the date fertilizer," he explained. His services cost us USD $1 a time, but, whenever the wizened old fellow arrived and started shinning up the tree in his bare feet, I worried that he would fall and impale himself on our spike-topped wall.

We had three guards (or gaffirs) – Joseph, Michael, and Amir – who rotated on and off duty in a routine that only they seemed to understand properly. Amir was later promoted to become embassy driver and was replaced by Santino. Joseph and Michael were Southerners, as is most of the servant population of Khartoum, and were loyal and friendly but always seeming to live on the edge. Their families were struck by tragedy after tragedy: Joseph's brother in the Army died of heat exhaustion, then he himself went down with malaria, while Michael spent all of his leave one year vainly trying to get on a cheap flight to Juba (which can only be reached by air) so as to claim the Army pension of his brother, who had been killed in action. They were always borrowing their meagre salary in advance, to purchase then kill a goat for a cousin's wedding, or to travel for a faraway funeral. It was senseless and inappropriate to argue that they should save their money; they were only paying their share into an informal social security network from which, in due course, they could also benefit.

We didn't really need guards: Khartoum is perhaps the safest big city in Africa. But they were expected to perform a multitude of other miscellaneous duties: turning the generator on and off, allowing the electricity- and water-meter men in, helping the gardener mow the lawn, watering (an endless job), supervising the car parking at receptions, opening the gates when we drove in. They also served to shoo away mischievous small boys and, when the water went off in the neighbourhood, to mete out carefully measured supplies to our neighbours (we seemed to be immune from these particular cuts).

We also had a gardener, or rather a series of gardeners. The first was a tall and silent Dinka called Zachariah, who spoke absolutely no English and very little Arabic; he simply disappeared one day, after announcing he was going to look for a job in the oilfields. Then there was Gabriel, who was rather lazy and also disappeared, having mystifyingly told us "my visa for the USA has arrived." There were one or two others whose names I forget, but the best was Peter, who was so keen that he would sometimes wake us up by mowing the lawn at 5 a.m. When the handmower broke (a frequent occurrence), he would go down on his knees and do the job with shears.

Sometimes, the gardeners had special requests. I made several trips to a mud-built slum on the edge of Omdurman, where a man kept some twenty or thirty goats, whose apparent only food was, true to form, plastic bags. Here we solemnly raked through goat droppings while Zachariah assessed their quality as lawn fertilizer, then offered a price; or we would go down to the main souq to buy bags of urea, which was apparently essential if you wanted your lawn to survive.

And there was Stella – dark, diminutive, and usually smiling bashfully – she was also a Southerner, from near Juba. A fervent Christian, she would sing very softly as she dusted and cleaned. But her life was not all happy.

Sometimes she would confide in Jenny. Her family had fled North after a raid by the rebel Sudan People's Liberation Army; two sisters had been hacked to death before her eyes. Her husband, a warden at one of the nearby Christian churches, had a baby with another woman, and Stella often wondered whether she should leave him. Once she spent nearly two weeks waiting all night, every night, to get a ride on a cut-rate military plane to Juba; a middleman took her money, gave her no receipt, then told her he had spent the money. She ended up paying more on a commercial flight. One day a cousin died, and it fell to her to host all the relatives who came into Khartoum for the funeral; they ended up staying for weeks, and she was expected to tend them, hand and foot. For a while she asked Jenny to keep her money at our house, because they were always asking her for pocket money, which she could ill afford to give away.

Stella seemed an innocent in a world of evil and hardship. Yet she was quietly determined to better herself. She assiduously learned new recipes from Jenny's mother and my father when they came to visit (Delia Smith's Shepherd's Pie ...), attended English classes through the church, and started taking typing lessons.

AN ARRANGEMENT HAD BEEN MADE WITH the British Embassy whereby it would lease to us a suite of three offices on the ground floor of its large twenty-year-old brown-brick building off Baladiya Street. The building included electricity, air-conditioning, telephone lines, a swimming pool, and a security perimeter; we could also make use of the British reception staff. It would have taken me months to set up something similar had I needed to start from scratch. This was called *colocation*, and Canada had similar arrangements in a number of other countries where the intention was to have only a minimal diplomatic presence.

Because bilateral relations between Canada and Sudan were none too warm (for reasons that will become apparent later), my establishment was not called an embassy (lest that imply an undue degree of recognition); rather it was an Office of the Canadian Embassy, formally dependent on the Canadian Embassy in Addis Ababa, and I held the dreary title of Head of Office. The ambassador was almost permanently in Addis.

It all worked well enough, although some visitors were understandably confused as to the exact status of Canada when they found our office inside the British Embassy past a dual-purpose watercolour of Queen Elizabeth. This confusion was only increased when I opened my mouth and they heard a British accent. "But isn't Canada independent these days?" they would ask.

The British themselves were friendly enough, but not effusively so. I wondered occasionally if there was an unspoken resentment at having in their midst someone who had been born and grown up in the UK but had then voluntarily renounced England for Canada. I had access only to the Canadian section and had to be escorted if I wished to see anyone in the main chancery; in fact I saw less of the aloof British Ambassador than of most of my international diplomatic colleagues.

Very usefully and generously, I had the right to frequent the Pickwick Club, the embassy's weekly Thursday-night bar, named after a long-lived (but now dead) parrot that had been the bar mascot for decades. The Pickwick was a very popular establishment in otherwise dry Khartoum. But to get in you had to be non-Sudanese, and you had to be on the "list" of one of the British expat staff or on my own. If guests disgraced themselves, for example by getting very drunk or falling in the pool, then their sponsor also lost visiting and inviting rights. I was always careful not to invite too many guests – and almost never anyone from Canada's controversial oil company, Talisman – because early on I heard a senior British diplomat complaining to a colleague that "the damn place seems to be overrun with Canadians these days." The oil men were in fact invited by other Brits, but I was determined never to be accused of abusing British hospitality.

Inside the main reception area, and at the entrance to the Canadian suite, I put up the Canadian coat of arms, in the standard sober mock-silver alloy. But I was then politely but firmly told that if I wished to keep this on the wall then, "for the purposes of symmetry," the British would also wish to put one up. "Fine," I said, nevertheless a little mystified, as there was no lack of British symbols on the exterior of the building. "And we expect you to pay for it," added the administration officer, "as we wouldn't have had to put it up otherwise." Two months later there arrived a full-colour British version and a bill for nearly fifteen hundred pounds.

KHARTOUM WAS THREE CITIES IN ONE: Khartoum proper, on the *h*-shaped tongue of land where the north-flowing Blue and White Niles converged; Omdurman (the traditional capital) on the west bank of the White Nile; and Khartoum North on the east bank of the Blue. The three cities were linked by two bridges over the Blue, two over the White, and one over the combined Blue and White – the Nile proper. As there were no mountains for hundreds of kilometres around, and the colour distinction between the Blue and White was not operative for half the year (when both were an identically muddy brown), getting around and keeping a sense of direction could be rather difficult. To compound the confusion, two of the bridges were to all purposes identical Bailey-style, reportedly brought over piece-by-piece from India in the 1950s after they had already served for a century on the subcontinent.

Although grid patterns were generally followed, in Khartoum itself this system was complicated by a number of diagonals, reputedly forming – if looked at from the air – a Union Jack; this made for some dangerous junctions. Street names were only marked very rarely, and then there might be several names for one street: Africa Road, for example, was also known as Airport Road and King Abdul Aziz Road. House numbers were not used at all. This meant that if you wanted to have a social life, one of the first things you had to do was make an easily reproduced map to your home using commonly known landmarks.

Favourite landmarks were the monuments that adorned many of the roundabouts in central Khartoum. Some of these were now being removed to create dangerous expanses of tarmac where you were supposed to obey traffic lights (but no-one did, and the lights didn't work half the time). Some of the more popular landmarks were known as The World, The Two Balls and a Cup, and The Coffee Jug. An old Mig fighter, which used to stand near the Hilton, was for a while another famous monument.

The streets were wide but borderless, sometimes paralleled by deep and half-concealed drainage ditches that often broke the axles of the unwary; while fewer and fewer roads in the downtown area were now of dirt, for much of the year they might as well have been, as a fine brown dust infiltrated everywhere. It wasn't for nothing that a feature of the traditional dress here was making your turban double up as a mask, so that only the narrow band of the eyes was exposed to dust and wind; at night, crossing poorly lit roads, ghost-like figures flitted across in your headlights. These days the streets were ever-more crowded with cars: some, bearing the legend GIAD, were Hyundais assembled in Sudan, but Toyota Hilux pickups had at least one third of the market, and old yellow Corolla taxis another important share.

It was wise to do a little bargaining before you got in a taxi and accept that the driver would want to overcharge hawaijas (white foreigners), but after that you could expect a positive experience. There might be some genuine confusion over the fare at the end. When the driver signalled "five" or "six," he was saying to himself "five thousand" or "six thousand," but that was in Sudanese pounds, a denomination of currency that theoretically had gone out of use several years earlier. The notes you had were in dinars, and actually you needed to pay five or six hundred of these (about USD $2). If the engine sputtered to a halt and the driver asked you to get out and push (as quite frequently happened), it was not a scam: he would wait for you as soon as the taxi chugged into life again. You had to beware of getting in with a good pair of trousers: the springs sticking through the faded red velvet upholstery would wreck them; you had to expect no air-conditioning, just windows with no glass. It was necessary to perform contortions to get out, sometimes spraining your wrist, as the inside handles and locks rarely functioned.

A cheaper alternative to taxis were the ever more ubiquitous rickshaws, or tuk-tuks: three-wheel made-in-India scooters with a small canopy that could seat two slim passengers. These could negotiate gaps much narrower than the girth of a taxi and could also manoeuvre between the obstacles on sidewalks. The disadvantage was that they capsized quite easily. A common scene was a tuk-tuk on its side, probably knocked over by a taxi or bus, with its driver (who was not usually the owner) making off before the police arrived.

The driving was atrocious, but many of the streets were so potholed, the cars so ancient, that no-one achieved any great speed; collisions in the city were not usually life-threatening. A particularly common cause of accidents was when a driver arrived at a roundabout and wished to turn left; instead of first going all the way round to the right in an anti-clockwise direction, he would simply cut the corner and frequently collide with a more law-abiding car or bus, hidden by the roundabout, coming the other way. In Cairo such a happening would cause a massive blockage of traffic, much honking of horns, and a violent argument in the middle of the highway in which dozens of people might become involved; in Khartoum everyone would get out very calmly to contemplate things and await the arrival of the police, usually there would be a rueful "Maalesh" ("Sorry") and the matter would be resolved quietly with a visit to a nearby panel-beater.

For the first six weeks or so of our stay, before our car arrived in Sudan, we used the services of the well-known Abdul and his old Corolla, usually to be found outside the Acropole Hotel. Abdul claimed to have driven for the British Army, during or just after the Second World War; certainly he was getting on a bit. In broken English he would mutter about the dastardly deeds of the current government, occasionally producing – apparently with no connection to the topic under discussion – a black and white photo of one of his several émigré sons. He knew Khartoum backwards but would not drive at night. Every few weeks, after we had our own car, we would bump into him; he was invariably cheery and asked how the embassy work was going.

THERE WASN'T MUCH TO DO for foreigners in Khartoum. One attraction, the archaeological museum, down near the Hilton Hotel, was usually empty of visitors. The labelling was poor, and there was no evident chronology. Most interesting were the reconstructed temples outside, rescued from the Sudanese portion of Lake Nasser when the Aswan High Dam was built.

The Republican Palace was a large wedding cake of a building reconstructed on the site of the British Residency, looking out over the Blue Nile; built between 1898 and 1900, it was reportedly in similar proportions to the original, but rather more grand. James Morris reports, in *Heaven's Command*, that in 1885 the Residency "was a dingy building of two stories, grey with green sunblinds, likened in one sufficiently macabre comparison to an Egyptian boarding house ..." The new Palace could not be visited by the general public, or even photographed. In the daytime you could drive – but not walk – past the front, on Nile Avenue, where two turban-clad dervishes kept guard. The young men of Khartoum's "in" set delighted in honking their horns as they approached; the guards would immediately come to attention, as the honking was supposed to indicate a general.

Tourists also took in the souq at Omdurman. This was interesting but very much a working market, where at most some trading beads might catch your fancy; many supposedly ancient beads had in fact, so said the experts in such matters, been cleverly aged by passing them through the gizzards of a live turkey. There was also the camel market on the desert edge of Khartoum North. Sudanese breeders claimed their camels were the best in the world, and indeed breeders and traders flocked here from the Gulf and Egypt to look for good racing and stud specimens; an average mature male camel would set you back about a thousand dollars.

Another stop on the tourist circuit was the Whirling Dervishes. About two hours before sunset every Friday evening, in a typically dusty and windblown cemetery in South Omdurman, a crowd would begin to assemble. The vast majority wore the simple white djellabiya, but a bearded and wild-looking few would be in bright green gowns and wore necklaces of large wooden beads; some of their outlandish outfits were stitched together from multicoloured rags. Small groups would begin to form around drummers; there might be some desultory dancing, and the group would dissolve. But after an hour the ever-larger crowd would start to coalesce and form a circular space before one of the larger stone tombs. The drumming would become more coordinated, more insistent, accompanied now by a rhythmic, hypnotic chanting. In the open space, six or seven individuals would start to twirl to the accelerating rhythms, while on the perimeter men rocked back and forth in a strange motion, as if sawing a log with both hands. Every few minutes, a climax would be reached and a few dancers fell to the ground in a trance. Then, as dusk settled, the whole thing would abruptly end, and the crowd dispersed. The dancers were Muslim Sufis, and they believed that in their trances they briefly attained communion with God; yet the anthropologists would say that there was here something much older than Islam.

Behind the Republican Palace and within its grounds, open at erratic hours, was perhaps the most interesting old building in Khartoum: now the Republican Palace Museum, but originally the chapel of the Residency and the de facto cathedral of the British condominium. The cornerstones of this modest but solidly built edifice, which was in red-brown sandstone with a red-tile roof, were laid in 1904, and the building had a Coptic or even Byzantine look about it.

Inside, a clutter of kitsch filled most of the glass display cases: three samples of fuel (gasoline, jet fuel, and diesel) labelled in Chinese, from the inauguration of the Khartoum oil refinery in June 2000; a "Rhino Desk Set" presented to President Ibrahim Abboud by the provincial government of West Java; a miniature old-design flag of Sudan, taken to the moon by Apollo 11 and presented by Richard Nixon. A three-metre-high traditional coffee pot, with an electric light inside, sat where the high altar should be. On the walls, beneath beautifully restored stained-glass windows that could have come from a medieval English church, was the poignant history of Empire. Many of the names molded in brass were aristocratic – Colonel the Honourable Milo George Talbot, Fourth Son of the Fourth Baron Talbot de Malahide; Douglas Henry Victor Bengough; Guy Bullen – but it was evident that life had not been easy in this distant colonial outpost.

Eustace Spencer Godfrey Blind, for example, was Engineer of Roads and Wells but died at the tender age of twenty-six in Gedaref. The unusually named Major Chauncey Hugh Stigana of the Royal West Kent Regiment was killed in action on 8 December 1919 during the now-forgotten Aliab Dinka Expedition. Leslie Reid Wharton "died as the result of a flying accident at Pibor Post" in January 1937, aged thirty-two; and twenty-nine-year-old Timothy Earle Ilbert was killed on 16 April 1933 while hunting near Mangalla. Bengough, of the Ninth Sudanese battalion, "Died at Wau, August 1907, Aged 28 Years."

Of Governor General Hubert Jervoise Huddlestone (1880–1950), it was stated – perhaps with excessive enthusiasm – that "It can be given to few Englishmen to have established so firm a hold as he did over the hearts of the people of every colour and creed with whom he worked and lived." The epitaph for Brigadier General Sir Herbert William Jackson Pasha, KBE, CB, was simpler and more touching (albeit eccentrically punctuated):

> He Lived at Merowe Until His Death
> There Where His Home Was And
> Where He Died He Now Lies Buried

Scattered around were various portraits in oil. The most arresting was the one with that famous moustache: Earl Kitchener of Khartoum, painted by the Hon. John Cullen. Nearby stood a large bronze sculpture depicting Kitchener's funeral, with one of the pallbearers wearing a fez.

Inside a large glass case but about to collapse in a heap of woodworm dust was an upright piano, brought by Gordon in 1884 and reportedly the first piano to enter Sudan. But the organ – a gift of Mrs Marie Duckett, of County Dublin, and consecrated in 1912 – appeared in better order, if hardly used these days.

If the wall plaques evoked a sense of long-lost romance and chivalry, the effect of the few post-independence black-and-white photographs that made up the rest of the museum was only rueful sadness. Two scratchy photos showed President Ismael Ali Azhari hoisting the new flag of Sudan on a sunny New Year's Day in 1956, but the rest were of one military dictator after another.

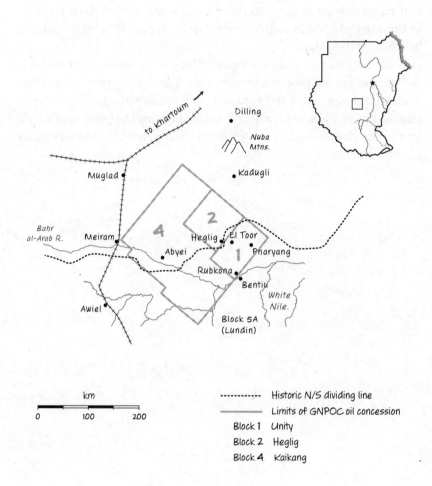

km

0   100   200

----------- Historic N/S dividing line

〜〜〜〜〜 Limits of GNPOC oil concession

Block 1 Unity

Block 2 Heglig

Block 4 Kaikang

The Oilfields

2

IN THE OILFIELDS
FUELLING THE FIRE?

THE REASON CANADA OPENED a diplomatic office in Sudan in 2000 was oil. But not because we wanted to get our hands on the precious resource; in fact, quite the opposite.

After some four years of exploration in Central/South Sudan's Muglad Basin, Chevron of the USA had made the first significant oil strikes in Sudan in 1978, close to the ramshackle riverside town of Bentiu. Estimates of reserves varied wildly over the next few years, but they were sufficiently optimistic to lead then-President Jaafar Nimeiri to adjust borders handed down by the British and redraw the map of Southern Sudan in such a way that the bulk of the known reserves fell into a new and specially carved-out state to be called Unity. In a related decision that would reverberate down the years, Unity was classed as a Northern state, not part of the semi-autonomous Southern region.

Sudan had been at war with itself since the very first day of independence on 1 January 1956. In 1972 the Addis Ababa peace agreement brought some respite, but by 1983 the civil war was on again. While the oilfields of Unity had yet to pump a single barrel of crude, the area now seemed to act as a magnet for violent conflict: in March 1984 three Chevron workers were killed by the Sudan People's Liberation Army (SPLA), near the Chevron base outside Bentiu, and the company ceased operations.

It was another four years before the Americans started up again, but the war was deepening and Sudan was sliding into instability and pariah status. Nimeiri had been overthrown in 1985 to be replaced by a government under the Oxford-educated Sadiq al-Mahdi, but Sadiq barely held on for four years before he in turn was deposed in a military coup by Hassan al-Turabi's and General Omar Bashir's fundamentalist National Islamic Front (NIF). In 1990, after pouring nearly a billion dollars into its investment and only two years after restarting, Chevron packed its bags once again – this time for good.

In 1992, Concorp International, headed by a senior Sudanese businessman close to the new regime, acquired Chevron's properties for the fire-sale price of USD $25 million and promptly resold them to State Petroleum, shortly afterwards to be bought by Arakis Energy Corporation of Canada. Over the next three years the shares of Arakis went on a roller-coaster ride as deals fell through and then were renegotiated; Arakis struggled to find the cash it needed to develop the Sudanese fields. In August 1995 Arakis was briefly suspended from trading on the Nasdaq and delisted from the Vancouver Stock Exchange due to perceived irregularities.

Modest production, trucked out by road tankers, had by now begun, but it was clear that, for the full potential of the field to be realized, greater investment and a 1,600 km pipeline to Port Sudan would be necessary. Accordingly, in 1996, Arakis entered into a four-way partnership, taking 25 percent of a consortium that also included the China National Petroleum Corporation (40 percent), Petronas of Malaysia (30 percent), and Sudan's Sudapet (5 percent). Unusually, the Greater Nile Petroleum Operating Company (GNPOC), as the new consortium was known, did not appoint one of its partners as a sole operator: all four partners would staff the operation in proportion to their capital shares.

With Sudan's oil imports reaching, by 1997, USD $400 million a year and the war proving ever more costly, Khartoum desperately needed the domestic oil flow to increase. Construction of the critical pipeline between Unity and Port Sudan, on the Red Sea, began in May 1998. Labour and engineering were provided largely by a subsidiary of the China National

Petroleum Corporation. The pipeline's designed initial capacity was 250,000 barrels per day.

But Arakis's financial problems were not over. It was still too small a company, too undercapitalized, to be playing in the big leagues like this. In October 1998 Talisman Energy of Calgary (formerly BP Canada) purchased Arakis for CDN $277 million, plus an advance of CDN $46.5 million to meet Arakis's immediate capital requirements.

Talisman, a blue-chip company that proudly boasted of being Canada's largest independent oil and gas company, brought to the project not only badly needed new capital from its deep pockets but also the last word in Western oil technology. Conveniently for the company, it faced no competition from US buyers because the United States Government had by this time slapped comprehensive economic sanctions on Sudan as a punishment for the country's alleged harbouring of terrorists. As a precaution against US retaliation, Talisman built a legal firewall around its Sudan holding and registered it in the Netherlands. At last, twenty years after Chevron's initial strike, there was a going concern in the Muglad Basin.

The pipeline was completed in April 1999, in what was a record time for the oil industry, and by year's end shipments were gradually working up to the pipeline's planned capacity. In direct proportion to the shipments, the money began rolling in to the empty coffers of the National Islamic Front administration in Khartoum. By 2001, notwithstanding disappointing prices worldwide, oil revenues would account for 40 percent of the Sudanese government's budget.

TALISMAN HAD DONE its geological and financial homework, but it had no idea of the political and public relations quagmire into which it was wading by acquiring Arakis and pursuing the Sudan project. In the first place, by operating in this particular country and by paying tax revenues to the administration in Khartoum, Talisman was doing business with an internationally vilified government.

The National Islamic Front regime that had taken power in June 1989 had done so by overthrowing the democratically elected administration of Sadiq al-Mahdi, the great-grandson of the same Mahdi whose forces had besieged Khartoum in the late nineteenth century. While Sadiq had (and has) many faults, and had shown himself incapable of economic management, he was committed to democracy and was in most respects perceived by the West as far preferable to his despotic predecessor, General Jaafar Nimeiri.

The NIF's coup, led by Lieutenant General Omar al-Bashir, was initially popular in that the new military regime promised to bring economic order; Sadiq's mismanagement had been such that long lineups for everything from gasoline to sugar and bread had become the norm in Khartoum. But the new regime soon showed its true colours, and Islamist demagogue Hassan al-Turabi was revealed by stages to have been the coup's mastermind. In April 1990, twenty-eight military officers who attempted a counter-coup were summarily executed; in August 1990 Sudan publicly cast its lot with Iraq in the Gulf War.

Over the next few years, the application of Islamic sharia (customary) law was intensified (it had been introduced by Nimeiri in 1983), political dissent was brutally stifled, and close relations were developed with both Iran and Iraq. Sudan also started to play host to foreign Islamic fundamentalist and terrorist groups, notably Hezbollah and Hamas, and there were allegations that training camps for these organizations functioned in the desert outside Khartoum. Other guests at this time included Carlos ("the Jackal") and the (then-unknown) Osama bin-Laden. In 1993 the USA added Sudan to its list of State Sponsors of Terrorism; in November 1997 it stepped up the pressure and imposed full economic sanctions, simultaneously blocking all Sudanese assets in the US. The previous year, due to an attempt on the life of President Mubarak of Egypt, allegedly launched from Sudanese soil, the United Nations had also imposed sanctions, albeit of a largely symbolic nature.

Sudan thus found itself isolated by the West. European countries, Canada, and the USA had cut all development assistance to the government and were now delivering only emergency humanitarian assistance to famine and war-affected zones. A number of countries reduced their diplomatic representation to bare-bones levels. In spite of its enormous level of indebtedness (at the time of writing Sudan owed more than half of all the arrears owed to the International Monetary Fund), the country was denied access to debt rescheduling.

US hostility towards Sudan reached a highly visible symbolic peak on the night of 20 August 1998 when several Cruise missiles rained in on a pharmaceuticals factory in an industrial suburb in Khartoum North; it was alleged that the Al-Shifa plant had been manufacturing ingredients for chemical weapons. A number of commentators doubted the justification for this attack – which was a convenient distraction at the height of the Monica Lewinsky scandal in Washington – but British Prime Minister Tony Blair immediately weighed in with strong support and closed down the British Embassy.

MEANWHILE, AS IT TURNED UP THE HEAT on Khartoum, the USA gave corresponding succour to the rebellion in the South, led by US-educated Colonel John Garang and the Sudan People's Liberation Movement/Army (SPLM/A). The stated twin objectives of the rebels were a secular Sudan and the option of self-determination for the South; whether *self-determination* was code for *secession* was – and is – a moot point.

The SPLM/A appealed to the USA because, most obviously, it was in complete counterpoint to the hated Islamist regime in Khartoum. The SPLM/A managed to give the impression that its cause was also a Christian cause, this in spite of the fact that most inhabitants of Southern Sudan are actually animists or of no particular religious persuasion. Its English-speaking black-African leaders were much more sympathetic to members of the US Congress and other opinion leaders than the "mad mullahs" in Khartoum, who were an uncomfortable and constant reminder of the humiliation inflicted on the USA by their Iranian counterparts a decade or so earlier. Perhaps most tellingly of all, Black Americans and Christian Americans were able to point to one especially egregious abuse that, if not actually orchestrated by Khartoum, was at the very least tolerated: enslavement of young Dinka children and women by Arab raiders known usually as *murrahaleen*.

The hostile stance of the Clinton administration towards the government in Khartoum enjoyed widespread, even fervent, support in the USA, where, to many, the struggle of the SPLM/A was an old-fashioned crusade, a clear case of good vs evil of a kind no longer easy to find in today's world. There sprang up in the USA dozens of support groups for the Southern cause. Black and Christian members of Congress were repeatedly – to the intense annoyance of Khartoum – escorted into Southern Sudan by the rebels, and on their return home gave moving accounts of the misery inflicted by the war and, specifically, by Khartoum's Antonov bombers. Christian Solidarity International and other similar groups raised funds worldwide for the redemption of slaves, (including through Marches of Dimes in elementary schools in the Southern USA) and, facilitated by the

SPLM/A, were seen in television documentaries freeing grateful slaves by the hundreds. On the internet, pro-South discussion groups proliferated and articulate intellectuals such as Dr Eric Reeves were able repeatedly to place anti-Khartoum op eds in influential journals. Non-governmental aid organizations, including even non-US ones such as Norwegian People's Aid, found that the United States Agency for International Development (USAID) lent an especially favourable ear to their requests for support, as long as the agencies worked in the South, not in the North. The Kenya-based aid community for Southern Sudan attracted not only a significant knot of people – including at least some Canadian pilots – who saw this as the last Great Adventure of the twentieth century, but many for whom it was its last Great Cause. Sudan was as much a domestic issue for the Clinton administration as a foreign policy issue.

Imagine how things now looked to this vast and fervent pro-SPLA and anti-Khartoum constituency when a Canadian oil company bought up former US assets at a bargain price, established itself on the ground, and promised – with the best of Western technology – to finally deliver to Khartoum the enormous promise of those oil reserves, whose dimensions seemed to grow with every telling. And imagine, too, how it must have looked to another quite different constituency: US oilmen.

IT WASN'T JUST THAT TALISMAN, by entering a country at war with itself, was – willy-nilly – about to deliver a very significant strategic advantage (in the form of tax revenues and oil) to the side perceived in the USA (and, to a lesser but still significant extent, in Western Europe) as being the bad guys. It was also that a convincing case had been made by very many highly respected groups, including Amnesty International and Christian Aid, that in order to allow the oil companies to begin operations in this region, the Government of Sudan forces and its ill-disciplined militias had, over the years, forcibly interdicted the land to its traditional inhabitants: the term "scorched earth" was widely used.

Unfortunately for the company, Talisman could not simply brush off these accusations as being, at worst, old history, for the enormous concession of the Greater Nile Petroleum Operating Company was still both a political and a military battleground, with the traditional North/South dividing line actually running between the two most productive fields: Heglig and Unity. On the one hand, the government was waking up to the realization that Unity State's oil could be the key to winning this never-ending war, while on the other the SPLM/A saw that the oil installations could be the regime's Achilles heel: deliver one sharp and effective blow, and the course of the war could reverse in an instant. Month by month, Khartoum sent more and more troops down to secure its assets (including a promising but less developed field immediately to the south of Bentiu known as Block 5A), while SPLM/A central command started to crank up its unreliable but extremely effective militia leader, Commander Peter Gadiet, in the area it still termed Western Upper Nile.

ALTHOUGH CANADA HAD, at the time of the Canadian company's entry into Sudan, no diplomatic presence in Khartoum, the looming Talisman problem had registered with steadily growing force at the Department of Foreign Affairs and International Trade in Ottawa. US church, human rights, and aid organizations worked closely with Canadian counterparts and were not slow to alert them to what they saw as a betrayal by Canada – through Talisman – of everything they had been working for.

The appeals soon got through and found a sympathetic ear in Canadian Foreign Minister Lloyd Axworthy. Once he was appraised of the situation, Talisman seemed to him a national embarrassment, a black mark on Canada's otherwise shining reputation. More specifically, Talisman was a major encumbrance to Canada's attempts to be seen as a neutral supporter and promoter of the stumbling Sudanese peace process.

Axworthy was sensible enough to realize that there could be more to the moral outrage of the Americans than met the eye, even though it was apparently and unusually shared by the White House, the State Department, Congress, and a large segment of the public. In particular, he smelled a rat when the normally hard-nosed Secretary of State Madeleine Albright, not usually one to pay any great heed to human rights for their own sake, started pressing him to "get Talisman out." He would look at the issue, but he wouldn't take the Americans' word for it. An investigative commission was organized and, with the reluctant acquiescence of the Sudanese authorities, sent down at the end of 1999 to the oilfields and Southern Sudan.

The so-called Harker Commission, as it came informally to be known after its head – John Harker, an expert on African affairs and representative in Canada of the International Labour Organization – travelled as extensively as is possible in a region where there were very few all-weather roads and where security considerations were serious. There was one particularly tense moment when SPLA militia leader Gadiet seemed to be contemplating holding the team hostage for an indefinite period. Talisman and the military authorities in the North cooperated fully with the Commission; the company even arranged for the loan of the oil consortium's helicopter.

The Harker Commission's fifty-page report was released in January 2000. Its most significant findings included:

- Oil is exacerbating the conflict in Sudan;
- Military use of the Heglig airstrip has been almost constant since May 1999;
- It is a prominent perception of Southern Sudanese that Talisman ... is in active collaboration with the Government, economically, politically and militarily; it is also the perception that the Government of Canada is either supportive of or indifferent to that collaboration ...;
- There has been and probably still is, major displacement of civilian populations related to oil extraction;
- Sudan is a place of extraordinary suffering and continuing human rights violations ... and the oil operations in which a Canadian company is involved add more suffering.

These findings alone caused Talisman's critics – and Khartoum's – to crow vindication. And yet John Harker stopped short of recommending what logic seemed to call for: the withdrawal of Talisman from the scene, voluntarily or through measures taken by the Government of Canada. Why did he seem (to some) to hedge? Perhaps because Harker understood – or was made to understand – that there existed neither the legal means for Canada to pull Talisman out nor, when it came to the government as a whole, the will.

The Harker report certainly got the attention at the Department of Foreign Affairs. But the departmental lawyers determined that the only weapon Canada could deploy against a Canadian company operating abroad was the Special Economic Measures Act of 1992. However, the SEMA was designed to be applied only in the context of a regime of multilateral economic sanctions, as had existed at one time against South Africa, for example, or as now existed in the case of Iraq – which was not the case of Sudan.

Couldn't a new law be enacted? In theory, yes. But it could be predicted that, in Cabinet, Minister Axworthy would encounter fierce opposition to the idea of, "at the whim of the Foreign Minister," Canadian investments being pulled back from countries "just because they might not be the flavour of the month at Foreign Affairs." The more so in that Canada's strength abroad was principally in fields always likely to be the most controversial: oil, mining, hydroelectricity generation. It was also perhaps whispered in Axworthy's ear, as a reminder, that the seat of Canada's oil and mining industries was in Western Canada, where the ruling Liberal Party's foothold was (and remains) tenuous at best and where it could not afford to lose any more popularity.

Talisman itself was not slow to defend itself, and quite ably. The only fair question to ask, the company suggested, was: "While a Talisman withdrawal might enhance Canada's reputation, and even the company's, would it in any way improve the lot of the people of Sudan?"

Yes, countered some: the withdrawal of a blue-chip Western company such as Talisman could damage the regime by beginning to reverse the tentative inflow of European capital that was starting in the 1990s – and it would at least be a major blow to Khartoum's prestige. But both of these assertions were doubtful: the Europeans seemed well aware of what they were coming into and had indeed watched the Talisman saga carefully; and they were still coming. And as for prestige, well, Khartoum, although struggling upwards, was already pretty much at the bottom of the status rankings.

What was sure was that, in the event of its departure, Talisman's 25 percent share in the Greater Nile consortium would be snapped up by one of its partners or by another oil company from the developing world and that – once the operation was well-established, as it was about to be – production would continue. Talisman, on the other hand, was a reasonable employer, had pushed for significant community development programs by the consortium – on top of its own – and, of course, its presence kept the Sudan issue alive in the West.

SO JOHN HARKER CAME AND WENT, and the company stayed. Every few months there were rumours of a sale that would make the Canadian business pages and give the news-starved habitués of the Pickwick Club much material for speculation. Talisman senior executives admitted that, due to "the Sudan factor," the company's shares (which typically made up a significant component of the senior executives' remuneration packages) traded at a considerable discount. If and when the right price was offered, went the mantra, Talisman would sell – just as it would any of its properties. But the right offer seemed never to be made and/or the political heat was never quite too much to take.

Meanwhile, the principal recommendation that Harker had made, which was taken up by Foreign Minister Axworthy – that Canada take advantage of its then-membership of the United Nations Security Council to bring "the Sudan question" forward for a high profile debate at the Council – failed in the face of indifference from the Council's Permanent Five members, including the USA. Gradually, political pressure on both Talisman and Sudan, on the part of the Government of Canada, faded.

This was replaced to some extent by two sources of pressure in the USA. Throughout 2001 and 2002 a piece of draft legislation known as the Sudan Peace Act made its way back and forth, from committee to committee, in the US Congress. It had a number of provisions, but the key one insofar as Talisman was concerned was one that would legislate full disclosure of a huge range of company practices and policies for any and all companies investing in Sudan and seeking capital on the New York Stock Exchange. Such disclosure, with the accompanying uncertainty, would – so Talisman said – make things impossible for the company. Chief Executive Officer Jim Buckee frankly admitted that if the Act passed "as is," Talisman would be forced to quit Sudan rather than face de facto disbarment in New York. Fortunately for Buckee, both the USA State Department and Alan Greenspan weighed in against these particular provisions. It became clear that, in spite of the enormous majority that the Act commanded in the House of Representatives (422-2), the president would never sign off on this version of the Act – due to the wider repercussions it would have for the USA as a capital market.

The second and potentially just as costly threat came from the Presbyterian Church of Sudan, which initiated a class-action suit against Talisman in a New York court on behalf of the Nuer population living in the vicinity of the GNPOC oil concession. A handwritten memorandum in Arabic was produced, allegedly from GNPOC security to the Army, stating that "the Canadian company" required to have certain villages cleared of civilian population so that oil exploration could be carried out unhindered. Talisman's defense, initially at least, concentrated on legal questions concerning the jurisdiction of the court.

Meanwhile the one positive and tangible outcome of the Harker report was that, due to its implicit admission that Canada needed to know more about Sudan, the decision was taken to open a small permanent Canadian presence in Khartoum. The idea was not to spy on what was going on in the oil concession – that was never a practical option – but rather to give us eyes and ears in this, the largest country in Africa, which we had thus far been trying to comprehend from the distant fastness of rainy Addis Ababa.

Was there also a secret desire to get a Canadian foot back in the trade/investment door, pending the anticipated thaw in the political climate? Certainly not as far as I was aware; the Talisman episode had in fact burned Foreign Affairs and Lloyd Axworthy badly, and there was no wish to repeat it. Canadians in Sudan would enjoy such consular support as our small office might be able to offer, Talisman staffers among them, but we were still far from keen about Talisman being here (if only because of the risk to the security of Canadian citizens posed by the sworn enmity of the SPLM/A). My final instructions actually included the somewhat unusual exhortation to "do nothing whatsoever to encourage further trade or investment."

In tacit response to the Talisman saga and the consequently increased profile of Sudan in Canada, Axworthy also named Senator Lois Wilson as a special Peace Envoy for Sudan; one of her main roles was to spearhead increased Canadian participation in the so-called Partners' Forum of the Intergovernmental Authority on Development. IGAD was the regional body that for years had been trying to broker peace in the Sudanese conflict; the Partners' Forum was a coalition of Western countries (including Canada) pledged to supporting those efforts financially and politically. Thus far, IGAD's principal achievement had been a May 1994 agreement between the rebels and the government known as the Declaration of Principles; it was quite an enlightened document, but talks had never proceeded as far as implementation. In the course of my tenure in Sudan, Wilson would be replaced (on her retirement from the Canadian Senate) by Senator Mobina Jaffer, an especially interesting choice in that, quite apart from her remarkable record on human rights and women's issues at home, she was Muslim and hailed originally from neighbouring

Uganda. However, with the USA, UK, and Norway becoming more and more proactive starting in 2001, Canada never shouldered its way to the front of the mediation process.

I MADE MY FIRST VISIT to the oilfields in September 2000, at Talisman's invitation and in the company of Wim van der Kevie, Chargé d'Affaires of the Dutch Embassy. Flying south in the GNPOC light aircraft, I became aware after a couple of hours that we were entering the 49,000 km² oil concession from the criss-crossing straight lines cut in the flat, green terrain below – seismic baselines from as long as thirty years ago. The first impression bore out the by now infamous utterance of Talisman President and Chief Executive Officer Jim Buckee, in response to allegations that the population of the region had been forcibly displaced to make way for the oil companies: "It's obvious there has never been anyone here..." But I knew better than to report this impression to Ottawa: Buckee had ignored the fact that many of the region's inhabitants were occasional and nomadic, their houses impermanent clusters of small branches and thorns.

We landed at a tarmac strip and were taken directly by Landcruiser to the nearby Heglig camp. It could have been an oil camp anywhere in the world: Portakabin huts on stilts, arranged in neat rows on the dusty red earth and in flat scrubland, with geraniums growing out of brightly painted oil drums. A sign displayed how many hours had been worked with no industrial accidents. From a set of flagpoles by the main door flew the national flags of the four principal partners in the GNPOC consortium. Only the heat served as a reminder that we weren't in Alberta anymore.

At our initial briefing over coffee and doughnuts, we were bombarded with figures and maps; there were at that time ninety-eight wells on line in the Unity and Heglig fields, with a further nineteen scheduled to be tied in shortly. Production, pumped through the 1,600 km pipeline to Port Sudan, varied between 180,000 and 200,000 barrels per day (bbd); the current maximum capacity of the pipeline was about 250,000 bbd, but this could be pushed as high as 450,000 with substantial upgrading of the existing pumping stations. One exploration rig and one drilling rig (Chinese-operated) were in constant use.

There were about six hundred personnel at the main Heglig Camp, and 120 at Unity, including one hundred or so expatriates, of which (at any one time) twenty were Canadians; as such, it was wryly suggested, this was "the biggest hotel in Sudan." I was interested later to note that the different communities didn't mix much: in the Canadian-run cafeteria, each language group sat on its own and, of course, preferred its national dishes: meat and lots of potatoes for the Canadians, along with pancakes and maple syrup at breakfast, and sweet tea served in those light green plastic melamine cups found in school cafeterias throughout Canada. The Malaysians sat well away and preferred fried rice, while the Chinese predictably opted for chow mein (with chopsticks). There was very little to do in the camp other than sleep and eat although there was a "video lounge" where the Canadians would occasionally gather to watch escapist DVDs; it was explained to me that working days were commonly twelve hours long (the compensation was that for each month worked you took a month off).

As is usual at oil camps, there was no alcohol to be had, although I was told conspiratorially that every Chinese New Year the rules were flagrantly broken and a few shamefaced drillers usually had to be shipped up to Khartoum the next day for repatriation. Rather less usually, women were not normally allowed to overnight here, apparently in deference to the sensibilities of the mainly Muslim Sudanese workers. Every time Margarite, who worked on the team responsible for Talisman's community programs, came to camp special permission had to be requested. Northern Mountain Helicopters – a Canadian helicopter crew from Prince George, BC – provided "around the fields" transport in a green and white Bell 212 helicopter for all four GNPOC partners, but most movement was by Toyota Landcruisers on the elevated red earth roads that bisected the oilfields.

The main pumping and generating station at Heglig was, of course, not especially attractive, and the Portakabins were unsightly. Their interiors were complete with fire alarms in English and French and would be eerily familiar to anyone who has stayed at logging or oil camps in the Canadian wilds; the cabins (inherited from Arakis) had actually been imported from Canada.

The site was impeccably clean. What I expected to find close to a war zone – but did not – was heavy security. The installations were surrounded by a flimsy cyclone fence; there were no video cameras, no patrols, no floodlighting at night. There was a considerable government Army contingent (one thousand men?) a few kilometres away down the road, and it had three tanks parked at its front gate, but the garrison itself seemed poorly defended, the tanks belonged on a junk heap, and the soldiers, with their outmoded weapons, ragtag uniforms, and flip-flops, scarcely inspired confidence. In fact, I was told, nearly all the serious injuries and fatalities that had occurred over the years in these oil fields were attributable to bad driving: rollovers when vehicles left the elevated roadways, or overtaking into clouds of dust and oncoming heavy trucks. On the airstrip there were no military aircraft, just a dark green transport helicopter loading tents for a relief operation in nearby Bentiu. Several people told me separately that there had been no repeat visits by the government's improvised Antonov bombers since that reported by John Harker in his submission to the Canadian Government. It seemed to me that, to a small, well-organized, and disciplined commando outfit, Heglig would be a sitting duck

The Canadians were not entirely complacent – they recalled the only attack on the camp in recent history, ten months earlier, when a shed in which sat a Canadian computer operator was raked by small-arms fire – but neither were they at all fazed. Perhaps, working twenty-eight days on and twenty-eight days off, they rationalized that the chances of anything happening while they were onsite were slim, or it may be that they had been hearing SPLA threats for too long.

At a formal meeting with Talisman staff in the Heglig recreation room and at another later in Khartoum, I did my duty and reiterated the concern of the Canadian Government vis-à-vis this situation. A number of individuals later thanked me for my frankness, but for the time being no-one was thinking about packing up and leaving. In fact, the only Talisman employee I ever heard of who quit due to security or ethical concerns worked for the office staff in Khartoum; he told me that on his periodic visits home, when people started to shun him at the golf club or in the bar, he really felt the pressure and decided that what he was doing was wrong.

Later, at the airstrip waiting to leave, I chatted with a friendly young Canadian rig control systems engineer from Calgary. It was his first job, but he was making nearly CDN $1,000 a day and had a girlfriend and a house in Spain; it was easy to see how he might be tempted to overlook the security risks. More bluntly, another Canadian oil worker (not with Talisman, but a subcontractor) said to me: "Yeah, we're economic prostitutes ... So what's your point?"

I LEARNED DURING THIS FIRST VISIT that most rural areas of the southeastern half of the concession were the scene of fighting and raids on the civilian population conducted by militias under Peter Gadiet, the

Nuer militia leader (warlord) who was the SPLA's principal ally in this region and whom Harker had met. Gadiet's latest incursions appeared to have been provoked by an attack on his Mankien base in early September 2000 by rival Nuer militia leader Paulino Matiep, who was at that time loyal to the government.

It was symptomatic of the confused dynamic of the conflict in this part of the country that until September 1999 Gadiet had been generally pro-government, while Matiep had been until late 1997 aligned with a pro-SPLA group – i.e., they had both switched sides. It seemed to me crucial to appreciate the facility with which these leaders and many others changed their loyalties: it gave the lie to characterizations of the Sudanese conflict as a black and white one, pitting the government troops against the SPLA (nor, for that matter, did the fighting here pit Nuer against Dinka: both Matiep and Gadiet were Nuer).

In practical terms, this situation of general mayhem complicated our travelling around the concession. Mohammed Mokhtar, the Sudanese Chief of Security for the GNPOC consortium, gave our helicopter pilots careful instructions for the approach to Bentiu, to avoid flying below five thousand feet (rocket range) until we were right over the town. For our same-day visits to Abyei and Mayom we flew two separate sorties from Heglig, because the open country between the two villages was not, as Mokhtar diplomatically and evasively put it, "fully under government authority."

I learned early on in our acquaintance that, although Mokhtar had attended a Talisman-sponsored human rights course in Nova Scotia, defending the ethics of the oil operation was not his forte. I found it difficult to draw him into a substantive discussion on either this issue or security; he would only avow, when it came to morality, that several fascinated late nights watching Jerry Springer on Canadian TV, when visiting Talisman headquarters in Calgary, had not left him with a positive impression of North American society.

When they were not fighting each other or the government's regular troops (which accounted for a relatively small proportion of their time), I learned from others, the militias were engaged in raids on the civilian population, stealing their cattle, their crops, and – sometimes – their young and adult males. For the past two weeks, Gadiet's forces had been the more active, driving upwards of seven hundred civilians into the small village of Mayom and, on the second day of my visit, hundreds more into Bentiu.

Displaced persons waiting for relief supplies; Mayom, September 2000

THE SCENE IN MAYOM WAS A SAD ONE. In the large open space between the small semi-ruined Army garrison and the thatched Tukuls of the village, about four hundred men, women, and children sat patiently in lines for food distribution, many clutching pumpkins, which were the only food they had been able to bring with them, and the plastic bags containing mosquito nets and blankets already given them by the aid agency present here, German Agro-Action. Flies buzzed everywhere. A woman leader of the Bull Nuer clan, her eyes hauntingly clouded by river blindness, told me (through a translator) how Gadiet's men had come into her village, Loung, five days earlier, beating people with sticks, driving away their cattle, and abducting many young men and boys. It had taken her three days to walk here; two members of her village had drowned when crossing a river. Minutes before I left, another group of about fifty women and small children (the babies were carried on the women's heads in reed baskets) straggled in from the open savannah. Their village, only a few hours' walk from Mayom, had been attacked at about the same time; the women had tried to tough it out, but, without their animals, with their crops stolen, and with many children suffering from malaria, they decided eventually to come to Mayom for assistance. The previous night, to keep hyenas and lions away, they had slept in an improvised thorn corral. As Mokhtar and the Talisman staff watched without comment, I took down the names of other nearby villages that had been ransacked: Quinam, Thorganen, Nurial, and Ramram.

At Bentiu and Rubkona, the two relatively large communities just on the southeastern border of the concession, the scene was peaceful, although over the past month the twin towns had received between forty and sixty thousand civilians fleeing from skirmishing and raids in the area. Most were housed in three camps over which hung a blue cloud of smoke from burning dung, which helped to keep the flies away and which kept the other smells down. Some had brought their animals (an estimated 100,000 head of cattle), and many of these were housed in a large corral specially designated for "internally displaced animals." Only hours after our visit, there began a new influx of several thousand more internally displaced persons (IDPs).

Armed and uniformed men whom the village elders described as SPLA had raided Abyei – the Dinka town from which the United Nations Secretary General's Special Representative on Internal Displacement Francis Deng hailed – on 11 August and (two days before my visit) 13 September. In the first attack the raiders had made off with fifty cows (in the Dinka and Nuer cultures cows have enormous financial and cultural significance – some even say they are considered as valuable as children). But in the second they had been completely repelled. The local Army garrison had sallied out to take on the rebels; from what I could gather, this was an exception to the rule.

In both Rubkona and the small roadside village of El Toor, I saw children as young as twelve in government Army uniforms and nonchalantly carrying AK-47s that were almost as long as they were tall. I questioned the wali (governor) of Unity State directly on the question of child recruiting when I met him in Bentiu. The scene was telling. With something of a smirk on his face, he looked around at all the other senior officials gathered under trees by the river, several of whom theatrically rolled their eyes and shrugged, as if to say, *another stupid foreigner come to bother us on the same old subject.* Then, whisking flies away, he slowly and painstakingly denied that any recruitment of minors by the government was going on.

I was not exactly convinced, but I do know that the question nevertheless struck home; the wali noted it down, and after my return to Khartoum I was pleased when an official from the United Nations Children's Fund (UNICEF) commented to me that she had heard that Canada had been asking awkward questions about child soldiers.

I also spoke with two young men who had each lost a leg to anti-personnel mines, one when fighting for the SPLA near Juba, the other in the ranks of Paulino Matiep. Erstwhile enemies, they were laconic and sat in the dust next to each other.

What was the connection between this fighting and the oil exploration/extraction? This was a question that exercised dozens of commentators inside and outside Sudan; it led to colourful talk of oil fuelling the flames of war. But there was no clear answer.

Certainly much of the armed activity and displacement occurring at that time (and since) in South Sudan was in or immediately to the south of the GNPOC concession, which formed a salient into rebel-held territory. But it seemed to me that much of the fighting was a function of the government having put in large numbers of troops to safeguard its assets and of the rebels and their allied militias responding in kind. Attacks on the installations themselves and on the long and vulnerable pipeline that snaked all the way to Port Sudan were mysteriously few and far between. This was in notable contrast to my last posting, Colombia, where rebels attacked the country's main pipelines on an almost daily basis. It was suggested, rather lamely, that good security had pre-empted such attacks, but it would have been no great challenge to infiltrate saboteurs among the hundreds of Dinka menial staff; and for almost all of its great length the pipeline was less than a metre underground, quite unguarded and easily accessed.

IN THIS SETTING, Talisman was spending about USD $1 million annually on community development and emergency relief work, this on top of the activities undertaken by the consortium as a whole (a figure that would later increase as the controversy over the company's presence deepened). Much of the investment was in the area of health.

The relatively large (with thirty-six beds) GNPOC-financed hospital at Heglig, which was opened in early 1999, would do credit to any small town in Canada, and later travels confirmed my initial impression that it was among the best in all of Sudan. Statistics over the previous year indicated that in the dry season (when roads are serviceable) this single-storey building served an average of three hundred outpatients per day, and 165 in the wet season. Contrary to what John Harker had found a year earlier, I observed the hospital to be full almost to capacity, its forty staff very busy. One of its two incubators (there were only thirteen in all Sudan) was in use. Medical treatment was given free to all comers.

At the Talisman-financed Pharyang clinic, on the eastern edge of the concession and operating since January 2000, things were a little more rustic (at best there was electricity two hours a day) but almost equally busy. I carefully jotted down some figures. The books showed that 3,781 patients had been treated in August, and there were about fifty people waiting when I visited. Half of the cases seen were of malaria, but the clinic was also treating fifteen to twenty cases of tuberculosis, along with cases of bilharzia and leishmaniasis. It had a staff of fourteen, including a midwife and a certified doctor. At Pharyang, Talisman had also installed a large water tank and the town's two sole stand pipes for drinking water.

The clinic in Mayom, where I had seen the results of Gadiet's latest depredations, was GNPOC-sponsored and had only been open two weeks. It was treating seventy to seventy-five patients a day, who suffered principally from malaria and dysentery, and – with the recent influx of displaced persons – it was short of key drugs. In the days immediately prior to my visit, Talisman had secured the services of a military transport helicopter (road access was impossible at this time of year) to fly in bell tents to house several hundred displaced persons.

Talisman had also supplied a hundred large tents to the Bimrock, Clermondock, and Tong displaced persons' encampments at Bentiu. It had contracted a doctor and support staff (including a midwife) to run a tent clinic here; the wali had tried to fire this individual and replace him with a nominee of his own, but Talisman forced his reinstatement.

Was Talisman loved by the local people? Many aid organizations, national and international, were frankly uneasy with the company's social programs, especially its relief work and the spin Talisman had put on it. It was pointed out to me that Talisman were amateurs in the business. Médecins sans frontières told me that drugs the company had purchased for use in its makeshift Bentiu clinic were inappropriate for the context; others saw the programs simply as "blood money" – conscience salvers. It was hard to argue with this. The local people and authorities with whom I spoke were uniformly appreciative, but several pointed out that, ironically, the clinics were proving so popular that they were serving as a magnet for population groups from outside the concession. The population of Pharyang, I was told, had grown from two thousand in June 1999 to an estimated seven to nine thousand in September 2000, putting a great strain on all local services. The Talisman Community Development Director subsequently admitted to me that he did think relief work was best left to the specialized agencies and that the company should concentrate on more medium- to long-term community work. However, he added that "Calgary likes the photo ops of tents going up ..."

In addition, GNPOC as a whole seemed to be appreciated for building the only (more or less) all-weather roads in the area, although these roads were widely criticized by the development community for also providing axes for government military pushes. At Abyei, the Sultan and village elders took the opportunity of my visit to ask Talisman to build one to their community; they were only slightly discouraged when it was explained that there would have to be an oil strike in the area before a road could be considered. And this did not prevent a Dinka elder from waxing poetic about Abyei (pop. five thousand) as a "beacon for all of Sudan, a power station sending out light in every direction ..."

Back at Heglig, I attended a final session at which senior management reviewed, with all the Canadian site personnel, the company's plans for implementing the Canadian Code of International Business Ethics, a set of guidelines that had recently been developed in cooperation between Canada's Department of Foreign Affairs and the private sector, including Canadian oil companies such as CanOxy (later Nexen). I was sure that this and a similar session were laid on partly for my benefit, but there was no doubt that the company was taking the issue seriously; it had identified a wide range of activities in support of each principle established by the code, with markers, dates, and persons responsible. Early in the new year, it would subject itself to an internal audit, to be followed by an external one, conducted by Price Waterhouse Coopers. I answered confidential questions for the auditors, and a number of staffers of aid organizations critical of Talisman also participated.

Talisman would, I believed, find that the most difficult section of the Code for it to implement would be provisions relating to the security forces that protected the oil installations and to the company's responsibility to ensure that they acted only properly. The company had made some timid steps in this direction, for example, requiring that the Heglig airfield maintain an accessible log of all incoming and outgoing flights, but it needed to be more aggressive here. What about the thirteen-year-old boy I saw in Army uniform, carrying a standard-issue weapon at El Toor? Should or could the company not speak out about this kind of thing?

A MONTH OR SO LATER, in November 2000, I was back in the region, this time as a guest of the United Nations' World Food Programme, in Bentiu. Bentiu, sometimes known sardonically as the Houston of Sudan, was a decrepit, woebegone kind of place on the south bank of the Bahr al-Arab River. Nearly all its buildings were the typical round thatched one-room Tukuls of the South, with a few government offices in weathered stone or brick that had not been repaired since the British left in 1956. The airstrip was a rutted and often flooded piece of flatland on the outside of town that doubled as a cattle run. On one side I saw a couple of enclosures littered with broken-down trucks painted in desert colours; on closer examination, these enclosures turned out to be military encampments, and what looked at first sight like drainage ditches and randomly placed logs were fortifications. This was a low-grade war.

The major displacement crisis I had seen on my last visit was now over. There were perhaps twenty thousand persons now in the town, as opposed to the thirty-six thousand counted on 13 August (aid agencies had found it impractical to distinguish between the internally displaced and the permanent population of Bentiu, which probably numbered seven to eight thousand). Most of the tent city that then existed on the outskirts of the town had been dismantled.

The outflux of displaced persons was due to two factors: the need to harvest their crops at home and a relatively improved security situation. However, I was told that the government-loyal militia of Paulino Matiep was in Bentiu and that the rebel SPLA-loyal militia of Peter Gadiet was not far away, likely near Mayom again; three days prior to my visit, Gadiet's forces, led by one Commander Majak, had launched a cattle-stealing raid as close as Rubkona (Hull to Bentiu's Ottawa).

What had not improved was the health of the displaced children. Two aid organizations – CARE and Action contre la faim – had seen their case-loads steadily climbing; when I visited their makeshift clinics they showed me their logbooks, which included many recent malnourishment-related deaths. Action contre la faim was now beginning a study to determine the exact causes of malnutrition in the region. The enormous quantity of cows here, as through much of Southern Sudan, was misleading: they were valued as currency far more than as meat or as milk producers.

Aid agencies operating in Bentiu were multiple: World Food Programme (WFP), UNICEF, Sudanese Red Crescent, CARE International, German Agro-Action, Médecins sans frontières/France, and Action contre la faim. Looked at coldly, this presence was disproportionate to the local need. The officials of the World Food Programme admitted openly that their regular food distribution exercises drew in hundreds of people from all over the region; in other words they were (like Talisman's Pharyang clinic) actually displacement-inducers. The phenomenon of international aid agencies grouping in a relatively few clusters was one I had seen in Colombia and answered partly to the mutual security that each offered the other, but I did wonder if dependency was not thus created.

And of course there was Talisman. The World Food Programme staff stated that Talisman's help during the last crisis (principally in the form of tents) had been appreciated, and the State Minister of Health told me that the company's facilities were a vital part of his infrastructure. But Action contre la faim staffers were more sour: they said that Talisman had made itself a laughing stock among the aid community by failing to include latrines in its clinic designs and that the local population did see the company as representing part of the problem (oil = conflict) rather than the solution.

FEBRUARY 2001, AND I WAS BACK ONCE MORE. On 25 January a force commanded by the government's eternal nemesis, Peter Gadiet, had attacked a drilling rig at Tamur, in the southern extremity of the GNPOC concession and close to rebel lines. No expatriates had been killed, but the night assault had been dramatic, resulting in a dozen deaths among government troops and perhaps as many as forty rebels dead. When dawn broke, an unexploded rocket round was found virtually at the foot of the rig; the oil workers had been lucky. For the second time since Talisman established a presence in Sudan, formal letters warning all Canadians in the oilfields of the risks they faced were sent by our government, and I was asked by Ottawa to reinforce these letters with a visit and simultaneously report back on the safety precautions in place.

From talking at length to one of Talisman's principal security officers (a highly experienced veteran of British special forces), to Talisman's people on the ground at Heglig, and to GNPOC Security, I reached the conclusion, first, that, of all of the partners, it was the Canadian company that – by far – took security most seriously. Every effort was made to keep to a minimum the number of Talisman personnel out on the rigs, which were the most vulnerable point of the operation; only Talisman maintained its own network of contacts with the military and civil authorities, and only Talisman topped up GNPOC's security briefings with its own more stringent and detailed requirements. Short of evacuation, the company was taking every reasonable measure on behalf of its employees.

Contrary to accounts I had read in generally reputable media, Talisman at no point placed armed personnel of its own in the field, and, as far as I could determine, neither did it employ any armed personnel; I am reasonably confident that the same could be said of its Chinese and Malaysian partners, although both of the latter were much more lackadaisical than Talisman in letting Sudanese military travel in their vehicles (and, later, on the Malaysian-subcontracted helicopter). One widely syndicated report by Christina Lamb in Britain's *Sunday Telegraph* (26 August 2000), to the effect that there were no less than 700,000 Chinese troops guarding the oil installations, was pure fantasy.

Lundin Petroleum, who operated in a much more exposed area to the south of the GNPOC partners known as Block 5A and who periodically counted Canadians among its staff, did not employ soldiers either, but it was much more difficult for that company to maintain any kind of separation from the Sudanese military, if only because the main access road to its concession was under constant attack and was the road used by the government to reinforce several tenuously held garrisons. A Lundin-contracted helicopter pilot suffered a miraculous escape from death when his machine was fired upon and he took several bullet impacts in the back; it transpired that the pilot was known to often transport troops at the government's request.

The significant number of other Canadians working for subcontractors to the consortium enjoyed less support from their employers than Talisman's people. A Western Canadian drilling services company (which liked to keep a very low profile and which consequently escaped all scrutiny in the international media) operated two of GNPOC's drilling rigs, and staff could avail themselves only of the laxer and less well-informed security services of the consortium as a whole. It was also more maverick, in the manner of the classic rough-and-ready oilmen of legend. Although I was very courteously received by the American rig manager at the company's Rig Fifteen, currently drilling at Bamboo Field (20 km north of Heglig), Canadian employees of this company who happened to be in camp at Heglig declined to meet with me; and, in Khartoum, company staff were always cagey about supplying the Canadian Office with any employee details.

How vulnerable were the rigs in the oil concession? It all depended on where they were.

Bamboo Field was considered a low-risk area. It was consequently protected by about fifty government troops who were housed in tatty canvas tents outside the main "berm" (a two-metre-high defensive earth wall/ditch surrounding the rig; about 100 m²). The surrounding scrub and woods were cleared to a perimeter of about 150 metres, with sentries posted at the four corners. The idea was that the berm would be high enough that the Portakabins and machinery within were immune·from small-arms fire, and the entrance roadway should be S-shaped, not allowing fire directly inwards. But at Rig Fifteen a standing rifleman could still have hit the cabins, and the entrance had not been finished and lay wide open.

At the foot of the forty-metre white-painted latticework rig, heavy machinery was arranged in such a way as to provide a safe haven in the middle, the muster point; drills were regularly held at which all employees were required to be at the muster point within thirty seconds. When in full swing, the rig employed about fifty persons, and it operated day and night, floodlit at night. Typically, rigs were at any given location for three to four weeks at a time.

The highest risk area in the concession was a triangular area in the extreme south, bounded to the north by the Bahr al-Arab River. South of this river (but still inside the concession) was the fief of Gadiet, and it had been from this sanctuary that he launched his January attack on the Chinese-operated Tamur Rig. Tamur was the highest-risk location operated by the consortium in the past several years, reflecting growing (now clearly excessive) confidence; for this reason, it was assigned no less than four hundred government troops with a couple of "technicals" (heavy machine guns mounted on pickups). The berm was built up to at least three metres, and the scrub cleared to four hundred metres out. Although the rig crew were lucky that the rocket-propelled grenade launched by the rebels failed to detonate, Talisman's security experts felt the rig was never in serious danger of being taken; indeed, government troops had performed "surprisingly well." The experts admitted, however, that GNPOC had probably gone a bridge too far in attempting to drill at this location at this time (following the attack, drilling nevertheless continued to the target depth only to discover a dry well).

Also at higher risk than Talisman employees per se were the crew of Northern Mountain Helicopters, although – realizing that shooting down a helicopter would be a major coup for the rebels – the consortium bosses had them fly circuitous and high-altitude routes to avoid territory thought to be in rebel control. My impression was that the crew were personally very professional and cautious, but their Bell helicopter was vulnerable to small-arms fire.

The Sudanese Government was taking the Tamur attack seriously. For the past month there had been two Russian-made Hind helicopter gunships stationed at Unity Field, and I was told they had been flying sorties almost every day, taking on large amounts of ammunition, "and unloading none ..." There was a third Hind out of action at Rubkona, having taken excessive dust into its intake. By some accounts, this represented one quarter of the government's entire fleet of combat helicopters. Talisman said it had indicated to the government its unease at the negative impression the helicopters might create by being based at Heglig or Unity airfields – in the light of Harker's criticisms of government use of company airstrips to launch attacks – and claimed to have sought assurances that the Hinds' presence was purely defensive.

Khartoum seemed to have been giving some direction to local militias under the command of Paulino Matiep and Peter Parr. No less than two thousand pro-government militia had recently been observed heading east from Rubkona recently, on foot, towards Gadiet-controlled territory.

Rounding off my visit, I again held a staff meeting, this time with about sixteen Canadians. I complimented Talisman on its serious and professional approach to security but once more insisted that in our view it was only a matter of time before there would be a serious security incident involving a Canadian. The only substantive reaction I received was a comment that Talisman's foreign partners were bemused by the attention that the Canadian oilmen (there were no women at Heglig) received from their government. By contrast, the Chinese and the Malaysian authorities were totally unconcerned by the security situation, even though their nationals were more nervous; during the attack on the Tamur rig, there was reportedly no space to be found under beds for a period of several hours. In spite of there being perhaps twenty or thirty British nationals in the area (some working for Talisman) the UK Embassy took a similarly laissez-faire attitude.

IT WAS NOT LONG BEFORE THE NEXT – and most serious – attack came. In the afternoon of 4 August 2001, government intelligence detected the presence of a group of regular rebel troops about 50 km to the west of the main camp at Heglig. This was most unusual in that the only SPLA-loyal soldiers normally active in the region were irregular Nuer militiamen under Gadiet, and these men were, moreover, in the very heart of the concession, well to the north of Gadiet's usual stomping grounds. Clashing with them at about 11:30 p.m., government soldiers soon put the group to flight but did not order a general alert.

Then at 4:50 a.m., with the brightly lit central processing facility still presenting an excellent target against the night sky, the first of thirteen 83 mm mortar rounds landed in the Heglig camp. A full-scale alarm was sounded, and all personnel (over five hundred) assembled at muster stations to the east of the main residential blocks. Four Ilyushin 76 transport jets based in Khartoum were put on alert, ready for a general evacuation.

Amazingly, the damage was minimal. The Canadian-operated helicopter was lightly damaged by shrapnel, but the crew was able to fly it up to Khartoum for repairs. As a precaution, all pumping was shut down for about twelve hours, and lights were doused for the next several nights. The rebels initially took the darkening of the facility as a sign that the attack had been successful, and many SPLA-leaning aid workers believed them, but I was later shown the daily production stats for the period in question; there had been negligible disruption.

When the location from which the rounds had been fired was discovered, about 9 km away, the conclusion was that the camp had been at maximum range of the model of mortar used (which, along with its 40 kg base plate, must have been carried in and out on someone's back). Probably the attack had been timed in anticipation of the other ground force – which had fortuitously been detected by the government the previous afternoon – hitting Heglig simultaneously. It may have been a coincidence or the result of good intelligence work by the SPLA, but the four or five Hind gunships that the government normally stationed at Unity and/or Heglig were that night all away undergoing maintenance at Muglad, well to the north. In sum, GNPOC and Talisman had been lucky – once again. Had there been a little more wind that morning, one way or the other, a few of those rounds might well have hit.

The common wisdom had been that the main installations were so far inside the oil concession that any incoming forces would easily be detected, and that, even if they did get in and inflict some damage, they would never get away. In fact, the rebel forces were able to escape unscathed. A short time after the episode, when I happened to be at the United Nations' forward base in Northern Kenya, someone said to me: "See those guys over there at the bar? They're the ones who did the Heglig raid."

THE WAR IN THE IRONICALLY NAMED Unity State dragged on and in mid-July 2002, it was time to check up on Bentiu again. Flying in to the same bumpy old cattle-track of an airstrip, I trekked off first to meet the new wali, John Dor. He was a distinct improvement over the one I had met the first time, nearly two years earlier.

He and his internal security officer expressed a breezy confidence in the security situation, following the government's recent recapture of Mankien (symbolically important as the home of Gadiet) and of Nhialldu. "Gadiet won't come back now," said Dor expansively but not prophetically; as an aside, he admitted that previous attempts to seduce Gadiet back to the government side he once favoured had for now been abandoned, on the basis of his fundamental "untrustworthiness." The rebel forces were now thought to be some 30 km to the west of Mankien; they had a good pool of heavy artillery but faced difficult supply-line challenges.

It was even suggested that "within a couple of weeks," Block 5A (to the south, from which Lundin Petroleum had now been forced to retreat, in the face of rebel activity) would soon be clear for oil operations. There now remained "only" 38 km before roadbuilders pushed an all-weather road through to currently beleaguered Leer. For what it was worth (probably not a lot), state officials did not consider Talisman employees to be in any great danger at this time.

Aid organizations did not share this optimism, particularly concerning Block 5A. In fact, I had heard in Khartoum from Lundin's boss, Ken Barker, that the company was very gloomy and foresaw waiting at least one more year before going back in. The aid organizations also said that although the government now held Mankien and Nhialldu, these towns were empty, with the civilian population still too nervous to return; instead, they were roaming the countryside, living off the land the best they could. They also suggested that such gains as the government had made had been thanks almost exclusively to militias, rather than regular troops, and that militias had of late been recruiting energetically and indiscriminately in the streets of Bentiu and Rubkona (including, once again, minors).

The wali admitted to the phenomenon of child recruitment, blithely saying "those children just love their guns." He also gave me an important and good-humoured pointer on how to distinguish between militia and government troops: the former usually wore flip-flops, but the government provided lace-up boots to its men (you never knew when you might need that kind of information, I thought, envisaging a scenario in which I might be desperately casting around for clues to the identity of my captors).

It was clear that some government estimates of up to 130,000 displaced in and around Bentiu were exaggerated (presumably in the hope of pulling in more humanitarian assistance). The Action contre la faim therapeutic feeding centre I visited – upgraded considerably since my visit of two years earlier – was dealing with about seventy cases daily, when at capacity (as it had been in 2000) it could take two hundred. CARE's centres were similarly busy but not crammed.

This was notwithstanding the heaviest fighting in years in this region. It seemed a point had now been reached when all those who were able and/ or willing to be displaced had displaced, while others wandered in circles in the swampy hinterland, living off wild food and what they could beg from one marauding band or another. As in other combat zones in Sudan, nearly all of the displaced were women and children; the men were dead or fighting in a militia – or had fled to Khartoum, usually forever.

This abandoned population faced a chronic, never-ending lack of food, which in turn compounded the many diseases prevalent in the area: malaria, tuberculosis, and kalazar (leishmaniasis). Because they were always on the move or holed up in alien semi-urban centres such as Rubkona and Bentiu, even when the rain came (unusually, it had not, thus far), they were in no position to sow crops.

The cheerful doctor, who did his best to tend to the thousand or so mothers and under-fives served by CARE, did heroic work in the most basic of conditions: there was no birthing centre, which meant that the half-stuffed armchair in his office did service for a dozen or so difficult cases a week. But understandably he had no time to ponder some of the more unusual afflictions of his patients. He told me almost in passing that he tended to an astounding four hundred disabled persons, most of whom were blind; neither he nor any passing doctor had been able to say why. When surgery was needed, he tried to send patients up to the good hospital at Heglig, which had been built by the GNPOC consortium, but usually there was no transport available.

Although the wali seemed to be in particularly jovial form, I asked him why there was a T55 tank posted very closed to his office, festooned with bandoleers of heavy machine-gun bullets. Did he fear a return by Gadiet? No, he said. The story was altogether more complicated.

There were two principal Nuer militias loyal to the government in this area (and here he launched into the confusing soup of acronyms that all students of Sudan must try to master): the large South Sudan Unity Movement (SSUM) force of Bull Nuers under Paulino Matiep and the smaller Dok clan under Tito Biel, who until recently had been fighting for the SPLA-aligned South Sudan Independence Movement (SSIM). So as to secure Biel's loyalty the government had been granting him more favours (i.e., guns) than Matiep. Tension between the two groups rose to such a pitch that on or around 1 July, a senior officer of Matiep's faction, at the time at Matiep's second residence in Khartoum, was murdered by a rival from Biel's group (Biel also had a home away from home in the capital). The tank, Dor explained, was to keep the factions apart on the ground.

Subsequent to this visit of mine to Bentiu, the situation escalated back in Khartoum. On 6 July at 1:00 a.m. a group of Matiep's men attacked Biel's residence; up to ten people were killed. Over the next couple of days there were running fights in Khartoum, one of which saw spear-carrying men attacking another band only a couple of hundred metres from our home. None of this was reported substantively or accurately in the news, but it was indicative and typical of the fighting that characterized what was so often and so misleadingly portrayed as a war between regular government troops and rebels: at least half of what went on was usually internecine disputes between militias, often with obscure or ostensibly trivial motives.

There were equally strange scenes to the west and south of the oilfields, as the government – with the assistance of three Wau-based helicopter gunships – consolidated its hold on Gogrial, which it had recently retaken after the rebels had held it for two years. While there was now no prospect of the much-feared annual supply train from Khartoum to Wau, with its posses of marauding outriders – all the track between Awiel and Wau having been torn up – the horsemen were finding alternative employment. Reportedly, it was they who served as shock troops to take Gogrial. A number came without their horses and were seen, white djellabiyas flowing and brandishing automatic weapons, riding into battle on Chinese-made Phoenix bicycles.

AS THE WAR EBBED AND FLOWED, Talisman executives wrung their collective hands and wondered whether to leave or to stay. In late 2002, the general belief grew that perhaps on account of brightening peace prospects and a promising oil strike at Daffar, near Abyei, they might after all tough it out. But simultaneously there were reports that the company was engaged in serious negotiations with India's Oil and Natural Gas Company (ONGC Videsh). While Talisman was no doubt hoping that the changing political scene would allow it to raise its selling price, suspicion grew that the decision had been made that the company was no longer prepared to live with continued attacks by human rights lobby groups, a 20 percent discount on its share price, and the persisting unease of many of its shareholders with the Sudan stake. Sooner rather than later, it would sell.

Confirmation came in the form of an announcement late in the evening of 30 October 2002 that a sale had been agreed, at USD $750 million. Terms were not actually finalized until mid-March 2003, as both Malaysia's Petronas and the Chinese National Petroleum Company objected to the sale to India (presumably wishing they could have snapped up Talisman instead), but, ironically, Talisman's share price hardly reacted to any of this.

While leaders of the campaign to get Talisman out – notably the academic Eric Reeves, who had gone so far in his columns as to put Talisman board members on a par with Hitler and Goebbels – rejoiced, it was in fact by no means clear that the Canadian company's departure was for the greater good of Sudan or Canada. Most obviously, it would do nothing whatsoever to staunch or even slow the flow of oil to the Khartoum Government, which – according to the human rights lobby – was allowing the administration to pursue the war on unequal terms. Nor would it stop whatever abuses may have been committed, or were still being committed, by government security forces in the name of protecting the GNPOC consortium. The Indians would simply step into Talisman's shoes, and the whole operation would go on as before.

Moreover, it was already clear from public statements by executives of the Indian company that they were not in the least perturbed by the controversy dogging Talisman and that they had no intention of speaking out about human rights, because these were sovereign concerns of Sudan. Being a state-run company (like the other three companies in the consortium, but unlike Talisman), the Indians had no need to concern themselves with shareholders or possible divestment campaigns.

Talisman, it is true, had not exerted as much pressure on Khartoum as Canada would have liked, not nearly as much as the human rights lobby would have liked, but I was nevertheless aware of a constant dialogue between the company and the government on ethical issues, and Talisman had taken concrete steps such as insisting the Heglig airstrip not be used for offensive military purposes. The company's efforts to draw up a memorandum governing actions by the military in GNPOC's name had failed, but it had at least attempted this (I saw a draft); it had also taken the unprecedented step of twice having itself independently audited on its compliance with the International Code of Ethics for Canadian Business.

Talisman had also facilitated a number of visits by journalists and European legislators to the oilfields – in full knowledge of their skepticism – and had shown itself always ready to dialogue with human rights groups. It had instituted a significantly funded community development program that, while it drew the scorn of aid agencies more experienced in the field, had nevertheless brought some concrete benefits to the communities of Bentiu, Pharyang, and Abyei. All of this would end with the Indian takeover.

More positively from Canada's official perspective, the Government of Canada could no longer be accused of sanctioning an unethical operation; Lloyd Axworthy had finally got his way. Presumably the SPLM/A would now accept Canada as a neutral player or onlooker in the Sudanese conflict, and presumably it would no longer be as perilous for a Canadian to travel into rebel-held South Sudan as it had been as long as Talisman was pumping oil. But whatever respect we had gained with the rebels, we had probably lost in equivalent measure with the hard-nosed apparatchiks of Khartoum, some of whom had only tolerated our complaints on human rights and other humanitarian issues because we were the largest single Western investor in Sudan.

ONE WAY OR ANOTHER I saw a lot of Ralph Capeling, Talisman's on-ground general manager. Ralph came over as very earnest and was clearly a capable oilman: he would not have got this far in the business were it otherwise, and the experts told me that he ran the Sudan operation in a driven, dedicated manner, constantly pressing for higher production, almost never sitting on his laurels. Ralph always facilitated my visits to the oilfields, answered my questions, and even volunteered to deliver letters, on behalf of the Government of Canada, advising Heglig staff that they were in danger of their lives. I could have no complaints in terms of cooperation.

But, as Ralph himself would periodically recognize, such was the controversy that Talisman's presence in Sudan had attracted, that as much as a technician the company needed a public relations expert, and this Ralph was not. He was unguarded in front of the media, famously responding to the CBC's Carol Off, who had asked him on camera about the value of the oil in a vast storage tank at Heglig: "It's to die for." And he was prone to miss the big picture that Talisman's critics were painting, seeking instead – fruitlessly, in my view – to undermine their credibility on points of detail such as dates and place names.

I saw a lot less of CEO Dr Jim Buckee and international Vice-President Jackie Sheppard: a couple of meetings in Khartoum, one in Ottawa. Buckee was not in the least your stereotypical oilman: as the media liked to point out, he held a PhD in Astrophysics from Oxford University. He was witty and usually relaxed; he and the harder-edged and sometimes sarcastic Ms Sheppard (whom my US colleague dubbed "the dragon lady") together made an effective good cop/bad cop duo. But for two intelligent type-A overachievers, Buckee and Sheppard showed right to the end a remarkable myopia when it came to objective judgement regarding where Talisman had gone wrong in Sudan.

In the first place, like Ralph Capeling, they tended to pick at the more foolish, hyperbolic, and/or erroneous utterances of the human rights lobby (and there were many) with righteous indignance. It seemed to me they were missing the point. Right or wrong, the human rights community hit a chord and, in the end, showed they were capable of outmanoeuvring this large, blue-chip oil company. The duo failed fatally at the outset to predict the waves their company's entry into Sudan would make (Buckee famously described early criticisms as "white noise we can live with"), and, once the company was in, their strategy of constantly denying there was any problem was manifestly ineffective. As one leading critic of Talisman in Khartoum said to me: "If they had once showed some humility, then we might have given them a break." They were also very impatient with expert advice and opinions from people in fields other than theirs: the company commissioned at very considerable expense a study based on aerial and satellite photographs of the oil concession area with the aim of showing that most of the oil-drilling areas had always been devoid of population and that other nearby areas had grown in population, i.e., that forced displacement was a myth. But they did not listen to warnings that the photos would be of limited value unless they covered every season of the year systematically, because of the nomadic habits of many groups to be found in the area. The photos were never shown to the public.

My last meeting with both was over breakfast one morning in the Hilton Coffee Shop in Khartoum, when the company's departure was all but a done deal. Looking for someone – anyone – to blame, Mr Buckee homed in on the Government of Canada. Now Ottawa had never been exactly enthusiastic about Talisman being in Sudan (there was an ongoing dispute between Buckee and Canadian Junior Minister David Kilgour as to whether Kilgour explicitly but privately warned Talisman off or not), but Foreign Affairs was always scrupulously careful in its public statements and actions to confine itself to concern for the physical security of Canadian citizens in the oilfields. Not once did we ever publicly say "Talisman should get out of Sudan."

Buckee refused to see this. He railed at how we had been shamefully negligent in not supporting the company more strongly (as though huge companies like Talisman needed the help of Ottawa bureaucrats to help them get business) and then picked at our worries about the safety of employees. "If you think we would ever sacrifice the safety of our staff to the bottom line, then you are being offensive to me," Buckee puffed when I noncommittally listed various of the close calls that Canadians had had in the oilfields; he irrationally moved the discussion into a condemnation of Canada's "idiotic" support of the Kyoto Accord.

In fairness, no other major resource-extraction company had ever faced the grilling Talisman had, and that campaign was not entirely logical. There was, for example, a great deal more Canadian investment in the oil and gas industry in wartorn and abuse-ridden Colombia than in Sudan, and yet Colombia attracted negligible controversy. The human rights lobby could sometimes be as wilfully blind as Talisman management: on my return from visits to Heglig, concerned groups reacted with visible disappointment and incredulity to my bland comments that the oil facilities were functioning smoothly, that I had seen no dead bodies, that there were not thousands of Chinese troops guarding the place, and that there were no bombers on the airstrip. They wanted in-your-face horror, and I could not deliver.

As the brunt of such criticism, Talisman was perhaps riding a wave of the future – it was "bleeding edge" – but understandably this philosophical musing was scant consolation to its frustrated senior employees as they packed their bags in May and June 2003.

EVEN AFTER ITS DEPARTURE FROM SUDAN, Talisman decided to maintain its various community development projects until they had run their natural lifespan. A small local office was kept open for this purpose, run by the ever-bubbly and enthusiastic Canadian Margarite d'Amelio.

But there was another purpose for the office: to serve as a home away from home for the expensive US lawyers that Talisman forecast it would be continuing to send to Sudan for some time to come. While Talisman had sold its stake in the GNPOC consortium and by mid-June 2003 only Margarite represented the company on the ground, it had not been able to shake off the class-action lawsuit in a New York court that many dismissed as frivolous but that, if successful, would surely break the company and send shockwaves through the entire oil industry. The Canadian company was being sued, under the little-used Alien Tort Claims Act, by the Presbyterian Church of Sudan on behalf of the Nuer people of Southern Sudan for no less than "acts of genocide."

The jurisdiction seemed dubious, the case itself undocumentable, and the fact that Talisman – on account of legal connections to the USA – was being sued alone, with no charges laid against Petronas, CNPC, or Sudapet seemed to be bad law. As a bitter parting gift to the company, after months of tantalizing silence and only days after it finally sealed the deal with India, the New York judge ruled the case could proceed. Talisman braced itself for another fight, potentially even more threatening to it than the SPLM/A – and this time with no easy exit in sight.

3

OPERATION LIFELINE SUDAN

WHEN SUDAN'S CIVIL WAR ENTERED its second phase in the 1980s and it became apparent that there was going to be no quick resolution, the international humanitarian community was faced with the major problem of how to access the benighted civilian population on both sides of the frontlines without infringing on the sovereignty of a recognized member of the United Nations. The answer was Operation Lifeline Sudan (OLS), the brainchild of then-United Nations Children's Fund (UNICEF) head James Grant. At the basis of OLS was a 1989 tripartite agreement between the Government of Sudan, the rebel SPLM/A, and the United Nations itself that governed the access not only of United Nations agencies to populations in need but also of aid organizations that formally agreed to subscribe to the principles of neutrality laid down by the UN and to constraints imposed by their respective security staffs. In a word, subscribing aid organizations delegated to the UN – with all its clout – the negotiation of their access to rebel-held territory, but in return they had to commit to play by the rules (for example, by not transporting arms or military personnel).

The agreement was unique in that a sovereign government, a member of the community of nations, ceded to the UN legal authority to access territory where the host government had no control and where, indeed, its sworn enemies were the authority. There was no such agreement in Colombia, where rebel movements had controlled enormous swathes of land for many years and where, consequently, there was no external humanitarian assistance of any sort; nor had there ever been similar arrangements in the civil wars that had over the years wracked Sierra Leone, Liberia, Angola, the Democratic Republic of the Congo, and Central America.

The OLS arrangement made the government in Khartoum nervous. It watched very closely any and all aid organizations who based themselves in the government-controlled North, manipulating them – to the point of harassment – through the denial of visas and/or internal travel permits, not to speak of planting informers within their operations. By such tactics, Khartoum was able to ensure that North-based organizations served only populations over which the central government had firm, consolidated control.

But over the much larger community of aid workers who chose to access the rebel-controlled South directly from Northern Kenya or Uganda – mainly through the small North Kenyan town of Lokichokkio – the government had very little control at all and had, for the most part, to trust the United Nations to watch things on its behalf. Khartoum's great fear of course was that some organizations would, under the guise of humanitarian assistance, provide help of direct use to the rebel SPLM/A itself rather than to the civilian population.

Given this fear, why did the Sudan Government ever agree to OLS? When Jim Grant came to them with this novel idea, the democratic government of Sadiq al-Mahdi was tottering and militarily on the defensive; only a couple of months later the fundamentalist National Islamic Front seized power from him and the government's international standing took a further dive. Cooperating with the international community in allowing humanitarian access to the war-affected population of South Sudan, even on the other side of the rebel lines, made Khartoum look relatively good. Khartoum knew, too, that, if it did not agree to some access framework, dozens of aid agencies would simply go ahead anyway, taking advantage of the government's inability to stop them.

Khartoum's ongoing discomfort with OLS was manifested in periodical – almost always groundless – accusations that the United Nations and/ or organizations under the UN umbrella had flown in weapons or otherwise abused the OLS agreement and, more perniciously, in flight denials. While the OLS agreement stipulated unrestricted access for humanitarian agencies, it did allow the government some latitude in that it could deny aircraft landing rights in specific locations where, in Khartoum's judgment, the military conditions were too unstable to permit humanitarian work. Some such flight denials were justified, but over the years the government too often used denial as a weapon to starve populations under SPLM/A control and thus deprive the rebels, as Mao would have put it, of the "water in which they swim."

The most egregious access denial in the history of OLS came, ironically, shortly after the signing in July 2002 of the Machakos Protocol, an internationally mediated framework for a peace agreement. Seeking to recapture from the SPLM/A the town of Torit, and thus to improve its stock of chips at the negotiating table, the government banned OLS from accessing all of Eastern and Western Equatoria and from overflying them. While Khartoum prepared its attack, all of rebel-held South Sudan was thus for a period deprived of any external humanitarian assistance.

More systematically, from 1999 to 2002, with oil finally coming online and new exploration being pressed forward in Western Upper Nile (Unity State to Northerners), nearly all locations in that region were denied on a constant basis; the effect was to drain the area of a large part of the civilian population and/or drive them into government hands. Later, the government applied the same tactic to devastating effect in the separate conflict in Darfur.

Frustrations of this sort, against which the United Nations and the diplomatic community that supported the agencies had little recourse, led a number of aid organizations not to subscribe to OLS and to work in South Sudan in defiance of the Khartoum administration. In theory, they ran the risk of having their aircraft shot down, but it seemed Khartoum never quite had the nerve to do this (quite apart from not having the ability to track small aircraft accurately so as to be sure that they were not in fact UN-approved).

These organizations gained a lot of freedom in that they could fly where and when they wanted; they were, they said, thus better able to serve the needy. But it was my sense, and that of many donor countries, that they did the humanitarian cause a disservice. In the first place, some did bend the rules and fly in people and merchandise that they shouldn't have. And it was interesting to note that on days when OLS did not fly – for whatever reason: bad weather or flight bans – then neither did the non-OLS players. In fact, they often used OLS aircraft to hide behind, shadowing them within a few hundred metres and only diverting from the flight path authorized by Khartoum for OLS at the last minute; they were gambling that the government would never take the risk of going for them, lest they hit the nearby UN aircraft by mistake.

WHILE NORTH-BASED PRIVATE AID ORGANIZATIONS had to content themselves with serving only Khartoum-loyal populations – much to the (undeserved) scorn of Kenyan-based groups who saw them as having done a deal with the devil – the United Nations itself based its air operations in two locations – Lokichokkio (Kenya) and El Obeid, a desert city of 300,000 in government-controlled North Kordofan, which historically had been a fastness of the Mahdi but was now served from Port Sudan by rail and had a good all-weather airstrip – and accessed government and rebel territory from both. At El Obeid, the UN's World Food Programme had its own apron and buildings, off the main airfield, which was also used as a staging post for the government's makeshift Antonov bombers and periodically for its helicopter gunships. Usually there were two large UN aircraft based here: a four-jet-engine Ilyushin 76 that was used for airdrops in the South (average two flights a day) and a four-turboprop Antonov 12 that served as a twice-daily air bridge to the besieged city of Wau. A smaller Hercules C-130 was sometimes also used. All were painted in UN white, with the World Food Programme logo and initials in blue.

Local United Nations staff were proud that their operation was significantly more cost-effective than Lokichokkio, due to Sudan's lower fuel costs, the higher payload of their Russian aircraft (which were too big for use at Lokichokkio), and the fact that El Obeid was closer to most drop zones in the South. This translated to savings of up to USD $350 per ton on airdrops and USD $240 on airlift.

The installations were impressive and well run. Semi-trailers bringing in grain and other staples from Port Sudan (1,200 km away) were unloaded into thirteen enormous Rubb Halls (framed tents) where the grain was then rebagged in preparation for air-dropping; a thickness of five bags was

World Food Programme Antonov loading grain at El Obeid, 2000

required. For air drops, wooden-floored pallets were then made up, each with an approximate weight of one ton, and loaded into the Ilyushin; for the Antonov that maintained the air bridge, no rebagging was necessary, and the sacks were loaded directly into the belly of the plane. The air crew of twenty-two were housed locally, and the entire operation employed about 180 persons.

Air drops were carried out from an altitude of 100 to 150 metres, over any one of the World Food Programme's 150 or so previously identified and marked drop zones. The altitude was carefully calculated so that by the time bags hit the ground they had lost their forward momentum; no parachutes were used. A prelocated reception crew was always on hand at the drop zone to supervise collection and distribution. Trial and error had reduced the bag breakage rate to 5 percent or less, and even then no food was wasted: the contents of burst sacks were almost invariably salvaged. OLS had only suffered two "home deliveries" (the euphemism for falling loads causing injuries or fatalities) in a dozen years of operation. In the two and a half years prior to my first visit to El Obeid, aircraft based here had dropped more than forty thousand tons of food and airlifted fifteen thousand.

The Antonov's Ukrainian aircrew proudly showed me around their cavernous ship, which was dusty with flour. Twice the size of a Hercules, this was an impressive but now very old-fashioned (thirty-year-old) aircraft, streaked with oil and the tracks of exhaust fumes. The crew were housed in Second World War-type conditions, and none of the huge arrays of panelling was electronic; the toilet was a bucket. Only one member of each crew spoke English, which had led at times to communications problems.

Calls at El Obeid (and I made many, in that all UN aircraft flying in government-controlled Sudan used this as their main refuelling stop) were not without their surreal moments. After a pilot had discreetly pointed it out to me, on every visit I looked over to the left of the apron where our aircraft normally parked. There would usually be a large orange truck with wooden sides, next to what seemed to be a shallow pit full of old oil drums. In fact this was a makeshift bomb dump, and several times I saw the bombs, which sometimes really were just oil drums packed with explosives and scrap metal and which sometimes were more recognisably pointed cylinders, being rolled up the rear ramps of Antonovs. I was told that the Antonovs bombed in exactly the same manner as their UN counterparts dropped food: the rear door was opened, the aircraft went into a steep climb, and the load rolled out of the back and into the void (hopefully without bouncing too much en route).

Once I watched three same-model Antonovs taxiing to the end of the runway: one was a World Food Programme aircraft en route for a food drop, a second was on charter to UNICEF and was delivering polio vaccines, and the third was a government bomber. All were bound for South Sudan. It was rumoured that the crews were all from the same pool, but I was never able to verify this.

While we waited in the terminal for our much smaller Cessna Caravan or King Air to be refuelled, the same little old lady would, every time, bring me over a strong and sweet black coffee. Huge wall-high air-conditioning units whirred eerily at all hours; the toilets seemed to have never been cleaned, but a small carpeted prayer area was spotless and there was usually someone asleep in it. Scattered around the invariably empty but always clean airport lounge were old baggage trolleys that read *British Airports Authority – Heathrow Airport*. There was no duty free, no baggage carousels, and, apparently, never any civilian flights coming or going.

Once, when our cargo charter from the Nuba Mountains called in to fuel up for the last leg to Khartoum, we found that the Shell crew had just gone for their Ramadan breakfast; it would be a long wait. From the back of the aircraft, someone found a dozen Hilton hotel lunchpacks; we sat munching hardboiled eggs on the grass by the bomb dump, as the sun set and the muezzin called the faithful to prayer.

EVERY COUPLE OF DAYS, 1,000 km to the south, a small convoy of dust-covered and mud-splashed flatbeds trundled into the Wild West-style Kenyan town of Lokichokkio (Loki), the other half of the OLS operation. From Mombasa it might have taken as long as five days to reach here, and on the final run north to Loki the trucks would have run into a gauntlet of mounted bandits. Local Turkana workers unloaded the trucks by hand into Rubb Halls or stacked the grain in pyramids inside the razor-wire compound of the World Food Programme. Occasionally, if it had been raining heavily in Kenya, bridges were washed out, and Loki was cut off: in May 2003 the UN Hercules fleet had to relocate temporarily to Eldoret, near Nairobi, because they had run out of aviation fuel.

At the beginning of each month, a detailed and very complicated flight schedule was drawn up, detailing the next four weeks' worth of air drops into southern and western Sudan. Up to 180 locations were designated for drops; some doubled up as small airfields, but many were simply flat spaces the size of two football fields on an island in the middle of a swamp. Most of the drop zones used from Loki were nominally under the control of the rebel SPLM/A, but some drops were made from Loki into government territory. The government sometimes scratched out six or seven of the chosen locations, ostensibly on the grounds of local insecurity; usually this meant that an offensive was planned in the area for the period in question; but sometimes it might simply mean that Khartoum did not want that particular population to receive food at that particular time; the SPLM/A almost never exercised a veto. Locations were selected by roving UN food monitor teams, who had the double role of assessing local needs and then receiving and distributing the drop. Early in 2000, I had a chance to see things for myself.

East Africa's busiest airfield: Lokichokkio, Kenya

MY FLIGHT, ABOARD A WHITE HERCULES chartered from the South African company SAFAIR, was scheduled to depart Loki at 11:00 a.m; our DZ was the village of Haat in rebel-controlled Upper Nile, southeast of Bentiu. I arrived at the airfield in time to see a giant four-engined aircraft return from its first run of the day, one of five or six Hercules or Buffaloes that landed over the next half hour, making Loki one of the busiest airfields in East Africa. The propellers were still turning as the rear cargo door opened, and the UN ground staff began loading the first of twenty pallets of a little under one ton apiece.

The pallets, each comprising thirty or forty bags strapped to a plywood platform, were loaded in two long rows, the length of the cargo hold, their passage smoothed by rollers. In each of the two rows, the pallets were linked by light nylon line, in such a way that they would fall out in a chain.

I was invited to climb up into the cockpit, to sit with the three-man crew and the loadmaster. We revved up deafeningly and lumbered out onto the runway, dead on time. Loki tower cleared United Nations 470, and we heaved ourselves up into the air, heading for the Kenyan border with Sudan, only a few miles to the north.

We were soon at six thousand metres over the Didinga Mountains, where only last week, at a much lower altitude, a Red Cross plane was fired upon and the pilot killed. We radioed in, first to Juba and then to Wau, where government controllers were warily tracking our course. Far below I saw the sinuous course of the White Nile, although it was so swampy at this time of year that for miles on end it lost itself in small lakes.

Ninety minutes out and we were descending towards the drop zone at Haat. The pilot made contact with the food monitors on the ground. Their call signs invariably began with "whisky," a no doubt unintentional dig at the sternly teetotal Sudanese authorities. As we dropped down, the co-pilot called out to warn of flights of large birds – it was migration season – and several times we lurched to take evasive action. At last Haat came into sight: a collection of a hundred or so Tukuls on what seemed to be an island in the middle of hundreds of square kilometres of swamp.

We levelled out at exactly 150 metres and started a dry run over the drop zone, so that the pilot could enter into his navigational system the exact coordinates of the centre of the zone as we passed over it. I made out the four corners of a wide muddy expanse, marked with empty white World Food Programme sacks; in the middle was a clumsy white cross, some ten metres across. As we passed over it and the pilot called "mark," I could clearly see a hundred or so villagers gathered together, waving at us enthusiastically.

We turned around and lumbered back for the first wet run, which I watched from the co-pilot's seat. Exactly nine seconds before we were due to pass over the mark, with the navigator counting down, the pilot yanked on the stick and we went into a screaming climb, while the loadmaster pulled a lever to simultaneously release the lefthand chain of pallets. Then there was a kick as the tail came up and a second of stomach-churning weightlessness as we levelled off again. I could see nothing of it, but eight tons of food was now hurtling groundwards, on a trajectory carefully calculated so as to fall vertically at the moment of impact.

From the ground, the monitors advised good-naturedly that we could have done with being about five metres to the right, but all the sacks fell within the drop zone. We went around in a wide turn and lined up for the final run.

This time I strapped in by the gaping rear door, into which a warm wind was howling. The sudden forty-five-degree climb, as the pallets rumbled past and fell into the void, was white-knuckle inducing: for a moment I felt as though I was suspended right over the zone and about to follow the cargo. Before we levelled off, I observed the wooden pallets sailing off like giant frisbees while the chain of white sacks ever so slowly undid itself and spread like confetti. I couldn't hear the bags hit over the noise of the engines, but this time I saw that they were spread in a neat line right up the very centre of the target area.

On the long haul home, there was some quiet tension when the load-master reported laconically that during the drop operation he had heard a noise from the flaps that sounded like a gear stripping. Plans were developed for a no-flaps landing at Loki; after ten minutes of tapping away at his calculator and consulting manuals, the pilot assessed that we might have to land at 190 knots instead of our supposed 130, but that we should have one hundred metres to spare on the runway. "Plenty," he said cheerfully. Fortunately, all went well – the flaps engaged as intended.

In his book *The Constant Gardener*, spy novelist John Le Carré recounts a similar drop from the standpoint of the team on the ground in a rebel-held South Sudan village. It is one of the few uplifting and uncynical parts of what is otherwise a very dark book. Le Carré acknowledges the troubling issues of dependency and political manipulation of aid; he recognizes that not all the food always goes where it should; but, he concludes, "it was like a communion rite; this was manna from heaven; surely this was not a bad thing ..." And his Judas of a villain is miraculously redeemed – for, in penance for his earlier sins, he now heads the air-drop ground team.

AMONG THE TRUEST SECTIONS of Le Carré's book is his largely unflattering depiction of the United Nations base at Loki. The first thing that struck me was Loki's resemblance to an armed camp. There was razor wire atop its high perimeter fence, and you entered through great steel gates painted UN-blue, where you had to undergo a lengthy registration process. All visitors were warned that they ventured out of the main compound at their own peril, and usually stories were circulating of recent muggings or shootings within a few metres of the base itself. Ironically, this violence was no overspill from the war in Sudan but a manifestation of extreme poverty and endemic tribal problems, exacerbated no doubt by the massive and incongruous presence of an affluent aid community that was interested only helping Sudanese, not Kenyans.

Inside, the place was laid out like a kind of equatorial Club Med. The standard accommodations were round cabins with straw roofs, each named after an African country or town (as a diplomat, I usually had the honour of staying at the deluxe Djibouti, which had its own adjoining bathroom), on "streets" named after UN notables, including a colleague of mine, UNICEF Country Director Thomas Ekvall. Catering was by a company called AFEX, which ran many safari camps for tourists in Southern Kenya and was of a very high standard; on weekends you might be lucky enough to coincide with an Italian theme night, held outside by candlelight, or a barbecue. Cold Tusker beer – immensely welcome to visitors based in Khartoum – was on tap at O'Brien's Bar within the compound, and outdoor televisions were usually tuned to the BBC or CNN. There was even a Cappuccino Bar, which served not only Italian coffee but also delicious mango and passion fruit slushes. Many first-time visitors asked if there was also a pool; but a succession of camp administrators had drawn the line at this, (rightly) fearing the wrath of donor countries, who already spent a fortune in maintaining this location.

The camp was home not only to United Nations agencies, the largest being the World Food Programme and UNICEF, but to the forty or more non-governmental aid agencies that operated under the OLS umbrella; their flags flew on rows of poles by the camp administration building. The organizations that didn't subscribe to OLS (among them many very respectable agencies such as World Vision and Médecins sans frontières) had to find their own accommodation outside; there were thus a number of smaller camps – some, like Trackmark and 748 Services, were commercial operations and even had pools – around Loki.

It was to these camps that you had to sally forth to learn about some of the more irregular things that went on in and out of Loki, or to meet SPLA commanders just back from attacks on Heglig. The pilots of Kingair, Ross Air, SAFAIR, and Air Afrique – the companies that regularly vied for and won the UN contracts – stayed here, but you could also find the US or Canadian pilots of smaller, ephemeral charter airlines that would fly any cargo and any passengers in their ancient DC-3s, Andovers, or Twin Otters, no questions asked. Many of them liked to think that they were fighting one of the last great crusades on Earth: "We go beyond neutrality" was the slogan of the famously maverick and pro-SPLA Norwegian People's Aid

– one of the principal clients of these rogue charter operations. But the truth seemed to be that most pilots were just in it for the adrenaline rush. Eavesdrop on beery conversations about dodging Khartoum's Migs in and out of Kauda, or using the headlights of cars to line up for illegal night landings at Loki, and you entered the derring-do world of Oliver North or Air America (a world described brilliantly in Deborah Scroggins's recent *Emma's War*). These people would have been just as happy flying for the Contras or for UNITA. One of them said to me: "Too bad they got old Savimbi; they had a good war going on there."

After a while, Loki got on my nerves. I once spent a week there, waiting for an SPLM/A travel permit than never came; I spent most of the time reading a very heavy biography of Karen Blixen, interrupting myself to make the occasional phone call back to Nairobi to see if there was any progress. Then Loki started to seem less like Club Med and more like a hearty and regimented US summer camp, minus the lake and the flag games. I started to sense the various cliques in the mess hall; the pancakes that I had gorged on the first few days began to taste leathery; I had already read all the notices on the bulletin boards (including the one seeking "Evangelists" for working in South Sudan). There was even a daily assembly, at 6:00 p.m. sharp, during which Jim Abelle, the former US marine who had forever been in charge of UN security, gave a laconic and humourless account of the day's fighting in South Sudan and indicated which sites were "Red No Go" for tomorrow's flights; he had a crew cut, and wore khaki bermuda shorts and tight white tee-shirts that showed off his impressive musculature; he looked every part the stern camp counsellor.

I started feeling irked by the constant casual references to the "liberation" of territory by the rebels and had to stop myself from actually starting to defend the indefensible: the Khartoum Government. Especially annoying were the outwardly humourous but inwardly smug and self-satisfied digs about my being "from the dark side." Someone asked me, "How can you sleep at night, dealing with those evil people every day?"

Every morning, as the tropical dawn chorus began and my room quickly lit up, I would hear the roar of plane after plane going overhead: the early morning runs into Rumbek and a dozen other locations in South Sudan. It was impressive, this well-oiled machinery that delivered the generous donations of Western governments and their citizens to three million people in need; those big white planes with UN stencilled in giant blue letters could make your heart swell. But once I'd been here a few days, there was a niggling doubt or two, as well. What would happen when back in London, Washington, and Ottawa people started to lose interest and there was nothing left for the planes to carry? The SPLM/A had been in control of a very large portion of territory for nearly twenty years now – wasn't it about time they started to feed their own people? And what kind of self-sufficiency and resilience were we encouraging by dropping hundreds of thousands of tons of grain out of the back of planes, however accurately, month after month, year after year?

Somewhere, OLS had gone wrong. So should we call it all off? No: if those planes stopped flying today, within a few months thousands of innocent and desperate civilians would be dead. However, if the government in Khartoum and the rebels in the South were compassionate or at all accountable to the people they governed, that in turn would drive them to the negotiating table and in the long run many more lives would be saved than lost. The problem was, they were neither: they simply did not care how many people died.

Couldn't we phase out the endless food runs by doing what all the aid manuals say: build roads, schools, hospitals, and the administrative infrastructure to support them – and, as the old truism goes, give people fishing rods rather than fish? In theory, yes, but this smacked too much of helping to build a new country; no Western donor country was ready to go that far in defying Khartoum and in betting on an independent, sustainable Southern Sudan. Doing this would also, in the short term at least, be more costly and less visible than food handouts and consequently difficult to sell to skeptical Western taxpayers with short attention spans. The planes droned on.

BACK IN KHARTOUM we all lived in a kind of Loki as well. The war was a long way away, and everyone in the aid world spent a great deal of time meeting each other, either at social gatherings or in a succession of meetings with acronyms that were initially bewildering.

There was HAF: the monthly Humanitarian Aid Forum, which brought together donors, the UN, and international NGOs. HAF also had its fortnightly HAF Steering Committee, which seemed to exist only because HAF was too big to be manageable, and the Steering Committee itself set up subcommittees. There was the Friends of the Nuba Mountains (FONM), which also met monthly, with the United Kingdom as its self-appointed chair; and the prestigious UNEOG (United Nations Emergency Operations Group), which, notwithstanding its name, had been meeting on a monthly basis for years and prided itself on starting exactly on time and never running for more than an hour; four big donors – the EU, the USA, the UK, and the Netherlands – maintained a firm grip on the chairing and agenda of UNEOG. There was the Like-Minded Human Rights Group, assiduously attended by all except the Americans and the Italians, and the Working Level Donors Development Group, and the INGO (international non-governmental organizations) forum ... the list went on. We all lamented the weakness of Sudanese civil society, but we actually included Sudanese groups in only one regular set of meetings – the United Nations-sponsored Peacebuilding Network. Shamefully, hardly anyone (including myself) spoke Arabic, and we didn't go to meetings unless we knew there would be translation into English.

Somehow, although everyone clamoured that we needed more coordination – and indeed all these groupings were in response to this – aid continued to be delivered in a muddled and inefficient manner. The international aid organizations were competing for the same pool of cash controlled by Western governments and would happily present impressive-looking proposals that in fact duplicated the work of other groups, in the hope that donor governments would not wise up. There were endless needs assessments, to the point at which one of the main findings started to be just that the poor and needy felt themselves to be overassessed and overresearched. With peace looming in early 2003, the UN was commissioned to undertake an ambitious and complex Contingency Plan for consideration at a high-level donor meeting in Oslo; the fact that donors had for the past two and a half years been financing an imaginative and creative Planning for Peace exercise with precisely this scenario in mind was simply forgotten.

The United Nations, at least until early 2003 when things began to improve significantly, was spectacularly uncoordinated between, on the one hand, its own agencies in Khartoum and, on the other, UNICEF and WFP operating in the South. On one notable occasion, UNICEF in the South actually hoodwinked WFP in the North to use its aircraft for an unsanctioned operation, leaving the overall head of the United Nations for Sudan, who was Khartoum-based, to make embarrassed and craven apologies to the governmental authorities. One food assessment in late 2002 by the UN's Food and Agriculture Organization (FAO) said that there would be a food surplus, but the World Food Programme – using the very same data – projected a deficit: donors were given a complicated story about "different emphases" and left to figure it out for themselves. WFP, the big boy on the block in terms of budget, often decided to ignore the advice of the United Nations' common security staff and was rumoured to buy the cooperation of the Sudanese governmental Humanitarian Aid Commission by judicious transfers of outdated radios and Toyota Landcruisers; none of the other agencies could afford such bribes and consequently suffered.

Most depressingly, when in mid-2002 the United Nations appointed an energetic and no-nonsense Australian as its overall resident coordinator – he actually criticized the government on its flight bans and told the whole truth to Secretary General Kofi Annan when he made his first visit – the government objected to his remaining and, defying all protocol and precedent, said it would simply not accept his authority. Western donor governments assured United Nations headquarters in New York that they would support the new coordinator; but New York said "thanks but no thanks," and the Australian was forced out, his tail between his legs. At a crucial time the entire UN system in Sudan was left leaderless, and the grim realization set in that, with New York having surrendered on this, it would be forced henceforth to cave on many more fronts.

But the United Nations is only a function of its member nations; and these can be selfish, vain, and uncooperative. The USA, with its big bucks and constant stream of high-level visitors, launched initiative after initiative with no prior consultation with its "friends," then expected them to help pay the bills. The Nuba Mountains ceasefire arrangement was one such example: the USA selected and contracted a private company called Pacific Architecture and Engineering to run all the logistics, paid for a large part of their bills, but then presented the outstanding accounts to other countries for settlement. Norway, ostensibly the co-chair of the multinational Intergovernmental Authority on Development (IGAD) Partners' Forum that had for years been backing peace bids, butted its way into the Machakos peace talks in Kenya then conveniently forgot entirely about the group of countries it was supposed to be representing; Italy, the other co-chair, was only interested in Somalia and unilingual Italian officials refused even to talk to Norway's flashy and glamorous but imperious Aid Minister, Hilde Johnson.

Even within their own respective administrations, the donor governments could be disorganized: in May 2003 the "Nairobi-based donors" (including Canada) wrote a letter complaining to the new overall United Nations coordinator for Sudan, Mukesh Kapila, that he was moving too fast towards a one-country approach to assistance (i.e., having Khartoum as the principal centre of action, gradually sidelining Nairobi). In their letter the said donors admitted that their points of view might not reflect either those of their respective missions in Khartoum or of their capitals; the inevitable impression (and it was a correct one) was that we were internally uncoordinated and unfocused in our thinking.

Periodically, there were serious and well-intentioned efforts to do things better. I participated enthusiastically in one such exercise, led by the United Nations' Sara Pantuliano, focused on a single geographical area where there was a local ceasefire. It was proposed that, rather than each Western government aid agency and non-governmental organization doing their own thing with no coordination (as was the usual pattern), we should establish a trust fund that would be jointly supervised by the donors, the aid agencies, the rebel SPLM/A, and the Sudanese Government. Project submissions would be carefully vetted to make sure that they did not duplicate existing or projected work and that they had the buy-in of all stakeholders. The plan was stillborn. None of the major donor countries was prepared to accept the loss of control over their own funds that this mechanism seemed to them to imply.

Over the years the tragedy in Sudan has attracted the interest, the dedication, and the philanthropy of a wide variety of individuals, organizations, and nations. We have busied ourselves, analysed, agonized, and examined ad nauseam, and we have expended fortunes many times over; but in the end it has to be said that if there are some places we *did* get it right (East Timor?), Sudan has to be an example of our thus far getting it badly wrong.

4

VICTIMS

FOR THE LAST TWO DECADES, Sudan has been one of the world's leading examples of the callousness of powerful men towards the common people whom they claim to represent. A million – or two million? – dead in the war, three million – or four million? – uprooted from their homes by violence, drought, or famine and forced to migrate hundreds of kilometres and start again, with nothing. And much of this, of course, has been done in the name of God – not just Allah, but the God of the Christians as well.

The Gulu and Kitgum districts of Northern Uganda, the principal home of the Acholi people, have for years been a hotbed of discontent: the Acholis, persecuted by Presidents Amin and Obote, still feel that they have been neglected by the central government of the otherwise more enlightened Yoweri Museveni in Kampala, that they have been given no share in the running of the country. In the late 1980s and early 1990s, a bizarre but terrifying guerrilla army came slowly into existence, building upon this simmering resentment: the Lord's Resistance Army, or LRA.

The LRA, created in 1989 as a successor to the Alice Lakwana's Holy Spirit movement, is half army, half messianic cult. Its avowed objective is not just to seize power in Kampala on behalf of the Acholi people but to install the Ten Commandments as the new constitution of Uganda. It recruits by force throughout Acholi-land, which also spills into Southern Sudan; over the years, literally thousands of children and young men have been abducted, brainwashed, and forced to fight for the LRA. Women and babies have been seized, too, to serve as wives for senior commanders and as camp followers. Discipline is maintained by the most savage means: persons seeking to escape are shot out of hand. But Joseph Kony, former altar boy and now the mesmeric leader of the LRA, is not just a wild-eyed dreadlocked cult leader: he is, unfortunately, a military commander of some talent, and the LRA until now has been able to evade repeated attempts to crush it.

Throughout the 1990s, the Government of Sudan gave open support to the LRA, not on any carefully studied ideological basis but as a means of getting back at the Government of Uganda for its more or less open harbouring of the SPLM/A. This support consisted of allowing the LRA to establish semipermanent encampments near Juba, whence they were well placed to make repeated violent forays into Northern Uganda, and of supplying them with food, weapons, and intelligence. When the LRA was not up to its usual misdeeds in Northern Uganda, it could in fact often be found fighting alongside regular Sudan Government troops against the SPLA.

By 2000 the formerly glacial relations between Kampala and Khartoum were starting to thaw, largely at the initiative of Khartoum, which was engaged in a more general campaign of rehabilitating itself internationally. The cement in this improvement was the Nairobi Agreement, by which both sides agreed to give up active support of the respective rebel movements and to move towards establishing normal diplomatic relations. The agreement was mediated largely by the Atlanta-based Carter Centre, which hoped, in encouraging greater stability in this conflictive part of the world, to improve access for its global campaign to eradicate guinea worm infestation.

Gradually, the LRA's bases in Sudan came under greater pressure. The Sudanese Army never did take on the LRA – that was perhaps too much to hope for – but the government largely ceased supplying weapons and food, and instructions were given that government garrisons were now to actively welcome escapees from the LRA and help them towards safe havens. At this point, UNICEF, with the support of Save the Children and a small group of interested governments, including Canada's, would take over and, after some initial rehabilitation, send the escapees back to their homeland, where they would receive further assistance and where the Government of Uganda had promised amnesty. In September 2000 I took part in the first groundbreaking mass repatriation.

In the days and weeks leading up to 17 September, a group of eleven males and five women had been brought, through varying routes, to an ad hoc reception centre at a recreational camp in Soba, a suburb in Southern Khartoum. Canada would finance their return home to Uganda, but we would need the cooperation of a number of other players – Save the Children, UNICEF, the Government of Sudan's Humanitarian Aid Commission, the International Organization for Migration, and, representing the Office of the President of Uganda, Mr John Baptist Okomo – to make this happen and, above all, to be sure that once home they would not be denounced as bogus (as had happened with the single other group that had thus far been repatriated). Sitting under the shade of a large mango tree and with the help of the Reverend Adi Ambrose, a Sudanese Acholi who interpreted for me, I interviewed all sixteen candidates: five adult men (who had been abducted as teenagers), a fifteen-year-old boy, five women, and five male infants.

Three of the men had been wounded in combat fighting the SPLA; one had lost a leg. These three had been treated at Omdurman Military Hospital, which told me clearly that they were at the time of their injuries serving under the LRA flag but alongside Sudanese Government troops. Four of the women were wives of the same LRA commander, one George Kormakech, who had died of natural causes in 1997; the small children were all his. Since that date they had been kept apart at a separate LRA Women's Camp. The four wives, plus a fifth young woman who helped with babysitting the four's five young children, broke out together in August 2000. They told me that two other ex-wives of the same commander remained in the LRA Women's Camp and another one died (i.e., he had a total of eight wives).

Fortuitously (or perhaps not – there was some suspicion that the Khartoum authorities had known where to find these abductees for some time) these interviews took place just as the Canadian-sponsored 2000 War-Affected Children's Conference was winding up in Winnipeg. Both Canada and Sudan were thus able to obtain a modest amount of kudos, although a headline in the Toronto *Globe and Mail* – "Canada Frees L R A Abductees" – was excessively flattering to us. I flew back with the abductees as far as Nairobi, where Bryan Burton – my counterpart at the Canadian High Commission in the Kenyan capital – took them back to Gulu and an extremely warm reception.

Over the coming months, I travelled many times to Soba and interviewed many more abductees. On 2 November I was meeting with a group of twenty-three.

This group included two small children who would require surgery prior to repatriation, and the doctor recommended that eleven of the group be tested for H I V. There was one anomaly: a forty-year-old man called Robert. He appeared to be a war veteran, having fought under Obote, and he'd had refugee status in Kenya at one point. Robert, it was clear, had joined the L R A voluntarily and was now taking advantage of our newly constructed pipeline to get a free ride back to Uganda. His case presented us with a quandary: I was firm that as an adult he should not be eligible for Canadian funding, but neither could he be left in Sudan forever in legal limbo. It would be nearly a year before his case was resolved.

By the time I was out at Soba again, in December 2000, there were more Roberts: seven former L R A commanders, who had jumped ship only a month ago. We had interesting conversations.

All admitted that they had been hardline L R A who had joined up with a vision: the armed overthrow of the Museveni regime (not just a better deal for Acholi-land). The L R A's current strength, they said, was between four and six thousand, including eight hundred women and at least five hundred children aged six or under. Anybody who could walk was considered a candidate to bear arms. Joseph Kony had at least thirty-five children and eight or ten wives.

As recently as a couple of months ago, they said, Kony had greatly reinforced his encampments and his defensive capacities. While the Sudanese Government had – in accordance with its promises to Uganda – effectively cut off supplies from outside, Kony and his men knew how to move freely through the bush and were in no danger of being starved out. The famous nineteen Aboke girls, a cluster of upper-middle-class Acholi girls seized in one notorious incident from a convent school, all of whom now had "husbands" and children, were kept at the very heart of the camp. The men expressed to me resentment that the Aboke girls had captured so much international attention, at the expense of hundreds of other abductees.

Why had the men deserted? They had concluded that, while Kony claimed to still have a vision and ideals, his cruel military tactics were in ever greater contradiction with his objectives. The men had planned their escape in the utmost secrecy and fled at night; there was no doubt in their minds that, had they been caught escaping, they would have been shot.

Could Kony be convinced to surrender? The men thought not. They believed that Kony would not compromise on his stated objective and that, even if his army shrank to three or four men, he would fight on. They doubted that the Government of Sudan would ever summon up the nerve to attack the LRA head-on ("they have been too useful to them in the past") and warned that, were they to do so, many minors and women would lose their lives. The men did not want to go back – they knew that, notwithstanding a formal amnesty, in Uganda their lives would be in great danger.

Meanwhile, repeated efforts were made to persuade the LRA to surrender or at least to hand over the women and children in its hands. Canadian Ben Hoffman of the Carter Centre was a part of these efforts, and in January 2001 he was sufficiently optimistic actually to attempt face-to-face contact with Joseph Kony. Accompanied by General Yassin of the Sudan Army, Hoffman first travelled to Nisitu, formerly Kony's major encampment. The location was abandoned and apparently had been for some time – this confirming government assertions that they had pushed the LRA deeper into the bush. Further in, the delegation met up with an LRA outpost. The junior soldiers on duty here told them that senior LRA commanders had been here as late as 8:00 p.m. the previous evening, awaiting Hoffman, but had then suddenly received word that Kony was seriously ill (it sounded like a bout of yellow fever; requiring at least five injections) and they had returned to tend to him. Various messages then went back and forth. Kony asked Hoffman to stay in the country a further seven days by which point Kony would contact him to set up another meeting.

But nothing happened. As on so many subsequent occasions, hopes were raised only to be depressingly dashed; on this particular occasion, it was later learned, Kony had probably feared a trap and had backed out at the last minute.

By September 2001, rumours of a split within the LRA and a possible surrender of at least one large bloc had in fact become so persistent that, with government encouragement, aid agencies prepared a reception centre at Juba that could handle up to seven hundred escapees; the idea was that we would process them rapidly and repatriate them by air straight to Kitgum. Again, it all came to nothing. I remember the date of our Juba meeting well because one evening as we ate ice cream with the Italian nuns who run a development program here, someone said that two planes had crashed in New York. There was no TV in Juba, and we didn't realize the full horror of 9/11 until we were back in Khartoum.

In 2002 Kampala began to lose patience, and the Carter Centre interest. Uganda negotiated with the Government of Sudan for permission to actively pursue the LRA on Sudanese territory with its own armed forces. To the surprise of many, Khartoum acquiesced, and Operation Iron Fist was launched. President Museveni boasted proudly that, within three months, the LRA would be crushed.

But he grossly underestimated the LRA and overestimated the capacity of his own army. Iron Fist was a miserable failure. The Ugandan Army soon bogged down, and the depredations of the LRA, inside both Sudan and Uganda, became worse than ever. The trickle of escapees all but dried up; the reception centre was never used. On one horrific occasion, the LRA interrupted a funeral feast, killed many of the mourners, then forced survivors to cook one of the bodies and eat it.

In early 2005, the LRA was rampaging as never before: a literally biblical scourge in an already much-tried land. And there were some signs that Khartoum had furtively renewed its support.

BY FAR THE MOST NUMEROUS GROUP of victims of Sudan's war were an enormous mass of people – disproportionately women and children – known in the aid world as IDPs: internally displaced persons (as opposed to *refugees*, who must cross an international border to earn that name). Nobody knew how many IDPs there were in rebel-held South Sudan, for they were shunted back and forth between bouts of fighting and there were no camps for them. In the North, the government had set aside four areas of common land in the forlorn, dusty outskirts of Khartoum and had designated these as camps, and most other towns had a quarter known wearily as the IDP settlement. Estimates of the total number of IDPs in Sudan varied from two million to four and a half. But the designated camps were nowhere near large enough for the sheer mass of humanity that had fled the war zones; most simply squatted where they could.

Soba, a prime area for unofficial settlement south of the LRA reception centre, was about twenty-five minutes' drive from central Khartoum. After the metalled road gave out, there stretched square kilometres of single-storey adobe dwellings divided by wide and dusty tracks. There were a few patches of waste ground with sparse bushes (where they had not been eaten by the goats), and everywhere windblown litter was caught in fences and on vegetation. It was very easy to get lost. There were no street names and no numbers; you could often only orient yourself by glimpsing a distant water tower. It always seemed extremely hot, and there were no buildings high enough to provide any significant shade. But the settlements were not especially cramped – space was not lacking in the Sudanese desert – and it was strange to see dwellings of a rural design, that is, with a large enclosure for domestic animals, cheek by jowl in an urban setting.

Most people living here had been moved on three or more times by the government until they had been able to afford the registration fee required to regularize their situation. In fact, when I asked what services the government provided in Soba, I was told – with a straight face – "Only a Registration Office." There was some state schooling available, but it was Islamic and far from free: there were fees for uniforms and books.

Most areas in Soba did not have electricity, and water was moved around mainly by donkey cart: two leaky oil barrels welded together, usually painted pale blue and hoisted onto a pair of old car wheels. Where there was a water hand-pump – often supplied by aid agencies – this was the centre of local activities. In the heart of this bewildering maze of dusty tracks, it might be five or ten kilometres to the nearest shop of any sort; the area was strangely quiet in the daytime as most of the men had made the long trek for work in central Khartoum.

At the Soba clinic, which served a population of thirty to thirty-five thousand, a midwife and a small staff with basic medical training tended to a variety of woes, with malaria, diarrhea, and dysentery at the top of the list. There had been some instances of AIDS, and the staff did their best to educate the local population in this regard, but there was consensus that for cultural reasons AIDS was severely underreported. The facility consisted of three adobe rooms with a straw roof and a separate straw-roofed waiting area, but the proudest edifice was an enclosed latrine in the centre of the square, with a locked door; the key had to be sought from its custodian. This was the only custom-designed sanitary facility in the entire quarter; best not to ask what most people did.

Patients here were charged a small fee, according to their capacity, and this was used to pay the staff; many patients were not charged at all. Medicine was supplied by the United Nations Children's Fund.

At another clinic – spotlessly clean and tidy if rather sparsely equipped – I met the man in charge: a wise elderly Shillook who (so he told me) had a brother in Hawaii and another in Regina. From the clinic log book, I was able to see that thirty to sixty persons attended every day; while I waited the man took a stethoscope to a small baby with bronchial problems. Again, the only state presence here had been in the form of bureaucrats who had periodically closed the clinic down on account of the staff's failure to produce immediately their operation certificate.

At the nearby women's centre, the local women were exceptionally well-organized and dynamic – in spite of (they told me) strong initial suspicions from their menfolk. Their preschool group was attended by fifty or sixty small children, and adult literacy classes were held through the afternoon and into the evening (typically, the women were far behind the men in educational standards). But the challenge was to find productive outlets in this extremely impoverished community where cash was a rare commodity indeed.

Like most IDPs, these people were mainly from southern and western Sudan. This did not necessarily mean they were Christian and/or English-speaking; to the newcomer, indeed, it was quite baffling to try and deduce who was who by their facial characteristics and/or their dress, the exception being persons of the Nuer and Shillook ethnic groups, who might have ritually scarred faces (six horizontal bands on the forehead for Nuer, one for Shillook).

The four formally designated "camps" were Mayo, Jebel Aulia, Wad el-Bashir, and Dar es-Salaam; they housed about 250,000 people. The term *camp* was a misnomer in that very few government services were provided and the new arrivals usually had to build their own accommodation, but the acquisition of land at a nominal rate was facilitated and the areas served as nodes where aid agencies were given full access and tacit encouragement for their activities. By worldwide standards and thanks to generous donor governments, the conditions in these camps were generally acceptable; indeed, health and nutrition surveys now showed higher levels here (after stabilization) than in the Sudanese population at large.

But with the camps only accounting for 10 percent of all displaced persons in the North and with up to one thousand individuals arriving every day in Khartoum the government had now largely given up on making what it saw as artificial distinctions between migrants; it was now allotting land and services (i.e., water) on a non-discriminatory basis. It was easy to understand how this had come about – indeed it seemed to be quite rational, given the bureaucratic (and essentially meaningless) challenges that would be posed by some program that attempted to determine who was war-displaced and who was an economic migrant.

What were the social effects of these huge influxes of people on the city at large? The principal result had been, in the case of Khartoum, the creation of a vast poverty belt on the fringes of the city, where families survived by drastically reducing their food consumption (usually to only one meal a day), by looking for work in the informal sector, and by putting the entire family (including young children) to work. There had been a great strain on infrastructure that was inadequate in the first place: for example, one third of a typical displaced person's income went to securing drinking water, while another third (and many hours of the day) might be spent on travelling to the distant city centre in search of work, this because there was no good water system and no system of widespread and affordable public transport. And precisely because there was no infrastructure (roads, electricity), no industries had sprung up in these shanty towns that might provide IDPs with more viable sources of income close to their new homes.

The optimistic answer to this enormous problem was that, once peace was signed, everyone would go back home. That was unlikely to happen. In the first place, many of the displaced had now been away from their original homes for a decade or more; they had children who had grown up in the new environment and who had likely lost their tribal language, if they'd ever had it. In the second, peace means much more than an absence of war. Years after the conflict in El Salvador ended, violence was at a higher level than ever. Peace also means social, judicial, educational, and economic structures: these could take years to rebuild in areas currently in dispute. And third, after you've been gone for a decade, how likely was it that your land and former home would still be unoccupied? Most aid workers conceded that at most 30 to 50 percent of the present displaced population would eventually return home if peace broke out tomorrow – and that in any case this would imply massive development investment in displacement-generating areas.

A second answer was to keep doing what was being done now. Bad idea. At this time, IDP-focused humanitarian assistance in Khartoum reached at best 10 percent of the affected population (although it had – under certain criteria – actually raised their standards of living above the norm). This was not efficient or desirable use of donor money.

The third answer was a cocktail of measures: increased protection of communities vulnerable to displacement (this could be in terms of a permanent aid agency or United Nations presence); strategies tending to reduce the economic motivation for displacement; small-scale agricultural, livestock, and water projects in potentially vulnerable areas; pilot return processes, with the aim of demonstrating to the displaced population at large that under certain circumstances returns were viable and could be safe; in IDP reception zones, strategies that also paid attention to host communities, resulting in a more even, fairer, and less socially divisive distribution of assistance; and investment and infrastructure projects in the Khartoum poverty belt. Little of this was being implemented, though. On the one hand the reasons were financial, and on the other political. In the short term, you got more visible bang for your buck by feeding x number of hungry mouths post-displacement, although, rationally speaking, it clearly made much more sense to try and limit the push and pull factors rather than wring hands and pour money, year after year, into dealing with the phenomenon post facto.

Political obstacles? Donors feared being seen to do anything that looked like development – and hence complicity – in a country that was at war and was governed so poorly (and where, until late 2002 at least, there was not much prospect of change in either area). Where there was some hope in this otherwise bleak scenario was in some of the innovative programming being done in areas housing displaced persons by aid organizations and the Christian churches, increasingly starved of funds as they might be. Starting in Wad el-Bashir, for example, Canada's Fellowship for African Relief had implemented a child-to-child educational campaign by which young children instructed each other on basic health and hygiene practices: washing your hands before meals, using the assigned latrine areas, using a mosquito net, and so on. Then, with the help of two successive young Canadian interns – the appropriately and biblically named Rachel and Rebecca – the organization had grafted onto this program an entire peacebuilding curriculum: how and why you should get on with people from different ethnic groups, how to deal with bullying in the playground, how to react when the neighbourhood toughs try to inveigle you into glue-sniffing or theft, how to deal with your father coming home drunk and beating up your mother.

The program was an inspiring one, and the kids loved the performing that it involved. They must, for example, learn the traditional songs and dances of each other's regions; and they adored dramatizing daily scenes from the IDP neighbourhood, with a gusto and a lack of self-consciousness not found these days in North American children of the same age. I well recall watching one vivid re-enactment by four adolescents of life on the street – the language barrier was not important, you could sense what was going on – when in staggered what for several moments I thought was the star turn: a grizzled old black man lurching around theatrically drunk. The entire company collapsed in near-hysterical laughter when it became obvious this was no brilliant act. The embarrassed old man, who reeked of homemade alcohol from fifty metres away, sobered up at record speed.

SURPRISINGLY, GIVEN THE RUTHLESSNESS and efficiency of the Islamist regime, the arrest and imprisonment of large numbers of people on account of their political beliefs was not a normal government practice. During my three years in Sudan, the only political grouping that was seriously and regularly persecuted in this manner was Hassan al-Turabi's Popular National Congress Party, but even in this case there would be months on end when Turabi himself was the only member of the party in detention.

A notable exception to the rule was when, in December 2000, the security authorities swooped on a suburban house and detained six opposition figures, along with USA Embassy political officer Glenn Warren. The Sudanese, all openly members of the "inside" (i.e., non-armed) National Democratic Alliance (NDA), including Secretary General Joseph Okello, were accused of plotting with Warren an intifada, or uprising.

Right from the start it was evident that the raid was prompted by pique at the recently concluded and unauthorized visit to rebel-held South Sudan by American Assistant Undersecretary of State Susan Rice; comments made by Rice had enraged the Khartoum authorities and left them thrashing about for some means of striking back. The only evidence against the six and Warren seemed to be handwritten notes by one of the persons at the meeting, in which quite innocuous questions by Warren were recorded

– along the lines of "How serious are the country's economic problems at this time?" Warren was expelled from the country within a few hours, and the six were thrown into Kober prison.

Having quite dramatically thumbed its nose at the Americans, however, Khartoum then had to proceed with things. There was delay after delay, as the NDA-Six's highly effective lawyers challenged one aspect after another of the case. Finally, though, in June 2001, the case opened in the old colonial buildings of Khartoum's Central Courts.

Along with representatives of the European Union and Switzerland, I made it a point to attend regularly what turned out to be a long set of sessions. This was patently a political show trial, and our aim was to demonstrate quietly to the authorities that we knew it to be so; theoretically the defendants could face the death penalty.

Trial procedures were interesting to observe, even though the need for interpretation prevented me from following things as closely as I would have liked. The case was heard by a single judge (government-appointed), with the defendants sitting in a group on his left and prosecution witnesses (principally police officers) standing at a lectern on his right. The large defense team, led by the avuncular and stately Abel Alier and seconded by Ali Mahmoud Hasanein (of the opposition Democratic Unionist Party) sat in cramped conditions around a table close to the defendants, while the prosecution – generally led by an uncertain-looking young man in a shiny suit – had a bigger table. There was usually a large public, made up principally of relatives and friends of the defendants; reporters were allowed in, but it seemed that they were not allowed much latitude by the censors, because trial accounts that appeared in the papers were always very sketchy. Although men with guns lined the walls, the atmosphere was actually quite informal, and in pauses in the proceedings I was several times able to go up and chat with both the defendants and the defense team.

The judge took things seriously. There was no court stenographer, and he insisted on taking down every single declaration longhand, which soon led to the witnesses learning to speak either extremely slowly or with long pauses while the judge caught up. The remnants of the old British justice system could periodically be seen when the gnome-like Ali Mahmoud, clutching his white goatee, would bound to his feet with the English "Objection!" – to which the judge, more often than not, dourly replied (again in English), "overruled."

Day after day (there were usually two sessions a week), the defense would make what seemed to be irrefutable, conclusive arguments: the president himself had frequently met with the National Democratic Alliance, and the same individuals now on trial had openly met as a group with other diplomats and even with the United Nations' Special Rapporteur on Human Rights, with no adverse effects; the meeting place was searched without the authorities being in possession of a warrant; the defendants had no history of armed activity; there was no conclusive documentary evidence at all, and so on. It became evident that, in spite of his known political affiliations, the judge was finding that he had no alternative but to see the strength of the defense's case. His questions towards the lackadaisical prosecutor became more and more tetchy, and the prosecutor began to resort to ever more far-fetched tactics just to prolong the trial, including calling witnesses whom he knew to be out of the country.

Eventually, some nine months after the initial incident, the whole case was dismissed. It was a demonstration both of the government's vindictiveness and of the ultimate integrity of a much deteriorated justice system.

AN OBLIGATORY CONTACT for all Western embassies and a must on the itinerary of visiting delegations with even the most peripheral interest in human rights was lawyer Ghazi Suleiman. Over the previous decade, Ghazi had been perhaps the most consistently outspoken of the government's many critics on human rights but had acquired such international celebrity that he enjoyed a certain degree of immunity. Having a brother as the president's top economic adviser may also have helped.

Usually I would visit him at his home in the suburb known unimaginatively as Khartoum 2, where most late afternoons and evenings he would hold court and alternately entertain and entrance a steady procession of acolytes with his deliberately outrageous and colourful – if often over-the-top and not always politically correct – rantings against the government. He would be dressed rather bizarrely in white trousers, a gleaming white dress shirt, dark blue suspenders, and a matching blue tie, and he would punctuate his most colourful utterances by stabbing his cigarette holder into the air.

For novices, his habit of speaking very loudly, of leaning forwards in seeming aggression, and of apparently wanting to provoke with every statement could be unnerving. I recall that when I took Canada's peace envoy, Senator Mobina Jaffer, to see him in early 2003, we had barely said hello when he launched into a condemnation of Saddam Hussein as The Mother of All Dictators and – consciously bucking the mood of the day in Khartoum – berated Canada for not enthusiastically joining the USA/UK alliance against Iraq; he then veered off into an enthusiastic defense of Talisman, lamenting that their departure from Sudan would expose the country to the "horrors" of Chinese, Malaysian, and Indian business ethics. Fortunately, just as the senator was bracing herself to make an energetic rebuttal of all of this, Ghazi's eye was momentarily caught by a mouse running under the chair of Canada's ambassador; his intensity collapsed, and the senator realized it was all said in good humour.

As a human rights activist, Ghazi merited failing scores on a number of counts. He was energetic in his condemnation of homosexuality as an "unnatural vice"; he blurred his human rights activism with political activism so that you could not tell the difference between Ghazi the opposition politician and Ghazi the lawyer; and he would accept no challenges to what he saw as his anointed role as leader of the human rights movement in Sudan. But in spite of this; I always went to see him. Ghazi had paid his dues.

In February 2001, I had visited him at the Blue Nile Hospital in Omdurman, where he was recovering from seventy-two days in illegal detention – only the latest in a lifetime of arrests. He was suffering from no major ailment, but he had lost a lot of weight, had bloodshot eyes, and looked generally very run down. Happily, his spirits were as high and combative as ever; he was sitting up and receiving many visits and phone calls (for example, from exiled NDA leader Osman al-Mirghani calling from abroad while I was visiting) and hoped to be out of hospital in another two or three days.

But the beating Ghazi had suffered at the beginning of his detention had been severe: he had been attacked with fists, knocked unconscious, and spent the best part of twelve days in and out of consciousness. He was told that this was to "shut him up."

He had been detained at Kober Security headquarters, an annex to Kober prison in Khartoum North. For the first thirty-two days he was kept in solitary confinement. At no time was he allowed to speak to a lawyer. He was given no access to radio, TV, newspapers, or any books other than the Koran. He did not see any of various other detainees arrested at the same time, and, whenever he was moved from one place to another, the immediate vicinity was cleared. There was no advance warning of his release. He was told he could be rearrested any day.

He vowed not to stay gagged and indeed said he would file for damages, following his beating. He did say to me, however, that "we need to be cleverer"; by this he seemed to mean that he and other activists needed to be more careful in the exact wording of what they said, so as to give no excuse for arrest.

Ghazi's alleged crime? To have stated publicly that he thought the arrest of the internal NDA-Six was wrong and that he intended to defend them.

IN APRIL 2003, much to the displeasure of the Western members of the United Nations' Geneva-based Commission on Human Rights, Sudan assembled sufficient supporters (among them Cuba, Libya, Syria, and Zimbabwe) to defeat a resolution sanctioning the country for its human rights record and mandating, for another year, a Special Rapporteur on Human Rights for Sudan. Officials crowed that it was a triumph for Sudanese foreign policy, the long-delayed and overdue readmission of Sudan to the Comity of Nations. Abruptly, the human rights situation deteriorated.

A fourteen-year-old pregnant girl was sentenced to one hundred lashes; her alleged rapist was acquitted for lack of evidence. Death sentences rocketed, along with arbitrary detentions. The *Khartoum Monitor* was closed down for two months, and other leading papers repeatedly had their daily print runs seized. Anyone suspected of connection to the nascent Darfur insurgency was shown no mercy. Ghazi Suleiman and a clutch of associates were arrested for calling a press conference at which they intended to air their opinions regarding the peace process; Ghazi's family was not informed of where he was being held.

In June, I was contacted by Amnesty International regarding a case of five men from the Nuba region who had been detained earlier – on 19 May – apparently for plotting something in connection with Darfur. One of the five men was beaten to death within twenty-four hours, by a group of eight plainclothes security police. Initially, outraged, his family refused to accept his body, but local Nuba leaders were prevailed upon to mediate and the body was finally accepted and buried without protest.

Although the remaining four men were kept in detention, no charges were laid. A second man (whom I will call Mohammed) had also been beaten especially severely – with sticks and thick plastic-coated electrical cable – and had sulphuric acid splashed over him. In mid-June his health started to deteriorate significantly: his kidneys had apparently been severely damaged by the beatings to his lower back. Panicking, security sent him under escort with one of the other four prisoners to the kidney unit of Khartoum General Hospital.

Amnesty was concerned that, if the profile of the case were not somehow raised, then Mohammed would quietly die in obscurity, and the authorities would have gotten away with a double murder. I contacted both Mohammed's lawyer and a family friend to make sure that associating myself to the case would not put them deeper into trouble. They told me things could hardly get worse, so I might as well come on board.

We went straight to the hospital. Mohammed was lying on a bed in a four-person ward; the place was hot and filthy but no more so than the rest of the rooms in the rambling colonial-era edifice; his mother sat quietly on a straw mat at one end of the room. He was fully conscious, but, just as I started introducing myself, a tall well-dressed young man in sunglasses hurried in and stationed himself at the end of the bed, listening; "Security," confirmed my lawyer friend in a whisper.

Thenceforth our conversation was stilted. But I could see for myself the extensive scarring on Mohammed's forearms and elbows that he said was caused by acid, and he showed me that it was awkward for him to lie in any position that put the slightest strain on his waist. He confirmed in terse "yes"s and "no"s that his injuries had been sustained at the hands of internal security; the young man at the end of the bed listened but made no attempt to interrupt.

Mohammed's lawyer had a fistful of medical papers, the latest of which was an order – in English – for an ultrasound scan. When I looked interrogatively at the security man he responded that security was covering all the bills. But, no, I could not see the doctors' reports; they were in the possession of security.

I asked him why Mohammed was in detention, as it was now well past the maximum three-day time limit by which an individual must be charged or released. He shrugged and said that, as soon as Mohammed was well enough, he would be taken back to his home town and released there.

That night Mohammed slipped into a coma. The doctors placed him in intensive care and all further access, including by his family, was denied. Fearing the worst, his lawyer concentrated now on somehow obtaining a copy of the doctors' report before it was too late; if this case was ever to be taken further, this evidence would be vital.

OCCUPYING A QUARTER OF A CITY BLOCK in Khartoum 2 was the Maygoma orphanage. Every day, the police would bring to the orphanage two or three abandoned babies, some only hours old; they had been picked up from police station doorsteps, from the steps of mosques, or even from garbage. In Sudan's version of Islam, the stigma of having a baby out of wedlock was so enormous that few Muslim girls – least of all in the urban centres – were prepared to endure the lifetime of shame that keeping the baby would entail. Although half the population of Khartoum was of black African origin, no baby of this description was ever brought in; the displaced camps were desperate places, but it seemed there was always room for one more baby.

The numbers that reached Maygoma were probably only a fraction of those actually born illegitimately; it was thought that most were killed at birth. For reasons that were not clear, the majority who were abandoned alive were girls – was it that boys were kept or was it that the mothers pitied their baby girls more and would not kill them?

It was not easy for a foreigner to gain permission to visit Maygoma, and once inside I was strictly forbidden from taking photographs. I was never sure exactly why. Was it because the authorities did not want foreigners to see that there existed "immorality" in Islam, or was it out of shame over the conditions to which the babies were exposed here? Maygoma in 2000 and 2001 was a vision from hell that wore down all the well-meaning foreigners (and there had been many over the years) who tried to do something for these hapless innocents.

Some months, forty or fifty of the sixty or so admissions would die. It was true that many were in a desperate state when admitted, but most simply expired from neglect. Although the local staff – with international aid agency support – were paid twice what they would make in a hospital, most saw the babies as expendable products of sin, and, if five or six died in a night because the duty nurse had slept through their feeding times, it was shrugged off as the will of God. Ironically, the times of greatest morbidity were the Islamic religious holidays. At Ramadan, all the staff would adjourn every evening for raucous and long-lasting "breakfasts" at sunset, ignoring the pathetic cries of the babies, to the despair of foreign volunteers who assisted with simple physical therapy and held the hands of the dying but were not allowed to help with feeding.

Early in 2003, a decree came down from the Ministry of Social Welfare that henceforth no foreign volunteers were to be allowed to work at Maygoma. No reason was given. The director of the board of trustees, an erudite but ineffectual man, surmised that it might be because there existed no formal agreement with the ministry governing their work. "But it makes no mention of Sudanese nationals ..." he said consolingly.

"There are no Sudanese nationals working as volunteers," Beth Pelletier, the US director of the thirty-strong team of volunteers, shot back through her tears. "We've never been able to get any to stay ..."

"Well perhaps it's because the foreign wives have no work permits," the Director suggested lamely.

"And why would they need permits if what they are doing is unpaid?" answered Beth.

"Couldn't the volunteers at least be allowed to stay on until some formal agreement is set up?" I finally asked. I was at the meeting because Canada was funding an upgrade of the facilities and the purchase of toys for the orphanage. The Director shrugged. "I'll see what I can do. But you must understand that this week everyone is away at the pilgrimage in Mecca ..."

Eventually the volunteers were allowed back in. But I wondered how many had died as a result of this utter callousness on the part of some self-important bureaucrat in the ministry. Of all the victims of the regime, the unnamed and unloved babies of Maygoma were perhaps the most innocent and the most pathetic of all.

THE GOVERNMENT OF SUDAN kept a very wary eye on the media. It had an effective monopoly on radio and TV, but print media proliferated in Khartoum, and here the government faced a much trickier job. One of the banes of the administration's existence was the only English-language newspaper, the *Khartoum Monitor*, which first appeared on the street soon after my arrival in Sudan.

Its circulation never exceeded five thousand, and it often resembled more an amateur school journal than a modern newspaper. Much of its column space was filled by wire-service reports that were several days old and for which no subscription was being paid; and there were large sections of Hollywood gossip and sports news lifted straight from the internet (complete with hyperlinks). Columns would end in mid-sentence or would be inexplicably repeated on consecutive pages; captions for an Elton John photograph would be transposed with David Beckham's.

But the *Monitor* did carry, relative to other newspapers, unusually extensive coverage of the war, and in its editorial and opinion columns it conscientiously sought to present Southern points of view that were conspicuous by their absence from mainstream Arabic-language media such as *Ray al-Am*. And because it was in (admittedly erratic) English and because a number of its columns were replicated on its website, it had a disproportionate effect in influencing the diplomatic corps and the Sudanese diaspora.

The two key figures behind the *Monitor* were the large and genial Equatorian Alfred Taban, who doubled as a stringer for BBC Radio and Reuters, and the two-metre-tall Dinka Nhial Bol. They were a constant fixture on the diplomatic cocktail circuit – and not averse to the illicit liquid pleasures on offer at these events – but they were also true crusaders.

Scarcely a month went by without the government attempting some new ruse to force the *Monitor* out of business. First, there was an arbitrary rule that said you must publish a minimum of twelve pages (the *Monitor* had eight until then) and that you must employ a certain minimum number of registered journalists: a blatant attempt to force the *Monitor* and other small papers out of business. Then there were the constant late-night visits by censors, who would "pull" one article after another, sometimes when the print run was already rolling; for a while the *Monitor* responded by printing blank spaces, but it was told it could not do this. Then it ran cartoons of a zippered mouth; these again were banned. Finally the code by which it indicated to readers that it had been censored was a series of anti-smoking drawings, against which the censors could find no reasonable objection. Twice, the government put money behind rival English-language papers that were much more cooperative – *The Journalist* and the *Nile Courier* – but both were short-lived.

And then there were the lawsuits. The *Monitor* was once taken to court because an article on HIV/AIDS suggested (quite reasonably) that its spread in the South could presumably be attributed in part to government troops and associated prostitution. Another time it was sued for publishing a historical article on the spread of Islam, recalling that it had arrived in this part of the world at the point of a sword; this was taken by the authorities as a dig against the campaign in the South, and the print run was seized. In May 2003 the paper was closed down for two months following a complaint by the Ministry of Religious Guidance, focusing on three articles: one about a Christian priest who had been imprisoned for objecting to the demolition of a church; another advocating peaceful Christian/Muslim coexistence; and a third suggesting that Islam allows for some latitude on the matter of alcohol.

Through these misfortunes, Alfred and Nhial soldiered on stoically. For weeks on end they would receive no pay, and they were always trekking around begging for assistance in paying their fines. Both were in and out of prison constantly, to the point at which they kept suitcases always ready. On occasion, Alfred had even had to file his BBC Radio report from a mobile phone in his prison cell.

They took a secret delight, too, in the fact that the censors never seemed to "get" many of the quite risqué jokes that they reprinted from the internet in the daily humour columns. On one occasion, after the paper had been briefly banned for another article on HIV/AIDS, which had touched upon the phenomenon of prostitution in Khartoum by recounting an erotic late-night encounter in a Khartoum taxi, the paper slyly printed a full apology along with the judgement of the Press Council, including the complete and full offending text in bold case.

The *Monitor* wasn't about to bring about the fall of a dictatorship and the restoration of democracy in Sudan all on its own. But Alfred and Nhial's perseverance against all the odds, in spite of the almost laughable efforts of the government to silence this nagging mosquito, was an inspiration. One day, I was sure, they would be able to say with pride that they helped usher in a better Sudan.

5

NORTHERN LIGHTS

CONVERSATIONS WITH THE ELITE

THE HOME OF Sheikh Hassan Abdullah al-Turabi was a local landmark in the Khartoum neighbourhood of Riyadh, east of the airport, now rivaled in local folklore only by the rambling house nearby that Osama bin-Laden rented for several years in the early 1990s. I paid the sheikh a call in January 2001; as he welcomed me at the door he gestured to the newly asphalted road outside and chuckled: "See, I still have some influence ..."

Active in politics all his life and related by marriage to the Mahdi clan, Turabi had risen to the rank of attorney general under Jaafar Nimeiri in 1979 but fell from grace just before Nimeiri himself; perhaps not coincidentally, he was thrown into prison immediately following a 1985 visit to Khartoum by US Vice-President George Bush (senior). After the fall of Nimeiri the following year, he became the secretary general of the National Islamic Front (NIF; later the National Congress), subsequently serving as Justice Minister in Sadiq al-Mahdi's government.

In June 1989 he masterminded General Omar al-Bashir's coup, which effectively installed the National Islamic Front; but this was by no means clear at the time, and in fact – in a flurry of intra-NIF and military power struggles following the coup – he was for a while detained again. Over the next few years, he was the acknowledged power behind the throne, but following his election as Speaker of Parliament in 1996 he became increasingly critical of Bashir and was unceremoniously dumped from his post – and a State of Emergency was declared – at the end of 1999. He then started up his own breakaway movement, the confusingly named Popular National Congress Party (PNCP).

What was intended as a courtesy call turned into a three-hour marathon; this man clearly loved to talk (whether in Arabic, upper-class English, or flawless French); as we sat in wide armchairs with fruit juices arriving every half hour or so, he would often lean forward to me to make his point, then sit back and let his crossed leg swing back and forth almost frenetically. Often, at some lighthearted remark, he would emit a disconcerting high-pitched giggle, his eyes twinkling through his thick, black-rimmed glasses.

Turabi's mind was exceedingly agile; he was capable in one breath of pondering the apparently contradictory tendencies of Quebec separatism and the drift towards a federated Europe, and in the next the halcyon days of Islam. His anecdotes included characters ranging from Ronald Reagan (who at a dinner let slip to Turabi that he thought Sudan was in Latin America) to the princes of the House of Saud. Much of his humour was self-deprecating; he related how, several weeks after Bush's March 1985 visit to Khartoum and his own immediate imprisonment, he received, in his prison cell, formal written notification that he had been relieved of his ministerial portfolio.

I had to remind myself that the genial Hassan al-Turabi, perhaps as much as any other individual, had led Sudan to the sad state in which it found itself in early 2001: he had been the driving force behind the implementation of sharia under Nimeiri; until a year ago he had been responsible for the steady escalation of the war; and he must bear the brunt of the blame for the terrible human rights abuses of the Bashir regime in the early 1990s, notably the infamous ghost houses in which opponents of the regime were tortured and often disappeared. Most days, I used to drive past one of these locations: the old Citibank building on Middle Road in Amarat. It was even suggested to me that he was personally responsible for the one-woman hate campaign against Sudan instigated at the heart of the Clinton administration's State Department by Assistant Undersecretary Susan Rice: at a seminar at which Turabi was a key speaker, attended by Rice, Turabi allegedly responded to a particularly probing question by her with a sarcastic response along the lines of "you belong barefoot and pregnant, in the kitchen" – for which Rice never forgave him.

Turabi's analysis of Sudan's post-independence history was a simple one: three times, attempts had been made to build a strong central government, but three times these had failed in the face of Sudan's fundamentally nomadic culture, in which parties were more sect and geography-based than politically inspired. "Coups are how we do things," he said, adding as an aside, "I should know."

The key to governing successfully, he said, was instead to accept the size and diversity of Sudan and to move towards a decentralized, federated state. Phenomena as diverse as the growth of the market economy (tending to break down regional borders and leading to labour migration), desertification, even the flow of displaced persons from war-affected zones could only be dealt with by devolution of powers to the regions. And what was happening instead? President Bashir – "as one might expect from a soldier" – was appropriating more and more power to himself and the central government "so that we are now truly in a military dictatorship"; witness his recently tightened security legislation, the extension of the State of Emergency, his retention of the power to name governors, and his gradual erosion of the principle of ministerial accountability.

I referred to the December 2000 elections, which had seen Bashir win another term as president. Didn't these elections validate him in any way? No, insisted Turabi: "This was the worst election in the history of the Sudan." Children were pressed into voting, some urns were found to contain whole books of ballots, and in half the ridings of the country there was only one candidate. Official participation figures (over 60 percent) were "wildly exaggerated."

So what did Turabi's breakaway Popular National Congress Party have to offer instead? "Initially we were an elite," Turabi said, "but now we have widened our base." He estimated that 85 percent of the country's students were with him and that he had the support of many women. At my raised eyebrows, he commented, "Our ambition, you see, is to use Islam to defeat negative cultural practices affecting women." The PNCP had no contemporary model for its "democratic Islam" (certainly not the Taliban of Afghanistan, whom Turabi described as uncouth, uneducated, and quite ignorant of the Koran), but Turabi said that such a state did once exist: for some three generations immediately after the death of the Prophet and among his closest followers when, he added, women also held leadership roles.

Moreover, Turabi said, the PNCP had a strong following still within the existing Bashir administration. Ministers saw Turabi himself on an almost daily basis, and their principal complaints were that they had been robbed by the president of their powers and that Bashir was operating increasingly as a one-man show, in secrecy. Even in economic terms, Turabi and his allies contested, the president was trying to hold all the cards, refusing to privatize industries that should be sold off.

Turabi emphatically rejected the "fundamentalist" tag in every sense: "Besides, we are not an extreme people; we are not aggressive and we have no tradition whatsoever of political assassination." Both Umma and the Democratic Unionist Party (DUP) – the two other principal opposition parties – were, he claimed, much more deeply based in religion than his PNCP, both being derived from Sufi sects; Umma leader Sadiq al-Mahdi derived much of his prestige and following from the fact that he was a direct descendant of the Mahdi (a "messiah"). If there were fanatics to be found anywhere in Sudan, Turabi suggested, it was in Umma's Wahabi-tending private army. He also rejected the secular/non-secular dichotomy as a false one, pointing out that "To describe a state where Islamic values predominate as a non-secular state is nonsense, because Islam has no established church – Islam is a set of beliefs and values, not a church." Having said that, his objective was indeed a state in which Islamic values would be entrenched at various levels. Some of these values might need to be legislated at a national level – for example, the prohibition of the concept of interest (in a financial sense), which could be substituted by the Koran-compatible model of depositors as shareholders. But the infamous punishment codes that sharia is sometimes purported to require could almost invariably be made discretionary, without contradicting the Koran, and left to regional constituencies. Sharia was not currently applied in South Sudan, and even in the North there were these days "a maximum of four or five amputations a year."

"Democratic Islam, in which everyone has direct access to God and in which everyone rules themselves according to God's precepts," Turabi conceded, might take some time in coming – the process would be slow, just as the radication of democracy ("which never arrived here") in Europe was slow. The neighbours (he clearly meant Egypt) would also be suspicious, he added: "Anywhere that people rule themselves, other people get nervous." Did Colonel Gaddafi, with his emphasis on shura (consultation) ever get it right? He sometimes came close, Turabi said, but in the end (and here he related a number of uncomplimentary anecdotes) Gaddafi was and is a bad Muslim – apart from anything "he is profoundly racist." Turabi recounted how once he had, over dinner in Gaddafi's tent, informed the colonel that *Adam* means *black*, a point which Gaddafi had vehemently disputed until reference books were brought proving Turabi right.

So how was Democratic Islam to be achieved? Turabi hoped that the present regime could be eased out softly but was not betting on it. He did not advocate a coup this time – he believed that the Army was no more capable of running the country than President Bashir himself – but considered one possible, as he did an intifada that could culminate in the military taking control. The situation, in sum, was "precarious."

In the short term, Turabi's aim was a strategic alliance between the three major opposition parties: his own PNCP, Umma, and the Democratic Unionist Party. The three groupings had enough in common – the need for a free press, full and meaningful elections, the ending of the State of Emergency, agreement on the Declaration of Principles for Southern Sudan – to make this alliance viable, he said. The objective: to shame the president into handing over power and calling meaningful elections ("failing that ... an intifada"). Would the Democratic Unionists come "in" to participate in such an alliance? Perhaps they were not yet ready for the alliance, he admitted, but they were certainly getting ready to come back: DUP leader Osman al-Mirghani's younger brother Ahmed was expected back in Khartoum any time, and it was reported that the house of Osman himself was being readied.

We talked about the war. The Popular National Congress Party, said Turabi, had always had Southerners among its ranks and had good connections in the displaced camps of Khartoum. The South must somehow be represented in any opposition front, and to this end he had been attempting to hold a dialogue with SPLM/A Chairman John Garang. Would a hypothetical PNCP Government let the South go? "We agree to a referendum, but we hope that we would then be able to persuade the South not to leave"; Southern Sudan, he believed, was quite unsustainable as a state. But, I asked, hadn't he at one point advocated a jihad against the South? "Jihad," he said, is a much misunderstood term – it can mean as little as "effort" or "debate," certainly never any more than "responding in kind" (this from the man who formed the Popular Defense Forces and sent hundreds of young people off to their deaths, assuring them that they would be instantly transported to paradise).

Turabi believed that 85 percent of the country's disposable income was now going to the war and/or the security forces. Much of this money was squandered or dissolved in a morass of corruption; the military hardware the government did make available to its armed forces (notably tanks) "soon ends up in the hands of the SPLA anyway." And the oil revenues? Turabi maintained that neither the Central Bank nor the Ministry of Finance knew how much was being earned from oil, nor where the revenues were going.

On to the Great Satan. "We are much misunderstood in the USA," Turabi unsurprisingly claimed. He believed that the USA still associated Sudan with the mad mullahs of Iran and could not efface from its collective brain those humiliating images of students occupying the US Embassy in Teheran. For the USA, Islam was now necessarily anti-democratic; witness their terror at the prospect of democratically elected Islamist governments in Algeria and Turkey. The issue of Islam was still a relatively new one to the USA, and Americans were profoundly ignorant of Sudan, their views particularly skewed by the allegations of slavery in Sudan. For Europe, on the other hand, anti-Sudanism was an extension of the Crusades and was more deeply felt; for this reason, if he was exiled from Sudan, Turabi would rather live in the USA or Canada than Europe. "Islam can be freedom, it can be democracy ... don't fear it," he concluded.

Turabi "knew and liked Canada" before he was attacked at Ottawa airport in May 1992 by an exiled Sudanese karate expert (!); "I bear no hard feelings." In that he had much to do with the arrival of Canadian oil companies in Sudan (first Arakis, then Talisman), he was quite familiar with our current stake in this country. Our cards here were, he suggested, the facts that we were not the USA, had no colonial past, and had no superiority complex. He was well aware of and quite admiring of Canada's agenda at the United Nations and particularly related to our position that the United Nations Security Council should be more truly representative. He felt there was great scope for Canadian investment in Sudan: in agricultural machinery, electricity generation, mining, cattle raising and meat-packing, and so on.

Yesterday's man? I wasn't sure. I had the impression that this man had an extremely active, agile, and political mind through which many schemes were running at any one time. He was possibly the most able politician in a country where everyone must be political.

Certainly Bashir feared him. On 21 February 2001, barely a month after I had met Turabi in his Riyadh home, he was arrested, ostensibly on account of his Popular National Congress Party having signed a memorandum of understanding (presumably as a result of the discussions to which he had referred in our conversation) with the SPLM/A. Government spokesperson and Information Minister Dr Ghazi Salah al-Dien, announcing the arrest, said that "the agreement ... is meant to create a political alliance between the two parties with the aim of toppling the present government ... the arrest was made to prevent anarchy in the country and to maintain order and stability." Salah al-Dien also said that Turabi had claimed he was "in contact with the USA authorities." (Turabi publicly admitted this: "But don't ask me at what level ... Of course they want to know what the Islamists think.")

For the next two and a half years, Turabi remained incommunicado and accessible only to his immediate family, at first in a prison-guesthouse on the banks of the Blue Nile, but for a period in August 2002, when PNCP supporters briefly staged riots in the apparent hope of triggering an uprising in Turabi's name, in Kober prison. He was not brought to trial: the common wisdom was that the government feared to release him, lest Turabi spill the goods on all sorts of nefarious deeds dating from the early years of the regime, including the attempted assassination of President Mubarak in 1995 and dealings with Osama bin-Laden. The Egyptian ambassador was plain to me when I asked his government's opinion: "The day they let Turabi out, I'm packing my bags." There were many who suspected the Americans shared this view. But in October 2003, with peace talks progressing well, Turabi was unexpectedly let out; and the Egyptian ambassador stayed in place.

NOMINALLY SPEAKING, Secretary General Dr Ibrahim Ahmed Omer was Turabi's replacement as chief ideologue of the National Islamic Front (or National Congress, as it had now become). Our meetings took place in the former Catholic Club on Airport Road; the National Islamic Front had seized it and made its headquarters here ten years earlier, placing an enormous pale green concrete Koran at the gate. It was an irony I thought it not politic to bring to Dr Omer's attention on our first meeting, although the Khartoum Christian community did not cease to complain.

The bearded and bespectacled Omer (who superficially resembled Turabi) was courtly, urbane, and sophisticated in his discourse, as are so many interlocutors at his level in Sudan. "We are no mad mullahs" was the not-so-subliminal message. Only once did I glimpse intolerance, when he let slip that, although there was room in his Sudan for Christians, Jews, and other "people of the book," there was clearly none for atheists; he took it completely for granted that a Westerner such as myself was a practicing Christian or Jew.

Sudan, he pleaded, was misunderstood – how many times had I heard that before! The West failed to recognize the facts: this was a multiparty state, governed according to an enlightened Constitution that was drafted by democratic means. This Constitution made explicit provision for all internationally recognized human rights. Now the government was not perfect on observing the Constitution – "What state is?" – but it remained the frame of reference, and the administration stood to be corrected whenever it erred. I pointed out when I first met Omer that a State of Emergency – overriding the Constitution – had then been in effect for almost eighteen months. Omer was not to be deterred. In the first place, he said, this would soon be suspended, and in the second "you will have noted" that the president had made only the most judicious use of the special powers thus conferred upon him.

Insofar as the international community was concerned, the National Congress Party was presently engaged in a campaign to "explain ourselves" to the world and to say "we are open for business." Thus far, Omer said, Sudan had found a relatively receptive ear in the European Union and the USA; within the region, bilateral relations with both Uganda and Eritrea nevertheless remained problematic.

Omer equated Canada with Talisman. He said that the company was doing a "fine job" and that the government was happy that the pressures put upon it had not resulted in its quitting Sudan (our first meeting was in 2001). The company had served to "encourage" Europe and the USA, he concluded. Generally speaking, the objective of Khartoum was to achieve a geographic balance vis-à-vis investment sources; hence the presence of

Talisman and a growing UK presence were set off by those of the Chinese and Malaysian national oil companies.

Why should anyone invest here? The economy was strong, Omer answered, and getting stronger, privatization was proceeding apace, relations with the international funds – especially the International Monetary Fund – were good. Moreover, Sudanese were renowned for their friendliness, and Khartoum was one of the safest cities in Africa (I had no quibbles there).

I pressed Omer to define the National Congress Party at this moment. Here he was evasive, clearly wanting to avoid the Islamist tag. He began by saying what the NC was not: unlike the Democratic Unionist Party and Umma, it was non-sectarian; it was middle-class and urban in origin – particularly strong in the universities – and now broadening its base into rural Sudan. "We are both modern and authentic," he went on; "We are leading Sudan with our values and our beliefs, but we are taking modernity along with us." Yes, "You could say that our vision of Sudan is one of an Islamic state," he conceded, but it was one where there was room for other religions, too. Moreover, Omer suggested, "the basic values of all religions are the same: a belief in God, keeping one's promises, being tolerant." And the economy? "We are convinced free-marketeers."

This led us to a brief discussion of Turabi's ouster from the party eighteen months earlier. The problem here, Omer said, was not one of ideology but rather of Turabi's style and profile. He had simply become too big for his own boots and for the party, and all sense of collegiality had been lost – for this reason he had to go.

Discussing the relationship between the party and the administration, Omer suggested that the party could be seen as a think-tank, with the government serving as its interface with society. The party's job was to feed both the central government and the regional governors with ideas and principles, and the government's was to shape those ideas into concrete form and execute them. Omer himself directed this at the working level, although President Bashir was also formally president of the party.

Looking ahead, Omer noted that traditional urban/rural divisions in Sudan were fading away, as they were everywhere in the face of globalization. The only practical model for Sudan was one of a decentralized state, with special recognition (à la Quebec) for the South, on account of its ethnic makeup and of what it had suffered these past fifty years.

Omer said that Khartoum did not believe it could win the war militarily ("although Garang still does"). The number one priority right now should be a ceasefire. After this, but only after this, peace talks stood a real chance of making progress. By all means the talks could take the Declaration of Principles of the Intergovernmental Authority on Development as a point of departure, although the party made no bones about not being happy with either separation or confederation. What would it take for the South to opt for unity? "Schools, roads, hospitals, development ..."

In true Sudanese style, Omer was clearly telling me what he sensed I wanted to hear: he was almost frustratingly reasonable. Frustrating in the sense that, if one took everyone at their word on the conflict that wracked Sudan, there seemed to be few if any serious points of disagreement, certainly insufficient to justify the degree of ongoing violence.

When I met the professor again, in early 2003, the regional context had changed dramatically: the attacks of 9/11 had cast the Muslim world into agonies of self-examination, and a war in Iraq seemed imminent. What we were now witnessing, he suggested as he warmed visibly to the theme, was a new kind of Cold War, that was no longer about capitalism vs communism, but rather Christians vs what they saw as savages, with the Middle East and its predominantly Muslim population now substituting for the Soviet Union and its allies. The implicit message of the West, he suggested, was that *Christianity* equates with *Democracy* and that, marching hand in hand, the two will inevitably lead to *Progress*; the converse is that *Islam* is equated with *Totalitarianism* and *Backwardness*.

So was this what we were seeing in Sudan, with the West aligning behind the nominally Christian SPLM/A to oppose the nominally Muslim North? Well, no, said Omer. The Sudanese conflict had no significant Christian/Muslim dimension: its roots were in the apartheid-like policies of the British in colonial times, which fostered the Southerners' sense of difference and left a legacy of relative underdevelopment and illiteracy in the South. It was unfortunate that the two flag-bearers of the new Cold War, the United States and Britain, also happened to be the two principal mediators in the Sudanese conflict, the professor admitted, but this should not distract Sudan: the approach should be peace at any price.

We returned to the subject of bin-Laden. It was both a virtue and a vice of Islam, Omer conceded, that Islam had no authorities, no priesthood; on the one hand this allowed for direct communion with God, but on the other it permitted anyone and everyone to state, without fear of contradiction, that he or she acted in the name of God. Hence Islam's failure or refusal to condemn bin-Laden as loudly as the West would have liked. But certainly there was consensus in the Arab world that what al-Qaeda did, in attacking the United States at home, was not legitimate jihad; for the professor, the term should be understood not so much as "Holy War" but as "Defense of the Right to Preach Islam," with the emphasis on defense, not offense.

A dangerous deepening of this new Cold War, he concluded, could only be avoided with ever more energetic attempts by all to pursue interfaith dialogue, to promote both Islam and Christianity as different manifestations of the same basic truths. Otherwise, the dire predictions of Samuel Huntington's *Clash of Civilizations and the Remaking of World Order* could not fail to come true.

ASSESSING WHO REALLY HELD the reins within government (as opposed to the party) was something of a mug's game: everyone had their pet theories, but no two sets of theories ever seemed to coincide. The common wisdom, nevertheless, usually listed five or six individuals after President Bashir (whose own degree of control was by no means evident or the subject of consensus): Ali Osman Tahaa, Qutbi al-Mahdi, Nafie al-Nafie, Awad al-Jaz, and Ghazi Salah al-Dien.

It was also in the post-9/11 context that I met Dr Qutbi al-Mahdi, senior political counsellor to the president, in his stately rooms in Gordon's old Residence. Qutbi, whose most recent period of residence abroad had been as ambassador to Iran, had studied in Canada and indeed was said to hold a Canadian passport. However, due to a reported investigation by the Royal Canadian Mounted Police (for alleged involvement in serious abuses when he held a high rank in Internal Security), I judged it not tactful – given my purpose – to allude to his Canadian connections; Qutbi himself was similarly silent in this regard.

I congratulated Qutbi on the very positive public statements made by the Government of Sudan in the wake of 9/11 and recent measures of political openness: the president's decision the previous day to release unconditionally the members of the National Democratic Alliance Secretariat and various members of Turabi's Popular National Congress Party (albeit not

Turabi himself). I also noted carefully that Sudan must be pleased with the recent suspension of United Nations sanctions and (temporarily) of the Sudan Peace Act in the US Congress.

On the peace process (which in October 2001 looked moribund), Qutbi admitted that Khartoum's stance must at times seem confusing; but this, he insisted, was due to the complexity of the issue and of Khartoum's keenness to respond positively to every initiative going. Commenting specifically on the process mediated by the Intergovernmental Authority on Development, he went on: "It has been a very useful exercise;" he said, "it enabled us for the first time to identify and discuss issues. It certainly wasn't a flop," but, he went on, "it has got stuck." He suggested that IGAD's Sudan Peace Secretariat had been uncreative and insufficiently forceful and that as a result there had developed in government circles "a growing feeling that IGAD has done what it could do – that it has become circular."

Qutbi agreed that the two stumbling points in this process, which were also the two issues that prevented its reconciliation with the rival Egyptian-Libyan Initiative, were on the one hand the question of the separation of state and religion and on the other the principle of self-determination for the South. Qutbi felt that on state and religion there was in fact room for accommodation, if the SPLM/A would just abandon its insistence on the national government explicitly labelling itself as "secular." He went on to suggest the rebels were using ostensible deadlock on this issue as a Trojan Horse for advancing their real objective – that the talks immediately jump to discussion of transition/referendum/self-determination. Qutbi noted in passing that Khartoum had first accepted the use of the term self-determination in 1991, but "the political context was quite different then" and the phrase had not been as loaded as it has now become – to the point at which "it is code for secession." Discussing the Southern movement in general, he was dismissive of John Garang's claim to represent all Southerners and skeptical regarding reports that he had mended fences with exiled fellow Southerner Bona Malwal.

On oil, Qutbi agreed with my assessment that disrupting the industry was at this time at the top of the SPLM/A's list of military objectives. Khartoum found this intensely frustrating because "Oil is the key to the development for which the South is clamouring." I pressed him on the need to be as transparent as possible in the expenditure of the oil revenues (likely to reach USD $1 billion that year): he took the point and said that Khartoum was involved in detailed and open discussions with the International

Monetary Fund on the use of the revenues but that Sudanese sovereignty nevertheless had to be respected. He also suggested that Western critics greatly underestimated the many demands made upon the oil revenues – which were not just by the defense establishment.

Moving on to the internal political situation following the 9/11 terrorist attacks, Qutbi said that Sudan's condemnation of al-Qaeda should not be seen as "climbing on the bandwagon"; rather, it reflected a studied determination to "do the right thing and take the moral high ground." He doubted the possibility of a Pakistan-type anti-Western backlash in Sudan but did warn that the USA must avoid slipping into the mindset of a crusade; "And whatever happens must not be perceived as retaliation pure and simple." Were such a scenario to develop, Qutbi suggested rather carefully, then "we could not be in conflict with our own people."

Qutbi would soon hit the international news when *Vanity Fair* magazine claimed in January 2002 that, at the time of Qutbi's prominence in the Sudanese intelligence world, Sudan had offered to deliver Osama bin-Laden to the US authorities on a plate (actually on a plane – it had been prepared to divulge the exact timing and routing of the personal aircraft on which bin-Laden would be expelled from Sudan). But the Clinton administration turned the offer down.

WHEN IN OCTOBER 2000 I first met Dr Ghazi Salah al-Dien (not to be confused with prominent human rights activist Ghazi Suleiman), he was the Orwellian-sounding Minister of Culture and Information and also government spokesperson. Educated at the University of Surrey (UK) and a Doctor of Medicine, he was – notwithstanding his reputation as a hardline and core National Islamic Front member – an articulate and sophisticated interlocutor and as such a good choice for government spokesperson (although, as he admitted, his task of projecting a positive image of Sudan was "sometimes uphill work").

At this time, he was engaged in ambitious plans to privatize radio and TV in this country (they were then largely state-controlled) and "to give the people of Sudan access to information from all over the world." Within this privatization framework, he had successfully convinced both the BBC and RFI to locate boosters in Khartoum, thus giving Khartoumers access to their Arabic programming on the FM band; Deutsche Welle (radio) would soon join this club. The minister was also proud of a legislative initiative that, with the aim of improving the people's access to information, had seen all state taxes removed from TV sets, radios, and newsprint. Radio remained by far the dominant medium, with the largest print run of any of Khartoum's daily newspapers reaching only forty thousand; Salah al-Dien admitted that the quality of most newspapers was low and that there was a lamentable tendency towards sensationalism but stressed that salaries for journalists and technical standards were improving fast, which should soon mean an overall improvement in the sector.

Ghazi insisted that there was no government censorship in Sudan (in this he was technically but not substantively right: papers were told they could print what they liked, but, if certain subjects were touched upon, the print run would be seized). The content of news broadcasts and newspapers was watched over by a twenty-one-member Press Council made up thus: nine elected by journalists, five elected by Congress, seven appointed by the president upon the minister's recommendation. The Council had the power to impose sanctions – for example, the suspension of a paper for a limited period – and indeed occasionally did so. Grounds for such suspension (and here is where things became a little grey) might include obscenity, immorality, and slander; famously, a month previously, one paper had been closed down for a week for alleging that Hassan al-Turabi was a homosexual ("You have to understand the gravity of such an accusation in this culture," the minister insisted).

Ghazi hinted that, following the December 2000 elections, he would probably quit this portfolio to work full-time on one of his other responsibilities: "external communications" for the ruling party. He did not define the National Congress as an Islamist party, "although that tendency is dominant at this time." "It is a conglomerate of affiliate groups," he said, "including Southern Christians." He wanted to see the party reaching out to other political parties – whether in government or in opposition – in sub-Saharan Africa, as well as to the Arab nationalist groups with which it was more normally associated ("And you must understand that there has been a coming together of all of us in the past two weeks over Palestine"). When I asked his views on the Taliban, he said that of course the government did not recognize its authority and that historically the party had had much more contact with the opposition in Afghanistan, "but I wonder how much longer we can go on not recognizing a de facto government."

It seemed to me that, as government spokesperson, the minister perhaps had his work cut out for him in explaining away the recent antics of the wali of Khartoum. The wali, who had recently tried to ban women from serving the public was, he agreed, "an embarrassment," but his very power pointed up a dilemma in which the government found itself and which the wily Turabi was exploiting to the full: on the one hand decentralization of some kind appeared to be the key to solving the war in the South, but on the other the ceding of power to "lunatics" such as the wali led to excesses of this kind (a long time later, after I had already left Sudan, I was dismayed to find that the wali had been appointed as the government's chief negotiator for Darfur, a negative omen if there ever was).

On sharia (what political conversation in Sudan could ever avoid this topic?) he took the party line: that secular vs non-secular was a false dichotomy, that it was more useful to consider what the ideal state would look like in practice rather than deciding on a label right from the start. But, in a new take, he told me, "The problem with the word 'secular' for us is that this means 'non-moral,' and that we cannot accept ... I believe most Western systems of government are based on morality – look at Germany's Christian Democracy – and that is all we are asking for ..."

A few months later, Ghazi found himself no longer with a ministerial portfolio but in a position that, as it turned out, would be absolutely key: as presidential peace councillor and thus the lead on the peace negotiations. He had become the most influential figure in government, after the president and First Vice-President Ali Osman Tahaa. It was in this capacity that I met him again, in March 2002.

Ghazi launched enthusiastically right into his new obsession: the peace process. He acknowledged that the peace dynamic was fluid but stated that, as far as Khartoum was concerned, the USA was unequivocally calling the shots. This did not necessarily mean that the administration was comfortable with this. There was a recognition that Washington's policy on Sudan could in the next few months fall victim to many circumstances and situations entirely outside Khartoum's control: the Middle East peace process (which in turn closely involved Egypt, one of the keys to a peace settlement in Sudan), the continuing hunt for al-Qaeda cells, and the eventual mobilization of an anti-Iraq coalition.

The immediate fear was that John Garang, then coming to the end of a supposedly private but in reality high-profile visit to the USA (which included a meeting with Secretary of State Colin Powell – an honour thus far denied to Foreign Minister Mustafa Ismael), had gone a long way towards undoing what Khartoum perceived as the framework of its new

relationship with Washington, which in turn was permitting "real progress" towards peace. Dr Ghazi suggested Garang was "playing the Israeli
game": mobilizing US opinion not just against Khartoum but also against
the USA Government, with the aim of forcing the State Department and
the White House back onto the SPLM/A side of the fence. He pointed out
that Garang had cynically and publicly described SPLM/A engagement in
the peace process as a stratagem to bring about the downfall of the Khartoum administration and that he had irresponsibly misled the US public
by describing the administration as "the African Taliban."

The government was also concerned at the prospect of USA peace envoy
Jack Danforth's eventual withdrawal from the stage, even if he did recommend to President Bush that the USA remain engaged. There was recognition that Danforth's command of the details of the Sudanese problem was
not good and that the US State Department, on the other hand, *did* have
expertise in this regard, but there was great fear that State might not be
able to withstand political pressures on its peace facilitation, in the same
way that Danforth himself might. Ghazi suggested to me that Danforth
had had a large hand in blocking the Sudan Peace Act.

Turning away from the USA role, Dr Ghazi said that the government
position on peace remained unchanged: the requirement was for a comprehensive ceasefire that would permit, first, the discussion of humanitarian
issues then, second, substantive political negotiations. Khartoum was not
greatly enthusiastic about the prospect of further regional ceasefires like
that just negotiated for the Nuba Mountains, but Ghazi agreed with my
assessment that the Nuba ceasefire was probably more advantageous to
Khartoum than to the SPLA. He also agreed with the concern that the
USA had thus far addressed only the symptoms of the conflict, rather than
the causes, but nevertheless held out some modest hope that US attempts
to persuade Kenya and Egypt to agree to some joint peace facilitation
mechanism might bear fruit.

As to what more the Intergovernmental Authority on Development and
the IGAD Partners' Forum (IPF) could and should be doing, in light of
all of the above, the assessment was that the Europeans (and here Ghazi
included Canada) had consciously decided not to play a key role, pending decisive action by the USA. Ghazi said that this was understandable
but suggested that the Partners' Forum could usefully be considering the
eventuality of US disengagement: "Don't be sleeping partners ..." Ghazi
grimaced expressively when I suggested that, if the USA should withdraw,

the United Nations (rather than the IPF/IGAD) might be a candidate to step in.

We discussed the new focus of the war in the oilfields. Ghazi candidly agreed with the assessment I had heard from the mouths of the SPLM/A – "Five more years of oil revenues, and Khartoum wins the war" – but was at pains to add that, if the war were indeed to drag on that long, it would be by social investment, using the oil money, rather than through expenditure on weaponry that the South would be "brought round."

He admitted that a successful major attack on the Heglig oil installations by the SPLM/A would be a first-order catastrophe for the government that could well bring about its downfall. He suggested that the Northern-based opposition groups, Umma and the Democratic Unionist Party, would in this scenario quickly jump on the SPLA bandwagon. He discounted the theory that the vision of Heglig in flames would cause a rally-round-the-flag phenomenon in the North.

It was in recognition of this danger, Ghazi admitted, that Khartoum was making every attempt to secure the oilfields. But he rejected my suggestion that scorched-earth tactics were being used. Instead, he said, the focus was on hearts and minds and on persuading into the government fold rebel leaders – especially Nuers such as Peter Gadiet – currently aligned with the SPLM/A. Ghazi suggested that Garang had failed (or refused) to see how oil – under the guise of discussions on wealth sharing – could be brought to the front burner of any eventual peace talks and turned into a political rather than a military football: "We recognize that we will have to bargain away a good share of the oil for the South, but Garang doesn't seem interested in testing us on this."

We had come to what Ghazi saw as the nub of the problem. John Garang was a military man, dominated by military thinking. His objective – said Ghazi – was to be president of Sudan, sitting in the Republican Palace in Khartoum. But he was currently having an enormous amount of trouble digesting the knowledge that this was utterly inconceivable to a majority of Sudanese, and also to most of the international community. He had not yet moved, mentally, to the second-best option – declaration of an independent South Sudan – perhaps because he also knew that would bring its own share of troubles. Notably he would have to deal with all the old South/South rivalries that were currently subsumed to some extent in the South/North struggle. Garang "is having trouble conceptualizing peace ... because he rightly senses there would be no place for him in a peaceful Sudan."

MEANWHILE, OVER IN THE TRADITIONAL CAPITAL of Omdurman, and perennially eyeing President Bashir, sat Turabi's principal rival to the title of leader of the opposition. Sadiq al-Mahdi was no ordinary politician. Twice prime minister, the first time at the age of thirty, great-grandson of no less than the Mahdi who put Gordon to the sword, Sadiq was careful not to deny his semi-divine status. The melodramatic circumstances under which he allegedly fled Khartoum in 1996, in one of the darkest years of the National Islamic Front regime (by night, on a camel, clad in a woman's dress), could have come from a sequel to the 1966 Charlton Heston/Laurence Olivier movie, and his return – on the night of 23 November 2000 – was equally theatrical.

The original plan had been for him and his large entourage to fly into Kassala from Cairo, and then undertake a 400 km triumphal procession to Khartoum, but this was thwarted by the uncertain security situation around Kassala; as it soon emerged, the SPLA was about to take the town. But the scene was still dramatic. A four-hour delay (carefully calculated?) meant that the route from Khartoum airport across the White Nile to Omdurman was well and truly lined with party faithful by the time of Sadiq's arrival just after dusk, and the crowd of twenty-five thousand people awaiting him by the al-Khalifa mosque well-primed with a combination of prayers, political diatribes, and friendly Western-style political jingles. Sadiq's motorcade swept in under floodlights, and he was immediately engulfed by a huge scrum of stick-waving djellabiya and turban-clad faithful who threatened briefly to swamp the clutch of suit-and-tied diplomats quietly occupying plastic chairs and munching dates in front of the main podium.

After the initial chaos, the night proceeded in an orderly fashion. With the floodlit Khalifa mosque behind him, his great-grandfather's tomb on one side, and a starry velvet night as a backdrop, Sadiq delivered what in the circumstances was a remarkably moderate and measured address to his party faithful. He would work, he said, for a Sudan in which all points of view, all religions, and all ethnic groups were represented fairly – no specific reference to a secular state here; indeed Umma usually evaded use of the term, preferring the concept "citizenship" – and would strongly support the efforts of the Intergovernmental Authority on Development to negotiate peace in Sudan. There was no direct reference to the SPLM/A other than, in passing, a condemnation of "warlordism."

Sadiq was short on specifics, even shorter on his immediate plans. It was widely taken as a given that for some weeks he would hold meetings across the political spectrum – likely including the ruling National Congress – and would travel the country, simultaneously consulting and rebuilding Umma. The party was divided along a number of lines: there were many who believed Sadiq's return was premature, a sellout; and there was also a byzantine internecine feud over the rights to occupy the tomb of the Mahdi.

Sadiq must meanwhile grapple with a problem of the most fundamental nature. The Umma Party had its roots in a Sufi sect and was headed by a person who was the party leader because his great grandfather claimed to be a messiah; much of its support was along traditional religious and/or ethnic lines. While most people were sick of the Islamist excesses of the current administration, Umma was not exactly a secular political party with a political/economic agenda of the kind we understand in the West. The dilemma Sadiq would face was that, if he modernized and Westernized, a large proportion of his traditional support base would fall away, but if he did not then he could not attract those who wanted a clear break with the present.

Sadiq must also convince the public that, in power, he could do a better job this time around than the last time he held power, when he had been a Salvador Allende to Bashir's Augusto Pinochet. The Messiah was back. Whether he could save Sudan was a very open question.

I met with him several times over the next two years, the first some six weeks after his return. We had tea – crustless cucumber and tomato sandwiches, fruit juice from silver-necked cut-glass jugs, an enormous and rich cream cake, Earl Grey served in fine bone Wedgwood – in a perfumed gazebo in the garden of Sadiq's palatial house in Omdurman. Dug-in tanks guarded the approaches to the house, taking away something from the romance. Acolytes and servants hovered in attendance; one shyly and mysteriously identified herself only as Princess Yussuf. There was a sense of the Far Pavilions, of visiting the ancient nobility. But the Umma leader was no decadent fop; he spoke excellent English, argued vigorously, and listened attentively.

What were Sadiq's impressions when he returned from his four years of exile in Egypt? First, he said, he was enormously impressed by the fact that people had "persevered." Second, the intransigence that characterized the early years of the Bashir administration and had forced him to flee were starting to recede: "There is now space of which we must avail ourselves." There were two wars to be won, he said: the civil war setting North against South, and the security war that was a secret one pitting Northerner against Northerner. To both, the answer was deeply rooted democracy.

Would Sadiq cut a deal with the government? This was the question on everyone's lips at this time. The Umma leader would not discard such a scenario: "We are not seeking this actively, but it is possible." Before accepting any role in government, though, the party was looking for a formal commitment by the government to a process of reconciliation and a broadening of democracy. As to why the government had not yet made such a commitment, Sadiq believed on the one hand that a group of fundamentalist ideologues still held undue sway and, on the other, that the SPLM/A had allowed the government no space for manoeuvre, supported as the movement was "by foreign patronage" (presumably the USA, and to a lesser extent Uganda).

These two obstacles could be overcome. The ideologues within the National Congress Party were losing influence, to begin with. And Garang "is in the end a pragmatist." But as long as the rebel leader had the overt support of the outside world, he would play his cards aggressively. In parenthesis, Sadiq here expressed perplexity and amazement at the USA's then-blatant support of the SPLM/A, which he characterized as quite out of keeping with what he perceived to be its genuinely neutral and helpful role in the Middle East peace process. "I can only deduce that these are lightweight people at the State Department – desk officers and utopians like Susan Rice – who have been given free rein to indulge in campus politics, while the big boys are occupied elsewhere." He also wondered "Why now?" when "Even in the darkest hours of 1994 to 1996, the USA gave no support to the National Democratic Alliance or the SPLA."

"Canada," Sadiq said in parenthesis, "is a country with all of the natural resources of the USA and none of its hegemonic intentions." But he would not endorse the Canadian-supported Intergovernmental Authority on Development as the main vehicle for the achievement of peace. Peace had to be anchored in internal democratization, he suggested. There was in fact a general preparedness for dialogue on the part of the population at large; what was needed now was a mobilization of that opinion in one sole direction. More concretely, democratization had to be achieved through four steps: (a) the government must admit that forced acculturation of the

South and of Southerners was a mistake; (b) there must be changes to the Constitution and changes to electoral law but, more fundamentally, citizenship – not the principles of sharia (which could be still applied regionally, and at a community level, but not nationally) – must become the basis of the Constitution; (c) all grievances and currents of opinion should be reconciled in a comprehensive national agreement; and (d) it might be necessary to establish an "observation mechanism" to ensure follow-up and implementation of such a national agreement.

None of this would be easy, Sadiq admitted. "But in the meantime, Sudan and Iran are the best movies in town…"

ONLY ONCE BEFORE had I met someone considered to be semi-divine: the Living Goddess, a prepubescent Hindu girl kept cooped up in a decrepit Kathmandu palace, who would come to a window and wave to you for a mere five rupiahs. Sadiq seemed to me a rather more worthy vessel of divinity but this did not mean he was infallible. Indeed, by the time peace talks finally got under way in Kenya in mid-2002, his leadership of Umma was being severely threatened.

On 20 July 2002, when the stunning news reached Khartoum that a framework peace agreement had actually been sketched in, Sadiq, who received me again in his gazebo, told me Umma's position was "unreserved support." The exact timing of the Machakos Protocol was perhaps a surprise, but it was actually inevitable; the fatigue on both sides meant that sooner or later they would both have to compromise on their ludicrous respective maximalist positions. The SPLM/A simply had to be offered self-determination, because "that was their only guarantee," while Khartoum had to be given a reasonably long transition period before a referendum on secession was held and the option of maintaining sharia over the majority of Sudanese territory. What made the difference now was US pressure. And why the US engagement? The late realization that it had nothing to gain by continuing to back the SPLM/A, something to gain by easing off on Khartoum, a lot to gain – after 9/11 – from a peaceful and stable Sudan (notably, oil).

But the maximalist positions the parties had maintained to the last moment would now cause them many difficulties. President Bashir now had to handle three disaffected internal constituencies that felt suddenly let down: the Islamists who had every reason to hope that the dream of an Islamic republic that had inspired the coup thirteen years ago was still alive, the unionists who thought Khartoum should never contemplate any arrangement that could culminate in secession, and the small caucus of Southern ministers in government who now saw their future disappearing fast. John Garang must meanwhile deal with similar challenges: while the SPLM/A "got" self-determination, Garang had repeatedly stated that his clear preference was unity, which would have displeased many. Key figures in the diaspora, notably Bona Malwal, could now be expected to return to challenge his own supremacy; and there were the usual intractable tensions with the Nuer factions within the Dinka-dominated SPLM/A.

A further difficulty for the government would be placating anti-secessionist Egypt. "Egyptian reservations can be harmful ... and may encourage further dissent; we must involve them ..." The main argument that had to be deployed for Egypt was that Sudan already was divided and that the principles spelled out at Machakos at least offered a reasonable hope for a pacific reunification. (Libya appeared to be losing interest; an official statement rather tersely and shortly welcomed Machakos.)

Predictably, Umma wanted to see a gradual process by which domestic forces other than the SPLM/A and the government were involved in the peace negotiations; it would also like Nigeria and South Africa brought back in. The challenge was to create national and international momentum in such a way that Garang and Bashir could overcome differences within their respective constituencies: "This is an historic moment, but now we must create a multilateral coalition." Democratic reforms must accompany the peace process: "What made the Addis Ababa agreement ultimately fail was that it remained bipartisan only."

The positive fallout of a successful settlement in Sudan could be huge, Sadiq added: the Sudanese model could represent a shining example for the current debate on how Islam and nationhood can be reconciled; it could represent a new benchmark in Afro-Arab relations; it could galvanize the ten-nation Nile Basin Initiative (a wide-ranging water-sharing project in which Canada had a large stake); the negotiation model itself could be replicated elsewhere. And, in a nod to present company, Sadiq rather sardonically added "Peace in Sudan could also be a big success story for the West."

By early 2003, the date of my next rendezvous, peace in Sudan still looked attainable but war in Iraq probable. In Sadiq's view the main preoccupation in Sudan was and would remain the country's own civil war.

With peace talks now apparently close to a definitive outcome, Sadiq described the Khartoum administration as "hydra-headed." In his typically methodical manner, he enumerated four schools of opinion jockeying for supremacy, counting them off on his fingers: (a) a group who believed the South was demanding, as a condition for unity, too many concessions that affected Northern identity and who would rather just let the South secede (hence the government's "allowing" to be published by a senior official a "personal" opinion piece calling for Northern separation from the South ...); (b) a group who feared peace would lead to the dismantling of the NIF regime; (c) a more liberal faction who saw change and democracy as both desirable and inevitable; and (d) hardliners such as Energy Minister al-Jaz who still believed the war could be won militarily.

At this time, the pro-unity forces uneasily held sway, if for no other reason than that unity had become the only possible justification for the regime, its radical brand of Islam having been rejected and discredited, not just nationally but internationally. But the situation was fluid, due to the vacuum at the top: "This is a dictatorship without a dictator." The best hopes for peace remained the Sudanese people mobilizing, constructive international engagement, and the existence, within the ranks of both the SPLM/A and the government, of a reduced but significant number of "true patriots and pacifists."

Umma's position was that it was prepared to let President Bashir serve out his current term (two more years), but at that point there must be free and fair democratic elections – the international community must chime in to insist on this. In the shorter term Umma was preparing what it described as a "popular parliament," an assembly that would serve first to increase pressure on the negotiating parties and second to endorse and reinforce an eventual agreement.

Sadiq pleaded for Western help in creating modern democratic parties in Sudan – "which is what I want Umma to become." Multiparty Canadian delegations should be invited/supported to come to Sudan to share their experiences and thus strengthen civil society and political discourse in a non-partisan way. Was there any point in working with the National Assembly as currently constituted? Sadiq was blunt: "No; it's humbug."

Musing on the regional context, Sadiq suggested that the West's inadvertent propping up of dictatorships and repressive regimes had fostered Islamic fundamentalism, not stifled it, but that, in all of the so-called Islamic republics, Islam was a sham; Sudan was less Islamic than ever before, he stated. Moderate, progressive, and authentic voices of Islam must be allowed to develop; "If we fail to encourage these voices, then we empower the extremists by default."

THE UMMA LEADER MEANWHILE faced challenges not only in having Umma heard at the peace table but also from within, in the shape of first cousin Mubarak al-Fadil. Mubarak had a large house in downtown Khartoum, cooled by industrial-sized Russian-built air-conditioners and decorated with kitsch gifts from his days as a minister under Sadiq (notably an enormous orange teddy bear presented to him at the Seoul Olympic Games). Rotund and invariably genial, Mubarak (who had a brother who ran a business in Toronto) blithely described himself, when I first met with him in August 2002, as the leader of a palace coup (or, in Arabic, a "white coup") against Sadiq. He insisted that Sadiq had over the years become autocratic, considering the party his personal property; he had surrounded himself with an old guard, a coterie of old Umma names, drawn largely from those who followed him into exile in the mid-1990s, ignoring those such as Mubarak who stayed behind and who had been entrusted with the thankless job of trying to keep channels of communication open with a suspicious National Islamic Front administration.

How did the split begin? Following Sadiq's return to Sudan in late 2000, said Mubarak, the two of them initially cooperated in a policy of careful rapprochement with the government. A deal was actually struck, under which Umma would enter government, in return for key positions. But Sadiq suddenly backed down, leaving Mubarak cast as a collaborator. Why the cold feet? The president, mindful of his bad experience with Hassan al-Turabi, and fearing that from a position of influence within government Sadiq would force a transition and himself take the presidency, would not offer Sadiq any real personal power (he wanted a position as prime minister, as in the French system); meanwhile other opposition parties – the Democratic Unionist Party, the Communists – were calling "sellout." Mubarak was left holding the baby.

There was more, said Mubarak. Sadiq was "excessively intellectual." Having only ever held one paying job – as prime minister – he had no understanding of how to run a party, no sense that a party in opposition must develop at least the promise of delivering services and programs, along with the reasonable expectation that there would be jobs for the boys.

By contrast, suggested Mubarak, the ruling Islamists had been masterly in delivering to their own. And Sadiq was remembered, too, not just as a prime minister, but as a failed prime minister, one whose ineptitude contributed directly to the mood and popular feeling that had allowed the NIF to sweep to power thirteen years ago in an unopposed coup. He was a loser from whom "we have to ease away ... just as India's Congress Party is easing away from the Gandhis."

Early in July 2002 Mubarak had organized his own Umma conference in Khartoum, attended by a thousand or so delegates from across the country. The conference provoked an immediate undignified spin spat, with the "real" Umma issuing press releases and appealing to diplomats to ignore the event, while Mubarak invited them and the media in to see how large his do was. The plan was to build on this conference and take the Umma into what Mubarak described as a "broad alliance" with the government, the objective being a smooth transition to democracy over the next six to ten years – a "soft landing." The process had to be gradual, because the Army could still represent a threat; "it's premature to speak of full-blown democracy in Sudan."

Could the NIF be trusted? President Bashir, along with the central cadre made up of Qutbi, Foreign Minister Mustafa Ismael, and Ghazi Salah al-Dien, were already starting to think about their political epitaphs. The Army was neutral; the only threat to a soft landing, in fact, was First Vice-President Ali Osman Tahaa, a notorious hardliner perilously close to the joystick.

Could Sadiq have a place in this? Yes, said Mubarak, but he must accept the imposition of internal democracy within the party and be prepared to retire to the position of grand old man of the Umma. And if Sadiq didn't accept? "Then he'll be sidelined; just like Bashir sidelined Turabi ..."

The great Umma leader and his followers, as might be imagined, had rather a different take on things. Of the thousand at Mubarak's upstart Umma conference, said his Foreign Policy Adviser Sara Nugdallah, "350 were NIF, 150 were security police in plainclothes, and two hundred were opportunistic freeloaders"; she supplied me with a list of a further forty-four senior Umma defectors whom she acknowledged were the real thing.

For Sadiq himself, Mubarak's faction was "a medley of ideologies, with no class-based interests, no affective loyalties." This was a personal quest for power by Mubarak, not a true ideological split. The government was running after Mubarak, even encouraging him, because it sensed – more so after the 20 July Machakos deal – that it urgently needed to broaden its political support base ("Turabi took the quality, Bashir was left with only the quantity") and it thought Mubarak, specifically, could bring in support from the currently disaffected West.

I MET MUBARAK AGAIN IN JANUARY 2003. By now the government had caught up with him and offered him a deal. He had, to the scorn of cousin Sadiq, accepted a post as a senior presidential adviser, which came with a newly refurbished office on the grounds of the Republican Palace. War in Iraq was looming and was the talk of Khartoum.

The presidency, Mubarak began grandly, by no means bought the US argument that this was a continuation of the war on terrorism – not that there was any great love here for Saddam Hussein. Mubarak suggested Saddam was an opportunist whom the Arab world could do without and compared him in this respect to Nasser.

Leaning over to me confidentially, he told a hoary old Nasser joke. All the Arab leaders are in a plane, which is about to crash because it is over-loaded. The pilot asks for volunteers to jump out. A dozen do so, each one proclaiming "I die for Palestine!" Soon it's only the pilot and Nasser. Nasser grabs the pilot and pushes him out, crying "You die for Palestine!" After a quiet chortle at his own joke, Mubarak went on more seriously that, quite apart from whatever the government thought, the man in the street would not see Saddam's opportunism: to him the Iraqi leader would seem simply to be a martyr.

Closer to home Mubarak believed that, although the issue of state and religion had already been addressed in the Machakos Protocol, it would return in various guises (the nature of a future banking system, the status of the capital) to haunt the peace talks and the post-peace era. Mubarak's own view was that an acceptable compromise could be found in the concept of equal citizenship, with Islamic laws and non-Islamic laws applicable according to how individuals identified themselves (a proposal most dismissed as unworkable in practice and about which Mubarak admitted the president had yet to be convinced).

As I had heard elsewhere, the presidency believed the international community could be most helpful by coaxing the SPLM/A towards realistic negotiating positions and away from what Khartoum saw as maximalist demands. But was the will there on the government side? "Certainly," insisted Mubarak. "We are all tired of the war now. Unlike in 1972, it's reaching into every home. And we should also learn from 1972 that the war must be resolved politically, not as a security issue."

IF TURABI AND SADIQ were the principal claimants to the title leader of the opposition, there was nevertheless a third: Osman al-Mirghani, simultaneously head of the Khatamiya Sect, the Democratic Unionist Party, and the National Democratic Alliance (made up of the SPLM/A, DUP, and an assortment of smaller Northern parties). An impressive list of titles. But the snag was that Osman had for years been in self-imposed exile in Egypt. His brother Ahmed (who himself only returned in November 2001) was the DUP's senior representative in Khartoum, when he was not – in the style of all of Sudan's great old families – summering in Alexandria.

Ahmed, who was once president of Sudan – but at a time when the presidency was largely formal – would usually receive me in a vast, silent, and empty rectangular reception room in his stately family home at a choice location on the banks of the Blue Nile; it was furnished with soft armchairs in a bilious bright green. The solemn and most dignified tone of our meetings would only be disrupted by occasional and very sudden bursts into the theme tune from *Miami Vice* – a "program your own tone" mobile phone buried almost inextricably deep inside Ahmed's djellabiya.

Meeting Ahmed for the first time in 2003, I found myself comparing him to Sadiq. Like Sadiq, Ahmed repeatedly expressed concern at the narrowness of the current peace process, but he was more cautious than Sadiq and less original.

Neither the government nor the rebel SPLM/A were truly representative, he believed, and any peace achieved would be very fragile if the "skeleton" of Machakos was not fleshed out with the input of other constituencies. It was all very well for civil society and other groups to be airing their views in the media – as many were – "but we must have a sense that someone is listening." Ahmed, who was not averse to name-dropping and perhaps sensed he was not necessarily on the A list for foreign dignitaries, added that he had several times told this to US peace envoy Jack Danforth.

But peace was the only answer. He complained bitterly at the decline in services – roads, lighting, health – since "his" day and recognized that this trend could only be reversed by an end to the war. Like Sadiq, Ahmed thought that separation of state and religion would be the key to a successful peace agreement: "If this is not achieved, then we will have constant flare-ups, like in Israel and Palestine." Digressing a little to discuss the violence that was at this time burgeoning in the far west of Sudan, Ahmed made one of his more perceptive comments: "There are many Darfurs in Sudan."

Vis-à-vis the government, the most effective pressure the international community could perhaps exert was the prospect or promise of investment; but with the SPLM/A, for so long nannied by the USA, it might be a time for sticks, including pressure from the neighbours (notably Uganda) and from Christian Churches. Change was frankly unlikely to come from within the currently existing democratic institutions. Ahmed had pretty much the same view as Sadiq when it came to the National Assembly: "No use at *all*" (and he waved his hand as if at a fly).

6

THE BORDERLINE
GOVERNMENT-HELD SOUTH SUDAN

IN THE COLONIAL ERA, Southern Sudan was defined by the British as the portion of Sudan that comprised the states of Bahr al-Ghazal, Upper Nile, and Equatoria: roughly speaking, the territory south of the tenth parallel. But a salient of Upper Nile projects northwards like a thumb, and its northernmost town – Renk, on the eastern bank of the White Nile – is almost at twelve degrees north and is only 500 km due south of the capital. Like a number of other pockets within the SPLM/A-dominated South, this settlement was controlled by the government. This was just as well for Khartoum, given Renk's relative closeness not only to the capital but to its main source of power, the Roseires Dam (to the east, on the Blue Nile).

Once out of the Khartoum suburbs, the main road due south runs just out of sight of the White Nile and is straight, very narrow, and bone-jarringly potholed. Kosti, a riverside settlement named after a Greek merchant, is reached after 300 km and lies on the west bank: it is accessed by a long humpbacked road bridge and a lower railway bridge, the first two

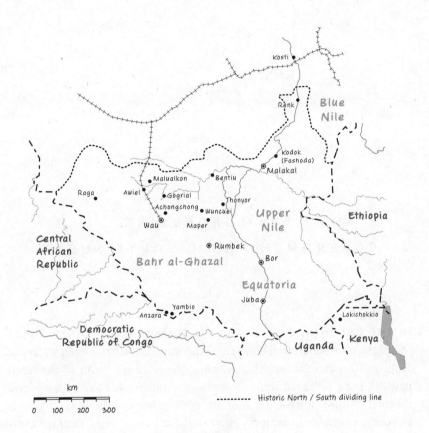

km

0   100 200 300

------- Historic North / South dividing line

SOUTHERN SUDAN

spans over the river since its exit from Lake Victoria many hundreds of kilometres to the south. There isn't much to recommend Kosti other than a remarkably pleasant roadside restaurant decorated with colour photographs of Mecca and Christmas ornaments at all times of year. It serves a very good fattur and the background music is Western muzak ("Take My Breath Away" and "Last Night I Dreamt of San Pedro" are favourites).

Carrying on south, the road starts to hug the White Nile, which here belies its name and is startlingly blue. You pass three huge and strange granitic mounds at Jebelein, and then the tarmac ends. It seems apt that the road gives out just here, where the South officially begins: one of the principal and best-founded grievances of the rebels is that the South was grossly neglected under the British and has remained so under Arab rule.

There are other signs, too, that you are entering a different land. Fewer and fewer of the men wear djellabiyas, and most of the women now seem to be bareheaded; a few are even bare-breasted. No longer can you see on the horizon the distinctive conical green or silver domes that indicate the burial place of a Muslim notable; instead, there are Christian crosses in most villages. You start to see more and more bicycles; although donkeys pulling their blue oil-barrel water carts are still ubiquitous. Every so often the road rises, and you pass over an east-running irrigation canal, but most of the ditches – meant to feed some vast farming scheme somewhere to the left – are weed-choked or dry, the pumping stations rusting.

Renk is a sprawling cluster of straw-roofed mud-walled Tukuls. Not untypically, the estimates I was given of its population varied wildly, from thirty thousand to an astounding 300,000: the local authorities had wised up to inflating their estimates whenever international donors came visiting. In the end, I decided that eighty thousand was probably a reasonable guess.

We were here funding the Canadian aid organization, the Fellowship for African Relief (FAR). It was the first agency to venture into Renk for many years, and it was just now starting to provide a varied package of services, including a therapeutic feeding centre for infants, a health and nutrition program, basic sanitation services (consisting principally of pit latrines and ingenious but low-maintenance bio-sand drinking water filters), and a household food security program – initially, training in fishing and provision of equipment, to be followed by vegetable gardening. The project had run into a number of bureaucratic obstacles put forward by the government but was now up and running quite well under the supervision of the locally recruited Victor.

Victor took us to meet the acting county commissioner, a Dinka named Peter. Peter was very friendly and not afraid to speak off script. He took a quick dig at Talisman for having "contributed to the problems of modern Sudan" (not what you were supposed to hear from government officials) and, when pressed, said that, although he welcomed the peace process, he and everyone he knew would – six and a half years hence, when the referendum came – definitely vote for secession. He laughed off my suggestion that an independent South Sudan might be confronted with some internal tensions and pointed to his deputy – a Nuer – as living proof that "we all get along together." Was he afraid for his job when the SPLM/A took over Renk, as was likely to happen under the terms of any peace agreement? "No," he shrugged. "They know us and we know them ... Many of them have families here." I was left with the clear impression that the SPLM/A had more than families: it probably already had half the local government.

Over dinner, we launched into a revealing discussion on ethics and value systems. Peter had two wives, both of whom he had bought with a significant number of cows ("more than thirty each," he said). What did the Dinka value in a wife? "Lineage, wealth, height, and a gap in their front teeth ..." He was intrigued when I said that the dowry system had all but disappeared from the Western world. "Why would she stay with you if you have not bought her?" he asked incredulously. He laughed scornfully when, a little embarrassed, I suggested that if two people do not love each other then there's not really much point in their staying together; I had gone down in Peter's estimation.

As part of our city tour, we were shown around the hospital, which occupied a large area, was very clean, and – by Sudanese standards – was not too badly equipped. There was only one doctor, a general practitioner, and his main complaint was that the hospital had almost no electrical power. There was a set of solar panels that fed three fluorescent lights, and there was – since the municipal generator had broken down "some time ago" – no city power. The doctor said that about one hundred of the hospital's 160 beds were occupied, but we only got to see two patients (and I couldn't see that there could be many more): a man who fell off a truck and who was now reclining on the concrete floor with an ill-defined back problem; and an unmistakably terminal HIV/AIDS patient on a pink drip in the corner of an otherwise totally empty ward. The doctor thought there was a lot of AIDS around, but there was nowhere nearer than Khartoum where they could test for it. This man had "about three or four days" to live.

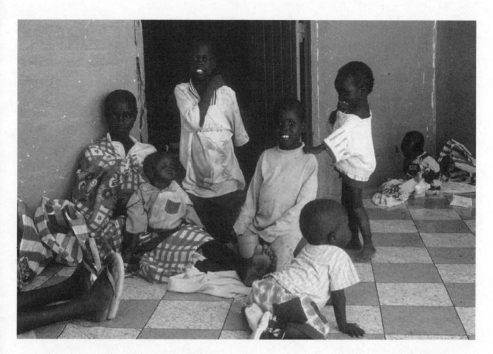

Outpatients at the hospital, Renk

All the action in Renk was down by the river. A surly policeman in blue camouflage pattern fatigues let us walk out to the end of the earth promontory that served as a ferry dock after we agreed to take no photographs. The steamer from Kosti to Malakal passed once a fortnight. There didn't seem too much of strategic significance for us to have spied on here. By chance, at 2 a.m., in the middle of an otherwise quite silent night, we heard the three horn blasts that heralded the steamer's coming.

As dusk fell, we sipped sugary tea, sitting on tiny stools by a straw hut at the gate to the ferry terminal. Nearby, small boys were loading up their donkey-driven water carts from a large hose running down from the water tank: although we were on the edge of one of the greatest water sources in the world, Renk had no piped water and no filtration service. Everyone bought their water from the donkey carts. Some of the donkeys were also loading up with freshly cut green reeds from the marshy land at the river's edge; their dinner, no doubt.

Knee-deep in a channel cut between the reeds, two men stood soaping themselves, naked, the sun setting behind them over the Nile. A flight of white cattle egrets flapped silently past, and we heard a far-off grunting. "Hippo," the tea lady confirmed with a shy smile.

300 KM SOUTH FROM RENK is Malakal. Bizarrely, it has the best airport in all of Sudan. There was a cannibalized helicopter gunship in the long grass and an artillery base just off the runway, but there were incongruously well-kept lawns and beds of geraniums by the terminal building, where a large blue and yellow sign proclaimed *Welcome to Malakal International.*

In the empty air-conditioned and marble-floored halls there were ultramodern chairs and tables in stainless steel and clear plastic, and there was even a small cafeteria where one might be tempted to sit and sip a bottled mango juice. In the course of 2002, the vice-president and other dignitaries officially opened Malakal airport at least four times.

Malakal, home to about 100,000 Shillook and Nuer, was in February 2003 in government hands, but the SPLA had the place encircled and was never more than 40 km away. Since the October 2002 ceasefire had been declared the barge from Kosti and Renk, to the north, usually had been coming through unmolested, but no-one was yet trying the overland route; the dirt track on the west bank, in fact, had been so little transited that it lost itself for long stretches.

I was here with our Canadian International Development Agency representative Marian, Catherine from the Human Security Division at Foreign Affairs in Ottawa, and Corry Slot, the country director of War Child Netherlands. We were supporting a project the Dutch were launching in Malakal, and it was Corry's locally based colleague Anna who met us in War Child's spanking new Landcruiser. We headed into town on a road that, surprisingly for Southern Sudan, was paved: the president had been here barely five weeks earlier, and the entire place had been spruced up in his honour. War Child's office was a crumbling brick-built house from the colonial era, reached by a plank over a foul-smelling ditch; I had the feeling that in the rainy season all Malakal would be rather malodorous.

We were given a warm welcome: as we walked into the main office, which was adorned with childish crayon drawings of fierce-looking men in green uniforms, a half-dozen of the project's local staff launched nervously into a lilting song of welcome, accompanied by a guitar. Twenty minutes later ("They never know when to stop," Corry whispered in embarrassment) we were served the mandatory Pepsi, and, through translator Peter, we started to hear about the project.

War Child had already identified various population sectors in which to seek out especially vulnerable groups of children: the camps and shanties of the internally displaced, street children in the souq, child prostitutes, the children's kalazzar ward at the local hospital, the women's prison, the makeshift non-official schools on the fringes of town. Working with other groups already active in town – UNICEF, Goal, Médecins sans frontières, the Children's SOS Village, the local Ministry of Education – War Child hoped to introduce a program of therapy through dance, traditional music, drama, and art. The drawings on the wall that I had mistaken for children's art were in fact the work of the would-be trainers: drawing for its own sake was something virtually unknown here. War Child's activities had barely started, and the office's shelves were laden with face paint, cartridge paper, and musical instruments, all in Dutch-labelled packaging.

We drove out to the southern edge of town, to catch an after-school dance and music session being given by two of the War Child staff. As we got out of the Landcruiser, a hundred or more gleeful children mobbed us, and we had to be forceful in pushing our way into the mud-walled straw-thatched classroom where this afternoon's class was under way. There were four large straw mats on the dirt floor, and about twenty-five boys aged eight to twelve were standing in a circle, along with Paul and Mary, the two instructors. Some of the boys wore improvised rattles around their ankles, and a few had string and bead skirts over their tatty shorts.

First, while Paul and Mary chanted, the children learned different clapping rhythms. Then there was a simple game in which the entire circle pointed and chanted at one individual, asking in singsong the name and provenance of the selected player. We were drawn into this, the refrain "Ana min Canada" drawing puzzled titters. Then Paul and Mary demonstrated various traditional dances; typically, Paul would approach Mary to a background of steady clapping, and they then launched into a Shillook, Dinka, or Nuer step. After a few moments, Mary dropped away, and Paul chose a new partner; then he fell back, and so the dance continued until everyone in the circle had tried a few steps. I recognized one of the dances as a favourite from North Kordofan: Mary put her head back at what seemed to be an impossibly sharp angle, then flapped her elbows back in a chicken-like strut.

As a variation, at one moment Paul simulated catching in his hands something small but fragile. He scrutinized it carefully then lobbed the imaginary item across the dark room to Mary, who caught it equally carefully. It took the children a few moments to catch on, but they soon got the idea and began to concentrate intensely, so that even the most timid and introspective of the boys in the circle was frowning as he looked into his cupped hands, then mimicked an ever-so-careful throw. Meanwhile, at the windows, more children craned to look in; at first they were giggling and noisy, but soon they too were concentrating hard as they followed the game, some unconsciously sucking their thumbs.

Once the session was over, we wandered for a few moments by the river bank – which, judging from the smell, was also the school's toilet. I tried to take a few pictures up and down the Nile, but the natural exuberance of the children was such that I couldn't get my camera out before a dozen grinning and laughing boys had posed in front of me, their thumbs up. The girls clustered around Marian, who was tall, dark haired, and freckled, and Catherine, who was slight, blond, and very pale; the girls could not resist tentatively touching the women's pale arms in wonder, then rushing away, shrieking in embarrassment. One pointed to Marian's freckles and evidently asked – in Shillook – what they were, but ran off laughing before anyone could answer.

Soon word came that it was time to visit the school principal. His office was a 4 m² dirt-floored hut, with an old desk and six metal chairs stringed with plastic. Mine had only three blue and white strings in each direction, so that I sank in deeply and briefly feared becoming wedged in the chair's steel frame. On the wall was an Arabic map of the world, a large yellow plastic protractor, and what I easily recognized as the school's timetable. There was a pair of geckos motionless on the crumbling wall; one suddenly moved its head as a large spider came within its circle of attention.

The headmaster was courteous but stood on protocol. After he had welcomed us in a rather grandiose manner and exchanged a few pleasantries, we tentatively got up to leave again, but he motioned us to sit down and – a little aggrieved, perhaps – complained that we had not formally introduced ourselves. I sensed that while he welcomed War Child into his school, he did not really understand the purpose of all this singing and dancing; such things had been absent from the school curriculum for these past thirteen years.

Back at the airport, the women passed through an unusually intimate body search. I pleaded diplomatic immunity; my card was scrutinized closely, with evident bewilderment, and I was waved through unmolested. Our World Food Programme Cessna Caravan was awaiting us. Ominously, its engine cowling was open; the alarmingly young South African pilot was peering into the engine. There had been some problems with the starter motor today, he said. Indeed, after we had clambered aboard and strapped ourselves in, several attempts at ignition failed. The pilot retrieved a large stick about the size and weight of a baseball bat from under his seat and climbed out again; there was some banging, he got in, and the engine started.

For three hours, we followed the Nile northwards. As always, the sunset over the desert to our left was spectacular, but there was scarcely a light to be seen until we made out Khartoum in the gloom ahead, the Blue and White Niles cutting dark ribbons through the glittering lights of Khartoum, Omdurman, and Khartoum North. The pilots muttered in frustration to each other when we were ordered to circle for twenty minutes to allow the KQ flight from Nairobi to land before us: it was Thursday night, and the bar at the British Embassy would be open in less than a half-hour.

THE TWO BIGGEST SOUTHERN TOWNS in government hands were Wau and Juba. Wau (pronounced *wow*) was the smaller of the two, nominally capital of Bahr al-Ghazal State in southwestern Sudan but in fact master of only a reduced area of countryside around the town itself.

Access to here from government-controlled areas was, for outsiders at least, only by air. When I first visited, in mid-January 2001, there had not been a train – from the railhead at Babanusa and through rebel-held territory – for over a year. In a mark of respect to the rebels, the pilots of the World Food Programme spiraled steeply into the city's red dirt strip from an altitude of six thousand feet: a tactic designed to minimize the risk of incoming small-arms fire or worse. Close to the runway and all too visible from high up were the wrecks of two large and not very old Antonov 26s; best not to enquire what happened to these.

Rice threshing, Wau

The town was a quiet, dusty, and litter-strewn huddle of red-brown bricked one-storey structures, the vast majority of which predated independence in 1956. The exceptions were an imposing Catholic cathedral (also in red brick) and an even larger (but almost unused) mosque that was more recent and that (symbolically?) overlooked the cathedral. Naive mural paintings inside the cathedral showed St Peter's, in Rome, set in equatorial jungle, complete with monkeys and parrots. The doors were of carved native mahogany.

With all external surface links cut, the only motor vehicles to be seen on the streets of Wau were Toyota Landcruisers, mostly belonging to the aid agencies and brought in by air; most people got around by bicycle or on foot. There was a 7 p.m. curfew for foreigners, 9 p.m. for everyone else; this was strictly enforced.

I met the wali in his brick-built offices, formerly the seat of the district commissioner. Gold-painted name boards reminiscent of some British private school listed all the regional administrators since the late nineteenth century, and the wali sat rather incongruously directly below an enormous mounted rhino horn, the trophy of a 1920s safari.

As walis invariably do (in my experience), this one insisted the security situation was "fine," and then proceeded to contradict himself. The most pressing problem was the presence in town, he said, of some four thousand murrahaleen who had recently arrived from the upline rail station of Awiel, where a long-awaited relief train for Wau was now empty and set to return to Khartoum (these trains to Wau were usually sacked well before they arrived, if SPLA attacks permitted their arrival at all; on one memorable occasion, the entire relief consisted of one lonely 50 kg bag of rice).

The murrahaleen were armed and horse-mounted mercenaries, typically but not always Arab; among the present group, I learned, were large numbers of Dinkas as well. They were paid by the government (and armed) to protect the supply train on its slow progress south from the capital, but all too often payment consisted of the authorities turning their backs on all manner of pillaging and abduction by the murrahaleen along a wide corridor around the railway. In this instance, it appeared the murrahaleen had become impatient with delays to the train and slim pickings near Awiel and had come to try their luck here. Many shops had been looted, and there had also been some attempts (largely frustrated) to steal from aid agencies. The incursion of the murrahaleen had not been without its surreal moments: they were observed carrying off computer monitors on the backs of their horses, apparently under the impression they were television sets.

The SPLM/A-maintained perimeter was in most places about 30 km from the centre of Wau, said the wali. Local people usually had no problems in crossing from one zone to the other on foot, although they had to pass through roadblocks maintained by both sides; most of the time an uneasy truce held. However, a military column that left Wau on 9 January 2001 to reinforce a position to the east of the city had been under continuous fire ever since; at several moments during my stay I heard sporadic firing from this direction. The wali (and others) speculated that an SPLA attack on Wau was unlikely and that Awiel was a more probable rebel target; but in fact most people believed the government might make the next move and attempt to retake Gogrial from the SPLA (which might in turn provoke SPLA pressure on Wau).

In his day-to-day running of this besieged city, the wali faced the same problems as most governors in Sudan: ever-increasing responsibilities delegated by the centre, but with deficient resources. When pressed the wali did admit to a slightly improved budget over last year (presumably a result in part of very healthy oil revenues), but this had only allowed him a little catch-up: for the first time since 1985, for example, this city of 120,000 now had piped water, but on the other hand salaries for teachers for December 2000 had yet to be paid and the town's two principal generators were out of action.

The wali (a Southerner) was well aware of Talisman and its Canadian connections; distribution of wealth, he suggested, had now become the central issue in the Sudanese conflict, which meant that, like it or not, Talisman was at the eye of the storm. Many years ago, he noted, Canada had been involved in hardwood extraction in and around Wau; he hoped (rather optimistically?) that it would not be long before we were back.

Most of the numerous aid organizations in Wau were involved, in one way or another, in addressing the needs of the forty-seven thousand internally displaced who were housed in camps on the edge of the city. Many of these dated from the major famine of 1998, but there was still a steady inwards trickle that rose to a stream as and when violence broke out in the hinterland, which was frequently. The World Food Programme maintained an air-bridge to Wau from El Obeid and annually delivered approximately seven hundred metric tons of food to the displaced through monthly distributions. The World Food Programme was also making a new push to incorporate peacebuilding into as many of its activities as possible, in particular the self-explanatory Food for Work. In this connection the WFP had been sponsoring an interesting and very productive set of dialogues between the Fertit (a grouping of some twenty-eight regional, mainly Arab tribes) and the Dinka – especially popular had been sessions at which elders had recounted the legends and tales of their one-time peaceful coexistence and joint schooling programs.

Action contre la faim maintained two wet-feeding centres for malnourished children from the camps for the displaced. Again happily, these were not at capacity. Whereas in 1998 this organization was treating three hundred children a day, it now only had thirty to forty cases registered, and few of these were cases of severe malnutrition.

Meanwhile, the small French aid group Enfants du monde was running a pioneering (unique in Sudan) psychosocial program with war-affected displaced from the camps, the dusty streets of Wau, and the region in general. Most of the eighty children – from across the religious and ethnic spectrum – who attended Enfants du monde's day centre for structured play, counselling, and other activities were orphans and/or severely traumatized. It was moving to see the staffers at the centre coaxing one extremely withdrawn child who had apparently not spoken since she had been found on the streets a month ago, into picking up a crayon and drawing a flower. After my return to Khartoum I started talks with the organization to see how Canada could put some support into this program.

Other organizations doing important work included the USA-based International Rescue Committee (IRC), which was teaching displaced women the making of fishing nets, fishing, and the smoking and drying of fish. One effect of this program had been the dramatic empowerment of women (who made up 60 percent of the displaced population) in their communities. The program was designed in such a way that women kept ownership of their nets and lines, even though it might be "their" man who did the fishing; this had changed family structures. And CARE International had a large operation with twenty-eight staff and two girls' schools. Abel, the Wau director for CARE, told me that both parents and the children wanted to learn (indeed to be taught in) English, but of course the law required that the national curriculum be taught in Arabic, and anyone who had not been taught in Arabic would find themselves unable to attend university in the Sudan.

Médecins sans frontières/Holland had a staff of four expatriates (including one Canadian) reinforcing the local three-hundred-bed hospital, which had an occupancy rate of about 60 percent. Malaria and tuberculosis were the principal problems, with HIV/AIDS then a growing but still undetermined threat. The local head of mission was candid with me: pending the next crisis, Wau did not actually need a hospital this big. She also noted surprisingly that cooperation with the local military hospital was "excellent"; in fact she had prevailed upon military doctors and nurses to help out with instruction here, which they had done on a voluntary basis.

I held a wide-ranging chat session with foreign aid agencies on national and regional politics. They felt that much of the conflict was an expansion of generations-old cattle raiding and related phenomena that was being skillfully manipulated into a political war by both the SPLA and the government. Even if peace were signed tomorrow, a great deal of fighting would continue, here at least (the 1972 Addis Ababa Agreement, it appears, had no discernible effect on violence in and around Wau).

Where education levels were higher and closest to the respective command centres of the warring sides random and traditional violence was reportedly much lower; but most territory in the South was in fact a no man's land, out of the effective control of either side. Here bandits (who might pass themselves off as one side or the other) held sway. Displacement was both economic and violence-induced; it was often exceedingly difficult to determine which factor had been predominant in a given group displacement.

What did people have to say about the SPLM/A? Not only the displaced population, said the aid workers, but the population of Wau in general was exceedingly reluctant to talk politics; it was simply too dangerous, with spies from both side everywhere. However, it would generally be true to say that the population of Wau would like a vote on separation and that, in turn, most would vote for an independent South. Some suggested that the international community accord the SPLM/A formal recognition "as it does to Khartoum"; none believed that the real agenda of John Garang was anything less than a separate South.

NEARLY A YEAR LATER, in December 2001, with financial support for Enfants du monde finally locked in, I made a second visit to Wau and took the opportunity also to have a closer look at CARE International, which was also receiving Canadian funds. The first thing I noticed was that the security situation appeared to have taken a turn for the worse. After another stomach-churning descent to avoid missiles, we dodged two Hind gunships that were taking off, nose down, for destinations unknown.

In daylight, you could see from Wau to the low hills beyond the eastern bank of the Bahr al-Ghazal that were held by the SPLA. Every day, there seemed to be big fires burning out there. This was not, I was told, traditional stubble-burning, but, rather, one side or the other clearing its view of the enemy.

At the outside end of the one-and-only bridge over the river, two armoured cars and a heavy machine gun all but blocked the road; however, the soldiers always seemed to be asleep in the shade. Easing our way past them to the Eastern Camp (the main displaced camp, located almost in a no man's land between government and SPLA territory) we passed several herds of traditional long-horned cows; "SPLA cows," said our guide laconically: "They graze them here, then come and get them when they need to eat one or two ..."

At night, the curfew was strictly enforced; this made for generally very quiet evenings. Sitting in the United Nations Children's Fund compound in the moonlight (main hazards: scorpions and bats in the toilet and a tame dik-dik that attacked all female visitors but allowed itself to be stroked by males), the silence would be total for half an hour or so, then a crackle of automatic fire might be heard, or perhaps the whump of a grenade or a light artillery piece. Once, our shutters shook. The locals didn't even pause in their conversation. As the wali disarmingly said to me: "Just light skirmishing, you know; nothing to worry about."

This past month, the government military had been hard at work securing the road west from Wau to Deim el-Zubeir and Raga, towns that were taken early in the wet season by the SPLA but that were now back in Khartoum's hands. One armoured convoy had thus far made it through, but this had not been sufficient to fill with confidence the several thousand displaced from Raga who were still crammed into the slums of Wau.

The train was at this time in Awiel, 100 km to the north and unlikely to move on until Ramadan ended (mid-December) and the government repaired the large stretches of track the SPLA had torn up since the train last passed. Just prior to my visit, the murrahaleen had actually become involved in a pay-related spat with their sponsors in Awiel that had left fifteen murrahaleen and at least one soldier dead. The government had then disarmed some of them, but only until the train moved on again; at that point the raiders would be given their AKs back.

In this difficult context, Enfants du monde's pioneering program for the psychosocial rehabilitation of children was getting under way. In essence, the program worked with community and displaced leaders to identify vulnerable children – orphans, street children, problem children at school – and then put them through an intensive two-month rehabilitation (with an option for extension to four months) at the organization's centre in Wau. Children were given psychiatric assessment and assistance where appropriate, but, most important, they were given the individual attention and love that were all too often the critical items missing from their lives; there was a great emphasis on playing together and on creative activities such as drawing, singing, and acting. At the end of their stay, the children

The children of war: Enfants du monde, Wau

got to keep their uniform smocks and were also given a care package – a blanket, mosquito net, school bag, exercise book, and pencils.

Undertaking such a program, which was then unique in Sudan but which would soon be imitated and varied by War Child in Renk, was especially challenging in an environment where the aid community was focused almost exclusively on logistics and numbers – how many mouths could the United Nations feed per month, how many children could CARE and Norwegian Church Aid get into school, how many malnourished children could Action contre la faim process through its centre. It had been difficult to communicate to community leaders that this was not just another relief program and that the children Enfants du monde wanted were society's rejects, not the smiling, playful children who were well-adjusted to their admittedly tough lives. And it had been difficult to do this with largely untrained staff who themselves were not much better off than most displaced parents and who were subject to all the climatic and health rigours of Wau; Corinne, the expatriate French girl who ran the centre, seemed to be coming down with malaria the day we left. I spent some time with Enfants du monde's local staff and with displaced leaders reinforcing the messages that the organization's two foreign staff had been trying to hammer home: that they wanted not the exuberant, interested child who ran over to see the newcomers, but the one who was sulking or crying in a darkened Tukul, or wandering alone in the fields, stealing from vendors in the souq, or refusing to go to school; that if Enfants du monde achieved success with all of its intake, then it was probably not finding the really hardened cases that it should be looking for; that there were some children to whom, sadly, even this dedicated program may have come too late.

CARE International's peacebuilding program was meanwhile getting under way. Women from different ethnic groups and camps had been identified and were undergoing a varied program of training in income-generation activities. At the women's own suggestion, these included the making of handicrafts; I was skeptical as to the existence of a market in Sudan (let alone Wau) for the admittedly beautiful items they were making, but the basic tailoring and dressmaking classes that were also being given were proving exceptionally popular and (hopefully ...) might displace the former. Was this peacebuilding, though? Well, the idea was that by bringing very varied groups of women together around these activities, they would start socializing and visiting across the usual barriers, and stereotypes would thus be broken down.

One of the most successful of CARE's peacebuilding activities turned out to be, ironically, the cheapest. There had for some time existed a tradition of Sunday afternoon Dinka dances: a time at which groups of Dinka musicians and dancers came together in a completely informal manner and celebrated their culture. CARE had cannily taken hold of this and, with a judicious injection of incentives (soft drinks, some advertising, some cajoling), had turned the formerly low-key event into a positive jamboree of different cultures and music. Now, every Sunday from five until sunset, as many as twenty different groups – Dinka, Xande, Lual, Juar, Balanda, Baya – assembled in the large open space below the mosque and launched a celebration.

The night we attended, almost half the town was there. Crowds of people excitedly wandered or pushed their bicycles from one group to

Dinka dancing, Wau

another, marveling at the high-kicking Dinka men courting their studiously impassive, tall, and graceful young women; at the exuberant body-painted anklet-rattling Awiel dancers; and at the Xande blowing into their weird didgeridoo-type tubas. The police kept an amiable eye on this cacophony, and it was amusing to watch one young lieutenant, evidently frustrated at being left out, thrust his automatic weapon into the arms of a surprised bystander and join – uniform and all – one especially frenzied Dinka dance that involved high energy strutting, stamping, and flapping of arms. The mood everywhere was one of good-natured exuberance and friendly competition. But as the sun set spectacularly, redder than usual on account of the smoke blowing in from the nearby fields of fire, we were reminded that the war was only a few kilometres away.

This visit also coincided with National HIV/AIDS Awareness Day. A two-hour program of speeches, music, and skits at the outdoor Wau

The backing group, Wau

Theatre (which had seen better days) was the centrepiece. The children of Enfants du monde sang two melodies, in counterpoise to the hilarious and surprisingly explicit skits put on by local high-school students. These featured what would in the North be taboo simulations of strutting and rap-listening young men frequenting tea ladies (commonly taken to be synonymous with prostitutes). The advice imparted was not always quite what one would expect or hope for ("Love and tend AIDS patients, but do not feed them too much; remember they will soon die anyway ... Give them the Koran or Bible to read; do not tempt them with erotic literature ..."), but the basic messages were certainly communicated and extremely explicit literature on condom use was nonchalantly passed around among the large crowd. The prevalence of AIDS here was thought to be very high, but there was no diagnosis whatsoever. The necessary testing equipment and supplies were not available.

MY LAST VISIT TO WAU was in November 2002, accompanied by Sylvie, the French country director of Enfants du monde for Sudan. I had had trouble getting a travel permit this time. In fact, about twelve hours before my supposed departure and on an especially sleepy mid-Ramadan Thursday afternoon, I had found myself obliged to call up the ministerial-ranking Humanitarian Aid Commissioner Dr Sulaf to complain that his agency had thus far spent a week processing my request and showed no signs of granting it in the near future. I heard out his complaints about the time of day, and then admitted I knew exactly where the permit was – at the offices of Military Intelligence, where he had referred it and where my driver Babiker was now waiting patiently. Might he consider giving them a call? There was a long silence. "I'm very embarrassed," he finally said. "You embassies are not supposed to know that Military Intelligence vets these permits ..." But my call worked.

Sylvie's plan was that we would get around the scarcity of free World Food Programme flights to Wau by getting a cheap ride down on a cargo aircraft and coming back with WFP. "There'll be no problem," she had said. "Everyone does it." Maybe, but best not to tell Dr Sulaf, I thought.

Our first attempt was not encouraging. As instructed by the staff of Sarit Airlines, we showed up at an unmarked steel gate on Airport Road at 3:30 a.m. There were a number of other people hanging around or sleeping under heavily laden trucks, so we seemed to be in the right place. But the word went out that our plane was currently in Port Sudan and would be flying to Heglig (in the oilfields) before returning to pick us up. This was the only plane of Sarit's that was currently serviceable, we learned; the other four were all undergoing urgent mechanical repairs. I went back to bed.

By noon, we were back at the anonymous metal gate. This time my stamp-covered travel permit was scrutinized with some perplexity. I had the feeling that, after all, few foreigners flew cargo class these days in Sudan. Amazingly, our tickets – handwritten notes in Arabic, on a scrap of torn-off paper the size of a bookmark – were accepted without a second glance. Finally we were ushered over to a pair of oil drums in the shade and invited to sit on them; we placed our bags on an old trolley with the familiar legend, in faded letters, *Heathrow Airport*.

Our red, white, and oil-streaked Antonov 12 finally appeared. Along with a man in a red fez, we clambered up a steel ladder, made our way past mountains of miscellaneous goods piled up haphazardly in the rear cargo hold, and stepped through a pressurized doorway into the passenger cabin.

No-one looked at our bags; so much for post-9/11 security in this haven of terrorism. On board, a swarthy and poorly shaven co-pilot in old track-suit bottoms and with a severe case of plumber's bum, directed us into a pair of incongruous Kenya Airways seats jammed into a corner. There seemed no point in doing up the seatbelts: the seats were not attached to the floor.

Our host, who turned out to be a Chechen (he admitted to smoking Russian cigarettes, though), served us coffee out of unwashed and chipped mugs and then subsided into his berth, in what seemed to be a large hole in the floor but was actually the space that in wartime would be used by a bomb aimer. The pilot lazily flicked a couple of dozen switches labelled in Russian – there was not a single LED display in sight – the four propeller engines sputtered into life, and soon we were lumbering low over the Blue Nile. The flight to Wau was disappointingly uneventful, although the spiralling descent was a little more exciting in this large plane than in the more agile craft of the UN's World Food Programme.

Wau was livelier and more bustling than I had ever found it, with several new shops open and the souq buzzing. This seemed to be one of the few positive side-effects of an ever-larger military garrison: gun-toting soldiers, on Phoenix Chinese-made bicycles adorned with plastic flowers, were everywhere. Ramadan was having little effect on this largely non-Muslim town: in pre-dawn silence, at 4:30 a.m., I heard a drum-beating parade of keen Muslims on their way to prayer being shouted at to "shut up" by lie-abed Christians, and the beautiful red-brick basilica was packed for the three-hour Sunday morning mass.

The security situation, with a nationwide cessation of hostilities then in force, was meanwhile as quiet as it had been in many months. This was the first time in Wau that I did not hear gunfire at night (at Médecins sans frontières' house, bullet holes in the walls were now marked, in pencil, with the appropriate dates). Although there had been an outflux of troops at the time of the government attack on Torit over a month ago, and a more recent influx, there had of late been no local troop movements and no signs of rebel activity either. In spite of this the local authorities, consistently with an enduringly hard line at the national level, were still restricting local travel by humanitarian workers and maintaining the irksome nighttime curfew.

The topic on everyone's lips was the peace process. Almost every conversation seemed to begin or end with "when peace comes."

Wau (like Juba) was home to an inordinately large government bureaucracy, most of whose members – with their nominal areas of responsibility under the control of the SPLM/A, and thus inaccessible – usually had very little to do other than collect their meagre paycheques. These people, including the police and military authorities, were slowly starting to realize that, notwithstanding reassuring messages from the SPLM/A that all would be forgiveness and harmony once it ruled the South, pretty soon their jobs would almost certainly be on the line, even though the rebels would on paper (and likely in fact) be less qualified administrators. Accordingly, there was an unusual and sometimes unseemly hustle on the part of many in authority to show to all – including the aid community – that they actually were useful and keen to contribute towards the sustainable and peaceful development of the South: everyone was trying to make themselves indispensable.

Interestingly, the international aid organizations seemed less alert to what a global peace settlement would – or could – mean to them. I spent some time talking to the highly professional staff of Médecins sans frontières/Holland. For all of their enthusiasm and dedication, they were hardly aware that as close as 70 km away, across SPLA lines, there were fellow MSF staffers operating at the far end of much longer, more tenuous, and costly logistical lifeline than their own. No thought had apparently been given to the huge efficiency and cost savings that would or could be made by reorganizing the agency's operations in the event of a settlement and ensuing crosslines mobility.

Why was this so? For so long now, the humanitarian community in Sudan had been accustomed to working as two separate entities – North and South – that not only developed different mindsets and views of the conflict but had also largely stopped talking to each other. This had been partly because of necessity (the government and SPLM/A had tended to make it difficult for people with experience on one side to be transferred to work on the other), but it had also now become a habit. The International Committee of the Red Cross was the most notable exception to this rule: it had a unique advantage in that it alone had always been able to move crosslines, but it had also been much more energetic in demanding the utmost neutrality and mobility from its staffers, insisting that they not become rutted in either North or South.

At Enfants du monde, Corinne could be very proud of what she had achieved in one year, largely with Canadian support. Even as we wandered around town, I noticed that she was being greeted with a cheerful "Khef!" ("Hi!") by ragamuffin street children on every corner; at the organization's centre, which I visited on a Friday afternoon, six-year-old girls were dancing to Congolese rhythms with tough-looking fifteen-year-old boys at the regular end-of-week party. At Corinne's home, there were always a few orphan children in the yard washing their clothes or having leg sores tended (while their friends calmly perused *Le Monde diplomatique* with every appearance of interest). The once-listless staff were smiling and motivated, the floors covered in homemade toys and half-finished drawings.

I spent time at the closing sessions of two parallel training sessions financed by Canada. At the first, teachers and community leaders from all over Wau had been asked to nominate child leaders for a week-long session of training about rights for children; the idea was that these children would then go back and become role models and mentors within their own communities. As we sat watching, they earnestly discussed, with only occasional intervention from the moderators, the formation of a network in Wau, among themselves, a Kids for Kids support group. At the second, a group of about fifty adult decision-makers, including senior police and Army officers, went through a similar exercise, not only to set up a network but also a whole range of activities and seminars aimed at embedding child rights consciousness in the community. Enfants du monde would offer its premises for some of these activities and would chivvy both networks into making good on their commitments; if only half of what the participants were planning came off, this would be a major – and unique – breakthrough.

Like most of Sudan in late 2002, Wau felt on the edge. There was a combination of hope and fear in the air that was all too movingly summed up by a deaf-mute little Dinka boy's desperate clinging to my hand as we stood to one side watching the Friday dancing. If only the grownups could now deliver.

7

BEHIND REBEL LINES

GETTING TO "THE OTHER SIDE" – rebel-held South Sudan – was complicated. Usually, from Khartoum, it meant taking the 3:45 a.m. Kenya Airways flight to Nairobi, spending a full day arranging a travel permit with either the SPLM/A and/or the smaller Relief Association for South Sudan (for areas controlled by the SPDF, Riak Machar's lesser rebel movement that was only periodically and uneasily allied with the mainstream SPLM/A), taking another flight northwards to the United Nations base at Loki, then boarding some combination of expensive and slow UN flights into South Sudan from Loki. I made no secret, in Khartoum, of where I was going as and when I set off on one of my periodical jaunts into SPLM/A territory, but neither did I ask permission, which would have run the risk of getting a "No."

As it was for everyone I have ever met who has been into the South, my first impression – from the air – was one of emptiness. The second, as an afterthought, was "Where did all the billions of aid dollars go?"

Even concentrations of population such as Rumbek were widely dispersed among luxuriant vegetation over an area of several square kilometres and scarcely looked as though they deserved to be called towns. Typically in South Sudan settlements only a few buildings from the colonial era (notably churches) were of stone and stood out. But on the ground and at this time of year (the rainy season) the villages were beautiful and bucolic, if run down.

Great avenues of teak, mahogany, and mango trees planted a century or more ago gave shade to the red earth tracks and homes to schools of monkeys and baboons (smoked arm, hand, and head of baboon were prized delicacies in Yambio). The large and stately (and also run-down) former residences of the district commissioners conjured up sundowners on the verandah and the long-gone but not forgotten days of the British administration.

Generally speaking, due to Talisman's well-known presence in the oilfields, going around in the South as a Canadian at this time was like wearing a *Kick me* sign on your back. More than once, as the little white Caravan left me by the side of a red dirt strip in the hands of the less than welcoming SPLM/A, I had the uneasy feeling that getting out of here again was not necessarily a given.

But there were actually other Canadians around, even if – for their own reasons – they might not have registered with the Office of the Canadian Embassy in Khartoum or the Canadian High Commission in Nairobi. Oxfam/Québec was at this time working near Tonj; a very capable Canadian on secondment from Save the Children UK ran the World Food Programme's Technical Support Unit at Loki; a Canadian photographer was documenting for UNICEF the Child Soldier Rehabilitation experience; and the USA-based Samaritan's Purse organization had a female Canadian staffer at the Child Soldier camp at Malen Gok, near Rumbek. And then there were two or three understandably self-effacing Canadians who worked for 748 Services flying Andovers (the original Hawker Siddeley 748s had all crashed some time ago) into the Nuba Mountains, dodging government artillery and – on at least one occasion – a MIG; I guessed that on occasion 748 Services flew more than just relief supplies.

On every trip, the first thing I did was check out the military situation from the Southern perspective. A couple of months before this first visit, the SPLA had captured (or *liberated*, in Southspeak) the remote Bahr al-Ghazal town of Raga from the government and, bloodied, neither side had

The former district commissioner's residence at Yambio, Equatoria, now the United Nations' guest house

since mounted a significant offensive. But there was sporadic skirmishing around the government enclave of Awiel in Bahr al-Ghazal, and from rebel-held Achongchong – barely 20 km from government-held Wau, whose low buildings I could see as I flew in – I could hear sporadic shelling in the night. Every day fifty to seventy civilians from Wau were crossing the lines to Achongchong, apparently partly in fear of an imminent SPLA attack.

After a lull in the early part of the year, bombing all over the South had intensified again. Wherever I went, people kept an eye on the sky and could readily tell me whether the droning we could hear was a Buffalo, a C-130 Hercules (both benign), or an Antonov (usually not so). At all of my overnight stops I was first shown the nearest trench or a more carefully constructed bomb shelter, and at Achongchong I was given a grab bag to be taken into the bush in the event of a land attack.

Here, more than the bombers or the government Army itself, people feared the murrahaleen, who in March 2001 had spent several days marauding in and around this community and had abducted several young boys (who were subsequently freed at Awiel). The Save the Children compound in which I slept – a clearing in the forest, with a fence of wooden stakes and a straw hut – had itself been raided. The commissioner (the local authority) had special reason to feel nervous: his two predecessors had been killed by murrahaleen and/or government raiders. At his headquarters, which I approached with some caution, a dozen or so bodyguards were hanging around, cleaning their fingernails with the tips of bullets. In a lighter vein but still in the same connection, a United Nations Children's Fund worker who had taken a small group of released child soldiers to see their first television, in Rumbek, told me that on seeing a Cowboys and Indians movie, the children had exclaimed: "They have murrahaleen in America, too!"

In the north and east of South Sudan, especially where Riak Machar's Nuer-dominated SPDF had influence, the security situation was much more chaotic. SPDF commanders and their men were moving wholesale to the SPLM/A, but not necessarily at the same time and – to confuse matters further – there were a few who were defecting to the government. In practical terms this meant that, when relief agencies flew into these territories, they were not certain who would be in control when they hit the ground. In one farcical saga, a local commander identified himself to an incoming World Food Programme monitoring crew as SPDF, went away, and then returned to announce that he had been mistaken: he was now SPLM/A.

SPDF boss Machar appeared in a kind of limbo as his movement disintegrated around him. Soon, he would negotiate for himself an ambivalent place in an expanded SPLM/A hierarchy, but for now his people were voting with their feet and leaving him with ever fewer cards to play.

Independently from the SPLM/A, the SPDF, and a multitude of other acronymic militias, I learned, there also existed the so-called White Armies: heavily armed gangs of cattle rustlers typically headed up by young bloods who would sell their temporary allegiance (or their mothers) to the highest bidder. Although these groups took their name from the preferred colour of cattle in these parts, the resonance with post-revolutionary Russia was apposite.

And then there were strange figures such as The Prophet: a Nuer man who claimed to be the reincarnation of a long-dead figure revered in Nuer history who would lead his people to peace. The Prophet had several thousand armed disciples in and around Akobo in the far northeast of rebel-held territory. He was rivalled by a younger messiah-like figure: a months-old baby born under a great star in the west (Twic County). Fresh from the womb, this baby already had teeth and was also prophesying (in English) peace in his time.

SPLM/A leaders talked bravely of unity in the South and dismissed the idea that a separate South Sudan would immediately implode, but aid organizations and the United Nations were much less sanguine. They acknowledged that a large proportion of the displacement that occurred in the South was due to intra-Southern conflicts and that at times only a shared hatred of the Northern "Arabs" was what united Nuer and Dinka. One SPLM leader, when asked for suggestions as to what Canada should be doing in the South, said that the best thing we could do would be to broker Nuer/Dinka reconciliation "so that we can more effectively pursue the war."

IN FEBRUARY 2001, six months before my first visit, the United Nations Children's Fund had mounted a spectacular operation by which, with the full support of the SPLM/A, 3,500 child soldiers then serving in rebel ranks in Northern Bahr al-Ghazal (Awiel East and West) were at a stroke demobilized and assembled in Rumbek in eight camps. Documentation and tracing of the children's families was by now almost complete and "returns," by Buffalo aircraft, were beginning; the process was planned to be completed within another three to four weeks. I was able to visit one of the eight Rumbek transit camps: at Malen Gok, run by Samaritan's Purse; the other seven were all directly managed by UNICEF.

The Malen Gok compound was no St Trinian's. The 360 children housed in straw huts were of all ages between five and eighteen, but mainly between eight and thirteen. Locally employed caregivers served as monitors in each hut, but these politically aware children did not hesitate to take matters into their own hands when they felt their rights were being infringed; the day before my visit, the expatriate camp supervisors had only narrowly averted an organized march to Rumbek by the camp occupants, who demanded mosquito nets. More constructively, the children had organized their own informal church under a tree and were cooperating in attempts to have some basic schooling delivered.

Samaritan's Purse, headed by Franklin Graham, son of Billy, was circumspect in its comments but clearly felt that the UN had mismanaged – and was continuing to mismanage – the program; Save the Children UK (another implementing partner) echoed these remarks. The non-UN agencies felt that they were being left out of the consultative process and informed of major movements of children into their areas of responsibility only a few hours ahead of the actual move. They also felt that UNICEF had underestimated the complexity and depth of programs that would have to be put in place in the children's home communities if re-recruitment was not to occur.

Everyone saw the desirability in principle of extracting child soldiers from military ranks and of making the entire process as speedy as possible. They also recognized the enormous inherent difficulty of undertaking any such exercise in an ongoing war and the fact that the lack of serious educational facilities in South Sudan – the primary incentive on offer to the child soldiers – was a problem too big for anyone to address at a stroke. In sum, UNICEF deserved credit, but should – they thought – make a greater effort next time around (and several further rounds of child soldier extraction were envisaged) at keeping its implementing partners in the loop.

AS WELL AS PRIDING ITSELF on its enthusiastic participation in the child-soldier program, the SPLM/A insisted to me that it treated women as full and equal participants in the struggle to create a New Sudan (the SPLM/A used this expression to refer to both the territory under its control at this time and to its utopian vision for a better country). In fact, the first SPLM official I met within the South was Mary, the county commissioner of Yambio. Wherever we went in Yambio, my SPLM/A guide (technically from the SPLM/A's "humanitarian arm" – the Sudan Relief and Rehabilitation Association, or SRRA – but the distinction was largely academic) pointed out to me women doing heavy "men's work" such as digging impressively deep latrine pits (he neglected to inform me that the United Nations had actually recruited and was paying them); in the souq he pointed to a bare-headed woman in a knee-length skirt and said, "She'd never get away with that in the North."

But a long talk with the commissioner of Wau County led me to the conclusion that the truth was rather less rosy. He gave me a very tradi-

Women digging latrine pits at Yambio, Equatoria

tional view of the place of women in the New Sudan (in the kitchen) and in the SPLM's decision-making process (subservient). He then commented facetiously on how difficult it was to keep four wives in line. Like many avowedly Christian Southerners, he was polygamous. There seemed to be little evidence that Southern women were substantially more emancipated than their Northern counterparts.

Whenever I visited the rebel-held South, one of the topics I always pursued was the degree to which the SPLM/A was attempting to administer the vast territory it controlled. Certainly there existed a formal structure, which the movement had modelled largely on the pre-1956 colonial pattern. Each of South Sudan's five regions (Equatoria, Bahr al-Ghazal, Upper Nile, Southern Blue Nile, South Kordofan – coinciding with the three states bequeathed by the colonists, plus two of the three "contested areas" where the SPLM held significant territory) had a governor who was simultaneously the top civil and military authority; each region was in turn divided into counties or districts, administered by a county secretary (or commissioner). Rumbek, for example, was one of Bahr al-Ghazal's twelve counties. Each county secretary then established various departments and appointed heads for them; in Yambio these departments consisted of health, agriculture, education, the judiciary, wildlife, prisons, and the police; the latter two were headed by military officers.

In theory, the activities of these departments and of the military were financed by taxes raised from persons of eighteen and above by the executive chief of each payam (large village). In Yambio County, such a village might have eight hundred taxpayers, who were required to pay 1,500 pounds (more on the value of money later) each November, for which they were issued a receipt. The county also received income from fines imposed by the courts. Most court cases involved litigation over cattle and marriage dowries gone wrong, with the horn size and skin colour of bulls providing much grist for learned legal debate.

I saw no sign of the records that such practice necessarily implied. In Rumbek, although I met officials at the main office of the county commissioner, the only furniture in the entire bat-infested building was the table and chairs at which we sat (under an old calendar of Chairman Garang), the only evidence of a "record" a scrap of paper on which the county secretary had at some point typed out the total number of taxpayers from two villages. The premises of the Wau commissioner were even more rudimentary: a two-bed straw hut in the jungle. I had the feeling that the bulk of collected cash revenues went straight to the military; certainly, all the social programs I saw (primary schools, water pumps, clinics) had been financed entirely by aid agencies or the United Nations.

The international humanitarian agencies confirmed that while the SRRA was generally helpful (and was thus not an exact parallel to the more obstructive equivalent in Khartoum, Dr Sulaf's Kafkaesque Humanitarian Aid Commission) neither it nor the county departments ever seemed to have any money of their own for social programs. At Achongchong, SRRA activities were limited to compiling a list of displaced persons as they arrived from Wau, passing that list to aid organizations, and serving as translators or accompaniers for visitors such as myself. The communities themselves weren't necessarily prepared to make even token contributions to projects from which they benefitted directly: stories were legion of well-meaning internationals attempting to introduce user-fee systems in the areas of health, education, and water and almost invariably failing. Tommy – a British pilot for Save the Children – had been flying into these areas for five or six years. He told me that aid recipients unloading planes expected to be paid handsomely for their work (i.e., they expected to be paid for receiving aid), which had more than once led him to take off again without unloading. World Food Programme staffers told me that the SPLM/A routinely and cynically pressured its food monitors and other representatives to exaggerate food needs and thus inflate food deliveries, this with the clear aim of securing for themselves the loyalty of the communities concerned.

Addressing the perceived right to aid of Southern Sudanese with SPLM officials was tough slogging. Only when I put the issue in very concrete terms was I able to get through: "Imagine Canadian citizen Joe, who goes to his quiet, safe office job in Hamilton every morning, taking the train to work. He has health coverage, electricity, water, education for his children, security on the streets, and the prospect of a good pension. Why should he send any of his money to a war-stricken land ten thousand miles away? Why should he care?" It seemed truly not to have occurred to the SPLM/A that much of the money spent by the UN's Operation Lifeline Sudan and aid agencies in Sudan came, ultimately, from the hands of private citizens to whom government representatives such as myself were accountable. Asked to respond, my interlocutors were generally at a loss, although genuinely appreciative of this crash course in aid politics.

SPLM/A officials seemed – at first – also not to realize that the political agenda of Western countries was not necessarily congruent with their own – a function perhaps of years of tacit US support for the cause? – and that our patience regarding Sudan might not be limitless. Again I found myself painting things in a stark manner, this time describing in concrete terms the daily realities, constraints, and choices faced by Western leaders in addressing issues such as Sudan. When I concluded by asking whether it really was justified for Canada to invest large resources here, given other demands and the limited prospects for lasting peace, more than once the question provoked nervous laughter and, after some hesitation, the comment: "Maybe you'd better choose somewhere else."

It wasn't just the fault of these mid-level rebel officials that they didn't understand the developed countries' agenda on aid and more generally on peace. It was, first, a natural product of an organization that was militaristic in nature and focused – for now at least – on almost exclusively military objectives.

But it was the international community that had let them get away with it for so long, by failing to insist that the rebels be more accountable to their own people and by extension to us, the donors. United Nations officials who had been too long in the field unhelpfully and irresponsibly fostered SPLM/A assumptions by referring in written reports to the "liberation" of places such as Raga. Some arms of the United Nations had also developed the custom of routinely inflating crises, in the self-fulfilling knowledge that Western governments were only likely to meet at most half of the requirements on their shopping list and also because – as in most organizations – career prospects were in direct proportion to your proven record in growing your particular operation.

To have an intelligent conversation in English with someone of influence in the New Sudan, I soon learned, one must look for grey hair. Almost no-one under forty had been to secondary school, for the simple reason that there had been no systematic secondary education in the territory for these past eighteen years. At various times there might be up to three secondary schools functioning, or more typically there might be none; on the occasion of my first visit, historic Rumbek Secondary had just closed for a month because parents had found they were unable to pay school feeding bills. At the primary level, the situation was better, but schools all too often consisted of a few tree logs in the shade of a large tree, with unpaid primary graduates working as teachers. A mixture of syllabuses was followed, with elements from both the Ugandan and the Kenyan systems. In theory English – the default lingua franca in SPLM/A territory – was the language of instruction, but I found few young people capable of more than a couple of words in English; Juba Arabic (a kind of pidgin) and/or Dinka were far more common.

Some steps were being taken to remedy the catastrophic state of education, notably by the United Nations with the support of the US Government's Sudan Transitional Assistance for Rehabilitation (STAR) program. In Rumbek and in Yambio small printing presses were being set up that were starting to turn out rudimentary textbooks. And in Yambio the Institute of Development, Environment and Agricultural Studies (IDEAS) was fast becoming a reality, under United Nations guidance.

IDEAS would be South Sudan's first tertiary-level educational institution. It would commence work with a distance teacher education program, which, starting in November 2001, would begin systematic training of seventy-five young teachers, through a diploma program being devised with the help of Batchelor Institute (Australia) and The Institute of Teacher Education in Kampala. IDEAS would also be the location for a US-funded centre for agricultural studies and would support a satellite institute in Rumbek that would deliver training in administration and bookkeeping. IDEAS was located on the former campus of an agricultural institute in Yambio, which had functioned until the late 1970s; it was hoped that over the next five years the campus would reach its intended capacity of seven hundred resident students.

This was an exciting project although, as with so many other aspects of development in the New Sudan, the issues of dependency and sustainability remained unresolved. There was no real prospect of IDEAS paying its way even in the medium term.

There was no planned economy in South Sudan. The economy was characterized by subsistence farming and cattle-raising at a usually very local level, with important injections of donor aid. Extremely poor surface communications, endemic insecurity, and lack of interest from the current authorities had combined to inhibit any further growth. Aping its Northern counterparts, the SPLM required all travellers to have travel permits – a further disincentive for small traders.

There was a popular perception that the reason for underdevelopment in the South was because "the North never did anything for us" in economic terms when it controlled these regions. There was some truth in this, although Khartoum hadn't actually done that much for the North either (if only Southerners had the chance to see). And the little the SPLM/A had inherited had been let go to rack and ruin. In Yambio a TV tower stood abandoned, electricity transmission lines hung uselessly from concrete posts, a water tower and water distribution system had all fallen into disrepair – all of these were prewar (i.e., "Northern") projects, now abandoned.

In the end, I was not convinced that, in objective terms and even counting the war, the South was necessarily worse off than large areas in the North. Never in my life had I seen harsher environments than those in which the desert communities of northern and western Sudan somehow eked out their precarious existence. By contrast, much of the South – especially the two Equatorias – was a land of plenty. Yambio was a case in point. With a completely straight face, County Commissioner Mary informed me that the problems the community faced included its inability to sell off its large agricultural surplus and that mangoes and papayas fell off the trees in such quantities that they had caused injuries.

A more serious but still bizarre problem faced by the regional economy was the lack of hard cash in circulation. Ugandan, Kenyan, and Congolese currency circulated in Yambio, along with obsolete pounds from some Khartoum administration of many years ago; it took a mathematical genius to keep mental tabs on the complicated exchange rates. Up in Rumbek, the Kenyan shilling and the US dollar prevailed; while in Wau County the current Sudanese Dinar was preferred. Nowhere were there sufficient notes.

In response to this problem, the SPLM was contemplating printing its own money, to be known as the Nile. No-one seemed to have any idea of the complicated economic consequences of such a move.

In 2001, peace talks still seemed a long way off. But all of the SPLM/A people I met with were well briefed as to the party line on Southern aspirations: insistence on the formal separation of state and religion and on the right to self-determination. After half an hour or so of conversation it invariably became clear that no-one thought self-determination would lead to a vote for Sudanese unity, even with a highly decentralized state. There was simply too much history, too long a litany of agreements betrayed.

The New Sudan would include – "this is non-negotiable" – the current sites of oil production. In fact, the war would be winnable outright by the South, I was told, were it not for the oil revenues that Khartoum had now been receiving for these two years past, which were sustaining the government military. Oil had taken centrefield in the conflict: "If the oil flow is not interrupted, then we can hold out for maybe five years. But, if we can shut it off, we have won." Following this line of logic, the principal objective of the SPLM/A (I was told) was now to close down production, either by forcing the international companies out, thus leaving the government unable to operate the fields (questionable, this – Northerners probably now had the expertise to run things on their own), or by inflicting sufficient damage on the installations so as to ensure that production was stopped.

If this indeed was the strategy, and it had a certain stark simplicity, then all of Talisman's efforts to dispel allegations of forced displacement and to implement community-friendly development programs were – it seemed to me – a waste of time. These were not issues for the SPLM/A, who thought it irrelevant that if Talisman left the Chinese would likely replace it and probably not care a fig for community relations. The rebels cared only that oil was flowing and that it was providing revenue to the enemy. If Talisman remained on the ground, "then they must be prepared to be caught in the crossfire."

When I asked how Canada could contribute to peace in Sudan, the most often stated serious suggestion I heard was that we lean heavily on Talisman to leave Sudan. Our contribution to the Intergovernmental Authority on Development Sudan Peace Secretariat was welcomed (when I brought it up). Most other suggestions resulted from very fuzzy logic and ranged from "Give us Stingers" to "Bomb Khartoum like you bombed Belgrade" and "Help us get together with the SPDF."

It was disappointing, but perhaps not surprising, to find that most people with whom I spoke were not prepared to find any positive features among Northerners and considered them as unredeemable in exactly the same manner as they claimed Northerners categorized them. I also came across a great lack of knowledge about what was going on in the North, explicable in part by the isolation from which the South suffered. Everyone with whom I met was avid for the latest gossip from Khartoum, and the SPLM/A was grateful for the back issues of the English-language *Khartoum Monitor*. Such ignorance of the North was also shared by many international aid agencies, although they were noticeably less keen – typically – to learn. "Don't confuse me with facts" seemed to be the attitude of a number of people when I tried to explain things from a Khartoum perspective.

How Christian was the South? Young soldiers often wore crucifixes, but they also toted heavy automatic weapons. Churches were empty and many looked disused; Sunday was indistinguishable from any other day of the week. By contrast, a number of the foreign aid organizations were overtly Christian, even proselytizing in nature.

I sensed that within the SPLM/A morale was probably quite high, certainly higher than among the Northern armed forces. But it was much more difficult to gauge the degree to which the common people shared this optimism. From the dead eyes of the displaced staggering into Achongchong and the listless manner in which they complied with the orders of their hosts, apathy and fatigue better described their mood.

BY MAY 2002, when I again ventured behind rebel lines, the government was on the offensive; government troops, who for some weeks had been reported to be massing in Wau, were breaking out of their enclave and heading north. Meanwhile, heavy fighting in Western Upper Nile (Unity State, to Northerners) was continuing: one account spoke of 1,500 dead on each side over the past six months. The focus was the newly constructed road south from Bentiu into Block 5A, with the government controlling most of the settlements on the road, and the SPLA and SPDF controlling the hinterland. The government was making extensive use of helicopter gunships (the Russian-built Hinds) and an Antonov bomber, backed with ground troops; it was reported that its operations were being conducted in an unusually organized and synchronized manner. Government troops had recently been reinforced by men freed up by the Nuba ceasefire. The government had denied access to any and all United Nations relief flights for the Western Upper Nile region.

The rebels were also fighting back more effectively, due to the early 2002 alliance between the SPLA and Riak Machar's formerly government-aligned SPDF. Although the two groups were nowhere fighting under a unified command and there existed general skepticism regarding the substance and durability of the alliance, in this area at least they were taking on government forces in a more-or-less coordinated manner. SPLA-loyal forces under Peter Gadiet seemed to control the area north of Koch, while SPDF Commander Peter Parr held areas to the south.

It was ironic that Machar's SPDF was now targetting the oilfields. A senior Talisman official had told me that Machar's personal assurances (when he was pro-government) had been crucial in persuading Talisman to enter Sudan three years earlier.

Both the government and the rebels were, as usual, making extensive use of irregular militias, and it was these forces – not discounting the disproportionate and indiscriminate use of the gunships and Antonovs – that seemed to be accounting for most of the serious human rights abuses now occurring in this region and driving thousands of civilians from their homes. Forced recruitment and indiscriminate killing, rape, and theft were the order of the day – from both sides.

I was also told that the rebels now had vehicles capable of moving through swamps. When I later commented on this to a senior figure in the oil industry, he suggested that this was likely a reference to a dozen Everglades-style "swamp buggies" seized from Lundin Oil in December 2001.

The other area of military activity on Sudanese soil at this time was a running battle between the Joseph Kony's Lord's Resistance Army and the Ugandan Defense Forces. Due to the increased fighting in the area, United Nations security had declared the area from Nimule and Pajarok, south of Juba, as "red no go" for humanitarian workers. Video images taken on 25 April 2002 by the UN while on a security reconnaissance mission showed what looked like localized shelling of (we could only assume ...) LRA forces around Ikotos. The footage showed steep, gully-filled evergreen mountains where long-term survival without assistance would most likely be possible. The UN said it had no information about the whereabouts of LRA escapees. While there was no evidence of direct Sudanese Government support to Kony's men, there was however mention of the Equatorian Defense Force, Martin Kenyi's pro-government militia fighting the SPLA, which might also have been providing some support to the LRA. Everyone agreed that this was still far from over; the Ugandans were not close to leaving Southern Sudan.

ON THIS VISIT, PURSUING MY ENQUIRIES on governance, I concentrated on the SPLM/A's judiciary, which was formally established (or reestablished) at the movement's 1994 convention. This provided for six tiers of justice, with a separate system for the military: a Court of Appeal (five members), which sat in Rumbek; six High Courts (each comprising four counties), four of which were operational; County Courts; Payam (or subcounty) Courts, each with three magistrates; Regional Courts; Executive Chiefs' Courts.

There was as yet no codified body of law in Southern Sudan, and no popularly endorsed constitution. A combination of British-style law and local restitution-based customary law was used. In a typical case, a murderer might be punished by having to pay to the family of the victim a certain number of cows ("bloodwealth") and – if the family of the victim so desired – by also serving a term of imprisonment; but imprisonment seemed to be applied rather arbitrarily. All death penalties were reviewed by Chairman Garang.

Customary law varied between the many ethnic groups that fell under the rebels' influence, principally the Dinka, Nuer, and Xande. Some attempt had recently been made to codify each set of customary laws, but there were major discrepancies and problems occurred when offenses involved persons of more than one ethnic group. For example, under Dinka law, an adulterer would be fined with seven cows, but a Nuer must pay only six. But a Nuer had to pay fifty cows to the family of his murder victim, whereas a Dinka would be fined with only thirty-one; a choice bride might well cost up to two hundred cows ("bridewealth") – the disparity between the cost of a bride and a murder was perhaps a comment either on the supreme importance of the mother figure in Nilotic culture or on the relatively low importance of human life. Grazing and water rights and disputes over bloodwealth and bridewealth payments made up the bulk of the territory's legal disputes.

Events of the past fifty years had had some effect on customary law, in that bridewealth and/or bloodwealth could also be paid in the form of automatic weapons. However, mariel (long-horned black and white) cows remained, against all the odds and defying logic, the prime measure of bovine wealth, ahead of cows that provided more milk and/or better meat.

Forty paralegals (payam judges) were currently undergoing training in Rumbek under the auspices of the New Sudan Council of Churches and the South Sudan Law Association, which was setting up a Judiciary Resource Centre, also in Rumbek. The churches' sponsorship of this activity arose from the realization that paralegals were an ongoing need in the context of the local Nuer/Dinka Wunlit peace agreement, which was still fragile. Judges and paralegals received no fees, other than a proportion of the bloodwealth/bridewealth involved in the cases over which they presided.

Police and prison officers received no special training of any sort, other than what they might have undergone in the Army. Police officers also served to prosecute crimes; in the courtroom the accused had no defense, other than the judge.

I also looked at two other critical areas of services. Health was left almost entirely to the United Nations and foreign aid agencies. However, there did exist a South Sudan-wide SPLM-administered Health Commission, whose task was to regulate health delivery and set policies. It had been responsible for developing an ambitious and enlightened HIV/ AIDS strategy: an AIDS counsellor, for example, had been identified for Rumbek. As elsewhere in the developing world, the condom promotion strategy was encountering a fundamental problem in that most families wanted large numbers of children. Agencies were now supposed to levy a fee for all health services delivered – usually two hundred pounds (about USD $0.08). However, there were many exemptions to even this very modest (by Western standards) fee; schoolchildren, soldiers, and the "very poor" were not required to pay.

Of the USD $0.08 levy, $0.02 went to the Health Commission for administration costs, the remaining $0.06 to the program deliverer. The funds thus far recovered were minimal, and the system was prone to abuse in that in South Sudan it was not difficult for anyone honestly to make the case of being "very poor." But even this low-aiming scheme had met with resistance from a public that, as a roundtable of foreign aid workers put to me, "has for the past twenty years been getting it all free." Tensions were also created when some agencies – the church or UNICEF – insisted on delivering free the same services for which a neighbouring clinic might be charging.

As in the North, the principal challenge to day-to-day survival for those who were not subject to fatal diseases or displacement and killing by the enemy was the scarcity of abundant and clean water, vital not only for drinking and cooking but also for the survival of the cattle – so central to life in this part of the world. There were worries in some areas that this year's rains were already late, and in many communities the nearest water source at this time might be five or six hours' walk away. While 2002 was not shaping up to be a year of extraordinary drought, it would neverthe-less not be a good year for water.

Anyone looking to spend some spare development dollars in Sudan could never go wrong by investing it in the drilling of boreholes or the supply of hand-pumps; the problem was that the demand seemed to be inexhaustible. SRRA plans were afoot to charge for water delivery in the same way as health services, but it was clear it would face similar problems in effecting any real cost recovery.

MY OTHER PRINCIPAL AREA OF INTEREST at this time was judging the receptivity in Southern Sudan to peace initiatives that seemed, for the first time in years, to be gaining momentum. But the mood in the SPLM/A and in other Southern circles was like a cool Nairobi rain shower.

Senior SPLM/A officials with whom I met in the Kenyan capital on the way into the South – "Foreign Minister" Nhial Deng, press spokesper-son Samson Kwaje, and Martin Okerruk – were very cautious regarding the eventual success or otherwise of US peace envoy Jack Danforth. They warned that it was too soon to see how the four "tests" of the parties' good faith that he had set could be a bridge to a political solution to the conflict and cautioned that the success of two of them – the Nuba ceasefire and the Agreement to Protect Civilians from Military Attack – remained to be seen. Nuba was "a purely humanitarian agreement and should not be polit-icized," while the agreement on civilians was " already breaking down," absent (then) its suggested verification mechanism. Unsurprisingly, Deng suggested that only one side – Khartoum – needed to be pressed and that the international community had a key role to play here; he added that he thought there had been a toughening of Khartoum's stance in direct proportion with Western engagement. The SPLM's insistence that over the years it had made all the concessions and Khartoum none was undermined when Kwaje handed over to me the Movement's diagram entitled "Solution Modalities in the Sudan Conflict"; the document was dated 1994: in eight years, the SPLM's position had not budged an inch.

I challenged Deng: was there, in fact, no "window" for peace now? Such potential as existed was, the officials hedged, due almost entirely to US pressure. The formation of a de facto USA/UK/Norway peace troika was welcome, but the USA was clearly the only possible mover and shaker. Pending some dramatic new initiative from the superpower, "The war may go on a long time yet ..." Deng underlined that there was still no resolution in sight on state and religion and insisted that – in spite of apparent backtracking by Khartoum, "at the behest of some regional countries" – the Declaration of Principles, including its enshrinement of the right to self-determination, was "fundamental."

Amplifying on the role of Egypt, SPLA old-timer and SRRA Director Elijah Malok (whom I met separately in Rumbek) said "there is nothing we can say to reassure Egypt." If Egypt's only problem was the Nile waters, as was commonly supposed, "then we pose no threat." Malok was skeptical that constructive US interest would last. He suggested at one point (the first time I had heard this) that the British Commonwealth might be able to play a useful role in the search for peace in Sudan When I asked if he had put this to British Ambassador Richard Makepeace on the occasion of the envoy's recent visit to Rumbek, he said no, with a smile; the message seemed to be *UK okay, Commonwealth better.*

Closer to the grass roots there did not seem to be any greater degree of enthusiasm or hope that peace was around the corner. As on my first visit, it was repeatedly suggested to me that nearly all Southerners had long since lost hope of a reconciliation with the North, that they felt irreversibly betrayed and bitter, that the agenda was not so much the abstract construct of self-determination but – rather – separation, plain and simple. Such interest as there existed in dialogue and reconciliation was almost exclusively within a South/South context. Youth leaders at the Rumbek-based Bahr al-Ghazal Youth Development Agency, for example, were noticeably uninterested in meeting any of their counterparts from the Muslim North; they talked of "unity" only with reference to milestones such as the Dinka-Nuer Wunlit Accords.

Aid organizations nuanced this bleak view by suggesting that a major problem was that the common people of Southern Sudan were far removed from information and intelligent commentary on the war; there seemed to them to be no options other than the status quo and separation, and people reasoned that separation could hardly be much worse than what they were experiencing now. The agencies also cautioned (as they had in Wau) that a great deal of what passed for a North/South war was a local conflict, with regional commanders interested almost exclusively in financial and other material (e.g., guns) gain rather than in pursuing a political agenda. As in government-controlled areas, access to water and grazing was at the heart of most local conflicts. Was there extensive war fatigue? Yes, but this did not mean that there was a "peace now" movement around the corner. There was as yet little realization among the common people of what benefits and dividends peace might bring – this again a function of the almost total absence of intelligent discussion and information on the war.

IN MAY 2002, as on my first visit, I was bombarded by SPLM/A officials with criticism over Talisman. But this time the local security situation (and better weather) meant that I was able to access two areas – Wuncuei (Tonj County) and Maper (Rumbek County) – into which civilians were reportedly fleeing from aggressive government operations in the oilfields so I could hear directly from those affected. The experience was sobering.

At the remote hamlet of Wuncuei, about forty-five minutes' flying north-northwest of Rumbek, the World Food Programme and Médecins sans frontières/Switzerland had recently completed an assessment of the tide of displaced persons that of late had been overrunning the area. They were mostly Bull Nuer from Western Upper Nile, to the east and north. Nuer access to this land, which was Dinka, was possible only because of the Wunlit agreement between the two ethnic groups, but not all was peace among the Southerners: intertribal conflict between Agar Dinka and Rek Dinka was still endemic to this area. The total number of displaced households here, as reviewed by the humanitarian agencies, was 1,020; multiply by five, said the rule of thumb, and you got the figure for individuals.

Along with colleagues from the Canadian International Development Agency, I met on a sweltering afternoon under a large tree with a group of a hundred or more people. Interpreting from Nuer to Dinka to English, with occasional forays into Arabic, made things slow and perhaps led to some misunderstandings, but the elders who were designated to speak to us were patient, stoical even.

David and his family (I have changed the names) arrived in Wuncuei in February from Koch and had walked nine days to get here. Koch had been bombed by a government Antonov and helicopter gunships every second day between 7:00 and 9:00 a.m., he said; the targets were apparently the cattle grazing areas and the village. David lost children of his sister, but none of his own. He also lost cattle and goats. In Bieh, Nydeng, Kuo (or Kot?), Rupnor, Gwadir, Loum, Kwernong, and Bauw, "the Antonov also killed animals."

I asked David, testing him, to describe the Hind gunships. "They look green, white, and yellow." Another translator butted in to say that David was using a term indicating "like military uniform." "They fired guns – they open the door and shoot from machine guns – flying very low. They would target living things. The gunship came seven times to Koch over a two-week period. We would have died if we had stayed as they were so regular." Aid organizations, David said, had been in the area previously but had left earlier because of the bombing.

John, aged forty, was from the town of Kuo, near Leer (in the heart of Lundin Petroleum's Block 5A). He had come to Wuncuei in March. It took him ten days to walk from his village. He had nine wives and twenty children, he said. Antonov bombings "and troops on the ground" made them all leave. He saw the government troops as he was running away; the SPLA was "pushed back" by the government. John saw an Antonov bombing his village and also saw helicopter gunships. His house was burned down.

Michael had left Leer on 10 March to walk to Wuncuei with his two wives and four children. Most of his animals were killed by gunships – only two goats survived, he said. He left "because of gunships and the Antonov. They came every second day, at 7:00 a.m. The Antonov came first and bombed, followed by the gunship firing machine guns. Four gunships came at the same time." There were both SPDF and SPLA soldiers in different parts of Leer, Michael freely admitted – adding "the commander of the SPDF is Peter Parr" – but neither group, he said, had anti-aircraft guns; they tried to defend themselves with AK rifles but "it was no good. I had no gun; I am not a fighter, and I was never trained as a soldier."

At Maper, in Rumbek County and at a similar distance from Rumbek itself, the story was a similar one. Here, the SRRA estimated there were seven hundred displaced households, comprising 3,783 individuals; I was told to write the numbers down.

Simon, one of the displaced, was aged twenty. It had taken him four days to walk here from the village of Sanor, a subvillage of Bieh. "The fighting made me leave." He had seen an Antonov over the village of Bieh at the beginning of April: "It came twice and dropped twenty-four bombs in the afternoon." He saw another Antonov in Koch in February 2002, this time a gunship was with the Antonov: "It was shooting, with machine guns." There were no SPLA in Koch at the time, he said.

Fifty-year-old Nicholas said he had left his village of Mayendit three months ago "due to the war." It was a four-day walk to Maper. "Many people were killed and also cattle; I didn't want to be killed, so I left. Gunships are killing us – we are so angry – we have no food, no water." The gunships "look like military uniform; they fly at tree level; there were three gunships together." When the Antonov arrived, gunships came with it, and so did government soldiers. "The government also took some of our people away ..." The SPLA still held Mayendit, said Nicholas, adding that Peter Gadiet (SPLA) and Peter Parr (SPDF) were working together.

It wasn't easy to talk to any women, and the elders muttered and shrugged with irritation when I insisted. Finally they pushed Norma forward. Her face was intricately and ceremonially scarred in concentric circles of raised dots.

Norma had left her village of Nimne (near Bentiu) due to fighting. She had walked from Nimne to Mayendit for five days. She arrived here in Maper fifteen days ago. She had walked at night time "to avoid the helicopter" and came with her family (five children; no animals). She fled "because of the gunships. Nimne is near the oil fields. The gunships came four or five times a day; there were three gunships and one Antonov. They came at 8:00, 10:00 and 12:00, even sometimes at 22:00." The gunships had "mixed colours, like a military uniform." Norma added laconically that she had lost one son, a three-year-old whom she had last seen running away from a helicopter. Some cows had also been killed; the rest ran away. The government soldiers had come; Norma saw them when she was hiding.

Was this evidence of "scorched earth" – of deliberate and systematic displacement of the civilian population in the oilfields – by government troops? Certainly all these people, notwithstanding some probable embellishment or filtering by my pro-SPLA interpreters couldn't be lying. They had fled from coordinated aerial and ground attacks, and many of them had lost animals and family in the process; they were now as destitute as anyone could be and dependent on the charity of their Dinka hosts, their erstwhile enemies. But it was clear, too, that the SPLA and SPDF were using them, mingling no doubt deliberately among civilians in the hope of deterring attack. If you had to relativize evil and cynicism, the government came out as by far the more guilty, but the rebels weren't innocent.

BY THE TIME I NEXT HAD ACCESS on the SPLM/A side, there had been some dramatic political developments: to the great surprise of many, the government and the rebels had, in July 2002, signed the Machakos Protocol, the framework for a peace deal. But a second round of talks, initiated in a mood of euphoria, had ended abruptly when the government side withdrew, alleging that the SPLM/A was attempting to revisit issues already agreed upon. In September 2002, everything was in an uneasy limbo.

First, In Nairobi, I attempted to get a sense of what was being said in the South about the one major achievement on the peace front that was holding: the regional Nuba Mountains ceasefire. There was criticism all around.

The multinational Joint Military Commission (JMC) charged with supervising the Nuba ceasefire was taken to task specifically due to a number of incidents. Many of these seemed at first sight minor, but in a climate of intense mutual suspicion even the most insignificant of issues can be a dealbreaker.

In connection with a recent fatal outbreak of measles, for example, the JMC had insisted on having the representatives from the government's Humanitarian Aid Commission and Ministry of Health enter SPLM/A-controlled regions without taking into account the political sensitivities concerned. The investigation into a landmine explosion that resulted in the destruction of a Samaritan's Purse tractor and the death of several civilians had been handled in a non-transparent manner. The JMC, it was said, described the government's placement of indirect-fire artillery as an "alleged infringement" of the ceasefire, when it was "clearly an actual infringement." Incoming flights from Lokichokkio to SPLM/A-controlled areas were monitored closely, but overland access to government areas from the North was unrestricted. More generally, the JMC did not "get around enough" on the ground and neglected Nairobi almost completely. Most significantly, the JMC did "not understand the reasons for the conflict in Nuba" and seemed constantly to be exceeding its mandate by pressing for a peace agreement rather than just monitoring and enforcing a ceasefire. As far as the humanitarian situation in Nuba went, the main complaint was that funding for aid and rehabilitation programs was still slow in coming, and there was a failure by donors to recognize the importance of including capacity-building (code for wage payments) as a component of every program.

In the face of conspicuous silence on the matter, it fell to me to raise the question of SPLM/A intransigence on the movement of civilians within the Nuba Mountains area, specifically its refusal to allow Sudanese nationals from humanitarian agencies based in government-controlled territory to enter SPLM/A-controlled lands; this seemed to be a breach of the ceasefire agreement. Neroon Philip of the SPLA-aligned Nuba relief organization (NRRDO) indicated that he did "not foresee any change of stance in the immediate future." It became clear that neither the rebel-loyal representatives nor the international aid organizations working in Nuba were greatly interested at this time in working in such a way as to erode the fixed lines on the map between government- and SPLM/A-controlled areas. They clearly saw this as potentially detracting from the strength of the rebels' bargaining position in future discussions on the destiny of Nuba, even though the ceasefire agreement called for Nuba-wide programs and for unrestricted crosslines movement.

Up in Lokichokkio, the eternal problems of humanitarian access into South Sudan continued to preoccupy the international aid world and contribute to a general mood of pessimism. There was a sense that Dr Sulaf's Humanitarian Aid Commission was becoming increasingly clever in its policies: while there were now fewer flat flight denials than before, the number of destinations not denied but reported as "unknown" was growing. The effect was that seventy-five thousand vulnerable non-combatants were inaccessible to humanitarian agencies. The most worrying area was, as ever, Western Upper Nile (Unity State), where effective access had now been denied for so long that some agencies were abandoning all plans for future interventions in that area. In Eastern Equatoria, the Lord's Resistance Army was another factor hindering access.

At this volatile moment, both the international aid agencies and the United Nations were extremely careful when it came to assessing the thinking of the common people in the South regarding peace. I had the disconcerting feeling that the aid workers were as wary of breaking the SPLM/A party line as the rebels themselves. In general, the populace was certainly aware of what had been going on at the peace talks, even if only through the government-controlled Radio Omdurman. And they did want a ceasefire. But they were skeptical as to whether the Machakos deal was the long-hoped-for breakthrough. Everyone agreed that close international involvement with Machakos was absolutely vital and hoped, above all, that the international community would be able to give the final agreement "real teeth"; there was fear that the Damoclean sword of a referendum six and a half years hence, as provided for in the Machakos Protocol, would not be sufficient to encourage the government to comply with its side of the bargain.

Generally speaking in Lokichokkio I detected an intellectual recognition that an enormous change in the role of the international humanitarian community might be just around the corner, but there was great inertia: nobody was yet looking seriously at what peace could mean for their mandates and/or their programs. There seemed to be a poor understanding that donor policies could change almost overnight, with major funding implications for aid agencies. While it would be recognized by donors that there would be a need for transitional humanitarian funding, many donors would be looking to get out in the medium term, rather than segueing smoothly into development.

I headed from Loki deep into the southwest of Sudan, to the remote rebel-controlled community of Malualkon in Awiel East (Bahr al-Ghazal), and made use of a two-hour meeting with County Commissioner Victor, as rain beat down on our straw tukul and lightning flashed, to explore what a typical mid-level SPLM/A official was thinking and saying at this time.

Victor, who had three wives and who used to be a senior military commander, claimed to have civil responsibility for the staggering number of seventy thousand households. Next day, his Health Commissioner told me the figure was actually four thousand.

How was the SPLM/A motivating its fighters, after nineteen years of war? Victor smiled ruefully. "How do you think? By promising independence ..." So the SPLM/A's acceptance that "the unity of Sudan ... shall be the priority of the parties" (Machakos clause 1.1) was less than sincere? He evaded the question but expressed his firm opinion that in six and a half years "everyone will vote for secession" and conceded that, when it came to the language of the agreement, most people fell into one of two camps: those who were actually quite suspicious that John Garang might be selling the movement out, and those who were happy to accept his ostensible pro-unity stance as a sly negotiating tactic.

He recounted an anecdote: when British Aid Minister Clare Short recently visited Rumbek, she had been greeted with a large crowd waving placards calling for separation. When she queried SPLM/A number two and top negotiator Salva Kiir on this, he shrugged his shoulders expressively, saying "that's what they want." After a moment, Kiir added "... and that's what I happen to want, too."

It was very difficult to know if this divergence between the SPLM/A's stated preferences and the actual preferences of the population at large spelled a significant problem for the leadership. Even in private, no-one would talk about this freely. A host of informal conversations that I initiated ended with the rather uneasy "You must ask our commanders about that. We will do whatever they say ..." (In liberated South Sudan, freedom of speech seemed very much to be of the Soviet variety, whereas in the North the diversity of energetically expressed opinion was positively bewildering.) I came to believe that this dichotomy was something that was possibly keeping John Garang awake at night – or at least, if he was concerned for his political survival, it should be.

Like the aid organizations, Victor would be "counting" on the international community to hold Khartoum to the referendum. His post-peace priority? "Roads ... so that we can get our goods to market and allow people to move again ..." – followed by education.

When we moved into a discussion on justice and human rights, the commissioner blithely foresaw the return of the traditional (and rather mediaeval) restitutive system of justice that had prevailed here prior to the conflict; he had no qualms concerning the death penalty. How did he reconcile his having three wives with the supposedly enlightened attitude of the Movement towards women? "You must understand," he said, "that, if I am to be respected in my community at all, I must have at least two wives ... and anyway the war means that there aren't enough men to go around for the women." Rather half-heartedly, he said that he would be advising his grandchildren to have only one wife each. He laughed a little uneasily when I said that Hassan al-Turabi had made remarkably similar comments to me when I quizzed him on polygamy just prior to his imprisonment eighteen months earlier.

Meanwhile, the Malualkon Health Commissioner had no less than five wives, one more than even Islam permitted. He was quite offended when I asked him how many cows he had paid for each; it appeared that such matters were highly sensitive. Like Victor, he wore a wooden crucifix around his neck.

Back in Rumbek, my old friend Elijah Malok, SRRA chairman, SPLA veteran, conservative, and member of the rebels' negotiating team, received me in his malodorous office again. First, we discussed the recent government walkout at Machakos. He recognized that there were pressures on Khartoum from Egypt and Islamists within the ruling party and suspected that Khartoum's chief negotiator – Dr Ghazi Salah al-Dien, "a criminal ... like Nafie al-Nafie" – might still be a closet fanatical Islamist, but Malok nevertheless believed that the principal reason for the breakdown was that discussions on power-sharing were starting to make the government exceedingly nervous; this would be the most difficult area when discussions resumed (which he thought would be "soon").

The SPLM/A, said Malok, was looking in numerical terms for at least 40 percent of power, to be matched by a 40 percent allocation for the South of development expenditure. This meant concretely that it wanted five of what it saw as the ten key ministries, with deputy minister posts in the other five. And it wanted an alternance of power at the top – Garang and Bashir to rotate. When these issues were mooted, said Malok, it became clear that the government was seeing them as red lines – "several bridges too far."

What about elections? Didn't Umma and the Democratic Unionist Party deserve a kick at the can as well? "All they have done for years," said Malok in an implicit no, "is talk in the streets ... actually we respect the NIF more than we do Umma and the DUP." I broached human rights. "That's a matter for you subjects of the Queen," Malok said dismissively. "In the interim period, our security will be our overriding concern ... and nothing else."

We fenced on the delicate question of South Sudan's borders. Malok chose his words carefully: "There are elements in Nuba, Ingessana [Southern Blue Nile] and Abyei that are part of the SPLM/A ... no comprehensive solution can exclude their aspirations." But he implied that the rebel movement would not object if these regions were to petition for their own self-determination mechanisms, separate from arrangements made for the South in the normally understood sense. I was left with the clear impression that the rebels were prepared to cut these regions loose, but probably not until the endgame of the negotiations. There was a persistent rumour to the effect that, in addition to the public Machakos Protocol, there existed other agreed-upon written material, which had been initialled but which would only be published in the context of a comprehensive deal; Nuba might be somewhere in this material.

On the mediation process, Malok was full of praise for Kenyan peace envoy Lazarus Sumbeiywo, the architect of Machakos, and not unhappy about the role the USA, UK, and Norway were playing (although "Jack Danforth has now become irrelevant"). But the mediation team should be kept small: "Canada should wait until a deal has been signed before doing anything."

Less bluntly (he was not a man to mince words), Malok suggested that one of the first priorities post-peace would be to open up North/South communications and commerce. If the unity option had a chance at all, it would be because the people of the South saw that unity made economic sense. "Personally I am a secessionist," he said; "Europe forgave Germany ... anything is possible. And, even if we secede now, it could be that my great grandchildren would petition for unity again in thirty years' time."

BACK AT THE RUMBEK HEADQUARTERS of the United Nations Children's Fund, I updated myself on the massive child-soldier demobilization exercise, whose initial fruits I had seen a year or so earlier. Phase One had seen 3,551 children extracted from rebel ranks, processed through camps, and returned home.

Phase Two (since October 2001) had focused on "clearing" Bahr al-Ghazal, with the exception of disputed Raga. A lower-key, more needs-adapted process had been devised: in cooperation with UNICEF, the rebels selected area focal points from their ranks (twenty-four in total) who – after training by UNICEF – screened children, registered them, and then worked through the UN agency with host communities to relocate children in small groups. While some children did still resist demobilization or refused to return to their parents, the process seemed to be working quite well, and a further six thousand children had been repatriated over the past year.

The task force was now beginning work in Nuba and Blue Nile. By the end of 2002, it estimated that a total of ten thousand child soldiers would have been demobilized (the SPLM/A had originally admitted to six thousand in its ranks). When this target was reached, the task force would not close down: constant follow-up would be required, and there was a burning need for new school places to be found for the children, lest they attempt to rejoin the military.

In more general discussions, I found on this visit a greater world-weariness than I had noticed before among persons working in the humanitarian field in South Sudan. This was perhaps a function of the sheer length of the war but also because, as peace seemed to be drawing near, the utter cynicism of those who had kept the war alive for so long was glaringly apparent. In the scramble around the Machakos peace table, personal power agendas (on both sides) were being glimpsed more and more frequently, and the desperate needs of the civilian population were ever more subordinate to political machinations and the cynicism of elites.

In parallel to this, many long-serving and unsung heroes in the humanitarian field were beginning to wonder guiltily if in some way, through their work, they had inadvertently colluded with these elites. There was more and more recognition, as the prospect of peace loomed, that we might all have created an awful lot of dependency these nineteen years and that this might now have become a problem almost as significant as the bombs and the droughts, one that would not easily be solved by a peace treaty or enhanced mitigation of the effects of drought.

It was not just that impoverished and hard-pressed displaced persons had come to depend on food drops by the World Food Programme, to the detriment of age-old coping mechanisms (although this was bad enough). The SPLM/A leadership had a worrying faith that the international community would stand by Southern Sudan for the foreseeable future, that hundreds of millions of dollars of aid, investment, and oil money would soon be pouring in and that all of the best brains in the diaspora would flood back to realize The Dream. This irrational optimism was dangerous not only in the long term but right now, for it was inhibiting serious thinking about the enormous challenges of the interim period and, later, of independence.

ON THE PLANE BACK TO LOKI, I jotted down a few unrelated South Sudan moments that in some ways conveyed the strangeness of this place that now found itself on the cusp of history.

When our tiny white World Food Programme Cessna Caravan stopped at Akon, a man approached us to see if we had room on board for a boy with a gunshot wound. The pilot hesitated, and the boy's father soon wandered off, unconcerned.

Also at Akon, a fat and sunburned US man was fuming that 748 Services, the commercial charter service that had left him here three days ago to deliver ten thousand vaccines on behalf of his home town in Arkansas, was a day late in coming back for him. He was worried that he would miss his KLM flight in Nairobi and was planning to start walking to Ethiopia. We pointed out that Ethiopia was 1,000 km away, the temperature was forty degrees, and there were no roads. He pleaded for a ride, but, as he had flown on 748 (thought also to transport guns and military commanders), we could not take him on a UN aircraft except in case of a medical emergency.

Driving in our Landcruiser from Malualkon to the Akuem river, where we would observe a Tearfund rice project, we came across a Russian tank by the side of the road. Over the turret hung a belt of ammunition and a bra, an unusual item of apparel in Southern Sudan. My driver assured me that, although the tank lacked one track, the turret was in fact in working order and was pointed down the lane along which attacking government troops would most likely come.

Further on, we got stuck behind a convoy of donkeys, prodded along by a boy in green fatigues with an automatic rifle. When we finally got past, I could see that they were carrying red and blue United Nations grain sacks. There must have been an airdrop recently.

At the Tearfund camp at Malualkon, I received the ritual exhortation to check out the compound's bomb shelter and slit trenches; "my" slit trench had a foot of water in it – and a dead cat. The trench smelled worse than the latrine. I decided to brave the bombs in my bunk.

The day's activities at Tearfund began with thirty minutes of Bible reading; today: Corinthians II and a fierce tirade against homosexuals and prostitutes. There was a pile of Dinka New Testaments on the table, along with some recent *Guardian Weekly*s. Outside, a gaggle of laughing children made their way to Sunday school.

After I met with the commissioner of Malualkon, his bodyguards (who had been waiting outside in the pouring rain for two hours, getting themselves and their AKs soaked) asked if the Tearfund Landcruiser would give the commissioner's a tow to get it started (it had no battery). Tearfund obliged but pulled off the entire front structure of the commissioner's vehicle. We left the bodyguards mutely pondering the wreckage as darkness descended and the rain resumed.

Wandering around the souq at Malualkon, I stopped for a cup of tea at the medical dispensary. I chatted with the pharmacist; he had an assortment of bottles of pills, mainly anti-malarial, and his counter was a large wooden box painted in military green; it bore a bright yellow sticker that read *Explosives*, with the legend *Ministry of Defence; Kampala*. The pharmacist assured me the box was empty.

I received the news that Madhol, the airstrip from which I was due to fly out, was now boggy and unlikely to be useable for several days. I resigned myself to a week in Malualkon. But in the morning there was a drama. Gibson, a young Kenyan driver for Médecins sans frontières, had been, the previous night, riding his bicycle down a dark track in the rain. He was struck by lightning and regained consciousness fifteen feet up a tree, sans shirt and glasses and with his face bashed in. A medical evacuation was called; it would have to use the dry but flight-denied strip at Malualkon itself. It was hoped that the government authorities would not wise up to this. After much deliberation, I was also given a "green light" to accompany the patient, ostensibly as his nurse. When our bare-bones Twin Otter (no seats) finally arrived, Gibson was laid out on the metal floor. I sat cross-legged beside him for two hours, wondering what I would do if he stopped breathing. We arrived intact at Rumbek, and he was placed under a tree to await another plane. Fortunately, he seemed to be still alive.

Across the central green of Rumbek there calmly wandered a grizzled old Dinka man. He carried a spear and he was quite naked. He attracted not even a glance.

Bumping along a rough track west of Rumbek, we encountered a chain of eight downcast prisoners trudging to town, tied to each other by a thin rope at the wrist. Walking nonchalantly beside them was their guard: a fifteen-year-old boy in flip-flops, chewing a blade of grass and toting an AK.

My flight from Rumbek back to Lokichokkio ("Lima Base") was delayed. We learned that at Yambio, its previous stop, the De Havilland Buffalo had been inadvertently refuelled with diesel instead of Jet A-1. No-one knew the consequences beyond that the plane would not be coming. I negotiated my way onboard the last flight of the day: a UN Dakota that had first seen service in 1947. As we droned east for three hours, I half expected a trilby-clad and cigar-munching Harrison Ford to poke his head around the cockpit door; instead a fresh-faced young South African grinningly apologized that there would be no inflight movie today, but that he would shortly be serving iced champagne.

BY THE TIME OF MY FINAL VISIT to the rebel-held South, in May 2003, a ceasefire had been in effect for seven months. South Sudan was more at peace with itself than at any time in the previous twenty years.

A year earlier I had met with civilians at Maper and Wuncuei who had been fleeing the scorched-earth tactics of the government Army in Western Upper Nile. This time, with hostilities in abeyance, I was able to get to the very edge of the government-controlled area. I was accompanied by a representative of the Canadian International Development Agency. Instead of heading to the north-northwest of Rumbek, we flew almost due north, putting down at Ganyiel and Nhial and then entering the forsaken, swampy wastes of the Sudd, the largest swamp on Earth.

The small Nuer community of Thonyor was only 10 or 12 km from the nearest government garrison, which was on the disputed road that linked Bentiu in the North to Leer and Adok in the South and which served as an axis for the oilfield denominated Block 5A. As recently as January 2003, government troops backed by gunships were forcing the civilian population away from the vicinity of this road and Thonyor (which had itself been "scorched" several times by government troops) was feeling the spillover. But now the village authorities with whom I spoke (SRRC – the new body formed by the merger of the SRRA and RASS) complained that local women were being lured back into government territory by the relative abundance of food and water at and near government garrisons.

This was Nuer heartland. The SRRC insisted that, notwithstanding rumours to the contrary, the alliance between the (Nuer) SPDF under Riak Machar and the Dinka-dominated SPLM/A under John Garang was real and functioning, as was the SRRC itself. Reportedly, Machar had recently paid a morale-boosting visit to Thonyor, which had lasted longer than intended: his rented twin-engined Antonov had disabled itself on landing; it was still parked by the dirt strip, its props irretrievably bent.

But even without open fighting, Thonyor was a desolate place. Cut off for half of the year by swamps inhabited by crocodiles, elephants, and hippos (the hippos sometimes came into town), it seemed always to get too much rain or none at all. With Canadian support, Médecins sans frontières/Holland had here established both a primary health care and a tuberculosis clinic. The clinic (which was one of only a very few truly free tuberculosis clinics in the country) had 190 patients on its roster; so much had it been a victim of its own success that people would brave the hazardous and arduous 1,200 km trip from Khartoum, across battle lines and largely on foot, to take treatment here. In the courtyard, small children with telltale humps on their spines played and shouted happily, tugging at the hands and skirt of Kate, the English woman who ran the place. Her blithe cheerfulness seemed to have infused everyone: with huge smiles on their grimy faces, the children posed gleefully for photos.

Back at Rumbek: the place was visibly growing in importance. As recently as a year ago, no aircraft had dared overnight here; now the US-sponsored Civilian Protection Monitoring Team based two aircraft in Rumbek, and there were commonly a couple of World Food Programme Caravans and a De Havilland Buffalo on the ground as well. The United Nations Development Programme, which hitherto had had no presence behind rebel lines, was setting up shop beside the United Nations Children's Fund. Significantly, its local staffer answered to Khartoum, not Nairobi. Such was the level of activity here now that the privately run AFEX company, which fed Loki as well as thousands of tourists in the Kenyan game parks, had set up a semipermanent tent hotel.

There was still that *On the Beach* feel to Rumbek, with most of the population still living in tukuls among the stone ruins, but another sign of the times was the very popular internet café and resource centre adjoining the United Nations base. For the first time in twenty years and for a modest fee, the people of Rumbek could now read the news and engage in correspondence (there was still no telephone service in South Sudan). European soccer matches and war movies were also popular fare when the VSAT was switched on. Meanwhile, speculation was growing that Rumbek, due to its geographical position and the absence of a pre-existing government garrison, might now be favoured by the SPLM/A as a potential capital for the Southern region over the hitherto preferred and much larger Juba.

On to Yambio, in the equatorial jungle and close to the Congolese border: this town was as lush and productive as Thonyor was sterile and precarious. In the village I engaged in some tourism and visited the brick-built Episcopal Cathedral, whose foundation stone had been laid in 1925. A blackened brass plaque near the altar commemorated, in Xande, an

English missionary – John Spencer Bates – who had toiled here, as far as I could make out, from 1939 to 1950. A tall dignified black man in clerical garb and dog collar invited me to a funeral service; it was for a young US deacon of the church – presumably an aid worker – who had recently died (at Albany, New York) of malaria contracted here.

All was not as bucolic as met the eye. When I renewed my three-year acquaintance with Commissioner (formerly Commander) Mary, the most senior woman in the Movement, she told me sombrely that HIV/AIDS was decimating the community. Everyone now had a close relative who had recently died of AIDS or who lay sick; her SRRC assistant, at her side, told me that his own daughter had passed away only last week. Ironically, it was Yambio's lifeline to relative prosperity – the awful track to Uganda – that also brought death, in the form of promiscuous Ugandan truck drivers.

When, following Mary's exhortations, I drove west for one hour to visit the once-famous multi-sectoral engineering workshops at Anzara, I was left even more depressed. Spread across acres of jungle was a complex of vast but now ruined sheds and hangars where all kinds of metalworking and engineering used to be done, where a steam-powered sawmill turned mahogany and teak trunks into planks, where fruit and meat were processed. The sawmill was now inactive, waiting for some donor to contribute a diesel engine; a few of the lathes in one shed were in working order but it was evident that most of the engineering now done at Anzara was of an old, improvisational kind: great piles of charcoal and three anvils in a dark corner were what the project had come to. "It's the war," everyone shrugged. No. It was neglect, pure and simple. And the irony was that the only reason Anzara was functioning at all was thanks to a Northerner, Engineer Mohammed, who had stayed on when almost all his co-religionaries fled North a decade earlier.

Anzara was a gloomy place, the more so when I learned a little more of its history. It was the location of the first known death from Ebola.

8

FALLEN EMPIRES

DOWN ON THE BANKS OF THE NILE, close to St Matthew's Catholic Cathedral and the blue-shuttered Sisters' School in Khartoum, was
the Blue Nile Sailing Club, where in winter, when the winds were steady
and strong from the north, the river low, clean, and not too fast-running,
Jenny and I would spend much of our free time. This was no ordinary
sailing club. The clubhouse was a relic of Kitchener's 1898 expedition: the
gunboat HMS *Melik*.

The *Melik* was originally commanded by Major "Monkey" Gordon, RM,
a nephew of Charles Gordon; among the captains of two of the *Melik*'s
sister ships had been David Beatty, who later commanded the British
Grand Fleet's battlecruiser squadron at the Battle of Jutland, and Horace
Hood, who died aboard his own HMS *Invincible* at the same battle.

The *Melik* was used to devastating effect in supporting British troops at
the battle of Omdurman, and its powerful searchlights were unexpectedly

Her Majesty's gunboat *Melik*, headquarters of the Blue Nile Sailing Club

useful in deterring night attacks by the dervishes. Following the battle, it lived a varied life around the junction of the two great rivers.

Legend has it that one day in the early 1930s the British garrison commander, finding that there was dangerously little for his men to do in hot Khartoum, appointed one of them to build a fleet of sailing dinghies for the use of officers and their wives. As there was no wood to be had for a thousand kilometres around, ⅛-inch galvanized steel was used in their construction, and the conveniently idle *Melik* was designated as the club-house.

Perusal of the club's rule book, last revised in 1972, was fascinating. It was noted that "the design of the Khartoum Class, in 1932 by Morgan Giles, is based on the Twelve Square Metre Sharpie modified to suit local conditions ... in good hands they can sail partly submerged, under jib only, to safe moorings."

At about 4 p.m. every Sunday and Wednesday, a dozen or so aficionados would gather to sip warm Pepsis on the lawns by the *Melik*. After fifteen minutes, Assistant Sailing Secretary Mohammed el-Hadi would pass around a sign-in sheet, and, as long as there were four or more two-person crews on hand, we raced. Club Secretary William would count off the final five minutes before the start, flipping a set of black and white discs around as signals; the start itself was signalled with the *Melik*'s bell. Many of the trophies listed in the 1972 rules were still contested but, in alcohol-free Sudan, the McEwen Mug had sadly been a casualty: rules for this contest specified that the winning crew would be the first, following the conclusion of the race itself, to quaff a silver tankard of foaming beer placed on the bridge deck of the gunboat.

There were maybe fifty Khartoum One Designs still in existence, all built between the 1930s and 50s, and of these about twenty were in good shape. The eighteen-foot boats were heavy at 280 kg, but their rigs were tall and they were capable of a surprising turn of speed; they would capsize without too much difficulty, but – as noted in the rule book – buoyancy tanks at either end kept them more or less awash (just beware the crocodiles if you capsized in the White Nile). Most still had wooden masts, which had been spliced together so many times that they snapped with disconcerting facility, but a few of the club's young bloods had pirated aluminium masts from more modern dinghies and, with a hacksaw, had adapted them to the One Design.

The round-the-buoys racing on Sundays and Wednesdays was aggressive but good natured: there was a lot more contact between vessels than would be approved of by the Royal Victoria Yacht Club, but these dinghies were made of steel and could take it. Many members' knowledge of the rules of racing was rather hazy: the cry "Starboard!" was used as a general-purpose *Get out of my way!* Sometimes there were regattas with cash prizes; on these occasions a protest committee was formed under club patriarch Khalid, and there could be much earnest argument. On Friday mornings there were longer races: perhaps around Tuti Island, or to one of the Nile bridges and back.

Things could get quite exciting on the White Nile, where the current was strong and a powerful winter norther could kick up large waves. On a long race south up the White Nile to Umm Shagira in March one year, the winds were so strong and – combined with the waves – put such a strain on our rigging that the mast snapped at deck level and came crashing down around us. The current was carrying us fast towards the pilings of the concrete Chinese Bridge from Khartoum to Omdurman – which could have made for a tricky situation – but unusually, there was a powerboat on hand to rescue us and tow us home; with some glue, two hose clamps, and a few strategic paper clips, the aged and rheumatic "boatboy" Mohammed Bahar was able to repair our mast within twenty-four hours.

A favourite was the annual race to a beautiful white sandy beach at Om Dom ("crocodile") Island on the Blue Nile, where a barbecue was held and the men went swimming, before racing back in time for sunset. This race had been held every year without fail since 1924.

One year we set off to Om Dom on a Thursday afternoon, after work, instead of in the morning. The roster was Mohammed el-Hadi and his Greek girlfriend Ellie in their pale green CIBA boat (many of the boats were sponsored); seventy-four-year-old Farouk in his blue *Pepsi*; Yasseen in his unnamed and extremely speedy orange boat; retired soldier Ninnis in his boat on permanent loan from Lundin Oil; Mike Wood, whose leaky, slow, and unnamed white boat sported both a Union Jack and an Ethiopian flag; the redoubtable and usually victorious Mohammed Medani in *Mobitel*; and one of the old club stalwarts who was persuaded to take part in his first race in years aboard the blue-sailed *Pepsi Two*.

It was an exhilarating reach east along the Blue Nile for forty-five minutes, all the more so as Jenny and I had – on account of our indifferent record – been given a three-minute start (thus we had most of the other boats on our heels). Then a slow turn to the right, with the wind steadily moving astern. Soon we were rushing along wing-on-wing as the sun sank and the hot afternoon began to cool. There were a couple of rather delicate gybes and a few tense moments when, coasting in shallow water, we scraped bottom, but two and a half hours later, just as the sun set, we were grounding at Om Dom, fifty metres behind Farouk, who had overtaken us on the final run.

As a three-quarter moon came up, we set up camp on a pristine white beach. Mike lit the primitive charcoal barbecue and put on some tea, and then we fried up beef sausages and kebab. A couple of bottles of pirate Raki circulated quietly, and we added a bottle of illegal Chilean wine. There were one or two lights on the other side of the Nile, but no cars could be heard – it was difficult to believe we were only a couple of hours' sail from the centre of Khartoum.

The return was a beat all the way – zigzagging across the Blue Nile but being careful (with centreboards fully down) not to venture into the shallows where some of us had grounded last night. We edged around the unfinished end of the new bridge being built from Manshiya to Haj Youssuf (another year, and perhaps this race would be impossible …) and then reached past the crowds of Friday morning families come to take advantage of the sun and cool waters on the beaches north of the Khartoum fairgrounds. We ghosted over the line at the *Melik* a full ten and a half minutes ahead of Yasseen – and were especially pleased to confirm that, while our handicap this time had unintentionally been longer than the previous day's, it had certainly not been as long as ten minutes.

In these longer races, it was not so much racing aggression as local knowledge that won the day. Club boat boy Farouk, who had been sailing these waters for fifty years and who surreptitiously scrubbed his boat's bottom and tweaked its rigging before every race, knew exactly where every pocket of calm was likely to be, where the current was strongest at particular times of year, and which sandbanks you could sail over. But he guarded this knowledge carefully. More than one hawaija sailor had blithely followed in his wake only to go firmly and inextricably aground: unobserved, Farouk had stealthily hauled up his centreboard all the way before leading the unsuspecting foreigner onwards, like some latter-day Cornish wrecker.

Another annual race was held at full moon, some time early every New Year. We would assemble at sunset on the clubhouse lawns, and as the calls to prayer echoed out all over the city and the sun sank behind the twin minarets of the new mosque by the Hilton, an enormous "tea" of cream cakes, sandwiches, and Lipton's would be served. By about nine, the moon would be sufficiently high over the Blue Nile to cast a shimmering reflection the length of the river. But the buoys that marked our usual afternoon race course were close to the bank and in relative darkness. One year we tried racing around the normal course, but there were complaints that overly competitive members were taking advantage of the obscurity to make short cuts, so the next year we held a more straightforward series of races up river to the railway bridge, around a piling of one's choice, and back.

There was easily sufficient light for someone on shore to see who had crossed the finish line first, but what had not been foreseen this time was the difficulty of crew members making out the five disks – black on one side, white on the other – that are rotated to signal the final five minutes leading up to the start. It was agreed that next year some better alternative would have to be found.

EARLY ONE MORNING IN LATE WINTER, with office driver Babiker at the wheel, we loaded up the white Pajero with new sand ramps, a shovel, a hemp tow rope, twenty gallons of extra diesel, and lots and lots of water. We drove through the still-deserted streets of Khartoum, then over the White Nile to Omdurman; by the time we reached Souq Libia, on the edge of town, the streets were coming to life, and we stocked up on some fresh bread.

200 km out from Omdurman, with the sun now well up on our right, the almost empty tarmac road simply stopped in the middle of an utterly barren Marsscape. From here onwards, there were only occasional and elusive tire tracks to indicate that other four-wheel drives had been this way before. But the road was not completely deserted: every half-hour or so a cloud of dust slowly neared and a white Toyota Hilux pickup – a Boksi – bounced past at high speed, crammed with passengers wrapped up to the eyeballs (like the Invisible Man) in dazzling djellabiyas and turbans. The occupants waved, and the vehicles were quickly gone, but when we flagged it down one was more than happy to stop and extricate us from an especially soft patch of sand. After we moved off, I found sticking vertically into the sand – where it must just have fallen – a beautiful razor-sharp dagger.

The trick to desert driving, I soon learned, is to keep moving fast, and if you sense you are sinking into the soft sand, start fishtailing. It makes for some alarming moments.

There were pleasant surprises, too. Later on the trip, on another long stretch – 260 km from Karima to Dongola – we navigated by the setting sun but were amazed to crawl laboriously up one dune to find on the other side three bright green trees, a well (water at 180 metres down), and two small boys serving hot tea. "I knew there was a restaurant somewhere on this road," said Babiker calmly over the strains of his favourite Céline Dion track.

Apart from the isolation, the heat, and the sand, there are other hazards associated with driving in these parts – such as the local wildlife. A story has it that one day a camel, a dog, and a goat wanted to take a Boksi into Omdurman, to the market. They flagged one down and climbed in. The

Driving in the desert, north of Omdurman

fare was five piastres each. The camel laboriously extracted his five-piastre note and tranquilly handed it over. The dog had only a twenty note; with much reluctance he gave it in, but only after the driver promised he would be given his full change later. The goat had only two piastres, but wheedled and whined so much that the fed-up driver took his money, saying he must pay him the full amount before getting off. But when they reached the traffic jam in Omdurman, all three animals jumped out without another word, the stupid dog having forgotten what he was owed, the goat anxious to escape paying in full. Ever since, dogs in Sudan have aggressively chased all vehicles, hoping to get their change; goats, fearing that the Boksi driver might claim the three piastres owed him, all run away in a panic, and the self-confident camel, who has paid in full and is proud of being a law-abiding citizen, stands superciliously in the middle of the road, only deigning to move out of the way when the traffic has come to a complete standstill.

Five hours out of Omdurman, we hit the Nile, where, after heading due north from Khartoum, it had made a long loop south and west before resuming its flow onwards to Cairo. It's a cliché, but all life in these parts depends on the great river, which is here four hundred metres across, with a 2 km-wide strip of intensely cultivated date plantations on either side. The plantations are watered by millennia-old channels, but these are now fed by Indian-made diesel pumps; the *phut-phut* of these pumps is the most characteristic sound of the region. Drinking water is in some places from boreholes, but in others the bedrock is too thick and it is drawn straight from the sediment-heavy Nile; the water looks like lemonade. It was on improving access to good water that most of the Canadian aid projects in this region were concentrated; this meant boreholes where appropriate, water tanks for storage and pressure, distribution systems to allow the women not to have to make daily hours-long treks to pick up water.

And it is water – and access to it – that dominates all local politics. Every village dreams of constructing a new and better water tank and of piping water to every home, and many are the machinations centered upon this. The most powerful and important group in any community here is the water committee (typically only men, unfortunately – especially since water gathering is traditionally women's responsibility).

Other themes in local politics are much as elsewhere in the developing world. There is much grumbling about regional government, and indeed in the ancient townships of Merowe and Karima the good citizens appeared to have justification. Early in January 2001 the main generator supplying a vast region with power had burned out – either from neglect or, according to some, because of sabotage by disgruntled electricity workers who were about to lose their jobs to privatization. Either way, there was no prospect of a new generator for years; there was no contingency fund, no insurance.

The war in the South was felt here, but only distantly. The main impact had been the forced recruitment, in every village, of young men for military service; most families (which were admittedly large) had lost one or more sons forever. No-one had any solutions to the conflict; it was something they had come to see as immutable, something they just lived with, like the prospect of the Nile flooding as it did in 1988, or of the rains failing and the river not rising at all. Did people vote in the last elections, in December 2000? My question to the water committee elicited laughter: apathy was such that electoral officials had to set up their booths outside the mosques after prayers, and even then they attracted only a few reluc-

Debating water, near Karima, North Sudan

tant participants. Nobody seemed to know who had been elected in these constituencies, but it was assumed that they were all candidates of the ruling National Congress.

People here were religious (Muslim, of course) but – it seemed to me – in no way fanatical. Anyway, the line between what is culture and what is religion was very blurred; in a discussion regarding appropriate behaviour for young men and women, for example, there was insistence that what we see as restrictive norms (for example, for an unmarried man just to be seen talking to an unmarried woman is taken as a sign that they will – indeed, must – marry) are cultural rather than religious. There was scorn for Hassan al-Turabi, who was widely seen as being responsible for most of the country's current ills.

The hospitality was outstanding. It was almost impossible to buy and pay for one's own food; everywhere, when the conversation appeared to be dragging a little, a veritable banquet suddenly appeared: evidence that the family had been preparing it from the moment you had arrived (unannounced). Even at the shabby restaurants by the tarmac roads, you only had to sit down for a moment for your neighbour to gesture and invite you to sit down and share his meal. It was difficult to run to a schedule in the face of such generosity.

The grip of civilization on this harsh land seemed very tenuous sometimes. But of course it was not. At Nurri the village guard was rustled up, and we were shown into the 2,600-year-old royal tombs that – though only two in number – were on a par with those found in Egypt's Valley of the Kings. By candlelight he pointed out Anubis with his jackal head, Horus, and the sacred baboons; and he translated some of the hieroglyphs. As in Thebes, the motifs of the sun and the Nile dominated everything. Heat and water – it's what life had always been about in these parts, and it still was.

Further east, close to Karima, is an Ayers Rock-type natural monolith, known as Jebel Barkal. At one end of the monolith, close to the river, is a curious pinnacle of sandstone that caught the attention of the ancient Nubians and around which they built an extensive temple and tunnel complex.

This is one of the more controversial sites in regional archaeology. The ad hoc guide thrust upon us at some cost by the local hostelry blithely told us that everything we could see was six thousand years old, and so we soon dismissed him for we knew better: this indeed is an ancient site, but Jebel Barkal's Temple of Amun was probably initiated by the Egyptian pharaohs of the eighteenth dynasty (1550–1295 BC).

Later, in the eighth century BC, Nubian kings turned the tables and conquered Egypt, where they ruled for a century. Jebel Barkal, then known as Napata, was thus for a period the centre of Egyptian civilization: the so-called Black Pharaohs of Kush ruled not only over these desolate middle reaches of the Nile but over the much-better known Thebes and other great cities of the lower Nile. Their domination came to an end when Assyrian armies routed the Nubian pharaoh from Thebes in 663 BC.

Certainly, Kush bequeathed to Lower Egypt the classic but rather unusual profile of Amun ("The Hidden One") that is carved into a hundred walls at the Temple of Karnak in Luxor and that, if you stand back a kilometre or so, you can clearly see in Jebel Barkal's great rock pinnacle. It's possible that the cult itself began here.

A few classical Egyptian archaeologists take this theory as an affront to their sense of nation, while at every presentation of the Sudan Archaeological Society in Khartoum, regardless of the period or topic under discussion, some Sudanese nationalist will stand up and try to elicit from the presenter the recognition that – "as Jebel Barkal clearly indicates" – Egypt was colonized from Sudan, and not vice-versa.

To appreciate the ruins, you need to climb Jebel Barkal. A steep scramble up a goat track at the other extremity takes you up to a rocky plateau in ten or fifteen minutes, and then you can tiptoe over to the steep precipice that overlooks the ancient site. Go when the sun is setting. As the shadows lengthen and the sand turns to gold and pink, you can make out every detail of every courtyard and colonnade far below, and, among the still unexcavated sand dunes adjoining, you can discern more mysterious structures.

Lift your eyes to the deep green strip of date palm orchards that starts immediately beyond. An ethereal grey-blue haze hangs almost at ground level, from the palm leaves that the fellaheen are burning. You can hear the soothing sounds of the pumps feeding the age-old irrigation channels. Beyond the trees is the great Nile itself, silver and gold at this time of the evening.

IN 1884 AN EXPEDITION WAS ORGANIZED to rescue Charles Gordon, besieged in Khartoum. With hindsight, the easiest route to Khartoum would probably have been through the newly built Suez canal, down the Red Sea by boat to Suakin (near the modern Port Sudan), then due west across the desert to the Nile at Berber (near today's Atbara), and up the Nile to Khartoum. But General Garnet Wolseley, the charismatic English commander charged with the rescue mission who had cut his teeth on the 1870 expedition to quell the Red River Rebellion in Manitoba, had no experience of desert fighting, and the dry 400 km from the coast to Berber followed by another 300 km up the Nile seemed to him to pose insurmountable supply and water problems. Wolseley thus decided the route to Khartoum lay up the Nile.

From Alexandria to Wadi Halfa ("Bloody Halfway," as the soldiers came to call it), the going was quite easy: rail then steamer. But at the second cataract, things got decidedly more difficult: the steamers could go no further, and it would fall to four hundred Canadian voyageurs recruited from the Ontario backwoods, civilians but under the command of Major Frederick Denison and Lieutenant Colonel William Kennedy, to shepherd the redcoats in their whalers up another 1,500 km of much more treacherous and fast-flowing muddy waters through five sets of rapids.

While most of the expedition took place in the Egyptian and Sudanese winter, the climatic conditions were still incomparably hotter and harsher than any in this army's experience. The voyageurs acquitted themselves admirably and remarkably few lives were lost to the Nile: Wolseley had initially noted in his diary that "they are a rough-looking lot," but when it was all over he wrote to Canada's governor general, Lord Lansdowne, that "the services of these voyageurs have been of the greatest possible value."

Everything went slower than planned, and the messages Gordon was able to smuggle out to the relief column became more and more desperate. Belatedly, Wolseley decided to split his force, sending one contingent (the Desert Column) overland from Korti, thus cutting off a large bend in the Nile, while the River Column persevered upstream. The major obstacle the River Column faced was the fourth cataract.

This is scarcely any more accessible today than it was 120 years ago. Heading northeast from Karima, we hauled our Pajero across deep ditches, through wadis and over glaring plains of black shale. Gradually the dark vegetation-free rocky hills on either side of the great river steep-ened, and the Nile narrowed perceptibly. Soon, below us and to our right, the river that had seemed so wide and placid at Karima was contained between rock walls barely fifty metres across, with right-angled bends and false channels sending the muddy waters careering off first one way then another. At one place, a full twelve metres or so above the present level of the water (this was the dry season), a thirty-metre-long river steamer lay wedged inextricably in a rock crevasse. The track petered out, and we had to walk the last 2 km to the upstream end of this maze of rocks and water; for a kayaker of today, the final cascade would have presented no problems (going downstream, that is), but it was not difficult to envisage how daunting and exhausting it must have been to drag, pole, and row all those heavily laden and old-fashioned whalers upstream through obstacles such as this. With Wolseley's River Column thus bogged down, efforts were concentrated on the contingent crossing the desert.

At Abu Klea, about halfway across the desert from Korti to Metemmeh, on 17 January 1885, fourteen thousand of the Mahdi's forces surprised the redcoats of Brigadier General Stewart's Desert Column. Eleven hundred dervishes were lost, for seventy-four British dead, but only two days later the Mahdists regrouped and fought again; this time Stewart was mortally wounded (although he did not die until 14 February). Command devolved to the inexperienced Colonel Sir Charles Wilson.

Wilson made what turned out to be a fateful decision. Instead of pressing on immediately to Omdurman, just across the Nile from Khartoum, he cut due east, to where he knew two of Gordon's steamers, which had escaped the siege, were waiting. On 23 January 1885 he rendezvoused successfully with the *Bordein* and the *Telawiyeh*, and, in temperatures of thirty-seven degrees, they set off south, up the Nile.

In the late afternoon of 25 January 1885, Khartoum finally fell to the Mahdi and Charles Gordon was killed. Wilson and his two steamers were at that moment still negotiating the relatively benign sixth cataract, 80 km north. It was not until the morning of 28 January that they reached the site of what is now the Shambat Bridge over the White Nile and saw, through the heat haze, that Gordon's flag no longer flew over the residency.

It had all been for nothing.

THE 1884–85 LESSONS OF THE LONG laborious haul up the Nile, were not lost when, eleven years later, the decision was taken to "smash up the Mahdi" (actually his successor, the Khalifa) and avenge Gordon. This time command fell to the British Sirdar of the Egyptian Army, General Herbert Kitchener (who had seen service as a major in Wolseley's abortive relief expedition).

Kitchener's approach was altogether much more methodical, less romantic. As Roy MacLaren notes in his authoritative *Canadians on the Nile*: "Brawn and bravery carried Wolseley far up the Nile. But steam and careful staff work took Kitchener to Khartoum." Kitchener realized that the key to the conquest of Sudan would be a secure supply line – something Wolseley never had. So he built a railway.

Kitchener used the same base that Wolseley had established, at the foot of the second cataract: "Bloody halfway." Captain William Butler, one of Wolseley's famous Ring and another veteran of the Red River Expedition, wrote that Wadi Halfa in 1884 "looked as if the goods station of a London terminus, a couple of battalion of infantry, the War Office, and a considerable proportion of the Woolwich Arsenal had all been thoroughly shaken together, and then cast forth on the desert." Over the ensuing ten years, as England grew increasingly nervous at the Khalifa's consolidation of his power in Sudan and the consequent threat to Egypt and the Canal, the dusty town grew steadily in size.

Kitchener selected for the task of building his lifeline a young Canadian engineer and soldier, Percy Girouard, who was educated at the Royal Military College at Kingston (Ontario) and had then entered the Royal Engineers. By 1895, when Kitchener recruited him, he had just completed five years running the network of railways that served the Woolwich Arsenal in London.

His first assignment was to build a line due south along the Nile to support Kitchener's September 1896 march on Dongola. Girouard proved himself capable of laying track at an astounding rate – up to 3 km a day – and the expedition was a great success. In October, Kitchener began to draw up plans for an altogether more serious operation, which entailed moving his advance base halfway towards Khartoum, past the dangerous fourth cataract, to Abu Hamed; he would bypass the most difficult stretches of the river by laying a 400 km railway track directly across the desert.

Girouard excelled himself. In the hottest months of 1897, May and June, as much as 1.5 km of track was being laid every three hours, and Abu Hamed was reached on 31 October. The official History of the Royal Engineers was later to glow that "The critics had been confounded by Kitchener's Band of Boys, who had accomplished what may justly be classed as one of the most remarkable engineering feats of modern times."

From now on, Kitchener's expedition acquired a sense of inevitability. Winston Churchill of the 21st Lancers wrote that "The Khalifa, his capital, and his army were now within the Sirdar's reach. It remained only to pluck the fruit ..." First came the battle – or carnage – of Atbara, on 8 April 1898: three thousand Mahdists killed for the loss of eighty-three British and Egyptian. By August 1898 Kitchener was advancing on Khartoum itself with a force of twenty-six thousand men.

The Khalifa – the anointed heir of the Mahdi whose forces had killed Gordon in 1885 – decided to give battle on the plain at Omdurman. By 11:30 on the morning of 2 September, eleven thousand Mahdists were dead, for only forty-eight British and Egyptians killed. Hilaire Belloc, learning of the scale of the killing at Omdurman, reflected wryly on its lessons for the future in his poem "The Modern Traveller":

Whatever happens we have got
The Maxim gun and they have not.

IN NOVEMBER 2002, I WAS ABLE TO HAVE a close look at the long stretch of rail track north of Atbara and south of Wadi Halfa. My pretext was visiting some possible and actual water projects on the 200 km stretch of the Nile between Atbara and Abu Hamed, Kitchener's railhead for the final attack on Khartoum.

Babiker, Canada Fund coordinator Salah, and I drove up in the Pajero. At the village of Korgis, on the west bank of the river about halfway up to Abu Hamed, we stayed the night in the courtyard of a gentle old man in his seventies. It was Ramadan, a season that encourages after-dark garrulousness. The man recalled well the time of the British. After spending most of his adolescence in Korgis, he had gone to work for the colonial police in Omdurman. "What's changed around here since 1956?" I asked.

He pondered long and hard. In fact I thought he had gone to sleep. "Everything has fallen apart," he finally decided. "We used to have a post office here, and a public telephone box. Now we have neither. And we would literally set our watches by the Express, as it passed on the opposite bank; in those days, they gave you your money back if the train was late. Now you are lucky if the train even comes on the day it's supposed to come ..."

On both sides of the Nile here, the road was terrible. For long stretches on the east bank, it consisted only of a series of white posts in the rolling desert, maybe 1 km apart. It seemed to me a comment on Sudan's underdevelopment that, although this route had been a major thoroughfare for at least four thousand years and appeared on my excellent *Michelin* map to be the main route northwards on the eastern side of Africa, it really wasn't a road at all but just a set of tire tracks in the sand.

Every couple of hours' driving, there was a chance to cross to the other side by rickety and underpowered steel *pontons* (ferries), capable of taking one or two cars. But two out of the four we tried were *baez* – dead. In compensation, the service on the other two was friendly in the extreme. When we arrived at El Bauga at 11:00 p.m. – another quiet desert night – looking for a ride across to Abidiya, we were not surprised to find that the ferryman had long since gone to bed. But he was not in the least perturbed to be roused from his shack at the edge of the village and asked to crank up his craft just for us. When he heard we were looking at putting in some water tanks or pumps hereabouts, he refused to accept our fare.

As everywhere else in Northern Sudan, the main topic of discussion and interest was water: there always seemed to be too much or too little of it. At Kadeita, just across the river from Abu Hamed, there had been severe floods for six out of the last twelve years, the last series ruining whole quarters of the village. Clearly, people needed to move further back and higher up – but here was the catch. By doing so they would be moving away from their normal water source, hence the need to drill wells on the higher ground near the new settlements. I wondered if the long-planned construction of the Merowe Dam, downstream and to the southwest, would mean that people would have to move yet again, but nobody seemed to know, even though construction was now starting.

WHEN THE ASSYRIANS DROVE OUT the last Kushite pharaoh from Thebes in 663 BC, he fled back up the Nile to Jebel Barkal/Napata. The Assyrians, and later the Persians, kept up the pursuit: their warlike demeanour is captured in dozens of friezes across Nubia that show them clutching by the hair the heads of their decapitated victims. In 591 BC, Jebel Barkal was in turn abandoned and the Kushites established a new capital at Meroe, much further to the south and only 200 km north of Khartoum (confusingly, the modern town on the Nile's left bank closest to Jebel Barkal is Merowe – identical pronunciation, different spelling in English).

This new capital thrived for six hundred years, fell into decline, and was finally abandoned in 350 AD. The southern Meroe is, due to its accessibility to Khartoum (a three-hour drive along the asphalted highway, built by the now-infamous bin-Laden Construction Company of Saudi Arabia), the most visited archaeological site in Sudan. Most people come and go in a day, and they try to see everything before noon, at which point the heat usually becomes intolerable. But you can do things in a more leisurely manner by spending the night at Shendi.

This outwardly unprepossessing Nileside town was described at length by the Swiss-born and Cambridge-educated explorer John Lewis Burckhardt (1784–1817; the rediscoverer of Petra), in accounts of his 1814–15 travels in Sudan that had been commissioned by the quaintly named Association for Promoting the Discovery of the Interior Parts of Africa.

Burckhardt found that in 1814, with six thousand inhabitants, Shendi was the most populous town in central Sudan; Khartoum did not exist at that date. Due to its location, at the point where the Nile came closest to the Red Sea and where trading routes to and from Arabia, Egypt, Ethiopia, and West Africa converged, it was a great market. The explorer wrote that here you could buy spices and sandalwood from India, antimony from Oman, swords and razors from Germany, saddles and leather from Kordofan, soap from Egypt, gold from Ethiopia. It was also a centre for slave trading: about five thousand slaves passed through here each year, with Ethiopian women as the most prized: "Being remarked above all other black women for their beauty, and for the warmth and constancy of their affection to the master who has once taught them to love him ..." Male slaves went for about fifteen dollars as long as they had survived smallpox (and had the scars to show for it) while females cost about twenty-five. There was also a trade in eunuchs, "but only about 150 a year."

Today, Shendi is about the same size at it was, but is more famous as the centre of the region whence President Bashir hails, along with many of the country's ruling elite. It is also known as being one of the consistently hottest and most windless locations in all of Sudan (which is saying something).

The railway line runs through the middle of town; parked alongside it, usually, are the place's half-dozen ancient Russian Volga taxis; large and plush but these days rather unreliable. In the dusty central streets there is on most days an active souq, but the wares are not nearly as exotic as two hundred years ago: red plastic buckets, cheap cassettes, and men's toiletries by the caseload. There isn't much to do other than sip chai or gahwa at one of the rickety steel tables out on the street, trying not to sniff the unmistakable odour of urine and feces that seems to dominate most small towns in Sudan.

The Hotel Kawartha, which is the only place to stay, is pleasantly located on the banks of the river, upstream from the depression in the bank that serves as a loading spot for a ramshackle three-car ferry. The hotel has a garden where le tout Shendi comes to sip juices and Pepsis after sunset. Its rooms are grimy and strangely designed – a noisy air-conditioner pumps freezing air across the bed at mattress height – and are a swindle at USD $40 a night.

From Shendi, it's 50 km north to Meroe. This city was first described to the West in 480 BC by the Greek historian Herodotus, based on stories told by spies sent here by the Persian King Kambyses: "... when thou has passed through this part in forty days, thou enterest again into another ship and sailest twelve days; and thereafter thou comest to a great city, the name whereof is Meroe. And the city is said to be the mother city of Ethiopia."

Later, Nero sent spies, too, disguised as envoys: their mission was to scout out routes for an eventual conquest of Meroe; they were also ordered to discover the source of the Nile and seem to have travelled as far south as the immense Sudd, in what is today Southern Sudan. Knowledge of Meroe's location then slid beneath the sands of time. In the late eighteenth century Scottish traveller and aristocrat James Bruce tentatively identified the site but it was only in 1910 that Liverpool University archaeologist John Garstang was able to confirm this.

Meroe is divided into two sites. To the west of the road, adjoining the Nile and half obscured by acacia trees, is the rambling Royal City, centered on its Amun temple; the City is a favoured dig site for a Canadian archae-ologist, Kris Grzymski, whom all the locals know as Doctor Kris. There are some good stretches of wall, and if you can find a guide he will brush away the sand in one or two locations to show you some well-preserved black and white mosaics, but the most interesting thing to see is securely locked up under a corrugated iron roof.

Here is the royal bath: a deep brick-lined pit, with steps down into it and stone pipes leading in from the Nile itself. Much decorative stone work still retains its original blue, yellow, and red. Next door is what some say is a set of steam baths, with what look like three large thrones in which one could sit and sweat. It is difficult to imagine the need or desire for a steam bath in a climate such as this, but maybe things were a couple of degrees cooler in those days. Or – the alternative theory – this was a set of three thrones dedicated to the cult of ancestors. Doctor Kris said that this is one of the most hotly debated topics in Meroitic architecture.

The main attraction, signalled on a weekend by the presence of a couple of sellers of dubious antiquities, is the Royal Cemetery, to the east of the road and a couple of kilometres north. The tombs of the kings and queens of Meroe are marked by fifteen or twenty moderate-sized pyramids, most of which have had their tops lopped off, so that they resemble a large set of broken, rotten dentures rising up from the reddish-brown sand.

The site is impressive, not so much on account of the scale of the pyra-mids (for they are a lot smaller if steeper than their famous Egyptian

The Royal Cemetery, Meroe

counterparts) but for the sense of abandonment that reigns here. Every time I visited, the sand dunes had shifted and threatened to engulf one pyramid, or newly reveal another. The decorated tomb entrances – porticoes, usually on the east side, that formed a gateway on the day of burial, but which were then largely filled in with rubble – have been protected with wooden doors, but drifting sands block many and you must content yourself with glimpses through cracked boards. On the sandstone wall are the familiar figures from Aswan and Luxor – Amun, Anubis, the ankh symbol – but absent are the Egyptian hieroglyphs, replaced by the unique Meroitic script that looks to be a cross between Greek and Amharic.

The tops of most of the pyramids are missing because Giuseppe Ferlini, a peculiarly misguided and avaricious Italian "archaeologist" sacked them for treasure in the 1830s, but there are lesser examples of vandalism that are interesting. In one corner is carved the name of Frédéric Cailliaud, a French explorer who on 25 April 1821 became the first European in more than a thousand years to see Meroe. Along with his assistant Pierre Constant Letorzec, he spent two weeks sketching and writing about Meroe and thus laid the foundations for Sudanese archaeology (and in particular for the still ongoing interest of French archaeologists); his careful engravings are still studied today. Meroe was one of our favourite places to take visitors. But I never tired of it: the place was invariably deserted, and you could imagine yourself as Cailliaud.

A FEW PHONE CALLS MADE BY SAMIA, my energetic assistant at the Canadian Office (who hailed from the Shendi area) meant that when Jenny and I, with our stand-in driver Amir, arrived in Shendi one muggy July morning the superintendent of schools – who also happened to be the local historian – was on hand to meet us. Along with two or three pickups, a herd of sheep, two camels, and a hundred or so people, we squeezed the Pajero onto the ramshackle old steel ponton and we launched out into the river. It was the height of the rainy season in Ethiopia and Southern Sudan, and the waters were muddy, high, and fast: it took us nearly forty minutes to edge across the river and a mere hundred metres upstream.

Shendi is the point of access not only to Meroe but also to Metemmeh on the opposite bank of the Nile, and thence to Abu Klea, site of the battle that fatefully delayed the British in 1885 and thus cost Gordon his life. Metemmeh – the point at which Wolseley's Desert and River Columns converged after the battle for the advance on Khartoum – is just a straight stretch of river bank into the soil of which a ramp has been dug out for the ferry landing. There are the inevitable tea ladies crouched on tiny stools under makeshift thatch shelters, and far away you can make out a couple of distinctive silver-painted conical tombs. The town itself has migrated inland.

En route to meet the local authorities in Metemmeh we rattled through two small settlements, which our guide told us were the homes of two of the federal government's most powerful (and conservative ...) ministers. President Bashir's home was also nearby. It was an interesting quirk of history that the local Shaygia, Jaaliyin, and Danagla clans still dominated Sudan just as they did when for so many centuries they had sat firmly astride the trading crossroads that was Shendi. According to a clandestine pamphlet circulating in Khartoum in 2000 (known as the Black Book), this region

The school superintendent at the monument to the Battle of Abu Klea

that accounts for only 5 percent of Sudan's population has since independence occupied from 47 to 70 percent of the government's Cabinet seats.

At Metemmeh, the commissioner (a Shaygia) received us under his carport with warm Pepsis and introduced us to his sidekick, the swarthy and rather surly looking chief of police. The commissioner, whom the school superintendent told me used to be a major general, awkwardly launched into a rehearsed panegyric on relations between Canada and Sudan, on which I tactfully declined to probe him; he seemed half-uncomfortable, half-mystified when I changed the topic to history and said I would like to visit the battle site of Abu Klea (pronounced "Tleh"). He and the police chief jointly mumbled about the "dangers" supposedly involved – did he mean bandits or the possibly boggy track? – but then diverted into an account of the battle by which the dervishes were the real victors, not the British. I sensed he was uncertain about the exact relationship between Canada and Britain (who could blame him? – Canadians were involved in

Wolseley's expedition, and, more to the point, I had already mentioned in passing that my office was physically located within the British Embassy).

I had perhaps been very insensitive in raising this 120-year-old conflict in detached and academic terms: quite possibly the commissioner and the police chief, who were from these parts, had lost ancestors at Abu Klea. For most Sudanese Gordon and Kitchener are (with reason) regarded as symbols of colonial oppression and arrogance, a matter of increased sensitivity in the Middle East post-9/11. I adopted a more respectful attitude, and the police chief soon agreed to accompany us.

The track wended its way through low hills that looked as though they had in the distant past been incinerated: the characteristic shale-like black rock covered everything, and even the few shrubs that somehow survived here look scorched. After about 20 km, the police chief started to point out low rectangular mounds close by or silhouetted against the horizon: these were the graves of the dying and wounded acolytes of the Mahdi, buried where they had fallen as they struggled back to Metemmeh after the battle. He was sombre and seemed moved.

Another 10 km, and the track ended atop a low rise. There was a simple two-metre-high monument in now-chipped cement. Not untypically, it listed the dead officers by name, then – almost as an afterthought: "65 NCOs and men."

For half an hour or so, we wandered from one group of mounds to the next. There were clusters of ten or twenty graves, while fifty metres away there might be another one on its own; none were marked. The larger groups must have been where the fighting was at its heaviest. Here, too, the dead seemed to be buried where they had fallen – and by the British: had fellow Muslims done so, the graves would have been aligned properly, uniformly facing Mecca.

By one grave I found a used and splayed-out cartridge: it looked original. I looked up to show it to the police chief, but he was a long way off: I could see his white robes, startling against the black desert; he was saying his prayers.

ON THE ROAD BACK TO KHARTOUM, it was well worth making a detour off to the left. A faded green road sign said it was 2 km to the ruins of Naga and Musawwarat, but in reality it was twenty or more. On

Camel and owner at the well, Naga

a first visit, you needed a guide to take you across the largely unmarked desert. Musawwarat is a large complex of reddish grey granite, whose exact purpose remains unclear; one of the more fantastic theories has it that this was a training school for elephants. At Naga, a few kilometres distant, there is an avenue of heavy stone rams – Sudan's answer to Egypt's sphinxes – and a delicate and fine structure, known to archaeologists as a Kiosk, that displays unmistakably Greek influence. As at Meroe, it is above all the setting that makes these places haunting: they are abandoned, and the only visitors for weeks on end are the nomads who daily bring their camels and goats to the ancient hundred-metre-deep wells they have used since time immemorial to fill their animal skins.

Initially, like the aborigines of the Australian desert, the nomads are invisible. But stop the car for a few moments, and out of nowhere a young girl herding a few goats appears; a man in a bright white djellabiya crosses the horizon on a donkey; a pair of hobbled camels graze into view. You realize that what you took for large thorn bushes are in fact temporary homes for these hardy, resistant people.

At night, when we camped, we would choose apparently remote and deserted gullies, but invariably and within minutes someone would appear. They would squat on their haunches a few metres away, wordless, perhaps fingering the tiny little leather bag around their neck that contains a verse of the Koran, and just watch us.

9

SOUTHERN VOICES

ASSESSING SOUTHERN OPINION from an office in Khartoum was, at best, a guessing game. While the Northern capital had over the past fifteen years become home to upwards of three million Southerners – many of them fleeing the war and famine in the South – it was, for obvious reasons, difficult to find anyone who overtly sympathized with the SPLM/A: quite apart from it being dangerous to express such views in public, the fact was that, if you believed in the cause, you would probably want to be in the South, or at least in Nairobi. There were nevertheless a number of Khartoum-residing Southerners whom I would seek out on a regular basis, because on the one hand they were well qualified to explain to me the history of the civil war and give me a Who's Who and on the other they were usually in touch with the South, at least.

My favourite source, and perhaps the most respected Southern figure in government-held Sudan, was Abel Alier, lawyer, former judge, former vice-president of Sudan, and president of the Higher Executive Council of Southern Sudan in the ten-year interregnum of peace that followed the 1972 Addis Ababa Accord. It was often said by Muslim Northerners that Alier was the one Southerner whom they could tolerate as president, but – although over the years his patience and pacifism had inevitably alienated many in the SPLM/A – Alier was no patsy of the National Congress Party. The title of his most well known book said it all: *Southern Sudan: Too Many Agreements Dishonoured*.

I would visit Alier in his sparse lawyers' office downtown, next to the Lufthansa office. Tall, white-haired, and dignified, he had something of the air of Nelson Mandela. Much in demand for his experience and wisdom, he was unstinting in his time with me.

My first meeting with him was in September 2000. At this time, Alier sensed already that the political climate in Sudan was opening fast. In his view, the monolith of the National Islamic Front was now breaking up, following the dismissal of Turabi from government. Alier attributed this ouster to a perception by the younger generation of Islamists (Turabi was then sixty-eight) that he had failed to democratize the NIF internally, failed to broaden its support base, and refused to share the spoils of power. But the West was mistaken, Alier believed, to rejoice in the fall of a "hardliner": in some ways Turabi was seeking to advance Western priorities; convinced that he had planted Islam ineradicably in Sudan, he was apparently ready to facilitate a degree of democratization, through relatively free elections, and he was genuinely committed to decentralization, including significant concessions to the South.

Alier warned that Turabi was not completely down and out. Although Turabi had failed to persuade large numbers of his followers within government to quit with him, he still had a large cadre of the faithful at the heart of the Bashir administration. Indeed, Turabi was a past master at working through others. Alier compared Turabi's position out of government (but at that time not yet imprisoned) as analogous to that of the Communist Party's secretary general in the heyday of the Soviet Union: apparently removed from power but still pulling the strings.

In the short term, Alier believed, the government faced three main issues. First, of course, the war, which was increasingly unpopular; pressure for a settlement was growing fast. But oil revenues that were now starting to come online might encourage those who still believed a victory by the North was possible. Key would be the Army: Alier felt they were at this time split evenly between the professionals who believed the war was unwinnable and more political elements who were prepared to go which-ever way they sensed the political wind to be blowing.

The second issue was the economy. Although the rich in Amarat swore that the economy was treating them better than it had for decades and growth was set to hit 6.5 percent for 2000, there had been little if any trickle down: teachers, health workers, and the Army had all threatened strikes recently, due to late wage payments. The general sense of grievance might have been accentuated this year by grandiose talk of the bonanza that oil revenues would bring. Common wisdom was that dramatically increased numbers of beggars on the street were an indicator of the true plight of the average Sudanese. Finally, the government faced the expectation – domes-tically and from abroad – of more openness: freedom of assembly, freedom of speech, freedom of religion, and a relaxation of unpopular dimensions of sharia.

On oil, Alier was well qualified to comment: in the 1970s he played a key role in bringing Chevron to the oil fields now being exploited by Talis-man and its partners. Alier believed that, as the government's principal cash cow (oil revenues had provided 35 percent of total export revenue in the first quarter of 2000), oil had inevitably become a focal point of the North/South conflict. Oil had now secured itself a position high on any agenda for peace talks – in part, ironically, because the government had so unwisely trumpeted its importance.

Prophetically, Alier judged that the USA – in mid to late 2000 – was weary of the war in Sudan and would in the New Year exert its influence to revitalize the peace process. As for Egypt, Alier found it frankly mischie-vous and its insistence on the non-negotiability of Sudanese territorial unity profoundly unhelpful. Why was it taking this stance? In the first place, Egypt evidently still felt that Sudan was an Egyptian province and that it had a pre-eminent right to dictate matters here. In the second, it was indeed concerned – as was often speculated – at maintaining the full flow of the Nile. Its fear was not so much that a new state on the Nile might interfere with that flow – for an independent South Sudan would at the most control 13 percent of the Nile's waters – but that such a state might be more inclined than the current government to negotiate with Ethiopia (which controlled most of the other 87 percent) so as jointly to press for water arrangements less favourable to Egypt. Third, Egypt feared that a new black African state in the region would necessarily be anti-Arab and thus upset the delicate regional balance. Alier felt strongly that Egypt's fears were unjustified and pointed out that the massive Jonglei Canal project, which was entirely favourable to Egyptian interests in that it promised to increase the flow of the Nile, was initiated precisely at the time when the South had relatively more power and autonomy than ever before.

By mid-2002 and the signing of the Machakos Protocol, when we next met, Alier believed that the context was more favourable to a sustainable agreement than it had been in 1972. Both sides were more fatigued than they had been at that time, and hence more motivated – although now it looked to be Khartoum that was the wearier, rather than the rebels. And there was – as Alier had pleaded for – active mediation. In 1972 Ethiopia had provided little more than a hotel (where delegates had to pay their own bills ...), and Haile Selassie only intervened when both parties petitioned him on the issue of post-agreement military arrangements.

Were the mediators, this time around, sufficiently neutral? Alier admitted to some doubts about the USA in particular, indicating that he and many in the SPLM/A worried about the Americans' stated and emphatic preference for unity as the final outcome. When asked to do so by USA peace envoy Jack Danforth, Alier had emphatically refused to go on the record as being pro-unity: "It is my democratic right to reserve my opinion on this," he said, and he suggested to Danforth that it was inappropriate of him to make such a request.

The protocol, as Alier saw it, did cover the principal areas of contention. Its weakness was that – from what we knew at this point – there was no clear path to elections and democracy (surely critical if the agreement was to stick), but this might be compensated for by the weapon it gave to the South: the internationally sanctioned possibility of secession six and a half years hence. For the perfect agreement to emerge, he suggested, some third party now needed to exert pressure on both sides so as to widen the margin of political freedom that Machakos allowed us to glimpse. Optimally, this third party would be an opposition coalition, but the opposition was severely fractured: Umma was split down the middle, and Sadiq was remembered as an indecisive failure (the day of my meeting with Alier, a gaggle of senior Umma figures, including Mubarak, accepted Cabinet positions); the Democratic Unionist Party was undergoing similar splits; and the Communist Party was now splintered into a multitude of small leftwing groups. What about Turabi's Popular National Congress Party? "They are a snake in the grass," Alier commented; "Dangerous, but no-one knows exactly where they are or when they might strike ..."

It was up to the mediators to force open spaces and ensure that a plural political system emerged. If they did not, then it was possible to foresee, a couple of years down the road, an intifada or coup that would lead to the abrogation of Machakos by the North.

Reflecting further on the Addis Ababa agreement, Alier said that a great mistake on the South's part in the ten years of peace that followed the accord was that it forgot that its military strength was its only defense against the North; although Addis formally left the South with its own forces, senior officers preferred to jump ship and enter political life; the Army decayed and, when the crunch came and Nimeiri challenged the agreement, the South had nothing with which to respond. "If I were Garang," said Alier, "I'd want now to keep the SPLA intact ..."

If greater realism was called for, it must be tempered by more mutual tolerance and "sportsmanship" than was seen post-Addis. Southerners needed to understand the need of even moderate Northerners to hold on to sharia and must give them time to move to a fully democratic system; and the North must not fear the South's calls for such democracy. There must be an energetic search for common points.

What were the threats to Machakos? As all Southerners seemed ritually to do, Alier reacted emphatically to the suggestion that an autonomous (or even independent) South would be so riven internally as to be unmanageable: "From '72 to '83," he said, "we had stability: this should be an inspiration ..." But certainly there would be a need for internal reconciliation processes, and in the short term the importance of Nuer leader Riak Machar's acquiescence to arrangements should not be underestimated.

Ever the perfect gentleman, Alier said that he had thus far been reluctant to speak out against Talisman, lest this be taken the wrong way by his Canadian friends and/or by the Canadian Government – "who have been so good to our people, accepting thousands of refugees" – even though until now he had been very firmly opposed to the presence of the Canadian company, and indeed to all oil exploitation pending a settlement. "But things have changed ..." Alier would never say this to the company, but he now did hope that Talisman would stay, because in a peaceful Sudan "this is exactly the kind of enterprise we need."

By early 2003, when I accompanied the newly appointed Canadian Peace Envoy Mobina Jaffer to meet with Alier, this time at his gloomy and hot home in Arkoweit, Khartoum (the area was undergoing one of its daily power cuts), the steadily growing pessimism regarding unity that I had observed on the old statesman's part over the past two years – notwithstanding positive developments in the peace process – seemed to have deepened even further. He was more critical than ever before of John Garang's ostensible pro-unity stances, implying that he was sacrificing the true wishes of the South to his own vain ambition to be president of all Sudan. But the idealism and vision of old had not entirely gone; he fussed over what Canada might be able to do in assisting the Sudanese diaspora to return home at the conclusion of the peace process: "We will need everything they have learned, everything they will know ..."

THERE WERE SOUTHERNERS WHO, for reasons mystifying to many, had accepted posts in government – the same government that at various times had declared that the struggle to reconquer the South was a jihad. In October 2001, for example, five of Sudan's twenty-seven Cabinet Ministers were Southerners, and one was from the Nuba Mountains: Colonel (Retired) Martin Malual Arop – Council of Ministers; Dr Riak Gai – Animal Resources; Dr Lam Akol Ajawain – Transport; Major General (Retired) Alison Manani Magaya – Labour; Joseph Malwal – Aviation; Ali Tamim Fartak (from Nuba) – Basic Education.

These were portfolios that had come to be traditionally assigned to Southerners. None were heavyweight; the post of second vice-president was also traditionally assigned to a Southerner; the then-incumbent was the pleasant but ineffectual academic Dr Moses Macar. Many Southerners looked upon all of these people with great bitterness, suggesting they had sold out to obtain a cellphone, a shiny black government car, and a few bodyguards.

Before meeting with any of them, I did background research. It became evident that, although all of these ministers were from the same region of Sudan and were ethnically African/Nilotic rather than Arab/Nubian, they did not function as a caucus. Lam Akol, Riak Gai, and Joseph Malwal were, essentially, lured in from the bush by two agreements – Khartoum (April 1997) and Fashoda (September 1997) – that had laid out a path towards self-determination, with a transitional period to end in a referendum. The mainstream SPLM/A stayed out of the agreements and fought on. In theory that transitional period was to expire (and did, only to be extended – with almost no-one noticing) in March 2002. Martin Malual, on the other hand, was a member of the 1989 Revolutionary Command Council, which seized power in a coup from then-Prime Minister Sadiq al-Mahdi; he, Alison, and Tamim could be considered card-carrying National Congress Party members. The presence of the six allowed the government to say truthfully that Cabinet was representative of the ethnic makeup of Sudan.

Reflecting their different career trajectories, Malual and Lam Akol expressed to me significantly differing views on oil and, specifically, on Talisman. Malual was an unabashed supporter of the company; he believed on the one hand that the use of oil revenues would be critical to the future development of Sudan – and to winning over Southerners to a more favourable view of Khartoum – and on the other that Talisman and its partners should be doing more in the area of community development in the meantime. Malual seemed to have a good understanding of the criticism Talisman had faced at home and agreed with me that his Cabinet colleagues had thus done an indifferent job in accounting for the oil revenues. Powerful Oil/Energy Minister al-Jaz, he complained, understood only the bottom line and was not sensitive to calls for accountability in expenditure. Lam Akol was more critical, skeptical, and uninterested in the putative good deeds of the Canadian company. In his days as an SPLA commander he had frequently had the oilfields in his sights. He said bluntly that "the people" had seen no improvement in their standard of living as a result of oil.

While Lam Akol's body language suggested some sympathy for the rebels' targetting of the oilfields, Malual elliptically suggested that he might be able to intercede on Talisman's behalf with the SPLA; he implied that Petronas (one of Talisman's partners in the Greater Nile Consortium) had already had contacts with the rebels with a view to "purchasing" their own safety. I didn't take him up.

On the then-rival Egyptian-Libyan and IGAD peace processes, Malual and Lam Akol shared a good deal more ground. Malual was emphatic that "IGAD has to be the one." He was quite critical of Egypt and suggested that Egypt's basing of its plan on the axiom of unity constituted inappropriate foreign interference in the internal affairs of Sudan: "This is something for we Sudanese to decide." He drew a parallel with Canada, saying that our referendums on sovereignty for Quebec should be an example for Sudan (when pressed, Malual's knowledge became sketchy – he was of the impression that the last two referendums had been about Quebec joining France).

Lam Akol was more emphatic still. He suggested that the pro-unity Egyptian-Libyan Initiative was being pushed by some elements in the Sudanese Government only as a means of definitively getting self-determination (read secession) off the table and went so far as to suggest that Egypt was not necessarily an essential part of any sustainable solution (not a common view, this). He named Ghazi Salah al-Dien, with some scorn, as the leader of the ELI-pushing faction (indeed Ghazi the previous week had said that anyone who spoke about self-determination should be considered a traitor – notwithstanding the Sudanese Constitution, which enshrined the concept). Lam Akol implicitly blamed the president for failing to provide decisive leadership on the whole issue and, "like John Garang," for "believing that the other side is about to collapse."

In agreement that self-determination must remain the guiding axiom, both ministers were also as one in that the principal challenge facing Khartoum on peace was the creation of conditions – in the Constitution and in the South – that might persuade Southerners eventually to choose unity over secession. Lam Akol was a lot more skeptical than Malual: the four-year transition period envisaged by the Khartoum and Fashoda agreements – which had brought him into government – had almost run out, with virtually nothing done. Malual agreed that the record was poor, but the way he looked at it – through the prism of the Intergovernmental Authority on Development initiative – there was still time, because the clock had yet to start running on IGAD's transitional period.

Malual was ostensibly relaxed on the internal situation. He suggested that within Cabinet the "liberals" were firmly in control: "Anyone who doesn't like this can quit." In specific reference to anti-US feeling at this time, there was "little risk" of people on the street taking matters into their own hands. The more maverick Lam Akol believed wariness was in order. There still existed a substantial and potentially dangerous National Islamic Front constituency, which still had men in Cabinet. The idea that the doves now had the upper hand in government was, he said, part illusion, and Khartoum's glasnost had been more by accident than design. Turabi was dumped, said Lam Akol, not for any ideological reason nor to appease the West but as the result of an internal power struggle, pure and simple. Ethiopia and Eritrea were making friendly noises in part for commercial reasons, and the USA – "well it's obvious that the rapprochement is not due to anything Sudan has done, but to their overriding security concerns ..." In other words, the hardliners should not be written off. There were two principal dangers: Turabi and First Vice-President Ali Osman Tahaa. The good news was that they detested each other.

A few months later, Lam was evidently no longer able to live with himself as a Cabinet Minister in an administration repellent to most of his beliefs (or perhaps he was starting to see the writing on the wall for that administration): he quit to join with two MPs in forming the Justice Party. After another year or so, he took the logical next step: he returned to South Sudan, revived his long-dormant private army, and realigned it with the SPLM/A.

I NEVER HAD THE GOOD FORTUNE to meet John Garang. For most of my tenure in Khartoum, Ottawa was undecided as to whether we should seek out an encounter, and if so at what level; certainly I would have liked to, if only to satisfy my curiosity. And there was another rather less savoury character whom I also regretted not meeting, in that he exemplified a dimension of the Sudan problem that I was sure would surge to the forefront following an eventual peace accord: Nuer warlord Paulino Matiep.

The closest I came to meeting Matiep was a long chat one day in my Khartoum office in June 2003 with the mild and entirely unobjectionable Martin Kenyi. Kenyi, commander of the Equatoria Military Area and a member of the South Sudan Defense Force (SSDF)'s High Command, resided principally in the capital, as nearly all of Equatoria was actually in the hands of the SPLM/A. He was thus rather more of a "shadow" commander than a number of his colleagues in the High Command but nevertheless claimed to have considerable forces within the important and well-populated government-held enclaves of Juba and Torit.

The SSDF was not simply the Southern branch of the Sudan Armed Forces, as might be imagined from its name and cosiness with the regime. It was a chameleon-like creature whose nominal commander was at this time Riak Gai, who also held the post of chairman of the Southern States Coordinating Council (SSCC) – a kind of Khartoum-sponsored government-in-exile based in the Northern capital but which in theory would rule the South tomorrow if the government conquered it militarily. The government fondly imagined the SSCC would have a role even if the South were pacified only by negotiation with the SPLM/A.

It was helpful, Kenyi suggested, to conceive of the Coordinating Council as a shadow government for the South, with the SSDF as its corresponding army – but the SSDF was in some ways more active and weighty than its political counterpart. It was composed principally of three forces: the Equatoria Defense Forces (EDF), the SSIM (South Sudan Independence Movement, commanded by Riak Machar until his defection to the SPLM/A), and the SSUM (South Sudan United Movement, under Paulino Matiep). Riak Gai was a reluctant commander-in-chief, Kenyi admitted: unlike his predecessors at the Coordinating Council (Brigadier General Gatluak Deng and Riak Machar), he saw himself much more as a civilian politician than a military leader: "More of a Jimmy Carter-type commander-in-chief than a George Bush Junior."

Next in the chain of command – and currently the real supremo of the South Sudan Defense Force – was Paulino Matiep himself (chief of staff), who for years had served as the government's chief defender of the critical oilfields. Matiep wore (in addition to the trademark sunglasses) the uniform of a major general in the Regular Army – but only because no-one had ever dared take it off him. He raised and paid his own forces and did pretty much whatever he liked. Usually this consisted of hunting down and attacking whatever Dinka forces he might encounter, an agenda that conveniently coincided with Khartoum's. So successful had he historically been in this that the central government rarely hesitated to back him up with regular troops and aircraft when Matiep required it.

Matiep, who was a singularly sinister figure whom some compared with the Marlon Brando character in *Apocalypse Now* (Joseph Conrad's Mister Kurtz), was thought to be seriously ill with diabetes. His erstwhile enemy but fellow Nuer Peter Gadiet, who had been bribed (my term; Kenyi did not demur) to defect to the government side only recently, was said to be jockeying to take over the SSDF as and when Matiep died; such was Gadiet's record that it was not difficult to imagine him seeking to hasten that death. In terms of cruelty, unpredictability, and general capacity for mayhem, Gadiet was unlikely to represent an improvement on Matiep. Kenyi disarmingly agreed that both were volatile and largely out of control but stressed (correctly, from what I knew) that they were nevertheless among the most effective field commanders anywhere in Sudan.

Matiep chaired the South Sudan Defense Force High Command, which consisted of six deputy chiefs of staff and three regional commanders: Deputy, Operations – Commander Gordon Kong; Deputy, Administration – Commander Ambrose; Deputy, Logistics – Major General Ismael Kony; Deputy, Political Orientation – John Machem Dit; Deputy, Military Training – Commander Benjamin Ater; Deputy, Security and Intelligence – Commander Elio Benson; Regional Commander for Equatoria – Martin Kenyi; Regional Commander for Bahr al-Ghazal – Major General Tom Anur; Regional Commander for Upper Nile – Brigadier Gabriel. Many of these personalities (including Matiep himself) had in the past fought on the side of the SPLM/A. Typically, they were seduced away from the rebels by the Khartoum Agreement ("now dead," Kenyi acknowledged).

So why didn't the SSDF go back to the bush if the Khartoum Agreement had brought them nothing? Some had of course done so, such as Riak Machar. But others such as Kenyi maintained that, although their dreams had not been fulfilled in the North, they would not go back and join the SPLM/A. They had three main reasons. First, unlike John Garang, they had never had any ambitions on power in the North: their aim was the liberation of the South – preferably through independence, but failing that through real decentralization and federation. Second, they perceived the SPLM/A as bent on Dinka hegemony, and the SPLM/A leadership as closed, elitist, and undemocratic. Third, command and control of the South should be regionalized, with Equatorian politicians and military commanders in Equatoria, Dinkas in Bahr al-Ghazal, and Nuers in Upper Nile.

The SSDF thus continued to sit on the government side of the lines, although its long-term military and political objectives were not at all those of the Khartoum administration. Put crudely, it seemed it was just that its members hated the Arabs who controlled the North marginally less than they did the Dinkas who ran the South. The long-term aim, Kenyi stressed repeatedly, was nothing less than independence for the South.

The degree of organization and coherence implied by the SSDF command structure outlined by Kenyi was optimistic. Essentially, this was a collection of warlords, some of whom (like Matiep and Kong) certainly had large numbers of troops at their command, while others were surely much less powerful than they made themselves out to be. But, to be realistic, the SSDF nevertheless did need to be placated and accommodated. Whoever replaced Matiep would likely be no more favourably disposed to the (probably largely Dinka) authorities of the post-Mackahos Southern Region than Paulino himself; in Juba, the creation of any peaceful modus vivendi would have to take into account the Equatoria Defense Force, and, elsewhere in Upper Nile, the faithful of Gordon Kong could not be expected to put down their arms quietly. The SSDF – however dubious its legitimacy and however bankrupt and incoherent its current pro-Khartoum stance might be – was capable of bringing the whole agreement tumbling down.

FAR BEHIND REBEL LINES, in Yambio (Western Equatoria) I was in May 2003 accorded the honour of an audience with the governor of Equatoria, Commander Samuel Abu John Kabashi: freedom fighter, warlord, war criminal, elephant poacher, taleteller – take your pick. The seventy-five-year-old is a legendary figure who participated in the 1955 Torit Mutiny, fought with Anyanya throughout the first phase of the civil war (1956–72), then rose through SPLA ranks through the 1990s. The UNICEF resident representative in Yambio, Eveline, warned me tremulously that Abu John could be peremptory, rude, and even threatening to his guests; it all depended what mood he was in. And indeed the manner in which his heavily armed personal escort came to attention when our small delegation arrived, and the trembling deference – even terror – of the servant girl who brought us water and lemonade testified to the awe he inspires.

Dressed in a blue Kaunda safari suit, Abu John received us regally in his earth-floored courtyard as the twilight gathered and bats squeaked in the trees. Initially frosty, he soon showed himself susceptible to flattery; over the next two hours he regaled us with anecdotes, politics, and ribald humour. He was especially proud of having just fathered a child (he was rather vague as to how many others he has), "and without the help of Viagra; my secret is slow but sure." At this point, his wife appeared; we had met her earlier that morning to discuss some small-scale development projects for which she was receiving Canadian funding. She had not told us then who her husband was, which made me cross: we should not be supporting projects so close to government, and she knew it.

Abu John was sanguine on the peace process. He was reasonably confident that a written settlement would soon be reached but stressed that the SPLM/A was not interested in "peace at any price." On the one hand he insisted that he and others of the senior leadership echelon were constantly being consulted by Chairman Garang as negotiations progressed, but on the other his questions as to our perceptions of how the talks were going indicated otherwise. I suggested that security arrangements seemed to be one of the major current stumbling blocks. He agreed and ruled out the idea of the SPLM/A and the Khartoum administration ever manning parallel garrisons in the key Southern towns of Wau, Juba, Malakal, and Bentiu, but he did seem to think that some kind of arrangement involving shared leadership of a combined army might be possible.

One of the principal reasons why the last peace agreement (Addis Ababa) failed, he opined, was that "it was too rushed." He saw no reason for concern that talks had thus far dragged out nearly a year since the July 2002 Machakos Protocol – quite the contrary.

As many (all?) Southerners did, Abu John largely blamed the Southern problem on the British, who in decreeing the South as a closed area – under the pretext of protecting Southern culture – ensured it remained chronically underdeveloped and generally cut off from civilization (it is a little-known fact that the British invented the concept of the travel permit, which is now the bane of every diplomat's life in Sudan). Neither Abu John nor County Commissioner Mary saw any irony in their vision of a post-peace South Sudan: a place where the Arabs (Abu John used the universal term of deprecation, "djellabas") would be frankly unwelcome, whatever attractive trading merchandise they might bring with them from the North. In other words (it seemed to me): back to the Closed Area approach.

In passing, Abu John was careful to deflate the myth that, whatever else their crimes may have been, the British colonial administrators were incorruptible. He recalled two district commissioners in Yambio – Major Wilde and Mister Grantham – and said that "both learned their tricks under the Raj." He had become aware that the late Mister Grantham was fiddling the books by entering road construction costs when no road had been built, but Abu John was able to turn this to his own advantage when he needed a loan and, on another occasion, when he needed someone to lie for him about his knowledge of Arabic on his application for military college in Omdurman (where Abu John was the first Southerner ever to graduate).

But getting back to business ... could the North be trusted to keep whatever promises it made at Machakos? Abu John was under no illusions. He recalled how after the Torit Mutiny of 1955 he visited a fellow Army officer who, notwithstanding an earlier offer of amnesty by the central authorities, was about to be shot. "Why are you crying?"Abu John recalled asking rhetorically. "We all knew the Northerners could never be trusted."

"But," Abu John went on, "Southerners are just as capable of betraying their own cause." For example, the Torit mutineers were fingered by a fellow Southerner (who was then in turn executed for his pains). And more recently, when the SPLM/A lost Juba, another Army friend of his stayed behind as a clandestine sniper, picking off three or four Northern soldiers a week, moving from one hideout to the next. "But he was betrayed too, by one of his own. The only good thing is that he took six or seven with him that day."

And what was Abu John's secret to survival, after so many years with the infantry? "God must be on my side."

I decided not to respond to that one and moved onto safer ground. How should donor governments be helping out, right now, with peace apparently imminent? I braced for the harangue on Talisman that I had come to expect. To my surprise I was, for the first time in five visits to the SPLM/A-held South, spared. With a straight face Abu John went on to echo another common refrain I had heard many times from senior SPLM/A old timers: "The best thing you could and should have done is support us with weapons ..." I refused to take him seriously, and, having accepted with feigned disgruntlement that the Canadian International Development Agency was not about to ship surface-to-air missiles to the SPLM/A, he went right to the point: roads ("if you had not flown in, you wouldn't need to ask that question") and education. But the old warrior was not exactly on bended knee. I was left with the clear impression that he saw these exceedingly costly tasks as the responsibility of the international community; if they didn't want to do it, shame on them – but the SPLM/A wouldn't do it either.

Abu John held out the prospect of internal Southern elections that year, regardless of the peace process – but how many times had I heard this before ... Neither he nor Yambio County Commissioner Mary would run: "I'm too old for that kind of stuff." And might we soon see a few more women in senior positions? "Well, we already have some in minor posts, but I'm not sure we are ready to see them at the top ..."

Intertwined with his more serious remarks, Abu John kept up a running commentary on his various physical ailments (gout, diabetes, and high blood pressure – all treated in Kampala by a "marvelous" Palestinian doctor whom Abu John insisted is "not really Arab"); on his wives (he had just sent one away for reproaching him, as a Christian, for polygamy); on his old schoolmate Saddam Hussein ("but I'd like a piece of that [USD] $25 million reward if he ever shows up here ..."); and on witchcraft ("I met Evans Pritchard [the famous anthropologist and author of *Witchcraft among the Xande*] once but I don't believe in it; when my father was sick, they put him under some special tree to cure him, but he died on the spot...") He recalled Abel Alier as "a little boy" at Rumbek Secondary School, nostalgically remembered inter-ethnic dorm-raiding, and then fondly segued to the time he won the jackpot on the fruit machines at Las Vegas. "But I'm putting it all in my autobiography, and I'll tell all," he concluded; his daughter would actually write the "autobiography," "but she'll put down exactly what I tell her."

Abu John was an entertaining villain who evidently liked to provoke and loved a stage. Underlying many of his more serious comments was a worrying – and in my experience not untypical – failure or refusal to see that most Western donors, along with the people they put into the field in South Sudan, were much less interested in the rights and wrongs of the SPLM/A cause and fifty years of grievances than in putting an end to the appalling suffering. It was not as though Abu John needed look far afield: while the old man had every reason to be bitter at both the British and the North, it was also an indictment of the SPLM/A that in lush, fertile, and peaceful Yambio there was no SPLM/A-funded and -administered secondary school, no SPLM/A-funded or -administered water or electricity services, no clinic, no road repair program.

The Movement must be given time, it might be said. Fair enough, but the thinking, the discussion, and the planning could not wait much longer. The SPLM/A leaders must move from fighting to governing; getting on with those long-promised elections would be a good start.

And, while they were at it, it would do no harm for them to try to remember what they had been fighting for. Abu John's wry "The only good Arab is a dead Arab" might be an all too human reaction, but it was not a promising slogan with which to usher in a new and peaceful beginning in South Sudan.

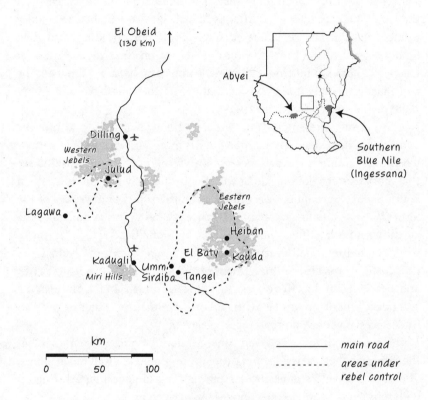

El Obeid
(130 Km)

Abyei

Dilling
Western
Jebels
Julud

Lagawa

Eestern
Jebels

Heiban

El Baty
Kadugli
Umm
Sirdiba
Tangel
Kauda
Miri Hills

Southern
Blue Nile
(Ingessana)

km
0   50   100

————————— main road

- - - - - - - - areas under
rebel control

The contested areas
detail: the Nuba Mountains

10

THE CONTESTED AREAS

WHEN IN JULY 2002 the framework for a peace deal was signed at Machakos the government, while conceding the principle of self-determination for Southern Sudan, carefully excluded from the deal three areas that over the next year or so came to be known euphemistically as "the contested areas" (as though all of South Sudan was not contested). These were three quite separate regions of Sudan where the SPLM/A had an active and armed presence and/or where the Dinka were populous; yet these regions did not fall within the commonly accepted definition of South Sudan – that is to say, below the zigzagging east-west line drawn fairly arbitrarily across Sudan by British administrators in the colonial era.

In the east, hard on the Ethiopian border, was the region known to Southerners as Southern Blue Nile, to Northerners as Ingessana. For the duration of my stay in Sudan, this region was inaccessible: because the government did not consider it part of the South, it refused to allow humanitarian relief flights until early 2003, and even then access was only from Lokichokkio. The area was particularly sensitive for the government in that it adjoined the Roseires Dam, which provided most of the hydro power for Khartoum.

350 km west, occupying a large part of South Kordofan, was another "contested" area: the Nuba Mountains, where the SPLM/A had steadfast allies among the indigenous people although the latter were not actually of Nilotic origin. A further 150 km south of Nuba, a stone's throw north of the Bahr al-Arab River and the "official" South, was the community of Abyei, firmly in government hands but never recognized as the North by the rebels.

OUTSIDE SUDAN, Abyei was known principally as the home of Francis Mading Deng, a paramount Dinka chief who rose to great heights in the Northern civil service (he was Sudan's first ambassador to Canada) but then left Sudan for the USA when the Islamist regime took power. In recognition of both his statesmanship and his ethnic origins, United Nations Secretary General Kofi Annan named him his personal representative on Internal Displacement (the Dinka being a people who, perhaps more than any other, have greatly suffered from this problem), and in this capacity he was periodically if rather reluctantly allowed back to his homeland by the Khartoum administration.

Sudanese journalists, historians, and politicians all knew Abyei as an untidy piece of unfinished business left behind by the British and perpetuated as such by President Nimeiri. Abyei was on the one hand predominantly Dinka, but on the other it lay north of the Bahr al-Arab that made such a convenient North/South dividing line; also, at certain times of year, it took on a decidedly Arab complexion. Abyei was a primary stop on the annual north-south migration of the Misseriya cattle-herding nomads and had been so for so long that the Misseriya were part of the landscape; mixed marriages are common.

The British solution, formalized by President Nimeiri as part of the 1972 Addis Ababa agreement that brought to an end Sudan's first civil war, was to propose that the people decide for themselves, through a referendum, whether they wished to belong to the North or the South. But the referendum never took place. Nimeiri abrogated Addis Ababa in 1983, and successive administrations in Khartoum tried to forget there had ever been a commitment to a vote. The SPLM/A did not.

I first visited Abyei courtesy of Talisman in late 2000. Abyei lay within the Greater Nile oil concession, and Talisman was anxious to show me how keenly the community of Abyei welcomed the company and its involvement. I supposed the good people of Abyei must be rather tired of being asked how many of them were related to Francis Deng, but the number of hands that went up when I posed the obligatory question to a group of a hundred or so "elders" under a large tree was nevertheless impressive: I counted at least seventy. They were happy enough with Talisman, acknowledged gratefully the refurbishment of the town clinic that the company was planning, then asked earnestly whether the company could not provide them with an all-weather road so that they would no longer be cut off for the five or six months that the rainy season lasts. Talisman's answer – that this would depend on whether or not oil was struck in the vicinity – left everyone ruminating in a rather discontented manner.

A year later, I made a flying visit to Abyei on my way north from Wau, in a World Food Programme aircraft. The place was buzzing. Oil had indeed been struck by the four-nation Greater Nile consortium, at Diffar – about 40 km to the north. The find looked promising and the longed-for road was under construction. Electricity lines had just been hung. The mosque was being repainted and expanded. Abyei was now one of the more developed towns in South Sudan.

There was a downside. The presence of oil brought troops. By mid-2003, with the road now complete and military movement easy, a quarter of Abyei's population was military. Heavy howitzers sat in the schoolyard of the Primary School ("Established 1955"). Around the entire town a one-metre-high defensive earth dyke had been thrown up by the oil consortium. In the ramshackle, fly-infested, and foul-smelling "restaurants" of Abyei's main street, soldiers lolled around with AK-47s slung casually over the backs of their white plastic chairs; others strapped their guns to the crossbar of their bicycle, where they made a bizarre complement to the gaudy plastic flowers with which most of the men decorated their Phoenixes. Many of the soldiers seemed to be fourteen or younger. Ingenuously, the commander of the garrison showed up at the United Nations compound where I was staying one day in June to ask if the Food and Agriculture Organization would supply his men with seeds and tools "so they can occupy themselves more usefully."

Much more promisingly, Ngok Dinka and Misseriya chieftains, after years of sporadic conflict over water and grazing, exacerbated by manipulation on the part of both the government and the invisible but close SPLA and made more lethal by an influx of small arms, had met and concluded a series of arrangements that amounted to a truce. This had required no external mediation. Both parties were simply fed up with losing dozens of their men, women, and children each year to fighting over grazing rights and decided it was time to try and rediscover the old ways of coexistence practiced by their grandfathers. In practical terms, it meant that a number of outlying villages that had been abandoned due to conflict could now be reoccupied by their old residents, who had spent most of the past decade in the relative safety of Abyei itself or in one of the teeming displaced persons' camps of Khartoum.

The international humanitarian community had decided to get behind the initiative of the local chiefs by designing an integrated project to support the return of the displaced. In deference to the need for anything aid-related to be given an acronym, this was known as PACTA, or Programme Advancing Conflict Transformation in Abyei, and our government was looking at supporting it to the tune of about CDN $250,000; the USA was also investing a large sum.

I decided that, within the limited time available, Abyei would be an interesting place to take Canada's Peace Envoy, Senator Mobina Jaffer, on her first fact-finding tour to Sudan in early 2003. By coming here we would both signal our approval of and support for the initiative of the chiefs, and we would send a public signal regarding the kind of initiative Canada wished to support as a complement to the more formal, high-level peace talks going ahead in Kenya.

Escorting us, for he was the brains and driving force behind PACTA, would be Canadian Marv Koop, now with the United Nations Development Programme but for many years the country director of Canada's one and only development agency in Sudan: the Fellowship for African Relief. There were a couple of other UN staffers with us on the twelve-seater Caravan we had chartered, and I was not that surprised when the newly appointed wali of West Kordofan arrived unannounced at the last minute. He did not ask, or offer to pay his way. This was unfortunately all-too typical of government officials, who seemed to assume that donors and the aid organizations were there largely to service the Sudanese bureaucracy.

We made the obligatory refuelling and coffee stop at El Obeid, then took off again. I was settling down, rather uncomfortably, to sleep when the corner of my eye was caught by the wali, who was fiddling with his white turban. He found what he wanted and brought it down to his lap. It was a small silver handgun, which he proceeded nonchalantly to load, before replacing it in his turban and himself settling down for a sleep. Clearly, the wali intended to take no chances on this first visit to one of the more unruly parts of his fiefdom.

To scare off wayward cattle, we made an initial swoop over the expanse of dry scrub that serves as Abyei's landing strip. I could see a huge crowd assembled off to one side: most of the town had come out. The crowd was not really for us. The wali had clearly phoned ahead and ordered the local police chief to arrange an appropriate reception for him. Rather indelicately, he pushed us aside so he could get off first and be the first – as welcoming traditions required – to step over the black and white cow that had had its throat cut just as our prop ground to a halt; the cow was still pulsing blood onto the hot earth. The senator was game: although she did not leap right over the cow, she did step over its staring head with a brave smile.

My uneasiness increased when we were ushered to a row of chairs behind a podium, a sound system, and a crowd of about three thousand men and a few ululating women. There was also the usual gaggle of curious small children who would periodically be chased off by a stern man with a large acacia switch. The wali was clearly seeking to give the impression to "his" people that he was responsible for bringing this high level foreign delegation here and that, accordingly, the people owed him gratitude for the munificence that would surely ensue.

There was another message in the various speeches that followed – one that was not exactly music to our ears. Conscious that within a day or so, in Nairobi, formal government/rebel talks on the three contested areas were due to start, the wali and his local cohorts launched into impassioned, histrionic, and multifaceted propaganda diatribes that left no-one in any doubt at all where Abyei firmly belonged: in and with the North. "Let us not forget the blood of our martyrs that has been shed for Abyei," the wali cried, brandishing his walking stick for emphasis, "and the mujahadeen who have died for you." I was partly consoled when the claque's politically correct "Allahu Akhbar – Alleluia"s were greeted by the crowd with total indifference.

Off we went to meet the local Peace Committee, in its newly refurbished meeting room. Happily, after having unilaterally declared to the nonplussed attendees that the Peace Committee was now obsolete and would henceforth be transformed into a Development Committee, the

Community leaders welcome Senator Jaffer, Abyei, January 2003

wali left to meet with more important people, and we were able to talk to Committee members freely.

The local peace process had not been without its hiccups: in September 2002 the SPLA had crossed the river from the South and raided the three embryonic peace villages that had been established only a few months before. A dozen or so people had been abducted, and most of the villagers had once more fled to Abyei. After some weeks of careful and low-profile negotiation, in which Marv Koop had played an important role, the abductees had been freed and the SPLM/A central command recognized that the entire episode had been a mistake; the only tragic, if bizarre, consequence was that one of the abductees was stung to death by bees. The three villages were now under reconstruction (again).

The Committee, composed in equal part of Misseriya and Ngok Dinka leaders under the chairmanship of Kwol Deng Majok (a brother of Francis Deng), and including some very articulate women, shied carefully away

FAR IN THE WASTE SUDAN

Misseriya women and children, Abyei

from the big political picture: only a few hours later, Presidential Peace Counsellor Dr Ghazi Salah al-Dien would pay them a visit and seek – unsuccessfully – an endorsement for placing Abyei in the North. But they spoke freely about the lower-level challenges they were now experiencing.

As always, water was at the heart of things. Most of the wells and bore-holes in the hinterland had lain disused for fifteen years or had been sabotaged by one group or another; reconditioning of existing water sources and the drilling of new wells was the number-one priority. It was, of course, not just a question of human survival: if tension between the two communities was to be kept at an acceptably low level, there had to be adequate supplies for the Misseriya's cattle (and the next rains were still months away).

The Peace Committee's representative for youth made a pitch for the creation of some basic sports facilities: the clearing of a football field and the supply of a few footballs. Not as frivolous a request as one might first think: it was the restless and underemployed young people of the two communities who were most liable to be sucked into reviving armed conflict. The women wanted funds for a women's centre; again, quite a good idea: if the women from both ethnic groups could be integrated and brought together for the discussion of common issues, then the men would be slower to resort to fighting as a means of resolving their difficulties.

We piled into the back of a Pajero, the aircon blasting out cool air but having no noticeable effect in the back, and bounced out of town along a rough track in the black cotton soil. The landscape was scrub and low acacia trees; the trees, Marv told us, had sprung up in the fifteen years during which this hinterland had been abandoned; previously this had been treeless cattle-grazing land.

First stop, about 15 km away, was the newly re-established village of Todaj (confusingly also called Um Bilayel). A posse of brightly dressed and enthusiastically ululating young women (I wondered if they had had a drink or two) greeted us, and we were escorted to the meeting tree. As we sat on rustic and rickety wooden framed chairs, with goat-hide straps, a succession of elders welcomed us more formally; the proceedings were slow in that their Dinka had first to be translated to Arabic for one of our escorts from the World Food Programme to then translate into English.

We sat in a broad semicircle in the shade with, before us, a hundred or so women and children squatting on the ground, and behind them the men of the village, standing. The tobes of the women were dazzling – red, purple, bright green, orange – and as I watched their patient faces I realized I could not tell Arab from Dinka. The only giveaway was the little girls: the Misseriya wore simple, ragged scarves tied under the chin, while the Dinka girls went bareheaded.

No doubt in deference to the (female) guest of honour, the women were given a chance to speak, although it seemed to me that what we eventually heard in English was a lot shorter than what had originally been said in Dinka. It was the same sad story as everywhere. For twenty years the women had been seeing their men and their boys lost to the war, or drifting away for work in distant Khartoum, never to be seen again. More than anything, they wanted peace. The men were more concrete in their demands: help in cutting wood for frames for new tukuls, more boreholes (of course), a school, a clinic.

We were careful not to promise too much. Not so much out of cheapness (although Canadian coffers were rather bare), but because there was an evident risk here of creating dependency. The rare self-generated initiative that had led to this local peace could easily be stifled with ill-advised and indiscriminate aid that took leadership away from the elders and gave it to the development wallahs.

It was another 10 km on to Noong (Naam, to the Misseriya), historically the home of the Ngok Dinka and birthplace of Deng, where we underwent exactly the same rituals. Here a new borehole was actually in the process of being dug, courtesy of the state government's ancient yellow rig. The process had inexplicably been stalled for days, and the people were worried the rig would be taken away before water was reached, but while we sipped hot tea from glasses, under yet another baobab tree, Marv butted some heads and obtained assurances that drilling would recommence the next day.

Almost immediately after we left, talks on the future of Abyei began in Nairobi. In May and June 2003 the United Nations orchestrated two modest but significant waves of returns of Ngok Dinka from the displaced camps of Khartoum to Todaj and other outlying villages. The exercise was not without its problems, but the almost ecstatic joy on the face of an old Dinka woman whom I met as she disembarked from a bus in Todaj – back for the first time in twenty years – spoke for itself.

A further nine months later, the SPLM and the government agreed that prior to the eventual referendum on secession for the South, a special referendum would be held in Abyei to decide whether it wished formally to be assigned to the North or the South. Only if the vote favoured the South would Abyei participate in the principal referendum.

THE NUBA MOUNTAINS are a collection of rocky and generally arid outcrops, interspersed with large areas of plain and covering an area about the size of Switzerland; nowhere do the "mountains" exceed one thousand metres in altitude. For two thirds of the year this is a hot, barren place apparently inimical to human existence. But once the first rains come in May or June it blooms into immediate greenness and streams appear in gullies and wadis that seemed to have been dry for eons. The land comes back to life and takes on a much more benign, even bucolic appearance.

The people of Nuba are ethnically distinct from their neighbours. Their features are Nilotic, but they speak either variations of the Nuba language or Arabic, are predominantly Muslim or animist, and are thought somehow to be linked with Nubia, 1,000 km to the north (and whence the name

Nuba is thought to originate). The people of Nuba are culturally proud and have their own music and dances that are found nowhere else in Sudan. Above all they are known for their male wrestlers; no Nuba celebration is complete without a set of matches. German photographer Leni Riefenstahl is among the many who have studied the Nuba culture: well into her nineties she was still visiting Nuba (she once famously walked away from a helicopter crash at El Obeid that cost several other lives). Her book of photographs *The Last of the Nuba* provoked a literary and political storm: Susan Sontag, in her essay "Fascinating Fascism," saw "the Nazi body cult" on every page, and her scathing critique dogged Riefenstahl until her death.

Successive administrations Khartoum neglected the Nuba people – perhaps due to their very difference and their refusal to assimilate into the Arabized sea around them – while tracts of relatively fertile land between the hills were snapped up for large-scale farming schemes by absentee landlords with the acquiescence of the successive governments of Nimeiri and Sadiq al-Mahdi. The indigenous inhabitants were gradually driven up to the drier and higher hilltops, where they languished for decades.

In the 1950s, Christian missionaries based at El Obeid started to move in, to the indifference of Khartoum. And then in 1985 came another kind of missionary: SPLM/A commanders sensed that here was a land fertile for rebellion. With considerable popular support, the SPLM/A was able to infiltrate the two principal groups of hills – the Eastern and Western Jebels – and within a year or so a thriving guerrilla operation was under way. The weapons for the creeping rebellion and most of the tactical advice came from the SPLM/A proper; while the first leader of the SPLM/A/Nuba, Yussuf Kuwa, was a Nuba, his successor, Abdul Aziz, was from Darfur; Aziz's deputy, Commander Ismael, was, notwithstanding his name, a Dinka.

By 2000 the SPLM/A/Nuba held a substantial area, but its territory was not contiguous; there was one egg centered on Julud in the Western Jebels (mountains), and another larger one on Kauda and Luer in the east. Between the two eggs lay the government-held towns of Kadugli and Dilling, joined together by a north-south road, that went south to the oilfields and north to El Obeid. A wide swathe of government-held territory stood between the two eggs and the SPLM/A-held South.

By the late 1990s the government was starting to become increasingly anxious about Nuba: the SPLM/A's presence here posed a threat to the oilfields from both north and south, and the country's principal oil pipeline ran through the heart of the territory. Khartoum decided to step up the pressure. The government had never officially sanctioned humanitarian relief flights coming in from the South, but now it actively harassed them: while no lives of aid workers were lost, a number of relief aircraft on SPLA landing strips were deliberately targetted by government artillery. Kauda was repeatedly bombed from the air, and on one occasion the school took a direct hit: twenty or more children were killed. Umm Sirdiba, on the frontline east of Kadugli, changed hands several times. The rebels were swept completely out of the Miri Hills, immediately west of Kadugli. By 2000, Khartoum looked poised to regain Nuba.

It was in this volatile climate that in 2001 US peace envoy Jack Danforth proposed his four-point test of good faith to the parties to the Sudanese conflict. One of the tests was that a humanitarian ceasefire be set up for Nuba. Danforth's geographical choice was a canny one: on the one hand the government was likely to respond positively to anything that might lessen the risk to the pipeline and neutralize the closest rebel threat to the heart of the country, on the other the SPLM/A – faced with an ever-better equipped and financed government Army – was starting to find that sustaining the Nuba enclaves was a major challenge to its logistical capacities and its limited military resources. Critics of the SPLM/A also calculated that, in the end, the SPLM/A's heart was not in the Nuba cause: in any definitive peace settlement, it would clearly be impossible for the rebels to define Nuba as the South, and they would thus have eventually to cut the region loose; they might as well start the process now and gain some kudos for doing so.

Under intense US pressure and with Swiss facilitation, a local ceasefire agreement was negotiated at the Swiss mountain resort of Burgenstock in late 2001. Maps were hand-drawn on art paper in the earlier hours of the morning, and an ad hoc and international ceasefire monitoring body – the Joint Military Commission (JMC – later to be more accurately renamed the Joint Monitoring Mission) was established. The ceasefire would formally begin on 19 January 2002, even though the JMC was nowhere near ready to begin operations on that date.

Amazingly, the ceasefire held. News filtered down from the hills of jubilation; traders immediately began crossing lines, and within days you could find in the souq of Kadugli glass jars crudely labelled as "Peace Honey." In more than one location, village leaders had to physically restrain people (who wished to revisit land abandoned years ago) from rushing through minefields. The World Food Programme immediately began delivering the first legal and large-scale external relief anyone had seen in fifteen years. Government troops and SPLM/A hardliners alike were nonplussed: it was clear that almost no-one, outside the innermost circles of the respective political and military command structures, wanted to ever fight in Nuba again.

IT TOOK LONGER THAN ANYONE had expected to establish the Joint Monitoring Mission, and the Canadian International Development Agency developed objections to Canada funding the operation, on the grounds that it was military and not sanctioned by the United Nations – hence ineligible for aid. I spent weeks lobbying Foreign Affairs in Ottawa and was finally able to obtain some relatively meagre support, in the shape of training for monitors to be executed by ex-Canadian military working through the Pearson Peacekeeping Centre in Nova Scotia. The team arrived in May 2002 and began work immediately, providing me with a good excuse to visit the JMM headquarters in person.

I found that the Pearson team, led by former artillery officer Bernie Saunders, had been doing Canada proud. After spending most of a week training international ceasefire monitors in Khartoum, they had moved to Nuba to start training fifteen government-nominated monitors, at the Tillo headquarters of the JMM, just south of Kadugli.

The monitors were all from the government's 5th Division, and held ranks ranging from captain to colonel. The trainers reported that they found their students (whose command of English was variable) initially passive; however, the students soon became very interested and involved, asking many questions. The training sessions concluded with a ceremony at the Tillo parade ground on 11 May 2002, attended by Brigadier General Wilhemsen (the Norwegian officer commanding the operation), the wali of South Kordofan, and the general commanding the 5th Division. Certificates were awarded and speeches made; the trainees gave a demonstration of driving the all-terrain vehicles that would be the monitors' principal form of transportation. At one point there was some fear that the trainees had actually taken off for Dilling, 100 km away, such was the enthusiasm with which they revved up and disappeared from the parade ground. But they eventually reappeared in formation, out of a cloud of dust, to much applause. The graduation ceremony was the lead item on the front page of Monday's *Khartoum Monitor*.

It had initially been hoped that training would be delivered simultaneously to government and SPLM/A monitors, as had been done a month earlier in Oslo – creating government/SPLM/A bonds being an important side-effect of the exercise. However, when the JMM decided to conduct the training at Kadugli/Tillo (in government-dominated territory) as opposed to the quasi-neutral village of Umm Sirdiba, the SPLM/A said it would not travel there and instead required to have its people trained within SPLM/A-held territory, at Kauda.

Accordingly, on 12 May we flew up to Kauda by MI-8 helicopter, and the Pearson team began a separate session for the twelve-person SPLM/A team; three persons had, for logistical reasons, been unable to reach Kauda from the distant western egg to which they were assigned. Training was conducted in the bombed and abandoned school that was the JMM base here; much improvising proved necessary, as there was no electricity or furniture.

Training in Kadugli was capped by a colourful and energetic performance by Radio Kadugli's Drama Team. This group of men and women in traditional costumes, led by the town dwarf, managed to inveigle a large public and a number of the JMM team into violent local dances that were interspersed by earnest messages about the ceasefire, the JMM, and the need for reconciliation. The highlight was an alternately hilarious and moving improvisation in which rebels and Army, complete with wooden rifles, re-enacted the war in Nuba, and were then visited, as they slept, by a nymph (immodestly dressed by Sudanese standards) of peace and thereafter lived in harmony. The show went on the road throughout Nuba, courtesy of the JMM, starting later the same week.

The physical conditions in which the JMM was operating were difficult. Temperatures in May were above forty-five degrees in Kadugli, and only a degree or two lower in Kauda. The JMM was in an old stone-built secondary school in the village of Tillo. The school's bare rooms had been cleaned and painted, and air conditioners had been installed in a few of them. However, it seemed to me that the JMM was not getting its money's worth from Pacific Architecture and Engineering, the company employed (with no competitive tender) by the US State Department to supply all logistical support. It was only on the day of the Canadians' arrival that the first latrine pit at Tillo was inaugurated; until that point staff had been using the woods (a euphemism for the litter blown expanse of sand and scrub that surrounded Tillo). Washing facilities were entirely public and consisted of buckets brought from a pump a short distance away and dumped over people's heads in the yard; it was only by their own insistence that Pearson staffer Susan Soux and the other female on the JMM staff, a German doctor, were able to arrange for more private facilities elsewhere. Bizarrely, there were only eight chairs in the entire complex; in frustration and to the disgust of General Wilhemsen (who thought them "soft") the Canadians went down to the souq and bought for themselves a set of bright green lawn chairs.

Similarly, at Kauda the accommodations consisted of the old school, supplemented by tents. Until ten days earlier, the staff had had no means of transport; it was forty minutes' very hot walk down to the airstrip, ninety to the military headquarters of Abdul Aziz. This deficiency had now been redressed following a successful but death-defying cargo flight into Kauda by an Antonov 26 bearing two Toyoyta Hiluxes – death-defying because the airstrip was only half the length theoretically required for such an aircraft, and one end was actually blocked by the wreck of another same-model Antonov whose pilot had evidently been less skillful.

Apart from the inbound flight, there was one more set of thrills to living at Kauda. The night before we arrived, an unexploded grenade was found in rubble underneath the bed that had been designated for my Swiss colleague to sleep in. Next morning there were two more discoveries. The cook, sweeping up outside the perimeter wall, caught his rake on something: it turned out to be the tail fin of an unexploded cluster bomb, buried nose down in the dirt. And four hundred metres away, a playing child unearthed a 100 kg unexploded bomb. All of these we inspected with experts from a State Department-contracted Mine/UXO disposal team; once they had the doctor on hand they would detonate them in place. The British leader of the team showed great interest in the cluster bomblet, which was apparently a US model. There had been no US arms sales to Sudan for twenty years; most of these devices probably dated from the major land and air attack by the government on Kauda in February 2001, in which twenty schoolchildren inside what was now the JMM headquarters lost their lives.

None of these various challenges to relatively comfortable and safe living were insurmountable; and sitting under the shade of a large mango tree in tranquil Kauda, where the only two cars seen in fifteen years were those of

An unexploded cluster bomb is discovered outside the compound, Kauda,
Nuba Mountains

the JMM, had its charms. However, one would have thought donors (well,
the USA in this case) could legitimately have expected better service than
this for the USD $5 million that had been paid to the logistics contractor.

There were other practical problems outside the mandate of the contrac-
tor. The South African company that was supplying helicopter services had
come up with only one of the two promised MI-8s and, more frustratingly
still, had said the dust at Tillo was so dangerous to the engine intakes that
building a concrete pad was required. The irascible General Wilhemsen
suggested that the company make do with a hosing down prior to takeoff
and landing, but the issue was not yet fully resolved. We flew anyway, with
the pilots grumbling loudly. As if to emphasize that they would not be
responsible for any accident, they had us test the round portholes to see
if we could squeeze out, and then – commenting on the lack of seatbelts
– dourly said "they wouldn't be any use in a crash anyway."

Although the demining team had been late in getting to work, they were now in place, complete with their four dogs. The good news, as I discovered when meeting with Commander Ismail in Kauda, was that the critical stretch on the Kadugli-Kauda track that had to be demined so as to open up Kauda to surface transport for the first time since the mid-1980s was only 12 km long. Ismail's engineer hedged when pressed as to exactly how many mines his men had laid on this stretch but promised to take the dog team to the vicinity of each one. The bad news was that even 12 km might take weeks, and the rains were imminent.

A further issue was flights. Although the ceasefire agreement stipulated unrestricted humanitarian access, the government insisted on authorizing any and all flights into Nuba, a position unacceptable to the rebels. Commander Ismael complained bitterly about this and intimated clearly that, if relief flights did not start arriving soon, the SPLM/A would "consider what benefits, if any, the common people of Nuba are gaining from this ceasefire."

ONLY TEN DAYS LATER, I was back again, this time in the company of diplomatic representatives from the UK, Netherlands, France, Italy, Norway, Japan, and Switzerland, along with military staff from Italy and Sweden. No doubt partly on account of the impending arrival of so many diplomats but also partly as a result of the arrival of the efficient (British) Colonel Symmonds as a replacement for the likeable but ineffectual (US) Colonel Giddens as joint co-chair, JMM personnel and the staff of Pacific Architecture and Engineering had clearly made a tremendous effort since my last visit to pull the JMM headquarters into ship-shape condition. A razor-wire perimeter had been installed; a fuel depot had been established; a helicopter pad was under construction at Tillo at a fraction of the cost originally feared, and another at Kauda; there were now tables off which to eat and chairs on which to sit; fans had been installed in bunking quarters; a two-bed emergency clinic had been established; the cooking had improved; and a cat had even been imported from Lokichokkio to deter rats. Generally speaking, the operation had an air of organization and purpose that it had lacked until now.

There was still only one helicopter in service, which meant that deployment of monitors could not occur simultaneously with demining (an activity for which the helicopter must be on medevac standby); a second

MI-8 was apparently en route from the Ukraine. There were also communications difficulties; outwards email from Tillo was by unreliable satellite phones at a cost of USD $7 per minute.

The verification by the JMM of the status of forces, a requirement of the Burgenstock agreement, had begun and was scheduled to be complete by 16 June. The operation was not as straightforward as might have been thought. While the government's 5th and 14th Divisions – the two units that covered Nuba – were in theory supposed to number ten to fifteen thousand men apiece, it seemed they might be as small as five thousand each, with battalions of only two hundred men; there was some speculation that these reduced numbers – and the redistribution of the armament of a unified artillery brigade throughout the two forces – were due to a thinning-out of ranks immediately following the ceasefire and to the government concentrating its remaining forces on the oilfields. Wilhemsen believed that SPLM/A forces were also much smaller than the JMM had originally been led to believe: although there had been talk of ten to fifteen thousand men, he thought real numbers might be as low as 1,500 to three thousand; the largest single grouping he had seen, on SPLM Day the previous weekend, was of only two hundred men.

A total of forty complaints had thus far been received by the JMM, but all efforts were made to investigate complaints before they were formalized. I witnessed one such incident. The government military had detained a non-uniformed SPLM/A member wandering around inside their military perimeter at Umm Sirdiba. A three-member JMC team was summoned: a US monitor, a Sudanese Government monitor, and a SPLM representative. After arbitration, the prisoner was retrieved and freed, and it was agreed that a letter would be sent to SPLA command in Kauda reminding that the military perimeters of each party were out of bounds to the other.

Less positively, a complaints box set up by the JMM in downtown Kadugli had the previous week been taken down, apparently on orders of government internal security. There was some debate as to the value of putting it up again; it was feared that persons using the box might have their names noted by the government.

Government and SPLM/A monitors were working well together. In a scene which a few months earlier would have been thought impossible, I spent half an hour wandering, in a relaxed way, around the First World War-style slit trenches and other defenses of the government-held Umm Sirdiba, accompanied by monitors from each side of the conflict (both

Canadian trained). As we waded through shell casings and spent machine-gun cartridges, both displayed a childlike enthusiasm in explaining the vices and virtues of the two heavy machine guns deployed, the Chinese 120 mm howitzer, and the 120 mm mortar; the SPLM representative recalled with relish how his men had once taken the town simply by skirting around the back of this east-facing defensive line and attacking Umm Sirdiba's undefended rear.

Monitors were also starting to be deployed in the remoter regions of Nuba. The challenges of providing effective coverage were enormous. One team reported over the radio from remote Sector Five (Lagawa) that their Toyota Hilux 4-WD had suffered three punctures; could the helicopter bring spares? The monitoring teams were undermanned: out of a planned international component of sixteen monitors, only nine were in place, and their rotations were shortly to end. There was an unresolved issue of whether the monitors should be paid. A government major made USD $50 per month, but an SPLM/A soldier was unpaid. How should the latter be recompensed by the JMM, without there arising a question of inequity?

The most important progress made over the past ten days had been on flight authorizations for relief operations. Patient but firm diplomacy by the British Embassy in Khartoum was pre-empted (or complemented) when the USA Embassy communicated to the authorities that, if they continued to insist on authorizing all inbound flights to Nuba (as opposed to leaving all control to the JMM), the USA would simply start financing and dispatching its own flights from Kenya, and they would bring nothing to government-controlled areas. The Sudanese Government caved. In the day prior to our visit, five flights from El Obeid had air-dropped thirty tons of grain, and as we met at Kauda with the SPLM/A a giant Ilyushin 76 repeatedly roared overhead and, in a spectacular operation, delivered twenty-five tons almost on our doorstep.

The two ten-person teams of a Mozambique-based demining team were now approximately six hundred metres into the critical 12 km stretch on the Kauda-Tangel road. The heat, however, was more than the four $25,000 dogs were used to, and work usually had to stop at around 10:00 a.m. every day (at which time the expensive dogs simply sat down). Complicating their task, too, was the greater-than-anticipated amount of military debris in the area in question; every buried bullet, cartridge, and piece of shrapnel gave off the same telltale odour as a mine and must therefore be carefully extracted. Also confusing things was the SPLM/A engineer who was accompanying the mission. He had initially indicated that he and his men had only sown "three or four" mines on this stretch but now changed his tune and said the number was more like three hundred. I later realized that this was all part of what the military analysts called "psy ops" – a good part of the value of mines was that the mere rumour of their presence could be as effective as the mines themselves.

The meat of this second visit was an hour-long joint session at the JMM headquarters in the mountains at Kauda with the rebel Abdul Aziz and his senior officers. Abdul Aziz's remarks were downbeat and of a complaining – even blackmailing – nature that, as far as I could tell, did not go down too well with my diplomatic colleagues. His thrust was simple: yes, relief flights had begun, but these were insufficient and very much overdue. The rebels had no confidence in the government not putting forward further obstacles in the near future: "They've only come now because you are here and [USAID Director] Andrew Natsios will be here in a day or so ... Moreover, regardless of the cost, we want these flights to come from Lokichokkio, not El Obeid. If you – the international community – fail here, then there will be no extension, and we will return to war ..." There followed a litany of the needs of rebel-held Nuba: water, education, tools, and seeds.

Aziz conceded that the ceasefire had been generally well-received by the people of Nuba but warned that the government had already breached it in various ways: by relocating troops to the oilfields (true), by obstructing and harassing movement (true to some extent, but probably mirrored by similar SPLM/A interference), and by not starting military disengagement, even though "everyone knew that in a few days' time" rains would give the military an excuse not to move. Aziz was not as charismatic or as coherent as I had been led to expect. He seemed tired and dispirited, his petulant attempt to blame the international community in advance for any eventual failure of the ceasefire a symptom of his frustration at being caught between a rock and at least four other hard places: his people's fatigue, the pressure of the international community, the investment of fifteen years' sacrifice, and the greater political ambitions of the SPLM/A.

Canada's peacekeeping trainers from the Pearson Centre had long since come and gone. Their contribution had been greatly appreciated, but Canada now had no physical and visible presence in the most promising development in many years of Sudan's debilitating civil war. The USA, Britain, Switzerland, the Netherlands, Norway, Germany, Italy, France, Denmark, and Sweden all had substantive contingents on the ground in

Nuba and/or large amounts of money going into the JMM pot; Finland and Australia had promised personnel. Of all the Western countries represented in Sudan, only ourselves and Japan were not now in this picture. I was to spend all of the ensuing year arguing vainly that we needed to be here: we were missing the peace train.

NOTWITHSTANDING OUR FAILURE to contribute directly to the JMM, Canada's International Development Agency did see its way to making an important donation to the development of a framework of humanitarian assistance and rehabilitation in Nuba – the other side of the coin to the JMM. In mid-July 2002, over the last three days of the the JMM's first mandate, representatives of the United Nations, national and international aid organizations, the government's Humanitarian Aid Commission, and the rebel equivalent (SRRA) met for three days on the neutral territory of the Umm Sirdiba camp to review the first six months of the ceasefire and this fledgling humanitarian framework, which went by yet another acronym: NMPACT (Nuba Mountains Programme Advancing Conflict Transformation). The meeting was a first in that it brought together, on Sudanese soil, governmental and rebel humanitarian aid facilitators, aid agencies that operated on both sides of the lines, and both North-based and South-based representatives of key United Nations agencies. Canada and the USA were the only donor countries that chose to participate.

Umm Sirdiba, which then consisted of three or four refurbished brick structures and a couple hundred straw tukuls many kilometres from the nearest significant road, was not the most convenient of locations, but, standing as it did on what was until recently the frontline, it was for the time being considered by both the SPLM/A and the government as an acceptable meeting place. Reaching the village involved coordinated flights from Lokichokkio (Kenya) and Khartoum landing (almost) simultaneously at the just-prepared dirt strip at Tangel and their fifty or so passengers then negotiating – on foot and/or by tractor – a wide minefield in very hot sunshine; accommodation was of the bring-your-own variety (i.e., tents).

There were no major mishaps in the well-marked minefield, but there was some anxiety when, on the return journey, the tractor spectacularly capsized while negotiating a steep hill, disgorging its passengers on the track. At Umm Sirdiba, a tropical rainstorm lasting three hours left the tents of the government delegates looking very sad and sorry (they had obviously never been Boy Scouts), and there were some scorpion and snake sightings. Not unexpectedly, the local population was bemused by the whole spectacle, but they turned out in large numbers to entertain participants with traditional singing and a display of Nuba wrestling (the USAID delegate acquitted himself honourably), and more than two thousand people saw us off at Tangel. For the farewell, SPLA members tactfully left their Kalashnikovs stacked neatly in the village church.

A significant portion of the discussions was dedicated to reviewing the first six months of the Nuba ceasefire from the perspective of the humanitarian agencies. Some of the perceived benefits listed included a dramatic reduction in killings; the population's ability to move crosslines for the first time in fifteen years, which revived regional markets and generally boosted prosperity; easier access to health facilities by large parts of the population; the reduction of military activity, accompanied by a lessening of criminal activity. Of more national significance, the success of this regional ceasefire had contributed significantly to the sense that a comprehensive cessation of hostilities might be possible and had generally energized peace initiatives, while the NMPACT meeting itself, supported by the JMC/JMM and bringing together government and rebel humanitarian officials for the first time, was an encouraging incremental step in the overall peace process. But there were problems as well.

Rebel representatives complained bitterly that the JMM had begun operations too late to stop government troops being transferred out to take the war to other fronts (notably the oilfields); that it had not yet been possible to negotiate crosslines movement for aid agencies; that in some areas withdrawing government troops had been replaced by an inordinate number of armed police; that mine clearance had been too slow; that developments in Nuba might have drained scarce aid funds away from more needy areas and might have given the impression that the peace process writ large would be easy (which it would not). Informally and off the record, a number of delegates were also uncomfortable with General Wilhemsen's stated intention to start exploring, during this second mandate, means of turning the ceasefire into a peace agreement. It was clear that the SPLM/A leadership in Nairobi did not yet want to go down this road and wished to settle Nuba only in the framework of a comprehensive agreement. Wilhemsen rightly noted that the populace at large wanted something more definitive and that they wanted it now, but injudicious pressure on the rebels at this stage could do more harm than good – *softly softly* should be the watchwords here.

BY NOVEMBER 2002 and the next meeting of humanitarian actors, the JMM, NMPACT, and the ceasefire in general were at last starting to get more favourable reviews. This time, sixty representatives of humanitarian agencies plus all the usual governmental and rebel suspects gathered at a specially erected tent complex at El Baty, near the JMM's Umm Sirdiba location. The Khartoum-based delegation had a close call when the wing-tip of our chartered Antonov grazed the ground at our rather short landing strip at Tangel but logistics were otherwise smooth; although a cheetah was reported in the vicinity of the latrines.

The meeting came on the heels of a multipurpose and crosslines two-week assessment in Nuba. Broadly speaking, team members now found that the one-year-old agreement had led to "a remarkable and tangible improvement in the quality of life of the inhabitants of Nuba." However, the principal consequence of the war – displacement – remained. Most visibly, large numbers of people from Nuba lingered in wretched camps in Khartoum, but even in the mountains tens of thousands of families were still not back in their homes.

Displacement lingered for several reasons. While freedom of movement was nominally protected by the agreement, memories of the war were raw; many in SPLM/A-controlled areas greatly feared the governmental Army, police, and Popular Defense Forces (mujahadeen) and were resisting the entry into their territory of anyone of whom they were remotely suspicious. Ironically, one peace dividend had been that "baggara" nomads, who for many years had detoured around Nuba on their annual migrations north and south, were now resuming their original routes, this (sadly) leading to a renewal of the kinds of pastoralist/sedentary conflicts that plagued so many other parts of Sudan. There were, predictably, tensions between communities that had stayed put throughout the conflict and recent returnees who were now competing for scant resources. The perception that large areas of Nuba were still mined generated a high degree of apprehension. More so than a perceived lack of services, this combination of fears – which could only be addressed properly by the entry into force of a comprehensive national peace agreement – inhibited a full return to normalcy. The key to making the agreement hold was not so much to bolster it with humanitarian assistance (although this remained important) as for the rebels and the government to reach a peace agreement.

Following this line of argument, NMPACT partners agreed that it was urgent for research to be done on the issue most commonly identified as being at the root of the Nuba conflict: competition over land. It was suggested that the current project by which the United Nations Development Programme, with Canadian support, was leading study of resource-based conflict in Darfur, North Kordofan, and the Sobat Basin be duplicated for the case of Nuba and its results fed into the Machakos peace process.

There were some negative issues/trends still to be flagged. The SPLM/A continued blocking crosslines access to nationals working for aid agencies, this in flagrant breach of terms of the ceasefire. This was not only a function of the local leaders' fears of infiltration but seemed also to be at the instruction of SPLM/A/Nairobi, whose overriding concern was to avoid, pending a definitive peace settlement, any blurring of the blue lines on the map between government-controlled territory and the two SPLA-held eggs in Nuba.

The divide between the JMM and the humanitarian community was becoming more evident, largely due to the very different characters of the two communities (serving or ex-soldiers vs aid agency staff), partly due to one or two ill-advised ventures into the humanitarian field by the JMM, and partly because of what the JMM perceived as the slowness of humanitarian agencies to implement their plans. The divide had most recently been exacerbated by what both the SPLM and the humanitarian community now saw as the "non-neutrality" of the location of the JMM headquarters at government-controlled Umm Sirdiba and by the consequent joint refusal of both the rebels and the aid community to use the JMM facilities for relief-related meetings. As well as hosting the JMM, the tiny community was also home to no less than eighty armed and uniformed government police; their presence was not technically a ceasefire breach, for the agreement nowhere provided for truly neutral territory, but unless the police left there was little prospect of the JMC/JMM and the humanitarian community working as one and being seen to do so – which was in principle highly desirable.

IN DECEMBER 2002, the initial six-month mandate of the Joint Monitoring Mission was renewed for a third time; it looked as though the cease-fire was here to stay. But the general perception among the public that the area was heavily mined was still bedeviling humanitarian assistance. In January 2003, I accompanied Canadian Landmine Ambassador Ross Hynes on a short visit to see what scope there might be for a Canadian contribution to demining action.

It was another of those excruciatingly early departures. Up at 4:30 a.m., just as a few prayers were starting to be heard from the city mosques, to the ever-more impressive headquarters of the Joint Monitoring Mission at the old French Embassy in Amarat, and then to the military entrance of the airport, where a chunky twelve-seater Antonov 28 on permanent charter to the JMM awaited us.

The service was better than World Food Programme's, it had to be said. Twenty minutes after we left the still-darkened Khartoum, the Russian co-pilot, in a decor of faux-marble formica, adorned with miscellaneous signs in Cyrillic script, handed around blue meal trays with the Sudan Airways logo: a boiled egg, some cold fish adorned with a hot chilli pepper, and the obligatory bottle of thick and incredibly sweet mango juice.

We landed at Kadugli and were immediately whisked by MI-8 to the JMM headquarters at Tillo Base, which was almost unrecognizable from the "old" days of scarcely nine months previously: in a large air-conditioned conference room, we sat on executive office chairs around a large conference table and were treated to a slick power-point presentation on the JMM's entire range of activities. I found myself wondering what had happened to the two-dollar plastic chairs the Canadian monitor-trainers had bought to the ire of General Wilhemsen.

We clattered away again by helicopter to Umm Sirdiba. The SPLA, the government, and the JMM were still arguing over the neutrality or otherwise of this location. Such crosslines activity as was going on was still centered at El Baty, some 8 km away. At El Baty, Danish Church Aid was busy. First, it was demining a relatively short stretch of track on a crosslines route that the general rather grandly called the Freedom Highway, where there had been a serious mine incident some months earlier and where it was thought there might still be anti-tank mines buried.

At a remote site in the bush we were given a careful briefing on the colour-coded rocks that the Danish aid workers used to mark their activities; most important to remember were the red and white rocks – red indicating the danger side of the line, white the safe side. Pale green rocks showed a potential mine site.

We watched as the four-dog team of German shepherds were "switched on." Their body-armour-clad trainers, two of whom were Kosovar veterans of demining in the Balkans, would toss a tiny fragment of TNT-contaminated rock onto a piece of open ground, then let their respective dog sniff it out. Dogs who behaved satisfactorily, that is to say, who found the fragment then sat patiently within one metre of it, were considered qualified for the day's activities. But dogs who were distracted, perhaps by the heat or strange smells in the vegetation, and did not find the fragment in the specified amount of time, would be excused for the day.

For an hour, the German shepherds patiently sniffed over 10 m² sectors of ground. The work was slow – excruciatingly so – but there was no alternative; although relatively few artefacts had thus far been found, there had been sufficient incidents to justify a patient metre-by-metre approach.

Back at the Danish tent camp, staff were engaged in an unprecedented training exercise: crammed into a military-style canvas tent, thirty men (and a few women) in blue boiler suits were listening intently as, through an interpreter, a young instructor explained the various types of mines that might be found in Nuba. This was a joint class of trainees nominated by both the government and the SPLA to undertake a five-week basic instruction exercise. The idea of such crosslines training taking place would have been unimaginable little more than a year previously.

It was de rigueur for all high-level visitors to Nuba to check in with both sides, so we took the MI-8 from Umm Sirdiba up to Kauda one more time. Once again Abdul Aziz, portly and this time colonial-looking in a khaki safari suit with a strange round hat resembling a pith helmet, received us under a mango tree outside the old school buildings. He was distinctly more jovial and at ease than on our previous encounter, no doubt buoyed by Chairman Garang's recent visit to Kauda and the fact that, one year on from Burgenstock, the blue lines around the two SPLA eggs in Nuba were still intact.

Abdul Aziz quietly reaffirmed the rebel movement's commitment in principle to the removal of anti-personnel mines in Nuba but did insist nevertheless that, as a security safeguard and pending a definitive settlement, the SPLM/A reserved the right to maintain anti-tank mines on the principal access routes to their strongholds. When Hynes commented that the government claimed it had no mine stockpiles and asked if the same applied to the rebels, Aziz went into a lengthy whispered huddle with his colleagues. After about ten minutes, he responded with an answer to a completely different question; it was clear that in fact the rebels had considerable stocks (as, we were sure, did the government).

The SPLM/A/Nuba supremo made his standard pitch for increased humanitarian assistance within his territory, coupled with an equally predictable accusation that government territory was getting the lion's share, but he lacked conviction; we had the feeling that in reality he was now much more comfortable than before with the status quo. He complained jovially that there were no Canadians assisting in Nuba, but when I pointed out that the Fellowship for African Relief was actually Canadian, he apologized with good grace and said how much he appreciated their work.

A MONTH OR SO LATER, Wilhemsen hosted the monthly meeting of the Friends of Nuba (as the loose coalition of countries funding the operation was known) at Tillo. After the meeting and an excellent three-course steak luncheon, we travelled out to see the most recently established (and final) location of the JMM: the Sector Four camp, in the Miri Hills, a ten-minute flight west from Kadugli. This area had once been the SPLM/A's third egg (in addition to its strongholds in the Eastern and Western Jebels). But Miri's proximity to both the pipeline and to Kadugli itself had been an embarrassment to Khartoum and in 2000 government forces had swept through, reoccupying Miri and effectively emptying it of most of its civilian population.

After Tillo, which now had not only chairs but also electricity, air-conditioning, flush toilets, and a coffee bar, Sector Four was pretty rough still. The camp stood on a rocky hilltop known locally as Koya and consisted of four tents and a couple of half-completed stone-walled tukuls. It was a sweltering day and hazy, but Captain Carlos, the young US commander, said that on a clear day his base commanded a radius of 20 km and that indeed he could sometimes see Kadugli Airport from here. The main danger, he said, was not mines and unexploded ordnance but (and here he dramatically drew out a jam jar he had been concealing behind his back) the wildlife: three enormous scorpions writhed uncomfortably within and Carlos told us a dozen were found every day. There were also a variety of venomous snakes in the vicinity.

General Wilhemsen poses with Nuba women, Miri Hills, Nuba Mountains

Standing in front of his map, the captain briefed us in the open sun; a hundred or so people milled around at a respectful distance. When Carlos and his team had arrived here only ten days earlier, there had been one old man living in a ruined brick building a couple of kilometres away at Ferek Al Droup, at the foot of the hill. But mysteriously the word had spread that there were foreigners in the hills, that there was no longer any risk of fighting, and that, indeed, work could be had: three or four families a day were now appearing, apparently out of nowhere.

Carlos was employing the locals in establishing the camp at Koya and clearing the helicopter landing area: there was a neat and very large H made in white-painted rocks. For the moment water still had to be brought in by vehicle daily along the rough track from Tillo, but Carlos was hopeful that one of the area's old wells would soon be rehabilitated and the returning locals thus become self-sufficient.

One year on, the ceasefire was holding remarkably well; better, in fact, than anyone had dared hope. Its popularity among the Nuba people was enduring. But I couldn't help feeling some trepidation: as the talks in Nairobi went back and forth, it became ever clearer that for both parties Nuba was above all a bargaining chip that would sooner or later be traded away for some quite unrelated advantage in another field. The good of the people had never really mattered to either the government or the SPLM/A.

11

THE WILD WEST

WHILE THE OUTSIDE WORLD focused on the conflict in Southern Sudan, it tended to be forgotten or ignored (until early 2004, that is) that the far west had its problems as well. Simply reaching the west was very difficult, as I found out on my first venture in this direction. Starting from Khartoum at dawn one April day in 2001, and heading for West Kordofan, Babiker (who was driving) and I were – encouragingly – past Kosti and coming to our first stop by noon: the small village of Kandua, in North Kordofan.

The tiny brick medical clinic Canada was funding in Kandua would serve a dozen villages within a radius of 10 km and would be staffed by a paramedic who had a couple of years' training in Khartoum but no formal qualification. Expectant mothers with potential problems would have to be brought in by donkey; for others, a midwife would be sent out. The paramedic would not perform but she would ask to be present as a health

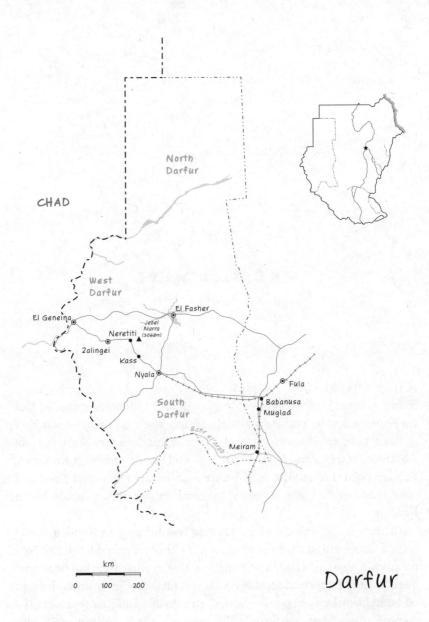

CHAD

North
Darfur

West
Darfur

El Geneina
Neretiti
Zalingei
Kass
Nyala
El Fasher
Jebel
Marra
(3068m)

Fula
Babanusa
Muglad

South
Darfur

Bahr el'Arab
Meiram

km
0   100   200

Darfur

precaution at ceremonies of female genital mutilation – an ordeal to which 90 percent of women in rural Sudan are subjected.

Few children attended school here. The leaders of Kandua had found it impossible to attract government-paid teachers, so most of the teaching was done by young volunteers with three or four years of secondary education. The leaders recalled with nostalgia the old days under the Anglo-Egyptian colony, when all the young men were sent away to boarding schools and housed in hostels in the larger cities (the women were not then educated at all).

In the medium to small villages, the local sheikh – usually a hereditary position – ruled; sensibly, the government made no attempt to interfere with traditional leadership mechanisms of this sort. At Kandua, even the military recruiters did not venture in without the permission of the sheikh, which was not normally given. The place's young men were thus safe from the horrors of military service and war unless they should be tempted by the bright lights of nearby El Obeid. The sheikh, dressed in a magnificent white djellabiya and turban, had a meticulously clean compound, comprising three or four straw-roofed tukuls and one large shade tree under which, in the company of the village men, he received outsiders. Women were seen only when the inevitable huge tray of food, covered with a traditional and brightly woven basket, was brought out, accompanied by a glass of hibiscus tea.

But at village celebrations the women played a key role and were much less inhibited than one might have thought in this nominally fundamentalist society. For an hour in Kandua, they led a traditional and periodically suggestive dance of welcome, each in turn playing the part of local game animals (some now locally extinct, such as the lion and giraffe).

AT 5 P.M., FAR BEHIND SCHEDULE and with the shadows lengthening, we tore ourselves away. At the railroad station of Rahad, Babiker judged that we could take a shortcut by heading diagonally southwest instead of following the main road west then south. All went well for a while, but the going became slower and slower, and the track – a set of ruts more or less parallel to the railway – steadily disintegrated, disappearing altogether for kilometres on end then reappearing as a pair of impossibly deep trenches, which meant you had to drive at a hair-raising angle, and fast, with one wheel in and one wheel out.

Darkness fell quickly, and we started to lose our sense of direction. Occasionally we would encounter some terrified locals caught in the headlights and ask them where we were, but no-one could give us a place name that seemed to figure on any maps. I recall one surreal stop at a row of straw shacks, lit by seven or eight candles. I could clearly see the stars of the Big Dipper, but the tea man said that was south. At about 11 p.m, suspecting by now that we were well off our route, we were stopped by a group of strangely dressed and heavily armed men; they wore dark double-breasted tunics with brass buttons and, apart from the AKs, looked as though they had stepped off the set of *The Three Musketeers*. I feared the worst, but after a few surprisingly desultory greetings and commonplaces they let us go on our way.

At 2 a.m. we at last hit a tarmac road. Turning at random to the right, we were soon entering the spectral outskirts of Dilling: a great avenue of old plane trees, no doubt planted early in the colonial era, floated on a cloud of vestigial fire smoke, bright in the headlights against a black night. Babiker knew how to find the Save the Children compound; after twenty minutes of banging on a metal door that seemed likely to wake half the town, we were let in by a sleepy and bemused nightwatchman. He gave us beds in the yard. We were off early next morning, hoping to avoid any nosy security officials, who would be sure to give us trouble for straying outside the areas specified on my travel permit. Soon, we again picked up our navigational lifeline, the railway running from Khartoum to Wau, which was known internationally for its slave train.

This portion of track was at this time travelled by maybe one train a month, and even here – relatively far north – it was subject to attacks by the SPLA; burned out wagons every few miles attested to this. It was also subject to delays of a more mundane nature occasioned by the unavailability of spare parts due to US sanctions. We came across some passenger carriages marooned many kilometres from the nearest habitation, with thirty men sitting despondently on the embankment awaiting a replacement engine; they had been there three days.

By late afternoon, we were finally at Fula, the small and quiet capital of West Kordofan. Only here, in all the state of West Kordofan, was there electricity, and then only for a few hours each night. In most villages water was extracted from the ground by the ubiquitous and robust hand-pumps installed over the past decade by the United Nations Children's Fund. These were the centre of village life, and rarely did we not encounter at a pump a huddle of brightly dressed women filling their plastic jerry-cans or loading leather waterskins onto camels or donkeys (always women's work, this). In bigger places, there might be a borehole, at least fifty metres deep, for which a diesel pump was needed; there was a line of thirty or forty donkeys at the only borehole in Fula, each harnessed to an oil drum on wheels.

We weighed up the possibility of reaching our intended destination – Meiram – carefully. We were already a full day late, and Meiram, to our dismay, was reported to be another day's drive ahead, in spite of its apparent nearness on the map. Things did not look promising. We decided to cut our losses, see if there was anyone interesting to speak to in Fula, and then head back.

The state's chief justice was located in a government-owned house in what passed for the government quarter of Fula. Unsurprised by our unannounced arrival and in refined English he explained to me that he was currently working on his doctoral thesis, which was to be on the theme of how – under the present Constitution of Sudan – a president might, in theory, be tried for a common crime. He repeatedly stressed to me that this was a purely academic exercise and that he had nothing but respect for President Bashir. The judge was evidently quite uninterested in talking about the day-to-day problems of Fula (which included slavery, war, and drought, as starters) but was rather surprised when I finally responded to his monomania and asked whether he thought the Constitution would allow for the president to be tried for taking power via a coup. "I had not thought of that," he said, finally.

Our return journey was eventful. Fortunately, many villages have a guest house (or, lakonda) for travellers such as ourselves, who are all-too-frequently stranded by flat tires or by boggy or sandy road conditions, or who are simply lost. When a resilient thorn penetrated our rear left tire, and after three hours changing the wheel (dust had penetrated and jammed the sensible wheel lock on the back door), we stumbled in the dark into Jebel Beja in search of such relief.

We paid three hundred Sudanese dinars total (USD $1 = 257 dinars) for the use of three rickety wooden beds, each strung with a dozen strands of old hemp rope, placed under the stars by the side of the track; there were no mattresses and no sheets; you just lay down fully clothed and went to sleep. A donkey tethered a few feet away brayed all night. I was glad to get back to the office.

Riding the rails to Meiram, November 2001

NEXT TIME, IN NOVEMBER 2001, in a second attempt to reach Meiram, I saved myself the long haul by road by flying first to Fula, then borrowing the United Nations' Landcruiser and riding (literally) the rail tracks to Meiram. The slave train was at this time in the government garrison town of Awiel, a little south of Meiram. There was thus no great danger of my UN driver and I running into it or the murrahaleen as we bumped uncomfortably over the railroad ties. One night as we slept out under the stars at Meiram an eerie far-off whistle did wake me and left me uneasy, until the village donkeys began their dawn chorus. And while the nearest SPLA troops to Meiram were a mere 10 km away, informal local agreements meant that the town was considered to be in no danger of attack; many Arab traders indeed ventured from here deep into SPLA territory. But the word was that the murrahaleen this year were more numerous than ever, attracted by the government's new policy of not only giving them free license to rape and pillage in return for their dubious protection

FAR IN THE WASTE SUDAN

but also offering a fee for every man who brought his own horse (forty thousand dinars, or USD $160), another for every one who had a Kalashnikov. The United Nations and the aid community were bracing for possibly hundreds of abductions after the train reached Wau and started heading north again.

In Fula, I raised the abduction issue with the state's acting wali. In an understatement of giant proportions, he acknowledged that there were usually "some discipline problems" associated with the train but insisted that the towns along the line needed the supplies the train brought annually and that the train needed protection. Khartoum, in the face of enormous international pressure and of the stigma of the world, had in fact taken some steps to address the slavery phenomenon, notably the establishment of the Committee to Eradicate the Abduction of Women and Children (CEAWC), which functioned simultaneously at the Khartoum level, state level (Fula in this case), and community level (Meiram and Muglad). At the community level, joint committees brought together five Misseriya leaders (the nomadic community of cattle-herders that provided many of the murrahaleen) and five Dinka leaders; their task was to identify, retrieve, and bring in abductees (or slaves) in the region under their care, in return for their expenses being covered. CEAWC had proposed posting monitors on board the train, but there had been no response from the Army and indeed it was most doubtful that the military would be able to guarantee their safety.

Since CEAWC had been established in May 2000, a total of three hundred local cases of abductees had been documented by the organization's representatives in West Kordofan; a conservative estimate was that there remained two or three hundred more to be found, but Dinka leaders said this number could be as high as one thousand for this state alone. Of these individuals, thirty-eight had been retrieved and sent home directly, a further sixteen had been processed through a reception centre run by Save the Children in Fula, and fifty-eight had been fostered out to Dinka families in and around Fula. The fostering was necessary because on the one hand it was often difficult to trace the parents of the abductee (some children were abducted as babies) and on the other their parents might be behind SPLA lines. The remaining 190 or so young persons remained in place (i.e., in a condition of slavery).

CEAWC had essentially ground to a halt over the past year, for two reasons: donor unease with the lack of transparency in the organization's accounting procedures and lack of will by the government. The first issue was being addressed at this time; in fact I met in Fula with the accountant recently engaged by the United Nations Children's Fund to thoroughly review CEAWC's procedures; he was now touring all points of reception to instil methods and accountability. The second problem was more intractable: Khartoum still had to put into CEAWC the funds it had long promised as a counterpart to international funding, and – most vitally – it had yet to make any effort to rein in the murrahaleen who were responsible for the abductions in the first place. What it all came down to was the Minister of Justice arguing for the murrahaleen to be laid off or at least brought under military discipline and the Minister of Defense replying he needed these ferocious outriders for the effective conduct of the war.

No-one had yet been taken to court for abduction: CEAWC felt that it was more effective to work through persuasion than coercion. Not all abductees were treated badly and sexual abuse was relatively rare, but at the Save the Children reception centre in Fula I was told that at least two of the sixteen recently processed children appeared severely disturbed and had been sent to Khartoum for more specialized care.

On from Fula, we turned south at Babanusa and stopped for lunch in Muglad; as always the only people eating or drinking coffee and tea in the place's few establishments were men; taking your wife out for lunch – or your wife venturing out for a girl's day out – was simply not done. Muglad used to be a major supply depot for Chevron in the 1980s, and test wells were still being drilled as close as 17 km from Fula. But no-one had knowledge of anyone from the local communities having been given jobs by the oil companies; all recruiting (even for road construction and menial cleaning jobs) was done through Khartoum. The acting wali, in Fula, had spoken approvingly of a Talisman-sponsored agricultural project at Keilak, and everyone was pleased with the all-weather road that now connected Muglad with Bentiu, through the Greater Nile oil concession, but he had gone on to tell me the Dinka story of the Lion Tree.

There is a particular tree that grows in South Sudan that gives abundant shade, fruit all year round, and even holds water in its enormous trunk. But it gives off a scent so repellent that even the bravest lion will not sit in its shade or eat its fruit: it is known as the Lion Tree. "The oil," the wali went on, "is like the Lion Tree. We can all see its fruit, its shade, its water – and yet we can have none of it."

Finally, after six months of trying, we reached Meiram. We came here to talk about a school.

Education, I had heard again and again, was second only to water as a priority for the small communities and the rural population of West Kordofan. There were particular challenges here: 65 percent of the state's population was nomadic, and another large proportion were Dinkas recently displaced from the adjacent war zone. The United Nations had devised a unique program of dispatching nomadic teachers to travel with the roaming Misseriya and of single-teacher schools in some of the more stable areas. Retention was a problem: at eleven or twelve, most children were taken out of school for agricultural duties by their hard-pressed parents, and at fifteen or so many boys volunteered either for militia groups or for the Army.

By the light of hurricane lamps under a starlit sky in quiet Meiram, with our Canada Fund coordinator Salah, we met with community leaders for a discussion that centered on two other critical areas of schooling, which we would need to address if we were to recommend assistance to the project they had in mind: forced Arabization or Islamization and access to education for girls. On the first issue, I was pleasantly surprised when Dinka displaced leaders – who here worked in refreshing harmony with the mainly Arab local officials – assured me that Islam was not thrust on their children at school and that they were indeed given time off to attend Meiram's Christian Church on Sundays. Classes were conducted in Arabic, but they were sanguine about that: "we know that learning Arabic makes sense for us, if we are to live and survive up here ..."

Everyone agreed that not enough girls went to school in Meiram. The reasons were complex. It was not that Islam required separate schooling and that funding for girls' schools was a low priority: at two schools I visited here, girls sat in the same classroom with boys for the first five years, and then there were two girls-only schools for the higher grades. Rather, the problem was economic. The school year was set up in such a way that children were freed up for the critical period of preparing the land and sowing fields. But year-round duties such as gathering water, milking the goats and cows, and getting the harvest in – not to speak of more domestic chores such as cooking and looking after the smallest children – were traditionally assigned to girls. Any family that had a girl and a boy would thus make every effort to send the boy to school but would consider the girl's presence at home indispensable. There was a further consideration. As one parent wryly put it to me; "Why invest in our girls when all they will do is get married and leave us? But the boys will always stay to work our land ..."

It was touching but sad to ask the children what they wanted to be when they grew up. Some of the boys would proudly say "a doctor" or, more commonly, "a soldier." But the girls seemed not to understand the question. At most, one brave soul might say "a teacher."

There were no easy answers to this problem. The United Nations tried to encourage increased attendance by girls by offering them (and not the boys) free school uniforms, special late-afternoon classes after the boys had gone home, and birth certificates (no-one hereabouts normally had any documentation; obtaining a birth certificate was practically useful and also conferred status). But the battle was an uphill one.

The picture of life in West Kordofan seemed to be a gloomy one. But it was with great and justifiable pride that a bevy of teachers, town authorities, and Dinka displaced chiefs showed me around the makeshift straw-hut school that served the displaced community and that they were looking to have us help upgrade. They had patiently rebuilt this school once a year for the eight years of its existence. The children in each of the eight classes (as many as sixty to a hut) sang enthusiastically to me and showed off their rudimentary English. In the staff room, the grizzled and djellabiya-clad chairman of the town council graciously ceded to the local Dinka chieftain (known as mowlana, or His Honour) when we asked embarrassing questions about Islam and girls; he was heard out gravely, and a lively discussion followed.

These were strong, resistant, but tolerant people who wanted to make better lives for themselves and their children; they were almost within earshot of the war, yet they had no time for the hatred and rivalries that engendered it and that the war in turn generated. And in this part of the Islamic world, at least, they knew little of Osama bin-Laden and cared even less; they were only effusively grateful that someone had travelled all the way from Khartoum to hear their petition for schoolrooms built of mud rather than straw.

When eighteen months later I paid a return visit to Meiram, I was pleased to see my faith had been justified. Now, thanks to Canadian support and the industry of the local community (who made the necessary bricks) the children had six airy, zinc-roofed, and solid-walled classrooms, the teachers a small room of their own. It was true that two classes still had to sit out under the trees, but it seemed to me no bad idea not to give absolutely everything that had been asked for. I was especially happy when the elders proudly informed me that of this year's first form of sixty-eight, forty were girls.

FOR THE CHRISTMAS HOLIDAYS of 2001, Jenny and I decided it might be interesting to actually travel on the railway that had served as an Ariadne's thread for my first two trips to the west. Our destination would be the fabled but rarely visited mountains of Jebel Marra, some way beyond Nyala and in the heart of the vast region known as Darfur ("Home of the Fur People"). The journey by train (and for a stretch by automobile) proved difficult, problem-laden, slow, and uncomfortable – notwithstanding the efforts of a very kind train engineer to accommodate us in his own berth. We decided we would probably try to fly back. Nevertheless, once we disembarked after a 30-hour ride to Nyala, our trek through the western mountains proved to be a rich and unforgettable experience.

Our first night camping out, at 2,500 metres up in the mountains north of Kass, was the coolest we had yet passed in Sudan; it seemed to be near freezing. The next morning was gloriously clear, and we were pleased to find ourselves camped in apparently deserted wild and hilly country, characterized by tussocky yellow grass and areas of apparently abandoned but ancient and well-engineered stone terracing. I switched on our small Thuraya satellite phone that doubled as a GPS but the latitude and longitude reading that it gave – although no doubt correct – did not jibe in any way with our outdated 1963 map: we would just have to follow our noses. After a breakfast of porridge and coffee, we set off up the nearest hill, with the aim of getting our bearings at the top. I clambered into a deep and very shady gully at one point to fill up our water bottles from a still, black pool that the sun could never reach; it was just as well I did, because from here on in, we were to find precious few sources of drinkable water.

We walked all day, not very sure of where we were but operating on the principle that if we headed for ever-higher ground we would surely eventually reach the rim of the huge circular crater that is the heart of the Jebel Marra range. We saw nobody, this despite the clear evidence – the terraces – that once this had been an intensively farmed area.

By late afternoon, hours longer than we had anticipated, we broached one final rise, and there before us lay a spectacle almost unimaginable in the bleak desertscapes that we had come to think of as the quintessential Sudan. Far below us, enclosed by precipitous and multicoloured rock walls, sparkled a great expanse of brilliant blue water, with a convenient pine-covered spur leading down from where we stood, right to the water's edge. This was the main "eye" of Jebel Marra, a lake rich in myths and legends, whose depths were reputed to be the home of evil itself. Partially hidden by a rock spur that reached out across the crater floor was the second eye

– its surface was at a lower level still, and it was thought to be bottomless. If the centre of a continent is the point furthest in all directions from the sea, then this crater is the very centre of Africa.

We spent the next two days camping on the crater floor. Although the twin lakes are the largest bodies of permanent, still water in Sudan, the larger is very brackish and polluted by cattle; the smaller is drinkable, but barely so. So we would periodically wade gingerly into the middle of a reed-surrounded tarn that fed the main lake, wait until the mud settled, then skim off the top centimetre of water for drinking. As the temperatures at this time of year were below freezing at night, this was not always an enjoyable experience.

We saw only one human being: a young goatherd who approached us and gingerly placed on the ground, wordlessly, a gourd full of fresh yogourt; we repaid him with two oranges and some rather stale bread, which he seemed to appreciate. In the still of the evening, large-eared foxes padded past quietly, while in the morning, as the mist cleared from the lake and the thinnest of ice melted away, we heard the raucous cries of baboons echoing around the crater; on dusty paths, tiny handprints showed that they had passed this way.

Continuing on our way, we used for guidance a rough hand-drawn map from a fifteen-year-old edition of *The Lonely Planet Guide to Egypt and Sudan*, which showed a path leading up the crater wall in the northwest: "Look for a large tree," said the note in the book, rather unhelpfully. Of course, it wasn't as easy as that. In several locations, we had to take off our packs, rock-climb up near-vertical stretches and then pass the packs up carefully; it looked as though it had been years since anyone had passed this way.

Once on the rim, the idea was to contour around to the west and then make our way down the outer slopes to Hoya Sochun, a set of year-round hot springs. But again, if there had ever been a path here, it was long gone. We could see where we wanted to go, but to our great frustration, every few hundred metres our way would be blocked by a deep, steep-sided gully, which challenged us either to go uphill again and around its head or to venture far downhill to a point at which it was sufficiently wide and less steep-sided to allow us to cross. Even more frustrating was the apparent utter absence of water sources. When we wearily reached the foot of one especially deep and dark ravine as night was coming on, it was with great relief that I found, buried deep in the undergrowth, a small dark puddle an inch or two deep: the water was the colour of tea, but we guzzled most of it on the spot and decided immediately to camp here, notwithstanding the narrowness of the path.

Next day we laboured onwards in the general direction of the northwest and stumbled on the hot springs almost by accident. The springs turned out to be warm rather than hot, and the water was scarcely less sulphurous than that of the lake, but the surrounding green meadow and palm trees were a relief from the otherwise brown and yellow landscapes of the crater slopes. As we followed the stream downwards, the greenery grew, and soon we were passing small but carefully tended orchards of oranges, tomato patches, and even plots of sugar cane: it was some of the most fertile land I had seen in Sudan.

Gradually we re-entered zones of habitation. The villages were tidily kept and composed of tightly grouped small clusters of round stone huts with conical straw rooves. At Dillesjur, there was a spectacular fifteen-metre waterfall; children played happily in the pools at its head while their mothers did their laundry. At Quaila, we coincided with market day, spent an hour or so wandering from stall to stall, and sat down to a glass of the usual oversweet tea. The local schoolteacher adopted us and, after half an hour or so of practicing his English, suggested that we camp in the school grounds, just on the edge of town. He showed us around his school – four bare rooms that one might have otherwise taken for stables – and brought more tea out to us as the sun set.

Next morning Jenny's feet were troubling her, so, an hour on our way, we flagged down some locals and, after much gesticulation and writing of numbers on each other's palms, agreed on a rental price for two donkeys – one for the packs, one for Jenny – plus the services of the donkeys' owner. We set off at a cracking pace, with which I was hard-pressed to keep up, and by noon we were at Neretiti, on the main road from Nyala to Zalingei, about 70 km northwest of where we had left it at Kass.

This road is actually the main road from Eastern to Western Africa. However, you wouldn't know it. By five, only three vehicles had passed us, two of them going the wrong way. The one going our way was a white Landrover belonging to Oxfam, which I thought would surely pick up two Westerners, especially as I worked for a government that was funding Oxfam in Sudan; but its occupants swept past without a sideways glance, and we went back to eating our oranges in the dust. The main action in Neretiti seemed to be the comings and goings of a "technical" – a 4x4

Toyota pickup with a heavy machine gun mounted in the rear, crammed with a dozen or so combat-ready soldiers. It roared round and round for minutes at a time, disappeared, then reappeared – this for hours on end.

At last, just as it was getting dark, a bus came along. We squeezed into the rearmost row of seats. Jenny's neighbour was a sleepy soldier with an AK-47 whose job was to get off at every stop and look alert; his rifle butt kept digging into her ribs, but she hesitated to startle him by waking him.

At 11 we were in the dark and quiet streets of Nyala. A small boy walked us to the equally dark and quiet Hotel Ferdous ("Paradise"), where after much knocking we roused a nightwatchman. He had us sign a visitors' book (the last guest had been our friend Angela from the United Nations, three months previously). The room was cockroach-infested and under the thin sheets there was a crinkly plastic coating covering the mattresses, but there was water in the shower. Next day we flew back to Khartoum.

The next time we saw Neretiti was on the TV news of the BBC World Service in August 2004. A breathless Emma Simpson was reporting that this was the epicentre of the worst humanitarian crisis in the world.

ABOUT A YEAR AFTER OUR VISIT to Jebel Marra, news had begun to drift back to Khartoum of what the government dismissed as isolated incidents of banditry in Darfur but which, from the scale of things, looked even then to be a lot more than that. Twenty or thirty people at a time were being killed in inter-ethnic raids, entire villages burned, many of them in Jebel Marra itself, and there was news too of police and Army stations being attacked, with a dozen people killed at a time. Darfur was placed completely off-limits once again by the authorities and, notwithstanding the efforts of Khartoum to play things down, started to grab more head-lines than the war in the South.

The region had been a semi-independent kingdom from 1596 until 1916. Charles Gordon appointed an Austrian adventurer who came to be known as Slatin Pasha to administer the place but who was forced to surrender to the Mahdi and spent twelve years as a prisoner before escaping to Cairo in 1895. After the defeat of the Mahdia at Omdurman in 1898, Sultan Ali Dinar was recognized by the British as the ruler of Darfur; he in turn revolted but was defeated in May 1916 after a now largely forgotten campaign that was overshadowed by the carnage at Verdun. The last Kings of Darfur were buried in the region's largest city, El Fasher, 1,500 km west of Khartoum, although the last one of all – Ali Dinar – has his grave near Wadai, in today's Chad, where the British ran him down in November 1916.

The flame of separatism flickered again in the 1960s, in the form of a secret underground organization known as the Soony, and more openly when the Darfur Development Front, led by Ahmed Ibrahim Diraige, came into being. In 1991 the SPLM/A attempted to spread the war into the west, under the leadership of Dawood Yahya Bolad, a former Fur activist who had defected from the Islamist government in Khartoum to the rebels. The enterprise was poorly planned and soon went wrong; Bolad was captured and executed. In 1997 a movement for the independence of Darfur briefly surfaced: a number of small villages in Jebel Marra were occupied before the movement disappeared from view again.

Partly in response to these events, the Khartoum Government, starting in the early 1990s, worked hard to develop a constituency in Darfur. To some extent this exercise was successful, but Khartoum abruptly lost that modest but growing support when its prime sponsor, Hassan al-Turabi, was ousted from government in 1999.

Since that time, government attempts to win the west seemed to have taken a much cruder and more violent form. There was some evidence to suggest that in a haphazard manner it had been arming Khartoum-loyal Arab militias (the Janjaweed group of tribes, including the Mahariya, Jalool, Hotiya, Saada, and Iraqat) to force off their own lands the historically more truculent and obstreperous native Fur people (who were also Muslim – religion per se was not at issue here) and to a lesser extent the Massaliet and Zaghawa. The Fur had in turn retaliated – including police and Army posts on their target list – and the result had been an escalating series of raids and counterraids in which hundreds had died. In one raid, on 23 April 2003, fifty-five Massaliet were killed.

As in Southern Sudan, disputes over water and grazing lands fed the flames. The Janjaweed recruited among nomadic herders of generally Arab origin whose herds were growing every year and whom desertification was forcing to migrate earlier and further all the time; while the Fur found support among sedentary farmers like themselves, whose land lay astride the old migration routes, whose families were also growing, and who could ill-afford to be generous to the nomads.

Out of this steadily escalating mayhem, the Darfur Liberation Front (DLF) was born (or reborn) some time early in 2003. In the early months of the year it seized and briefly held a number of towns of varying sizes in remote locations and generally led government troops on a merry chase around the region; in the midst of things it changed its name to the Sudan Liberation Movement (SLM). The DLF/SLM seemed to have its power base within the Fur and Zaghawa population: its political leader was thought to be one Abdel Wahid Mohamed Nur, a Fur lawyer, and its military leader a Chadian-born Zaghawa called Abdulla Abakr.

These events reached their first peak on Friday 25 April 2003, when the SLM launched concerted attacks on El Fasher and Nyala. El Fasher airport was seized and briefly held, a commercial airliner (Libyan) was destroyed on the ground as were two or three Hind helicopter gunships; the military headquarters was also briefly overrun, and it was thought that the rebels had made off with a considerable amount of munitions. In Nyala the central bank was attacked. By the government's own admission, the rebels used heavy artillery and numbered at least four hundred. The United Nations estimated that seventy-two persons were killed in these attacks, the majority on the government side.

Rebels also captured Major General Ibrahim Bushra, the regional Air Force commander for Darfur. A week after the main wave of attacks, a Sudan Liberation Movement "technical" was intercepted by government forces close to El Obeid – alarming because El Obeid was 1,000 km east of El Fasher and well within striking distance of the capital.

Government representatives were almost laughably uncoordinated in pointing the finger of responsibility. The SPLM/A was alternately blamed (by the wali of South Darfur) and exonerated (by Foreign Minister Mustafa and Professor Ibrahim Omer). The wali of North Darfur also blamed the SPLM/A (saying it had lent a plane to the rebels' operation) but named the military brains behind it as Abdulla Abakr. The Minister of Foreign Affairs saw an Eritrean hand in things, later the Kenyans and Chadians, while others frothed about "Zionist-American conspiracies." The accusation of Chadian involvement was fuelled partly by the fact that Chadian President Idriss Debby was a Zaghawa, born on the Sudanese border at Tina.

Interestingly, government spokespersons largely ignored the claims of the London-based Justice and Equality Movement (JEM) to have been responsible for the whole affair. The idea that this might be an exclusively Sudanese operation, albeit managed from abroad, was clearly distasteful to Khartoum.

Justice and Equality was led by Dr Khalil Ibrahim, an erstwhile associate of Hassan al-Turabi, although the initial common wisdom was that they'd had a major falling out some time earlier. The Movement's charter, which was available on the web, seemed to be national in scope, leading some to suggest that Justice and Equality had cashed in on the Darfur Liberation Front after the fact, first persuading it to go national (hence the midstream name change to SLM), then – encouraged by the SLM's relative success – starting to recruit its own army in parallel to the SLM.

By 2004, to cut a long story short, there appeared to be two rebel armies – SLM and JEM – functioning in Darfur. In very crude terms, the JEM seemed to be national in scope, with a moderate Islamist ideology, while the SLM was more regionally focused and explicitly secular. Poor old Turabi, just released after nearly three years under house arrest, was detained once more, this time under suspicion of links to Justice and Equality.

In judging the seriousness of the initial uprising, observers noted that the attacks on El Fasher and Nyala displayed an impressive degree of resources, planning, and audacity; the rebels appeared to have gotten the best of things, too. What the rebels had going for them was intimate knowledge of the unique and rugged terrain of Darfur (and of Jebel Marra in particular), a large and disgruntled population who perceived that Khartoum had never done anything of great significance for them, recent savage law enforcement policies by the government that had served not to quell ill-feeling but to inflame it, and an evidently well-organized diaspora. Fur mediators who had met with the SLM's leaders in Jebel Marra in March 2003 reported that the movement consisted of up to eight thousand men, including a considerable number of disaffected former government officers with good military training.

All this looked – understandably – worrying to the government. And worrying to not just the usual hawks and hardliners but also the pragmatists who one year earlier had overcome the odds and persuaded their skeptical partners in government to do the unthinkable and concede self-determination for South Sudan. For now the warnings of the hawks – allow self-determination for one group and everyone will want it – looked to be coming true; already there was talk that Red Sea Hills (where the objective poverty and marginalization were worse than anywhere in all of Sudan) might be next.

PRIOR TO THE UPRISING IN THE WEST, I had made a number of visits to El Fasher. Sudan Airways left both Khartoum and El Fasher at apparently random times on random days, but possibly twice a week and usually in their venerable Russian-crewed Yak 42; appropriately, there were lengthy prayers of thanksgiving in the cabin before every takeoff and after every landing ("Hamdullillah" – *Thanks be to God* – was a great catch-all phrase much heard on this airline). The alternative to the Yak was seven days across the desert from Omdurman, in an open-sided truck-cum-bus, with no oasis for the last three days.

The wali was invariably stoical when I met him. A former Minister of Defense, Ibrahim Suleiman was a contemporary of the president at officer training school and still held the rank of lieutenant general; he told me he thrived on challenges but missed the unquestioning loyalty he commanded in the Army: "The trouble with politics," he said, "is that you have to listen to everyone and you have to explain everything ..."

His principal concern on my first visit in August 2001 was not the crisis of the famine and drought that had loomed two months earlier. Rather, he was concerned at the almost total lack of electricity in the state capital. In a half-ruined shed on the edge of town that he took me to see there were in fact no less than nine diesel generators of one to two kilowatts apiece. This should normally have been sufficient for this town of 130,000, but only two were running – and at less than half their capacity. The causes were multiple, including US sanctions on the purchase of spares, but the bottom line was that there had never been any forethought applied to the question of the city's power supply (for example, in choosing a uniform brand of generator); corruption had accounted for most of the funding sent from Khartoum to remedy the situation over the years; and Khartoum was anyway sending the states virtually nothing these days, arguing that, if they were to have greater responsibilities and more programs (which not all of them wanted, it must be said), they must raise the necessary revenue. As the wali gloomily pointed out: how do you raise revenue in a place like this, which had been in a state of emergency for the past six months? In this respect, North Darfur resembled most states away from the centre of the country: it was crumbling.

Neither the wali nor his guests, of course, actually suffered personally from the more general problems that afflicted El Fasher. The Official Residence, which adjoined the ancient cemetery of the Sultans, had a beautiful shady and bougainvillea-full garden in which hornbills and egrets roamed romantically and where servants hastened through the shadows to fulfil the elite's every whim. One of the two functioning generators was dedicated solely to cooling the rooms of the Residence and diplomatic guest house. Life here was relaxed and, one suspected, not much changed from the 1930s, when Wilfred Thesiger and the legendary District Commissioner Mr Moore ran Darfur on behalf of the British Colonial Service. Indeed, I was so lulled into thinking myself a few generations back that I was not in the least surprised when the courtly white-robed Education Minister, following evening prayers and a cool grapefruit juice on the lawn one day, asked me earnestly if I had had the pleasure of meeting Mr Moore. It took me a moment to realize that, if alive, he must be around 110.

Close by was the home of the legendary Ali Dinar himself, last of the Sultans. It was now a dusty museum with motley artefacts in cracked glass cases; although two or three quiet and attentive staff were on duty, I had the impression that visitors were exceedingly rare. Only a faded but once magnificently painted and carved wooden ceiling in the Sultan's throne room gave a tantalizing hint of past splendours and military glory. Thesiger, who first arrived here in 1935 and found el Fasher "an attractive place," described Ali Dinar's palace even then as "retaining an atmosphere of the past"; at the time, Thesiger noted drily, it was occupied by one Major R.S. Audas, veterinary surgeon.

OUTSIDE THE WALLS OF THE RESIDENCE, things were in darkness after sunset. And there was a hint of the horrors to come in Jebel Marra. For some months, the wali admitted, large gangs of "bandits" – with hindsight, they were probably the precursors of the Darfur Liberation Front, Sudan Liberation Movement, and Justice and Equality Movement – had been ransacking much of North, South, and Western Darfur, armed not only with Kalashnikovs (which went for the price of two sheep hereabouts) but with machine guns and rocket-propelled grenades. Their weaponry, he admitted freely, was the heritage of years of random arming by the government of militias to defend one village against another, and there was also much traffic over the unpoliced border with Chad. Mostly, said the wali, these "bandits" seemed to serve as mercenaries for any village or ethnic subgroup that had a longstanding feud with another, typically over land or water resources (disputes exacerbated by the only recently ended drought), but they also liked to attack vehicles on the road south to Nyala, meaning that the Army often had to arrange for escorts and convoys. While at this time the wali did not detect any great degree of organization behind the violence, the situation was sufficiently serious for him to have made use of his military connections and have two Hind gunships stationed at El Fasher. They were loading ordnance in front of the passenger terminal when I arrived and the nose gunner of one waved cheerily at me.

Of the natural hazards hereabouts, drought was of course the perennial and most dangerous one. On one visit, an hour south of El Fasher on the way to look at a possible development project, Canada Fund coordinator Salah and I passed a large village where I noticed dozens of oil drums and other large containers by the edge of the road. The village had no well, and the containers were there so that when it rained (something that might happen only three or four times in a year) the entire village could turn out and bail water from potholes in the road into the oil drums. Puddles were the only close source of water for this community of one thousand or more.

As luck would have it, at the traditional market village of Tabbit we ran into a traffic jam of trucks and ludicrously laden buses. The reason soon became evident: the track ended in a sandy cliff, to continue atop a similar cliff one hundred metres on. In between was a fast-running torrent of muddy water at least two metres deep, the result of heavy overnight rains in the mountains. After three hours' wait, one truck attempted a dash across but bogged in deep water and mud almost immediately. A train of camels was eventually persuaded to swim across, but no donkey would even put his hoof in. It was a further two hours before the water had receded sufficiently for us to find a place shallow enough to cross, and even then the water was over the floorboards. At our destination, the village of Sheng el-Tobar, we found the entire community was cut off; we had to wade waist deep (with a cheerful gang of teenage boys testing the depth for us) for nearly half an hour before reaching the island on which the village now stands. If it's not a drought, it's a flood.

Like in Kandua, the Southern war in these rural parts seemed distant. Forced recruitment was not a problem: only in El Fasher might a young man be asked for his identity card and bundled off to a training camp. Given the perennially desperate economic straits in which North Darfur found itself, many volunteered: the Army offered a relatively lucrative career opportunity. If the young man in question was killed, his family would receive a pension up until what would have been his sixtieth birthday.

Government was hardly present at all. But the state paid the basic salary of the semi-trained paramedic who ran the clinic we hoped to be supporting in Sheng el-Tobar. He served a population of thirty thousand from his smelly, bat-infested two-room hut in the middle of the village, seeing thirty to forty patients a day. By far the most common complaint was malaria, which afflicted almost all of the population at some time of the year, especially during the rains. He had a small cupboard with two shelves of assorted drugs. There were no vaccines, for there was no means of keeping a fridge going. There was a primary school but so few teachers that classes numbered up to one hundred pupils, very few with the means of buying exercise books, let alone textbooks.

Yet there was enormous resilience – and of course the hospitality for which the Sudanese are renowned. With the sun setting and the wali no doubt fretting back in El Fasher (for we had told him we would be back at three), we were taken to the straw tukul of the village sheikh and, while the men went about their prayers, treated to a traditional feast of fuul (beans), kibda (liver), mutton, and other delicacies of unquestioned origin. The only damper on things was the prospect of the wade back to the road through what would likely now be ankle-deep mud rather than waist-deep water.

When the homegrown rebel movements burst on the scene in early 2003, my friend the wali, who was no fool, seemed to sense their strength and the at least partial justness of their cause; he argued hard with Khartoum for a policy of firmness tempered by negotiation and discussion. But his old military schoolmate, President Bashir, would have none of it: the response was to be exclusively military. The wali was overruled, and in mid-May 2003 he was summarily fired.

THE FURTHEST POINT WEST IN SUDAN is the low desert town of El Geneina, on the banks of a generally dry wadi a few kilometres from the Chad border. There's not normally much reason to visit here, but in late 2002 El Geneina was selected by the Federal Ministry of Health as the launch location for Sudan's eleventh round of National Immunization Days, or NIDs as they are known in the humanitarian world.

NIDs had been held in Sudan once or twice a year since 1996. The principal target was the eradication of polio, which necessitated constant and hopefully ever further-reaching waves of immunization of under fives, coupled with intensive surveillance, until a clean sheet was recorded for three successive years; at that point Sudan (which was by 2002 one of only seven remaining countries where the virus was found) would be declared polio-free.

The principal challenge in Sudan was accessing out-of-the-way and difficult locations. In 2001 Kadugli, in the Nuba Mountains, was chosen for the NIDs launch because of its symbolic value: a ceasefire had just been negotiated there. In 2002 it was El Geneina's turn, partly due to the difficulty previous campaigns had found in accessing the mountains of Jebel Marra and partly because a concerted attempt was being made this year to coordinate immunization in Sudan with a similar campaign in Chad.

For many years Canada had supported the worldwide campaign to get rid of polio, with cash, vaccine, and, more lately, with supplemental vitamin A immunization. Accordingly and along with the ambassadors of Japan and Holland (other key donor governments) and Rotary International (a nongovernmental sponsor) I was invited to accompany the minister and a posse of journalists to the launch ceremonies. It was a three-hour flight all the way across Sudan from Khartoum to El Geneina.

The most striking aspect of El Geneina's airport, which had been built during the Second World War, was – as at so many Sudanese airfields – a crashed aircraft, in this case a large Aeroflot Antonov 12 that had met its comeuppance when delivering relief supplies here in the catastrophic 1989 famine. Off the airstrip, dozens of robed nomads on horseback, waving their whips and AKs and shouting "Allahu Akhbar," greeted us and escorted our cavalcade of Toyota Landcruisers into town. For a brief moment I had thought they might actually be hostile – the natives had been notoriously restless for weeks here and mounted gunmen had killed twenty police at El Geneina only a week previously – but the growing friendly crowds by the roadside reassured us; this was clearly the biggest thing to happen at El Geneina since the famine.

In the main square – a vast expanse of soft sand surrounded by one-storey buildings and spotted with an occasional thorn tree – a great tent of red carpeting on a steel framework had been set up, as is customary, and we were ushered into armchairs in the front row, there to be plied for the next two hours with peanuts, dates, boiled sweets, and Pepsis. There were the usual speeches on a central platform and a few songs by the local children's choir. There were many plaudits for Canada, many more *Allahu Akhbars*, and much waving of walking sticks in the air to make points. Impressively, the Japanese ambassador made a speech in Arabic, which was greeted with wild applause; I was told his accent put the locals to shame. At the end we were presented with gaudy green sashes and walking sticks, to the strains of "Auld Lang Syne" on a tinny electric organ.

But what caught my eye throughout the ceremonies were the camels. This part of Sudan prided itself on breeding the finest camels in the world, and throughout recorded history El Geneina has been the approximate start location of an annual trek across the central Sahara – the Forty Day Road – to Aswan, in Southern Egypt, where half the caravan (which might consist of several thousand animals) is sold.

Thirty or more haughty camels had been assembled and formed an outside ring for the thousands of townspeople who had assembled. As they looked on patiently and serenely, it was not hard to imagine that they were actually listening to the speeches; they seemed faintly amused by it all. Most impressively, a half dozen had been kitted out with the full howdahs in which the nomad women are jealously hidden away for the great trans-Saharan treks. These were great cubical contraptions constructed of baskets, pots, blankets, and rugs, all brightly coloured in red, orange, or yellow, inside which the lady might be glimpsed with her equally colourful tobe spread out before her and flowing onto the camel's neck. The camel itself was bedecked with a set of three plumes over its head, and swinging curtains of shells that hung down 50 cm on either side of its face. As the camels were led around (it was impossible for the nomad women to exert any control), the howdahs, the plumes, and the curtains of shells all swung and swayed gracefully; the effect was entrancing.

After the speeches, we trailed the minister to three nearby houses where model families had been assembled with their children. Everyone took a turn at administering the requisite two drops of vaccine, but I made a near-disastrous faux pas when I was given a small red vitamin A capsule to deliver. I popped it into the nearest young mouth, but there were immediate cries of horror: I should have actually squeezed it. Some quick finger work was necessary to save the day.

After the festivities the wali took us on a lightning tour of El Geneina's sights, which consisted of a new Bailey bridge over the (dry) wadi, a generating station that, so we were told, delivered electricity fifteen hours a day (better than Khartoum, some of us grumbled), and a small house on a hill that was once the property of a local Sultan who had defeated an invasion by the French. Then it was off to lunch with the wali. Although the three foreign women on our delegation were all senior United Nations

Children's Fund staff, they were politely but firmly instructed that they "would enjoy it more" and "allow the men to rest" if they ate separately. It was noted that the authorities of El Geneina could do with a gender awareness workshop.

On the way home, we were presented with many more gifts. I collected an entire case of Cussons' Imperial Leather Soap, some faux Brut for Men, an equally faux tin of "T. Wood" Eau de Toilette, and some lemon spray of indeterminate purpose. The journalists were more than happy: it seemed El Geneina's main claim to fame, as far as most Sudanese were concerned, was as a source of contraband toiletries from Chad.

12

THE EAST

JENNY AND I SPENT MOST of an afternoon and all one evening rummaging around the house for a mislaid travel permit; the plan had been to spend the long Eid (post-Haj holiday) of 2003 at Dinder National Park, located on Sudan/Ethiopia border. But the paper was nowhere to be found. Should we hope for the best and seek to bluff our way through the many checkpoints we were sure to encounter on the 400 km drive southeast, or should we play safe and sit quietly doing nothing for the best part of a week in closed-down Khartoum? I made numerous photocopies of our diplomatic passes, we dug out our passports, and I drew up a worthless but impressive-looking note on embassy letterhead informing the Foreign Ministry of our planned travel (no lie, but anyone who could read English would soon realize that what mattered was the ministry's response, not our request).

All went well as far as Wad Medani, four hours south. Here we got lost and spent half an hour bumping across ploughed fields in the embassy

Pajero in search of the road onwards to Sennar. At one point, we drove past an eerie lineup of abandoned and ancient crop-dusting biplanes, all of whose tires were irremediably flat. But soon we were back on the dangerously potholed road to Sennar, much of it running parallel to, on the right hand side, a monumental canal. As the sun set, villagers squatted on their heels in the shadow of its eastern dyke, to watch their mud and straw villages turn golden in the twilight. We were now in the heart of the Gezira Scheme, for decades the largest irrigated agriculture project in the world and a showpiece of the British Empire. When established, Gezira was not just about agriculture: it included new social organizations, special agricultural institutions, high-minded film and discussion groups, and even a special newspaper, all in a novel arrangement combining public (the Government Irrigation Department) and private enterprise (two British companies).

Gezira reached peak productivity in the final years of the British colonial era when, with its three million acres of hitherto sterile land now made arable thanks to a web of canals leading out from the Sennar dam, Sudanese cotton became known as the finest in the world. But Gezira has been in decline ever since. Only at Kenana, 200 km west, where the original canals and dykes have been upgraded and rebuilt with Saudi and Kuwaiti money and tens of square kilometres of sugar cane planted, are the waters of the Nile still harvested to good effect: Kenana Gold sugar is exported all over the region.

At Sennar, it did not take us long to locate the only hotel in town: three storeys at the top of a decrepit office building on one of the dirt- and litter-strewn central streets; outside was an illuminated red sign indicating (in Western script) that this was the Al Raeba Tourist Hotel. Before we could check in, the young man who seemed to be minding the front desk ushered us out again and back into the vehicle. We must first visit the muktub (office); the police, I presumed.

In an unmarked villa ten minutes' drive away, a man was eating goat meat straight off the surface of a metal desk in a darkened room; an Egyptian soap opera was playing on a small TV. He gestured us to sit down and attempted to wipe the desk clean with an old plastic bag. Sundry men in sunglasses and plainclothes looked in and out, and eventually a dog-eared exercise book was found. We were asked in turn for our diplomatic passes and passports. These were scrutinized carefully and from all angles and passed around. Eventually, my name was inscribed in the book as *Charge* (one of the lines on my diplomatic pass, describing my functions), while Jenny was entered simply as *Wife*. Our explanation that we were on our way to see the "hiwarna" (animals) at Dinder provoked knowing nods, but then everyone seemed at a loss. We were offered a stainless steel mug full of iced water, and then the interview was abruptly over. I figured that, if we had got this far without a travel permit, we should succeed in making it all the way.

Back at the hotel, we walked up an unlit concrete stairwell for four floors, then reached a kind of steel cage blocking the way. Our boy unlocked the cage and took us up a further two floors; our room was numbered, mystifyingly, 405. There was a small TV on which the moderately intriguing Egyptian soap had now been replaced by a static talk show in which six men in Western clothing, presided over by a stately and tall figure in a djellabiya and headdress, sat in deep couches and passed a microphone from one to the other, all appearing to agree on everything. This was prime-time TV in Sudan. There was an adjoining shower/bathroom, with the inevitable clogged stand-up toilet and with two used razor blades and a clump of black beard hair on the floor, which seemed to be sprinkled with fresh cement powder (bare footprints showed clearly).

Down in the souq, we ate beans at a rickety blue steel table in the middle of the street; the Pepsi came not in a bottle but (flat) directly in a green plastic mug. A generator hummed, flies buzzed, and unhealthy looking dogs nosed around at our ankles.

Next morning we were so glad to get out of Sennar that it was a full hour before we noticed – from the angle of the sun – that we were heading west (and likely already halfway to Kosti), instead of south. The good news was that we seemed to be going through each and every road block without the slightest problem, although the police at Sennar seemed bemused to see us back so soon. Outside Sinja we passed a crowd of more than a thousand men in their finest and whitest djellabiyas, all lined up to face Mecca and pray together on this especially holy day. No-one seemed the slightest perturbed as we rather uneasily wove our way through the throng, having to honk a couple of times so as not to hit people. As we emerged from the crowd and started to accelerate again, I noticed that there were about a dozen women in a line some fifty metres behind the main group; unisex praying was clearly not the done thing here.

Following a friend's handwritten instructions, just south of Sinja and its southern roadblock, we turned left and bounced due east for a few kilometres. Things did not look promising, but all of a sudden we were at the approach to a modern and vaulting bridge over the Blue Nile, newly tarmacked and adorned with high stainless-steel lights. At the western end a man sat in a booth adorned with Chinese writing; he waved us on without even looking up. I couldn't make it out: the bridge seemed to have been accidentally teleported from some bustling Chinese city and dropped here, in the most unlikely of spots, going nowhere from nowhere.

On the eastern side of the Blue Nile, we zigzagged across a strange landscape of stubble fields, interrupted by disused drainage ditches, an evidently abandoned railway line, and dirt tracks that ran dead straight for five or ten kilometres then inexplicably turned sharp left or right. It was only by dint of frequent stops, much asking, and sign language that we finally reached Dinder village. At the park headquarters, which doubled as a police station, a man in a camouflage blue uniform was picking his teeth with one hand, nursing an automatic rifle with another, and keeping a wary eye on some shifty looking prisoners in a cage; the prisoners grinned at us. We pulled out letters of introduction (or at least, that is what we hoped they were, for they were in handwritten Arabic), and these seemed to have an effect. We were ushered into an office and, while we watched with some interest Osama bin-Laden's latest taped message being read out on Al Jazeera TV, a man filled out reams of forms on our behalf and eventually asked for about USD $60.

Our fee covered the company of one of the policemen: a friendly seeming fellow called Ibrahim who happily clambered into the Pajero front seat, letting his automatic rifle fall with a clatter onto the floor, and promptly went to sleep. Jenny nudged him to put on his seatbelt, but he was mystified by this and, after wrestling with its inertia mechanism for some minutes, he gave up. For the next four hours, our conversation consisted of "yameen," "tawaali," and "shimal" (*right, straight on,* and *left*) as we bounced on southwards, over kilometre after kilometre of more stubble and black cotton soil. At about three, we finally rolled into the small camp settlement of Galegu, on the banks of the (currently dry) Dinder River.

DINDER HAD A PECULIAR CHARM. We were told that elephants wandered into the wooded scrubland from Ethiopia in the wet season. About ten years ago there had been giraffes in the area, but, no doubt deterred by poachers, they had also gone to Ethiopia, never to be seen

Tourist quarters at Galegu, Dinder National Park

again. There were lions in abundance (we would hear them roaring at the moon), cheetahs, several species of antelope (including the rare red-fronted gazelle and the roan antelope), large herds of ostriches, three or four species of monkeys, baboons in packs numbering a hundred or more, guinea fowl, warthogs, and buffalo.

Most of these we saw in three days of leisurely drives around a complicated network of tracks that radiated out from Galegu; Ibrahim was replaced by Ali, whom we hoped might have a little more English, but it was not to be. He had a knack for spotting animals but was not forthcoming when we asked for the names of some of the more unusual species, even in Arabic. Several times we stopped at police outposts meant to deter poachers: Ali would catch up on the news with his friends while we poked around in the bush. At the large Amir waterhole where guinea fowl teemed in thousands, we found a series of sticks joined together with strong black twine; these were evidently traps, but we hadn't the heart to denounce the police; they seemed to be living in very rigorous conditions, and an occasional guinea fowl into the cooking pot would not lead to the extinction of the species.

The United Nations Development Programme was financing a project to encourage ecotourism and simultaneously provide men from villages adjoining the park with livelihoods other than poaching. It seemed like a good idea, but the scheme had – typically – become bogged down in Sudanese bureaucracy; for the first eighteen months of the project's duration, the security authorities had declared Dinder off limits to all foreign visitors, which had prevented not only visits from tourists but also from the United Nations staffers charged with running things. Some of the most obvious steps that one might expect of an ecotourism project had not been taken: there was no checklist of game to be had, and no-one to tell you how to distinguish one antelope from another; all the way from Khartoum, there wasn't a single sign to the park. I wasn't that surprised to see from the visitors' book that we were only the third group of foreigners to visit in the last nine months.

Some ugly-looking round concrete structures were under construction – for the tourists, we were told. We were very happy to be in the far simpler and cheaper straw compounds that served as rooms in the interim. We slept in the open on string beds, listening to the animals into the night, and showered with a jerry-rigged system in one corner. We brought and cooked our own food. Although there were two technicals parked outside in the compound, the main danger seemed to be aggressive baboons: we took the precaution of locking our food into the car when we weren't around.

On the way back, we again got lost four or five times and also suffered two punctures in the space of thirty minutes. Fortunately, almost every roadside settlement in Sudan has a shack with a tire stuck vertically in the sand outside: the sign of a tire repair shop. Having a puncture repaired cost about USD $2 (although if you need to get a new inner tube you will likely end up with some specimen of the wrong dimensions that may only last long enough get you to the next repair shop).

These delays meant we were forced to do what we had sworn not to: drive the last stretch of the busy Port Sudan to Khartoum road in the dark. A good 50 percent of the trucks we followed were carrying charcoal or grain – piled up to a frightening height that led to dramatic capsizes on windy days – and these trucks seemed to obey some law that exempted them from carrying any form of illumination. Every 10 or 20 km, there was spectacular wreckage on one side of the road or the other, but this deterred no-one from overtaking in the most foolhardy situations and seemed to faze neither goats nor humans as they wandered casually into this stream of death on wheels. It was with great relief that we hit the congestion of Southern Khartoum at about 9:00 p.m.: here, at least, the traffic was so heavy that cars and trucks could rarely reach dangerous speeds.

As we unpacked the Pajero, something dark on the floor behind the front passenger seat caught my attention. I put my finger down to touch it and an astounding pain shot up through my right arm; for a moment I thought I had been electrocuted. It was a scorpion, and it was good six hours before the pain receded sufficiently for me to sleep.

SOON AFTER ARRIVING IN SUDAN, I learned that, when taxi drivers in Khartoum or development workers in Sudanese organizations talked excitedly of "The Canadian Project," they were often not referring to Talisman's controversial oil operations but to the large experimental farm that was established in the eastern state of Gedaref (the breadbasket of Sudan) with a major contribution – CDN $23.14 million – from the Canadian International Development Agency in the 1980s.

The general objectives for the project, which were more fully stated in a Memorandum of Understanding signed in October 1980, were: "to establish the economic viability of medium and large-scale mechanized farming in Sudan; to develop improved agronomic practices; and to effect a transfer of technology to farmers in the Sudanese private sector." To this end, a model farm was established near Sim-Sim ("Sesame") Mountain, 130 km south of the city of Gedaref proper. The site was chosen because Gedaref was the state whose conditions best lent themselves to large-scale mechanized agriculture of the kind practiced in the Canadian prairies: enormous extensions of flat, fertile land with a paucity of population (on account of the lack of groundwater). One version had it that Canadian farmers became interested in the area as early as the 1940s, when there were Canadians serving with the British Army in Sudan.

We reached Sim-Sim after five hours of driving on blacktop from Khartoum and a further abominable five hours of bouncing cross-country in the Pajero, an experience only mitigated by a dramatic prairies-style

Tea break en route to the Sim-Sim agricultural project; centre right is Jake Hamm, Canadian veteran of the Sim-Sim project

blazing sunset, *The Phantom of the Opera* on the tape deck, and engaging encounters with the local inhabitants, who did not often see diplomatic plates in these parts.

The farm was really a small village – complete with prefabricated houses originally imported for Canadians; the walls were still adorned with calendar pictures of icebergs, polar bears, and now-retired National Hockey League stars – at the centre of ten thousand hectares of prime agricultural land. There was a staff of about fifty, the majority of whom had been with the project since its inception. The farm was home to the largest agricultural machinery workshop in the state (i.e., one of the largest in Sudan). Sim-Sim experimented with various techniques for growing, fertilizing, and harvesting sorghum, sesame, sunflower, and cotton. It developed custom machinery for this purpose, using Canadian equipment as models, and tested it out. It conducted weed-control research and developed new strains of seed; it also had a mandate to undertake field days and other outreach activities.

Was it actually useful, or just another ill-conceived development project to foist Western agricultural techniques on a country where they were totally unsuitable? Barely a week earlier I had visited El Obeid and seen the streamlined and highly effective operation by which the World Food Programme imported to Sudan hundreds of thousands of tons of grain, shipped it around the country, air-dropping it in some of the most needy areas – and then I saw the fields around Sim-Sim: this country had the capacity to be self-sufficient in grain – and indeed to be a regional exporter – and Sim-Sim, even years after the Canadian contribution had dried up, still looked well placed to lead the charge, if given half a chance.

Sim-Sim had already made important contributions: the development of four new strains of sorghum, and four of sesame; the production and national distribution of improved seeds; extensive research on weed control and the development of a custom-designed cultiplanter. A much less impressive job had been done when it came to outreach and education. What had happened was that with an ever-more pressing financial situation, these areas – which produced no immediate cash benefit – had been the first to be sacrificed. Sim-Sim no longer published, and it had been some time since a field day had been held.

Superficially, the principal constraints on the farm at this time were that most of the heavy equipment with which it had been fitted out in the early 1980s was now at the very end of its useful life, that there was no money for fertilizer, and that the road was in terrible condition, which increased transportation costs and in turn cut into the profit margins of Sim-Sim's commercial production. These symptoms masked an underlying sickness – why was it that Sim-Sim had been unable to generate the funds projected by Canada early on, which would have allowed it to replace its equipment in good time and to keep the road well-maintained?

An expert needed to look at the situation. Some of the questions to be looked at would be the regional, national, and international context – what effect had international grain prices and the domestic tax regime had on the viability of Sim-Sim? – and the two disastrous floods Sim-Sim had suffered in the past ten years – did this mean Sim-Sim was simply in the wrong place, or could measures be taken to mitigate the effects of such floods? Was it fair that the government had now withdrawn all state subsidies for Sim-Sim? Could a research institute not reasonably expect a degree of external support?

Meanwhile, the farm was just keeping its head above water. The loyalty of the past and present Sim-Sim employees was remarkable and moving. In Khartoum they maintained a kind of old boys' network; anyone who was anyone in agriculture in Sudan, from the minister on downwards, knew of Sim-Sim or had done research there, and they often met over a coffee to yack about the old times. At the project itself, mechanics and labourers who had been with Sim-Sim from the start did miracles in maintaining twenty-year-old equipment that in Canada would long ago have been consigned to the junk heap; they survived without complaining about wages that were sometimes paid months late.

It couldn't last this way much longer. This project needed to be galvanized – not necessarily with a large cash infusion, but with some objective, even hard advice as to future directions. It seemed to me that at the very least the Canadian investment of more than CDN $20 million merited, nearly twenty years on, an evaluation of some sort. But I couldn't interest anyone in Ottawa – the most I ever got was the dismissive response, "Don't you know that those megaprojects are out of fashion these days?" And while Sim-Sim, which had the potential to revitalize the domestic grain industry languished, the international aid community continued to spend millions on dropping donated grain onto the country from the rear doors of chartered Hercules aircraft.

PAST GEDAREF, THE EASTBOUND ROAD gradually starts to head north. It passes through Kassala – briefly but spectacularly captured by the SPLA in late 2000 – then climbs up into the rocky and barren Red Sea Hills. Just before Sinkat, there is a turn off to the right, to Arkoweit.

A gradually deteriorating metalled road heads across an empty plain. There's an abandoned tarmac airstrip, with eight or ten high horseshoe-shaped walls flanking it – presumably shelters behind which aircraft could hide from the often strong northerly winds. There are concrete pads that evidently once served as the floors of quite a large community of houses or huts. Later, when I mentioned this to a friend in Khartoum, he smiled and said: "Oh yes, there used to be a Palestinian training camp there until two or three years ago. But when the Americans put the heat on, they closed the whole place up and went away ..."

In the middle of nowhere, the road passes through a mock-mediaeval archway in stone and then starts to wind its way deep into the barren mountains; there is nobody to be seen. After twenty minutes, the road reaches the top of a rise: atop outcrops in a huge rocky bowl, are a dozen or so heavy-looking and squat buildings in grey stone, the only splash of colour their pale green shutters – firmly closed – and, on one hilltop in the centre, what appears to be a small white-painted shrine.

This is Sudan's answer to Simla or Ooty in India, or the Cameron Highlands in Malaysia: a hill station built by the British circa 1951, in the dying days of the colony, intended initially as an escape from the sweltering heat of Port Sudan a thousand metres lower down, then briefly taken over as a presidential retreat. As recently as three years ago, I knew, you could still stay at the main guest house; although the entire valley now seemed deserted. I wondered if the guest house was still open.

We approached via a rutted dual carriageway whose surface had washed away a decade or so ago but which evidently had once been bordered by flower beds and lit at night by fluorescent lights on tall steel posts. The building was boarded up; in the car park there were a couple of rusting wrecks, their wheels long ago removed.

We located a somnolent guard on the sunny side of the building. "Everything is closed," he said superfluously, and indeed as we peered in we could see no signs that anyone had stayed here recently; in what was evidently once the restaurant, tables, and chairs were piled up under dust sheets. It was cool in the shade, and a brisk wind was blowing; here and there, a shutter banged. It was all rather spooky and reminded me of the old and abandoned mining towns of the Mojave Desert. But the guard said that only that afternoon a group of Korean or Japanese businessmen had been here, to see whether Arkoweit was worth reviving as a resort.

The hexagonal white-painted building we had spotted on one hilltop was indeed a shrine: the grave of revered Mahdist chieftain Osman Digna, who came from these parts. For a decade or more at the end of the nineteenth century, in the period known as the Mahdia, he was a thorn in the flesh of the British: a carved stone inside the building recorded in Arabic no less than fourteen battles in which he fought. But he was finally captured in this remote fastness by Kitchener's men and transported as a prisoner to distant Wadi Halfa, where he languished until he died there in the 1920s.

I wasn't sure if non-Muslims were really supposed to be here, so it was with trepidation that we lifted aside the red curtains that enclosed a rectangular space in the middle of the building: they were hiding only the simplest of stone monuments, with no inscription. Salah, my companion on this day, reminisced about what his grandparents used to say about the period when the Mahdi ruled and Osman Digna held eastern Sudan in thrall; whenever the children were running riot, making a racket and in need of discipline, Grandpa would throw his hands up in mock despair and cry out: "It's like the Mahdia ... just be quiet, will you!"

AFTER SINKAT AND EL GEBEIT, the road parts company from the railway and starts to work its way down to the coast, through a series of rocky defiles. At every curve there is testimony to the poor brakes of the many trucks that ply this road: wrecked and burned out oil tankers, concertinaed cars, pools of oil in the dry stream beds. Then the road emerges onto the hot coastal plain. Scattered among the scrubby bushes are the tents of the nomadic Rashayda clans that roam up and down the coast, from Egypt to Eritrea, searching constantly for water and grazing for the goats and camels. The road reaches the sea at Suakin.

Salah and I stopped here one day for mid-morning fattur. Sitting on uncomfortable metal chairs at a roadside stall as they brought us beans and an omelette, we watched a truck loading up with passengers. The young men all wore the distinctive natty black waistcoats of the Beja people over their white djellabiyas, and a few even carried ancient-looking swords in leather scabbards that broadened just before the tip. A novel variation of the Indian-made Khartoum tuk-tuks (rickshaws) passed by: the hooded body of a motorized tuk-tuk on top of a donkey-pulled cart.

Walking down towards the sea from our breakfast stop, we passed what I recognized as the original of the fortified gateway that had marked the entrance into the Arkoweit estate: two squat and solid rock-built towers, joined by an archway, built by the British in the late nineteenth century. A little further, there was another less imposing wooden gateway, where a little old man came out and sold us tickets, five dollars for foreigners, a few cents for locals: "Welcome to old Suakin," he grinned.

Suakin: an ancient port that lies at the exact point where the seasonal southerly winds give out – and was thus the furthest point up the Red Sea that the sailing dhows of old could comfortably reach. Its name has been found on inscriptions dating back to the tenth century BC; this was reputedly used as a port by Ramses. But it was after the seventh century AD that Suakin truly rose to prominence, with the spread of Islam throughout Northern Africa, and the consequent need of pilgrims from the entire continent to reach Mecca, only 300 km north and across the Red Sea. First rest houses were set up on the small circular island at the centre of Suakin's perfect protected harbour, then merchants came, and gradually great families established themselves here with rambling and stately cool houses built in the soft malleable coral that is plentiful on this part of the coast.

In 1215, so the annals record, Suakin was absorbed into Egypt; but by 1429 it had established itself once more as an independent city-state, the most important trading centre on the Red Sea and a significant rival to Venice. In 1520 it fell to the Ottomans, and a period of decline began, but, when construction of the Suez Canal began, diverting into the Red Sea much of the traffic between Asia and Europe, Suakin boomed yet again.

As the traffic through Suez grew, so shipbuilding technology developed, and soon captains were finding Suakin's calm waters too shallow for them. After the British seized Suakin from the forces of the Mahdi, they began to ponder its future and scouted around for other harbours in the vicinity. Starting in about 1910, banks, shipping offices, the post office – everything – slipped inexorably away to the north, to Port Sudan, 50 km up the coast. By 1923 Suakin was almost dead, although a few Sheikhs continued to visit their grand old waterfront houses until the 1960s.

Now it is an eerie ghost town, quite uninhabited. The timbers that once held up doorways and stairs have rotted in the humid air; most of the larger buildings have collapsed, or are too dangerous to venture into. It's as if the place had suffered an earthquake. At what must have been one of the government buildings, there still survives a majestic gateway with the letters SG above it – Suakin Government? – and inside there is a plaque that mysteriously shows just the date – 1884 – and the insignia of a cannon. The fretwork balconies are crumbling, but above some of the doorways you can still make out finely crafted plaster moldings of quotations from the Koran. On the waterfront, cool high arcades are topped by heavily shuttered wooden verandahs in which birds and hornets now nest; great iron rings anchored into the coral are rusting away fast and will soon be gone.

The island must only cover a few hectares, but there seemed to be at least a dozen mosques, and it looked as though some effort had been made – at least – to keep these and their stubby minarets standing; a couple seemed even to have had some recent whitewash. Like Arkoweit, this would be a great movie set, not so much for a post-apocalyptic drama as for some M.M. Kaye moonlit romance involving sheikhs and daggers.

The outer reaches of the harbour are still used by a ferry that runs to Jeddah, but these days the only boats that come right into the shallow translucent waters of old Suakin are cruising sailboats from Canada, the USA, and Europe. Like the dhows of old, they ride the southerlies from the Bab al-Mandab, then they wait until the fiercest northerlies of winter, which reach this far down from Suez, start to weaken in April. At this time they can hope for a beam wind from the northeast if they're lucky or, unlike the dhows, take advantage of a day or two of calm to motor northwards.

PORT SUDAN ITSELF IS LESS APPEALING, with scarcely a build-ing more than eighty years old. The new Hilton in the port is far better finished and generally more comfortable than its sister in Khartoum, but rarely are more than a dozen of its 120 rooms occupied. It has an English-style bar on a mezzanine level, complete with big black leather armchairs, a dartboard, and mirrors behind the bar; Pieter, the Dutch-Canadian who also managed the Khartoum Hilton, loved to tell horror stories about his struggle to build this place (every single doorway was of slightly differ-ent size, which meant every door had to be made to measure). But he was optimistic that one day offshore oil would be struck and simultaneously he would receive a liquor license – "then I'll be sitting pretty," he finished, triumphantly.

Shortly before opening, he decided to inspect Port Sudan's firefighting capacities. In a ramshackle old garage in the city centre there was indeed a fire engine that, although empty, looked as though it might be in working order, and there was an official on the phone in a back room. Pieter waited

... and waited. It was evident that the official was calling some good friend or relative in a very distant location: he was swinging back in his chair, feet on the desk, laughing uproariously. After about twenty-five minutes Pieter caught his attention, and reluctantly he hung up. Pieter asked what was the routine in case of an emergency. "Well, they call us ..." and the official gesticulated to the phone. "But what if there had been an emergency now? They wouldn't have been able to get through."

"Well, yes, I suppose so." The official shrugged. "But they can always come by bicycle, there's usually somebody here ..."

The Hilton was a little outside my normal price range, so whenever I came to Port Sudan I usually stayed at the Bashair Place or the older Olympia. The Olympia had seen far better days, but it was one of the few buildings downtown in what I deduced to be Old Port Sudan style: the same high and shade-giving arcades I had seen in the ruins of Suakin, with an upper balcony covered by wooden shutters and a wooden roof.

There weren't too many destinations for a seafront walk. There was the Port Sudan International Club, but when I peered in it seemed to be abandoned and overgrown; and you could eat nameless fish at a place perplexingly named The Tennis Club (there was no tennis court in sight). At the east end of the harbour, there was a small restaurant where you could sip a cold Pepsi and watch the ships come in and out – the *Gold River* from Hong Kong, the *Pearl of Jeddah*, the *Diamond Atlantic* – and, if you felt the need, use the "Man Towlitt," or as appropriate, the "Wommann Towlitt."

Sitting here one afternoon, I watched what must be one of the local cottage industries in action: two men were rinsing used plastic bags in the harbour, then cleverly propping them up with rocks in such a way that their mouths were open to the breeze; the bags would thus dry in a matter of minutes. Over on a small stone jetty, a raucous crowd of young boys were blatantly ignoring the sign that said – in English – "No photograph; no swim" – when a uniformed policeman appeared at the head of the jetty. There was a moment's complete hush. Then he swung into action, brandishing a large stick, shouting and scattering the boys in every direction: some swam clean across the harbour to get away. As they then eyed him from a safe distance, he proceeded calmly to pick up the little piles of clothes and shoes that they had tidily left on the jetty, and he strode off without a backwards glance. There would be some angry mothers later that afternoon.

PORT SUDAN, IN SUMMER, is one of the most hostile environments on Earth; in 2001 temperatures daily reached fifty-five degrees in the shade for a period of three weeks, with high humidity; hundreds died. At the best of times the water supply, critical in this environment, is unreliable: it comes in by pipeline from two distant reservoirs and/or is expensively trucked, then transferred to donkey carts and small privately owned underground tanks, with middlemen taking a cut at every stage.

But for five years now, there had been a drought. The reservoirs were virtually empty, and the region's few wells were either dry or excessively salty. At the Khabila and Ingaz camps for the internally displaced (combined population about 20,500) a ten-litre jerrycan of water cost fifty dinars (USD $0.20) this season: an apparently modest amount, but here the total daily income of a five- or six-person family might be only two hundred dinars.

Water was of course not only critical for drinking, cooking, and washing; its lack greatly inhibited such efforts as had been made to set up small nurseries and market gardens in these communities. The drought had also depleted livestock in this predominantly pastoralist society, and it had exacerbated an already delicate health situation; it was estimated that at any one time four in ten children in the state were suffering from fever, and one in two from diarrhoea. Overall malnutrition rates were 29 percent "moderate," 6 percent "acute" (according to Oxfam). Local associations in Port Sudan for the internally displaced planned their own underground or aboveground reservoirs, which should cut the cost of delivering water by 30 to 40 percent, but even so the cost would still be higher than in Khartoum's equally miserable camps. About 30 km north of Port Sudan, at the desert village of Khor Arba'at, where we were looking at a potential development project, things were tough, too: it was a one hour walk to a water point that was the terminus of a black plastic hose that had come 8 km from the water main. As often as not, the hose was broken or blocked.

These problems were occurring in the most conservative society in all of Sudan. Beja women were as heavily veiled (if a little more brightly) as their counterparts in the Gulf, and at all my meetings to discuss possible Canadian aid, they would initially sit looking away to one side: eye contact with men was "haram" (forbidden). Coeducation at any age was also forbidden (in contrast to the wider Sudan, where girls were usually allowed to go to school with boys for at least the first three or so years of primary schooling), and yet there was not one single girls-only primary school in the entire state. Women did not visit the doctor's: instead men were sent on their behalf, with more or less detailed accounts of their wives' complaints. In the Hadendawa tribe, society's most prized women were said only to leave their houses twice in their lifetimes: once to get married and move to their husband's home, and once to go to the cemetery.

The few Western development agencies working here (Oxfam-GB, SOS Sahel, Ockenden International) had made women's empowerment their highest priority after the provision of clean and plentiful water. I agreed. Unless women could be given the ability to become useful, productive, free-moving members of this society, ultimate emergence from under-development would surely be impossible.

In Khor Arba'at, the local community had, to its credit, set up two informal and non-approved bush classrooms for primary-school-age girls only. These two thorn-bush and dirt-floor shacks, with no furniture at all, were the only such facility in the entire state; we would support their upgrading and amplification into proper structures. This plan was already the talk of the desert. With mixed amusement and mystification, I watched a lengthy and elaborate greeting between two Beja men who met in the wasteland near a water outlet we were inspecting. Between every ritual embrace and placing of hands on opposing shoulders they would look over to us. After fifteen minutes I asked for an explanation. First I was told that it was normal for the Beja to spend half an hour or more greeting each other: in a society with no newspapers and hardly any radios, greetings were used to convey information on pasture, local politics, and village gossip – all in a structured, formalistic way. In this instance, one of the two men was talking about the planned primary school, while the other was reciprocating with news of a fine patch of grass he had found for his goats (he pulled out from his grimy robes a hand-held GPS and showed his friend the position).

At Khor Arba'at, as well at Sinkat and at El Gebeit, aid organizations were also supporting adult literacy classes for women. To observe one of these was a moving experience. A gnarled forty-year-old woman with a nose ring (they aged prematurely here) proudly spelled out, on the blackboard, for the first time, her own name in Arabic; women simulated basic grocery bills from the souq and checked each other's for accuracy. I passed around a digital watch and asked women to tell us the time. I asked several women why they wanted to learn to read and write. Their answers were simple: "We want to know what's going on ... We want to know we aren't wasting our money ... We want our dignity."

Men were still heavily involved in selling projects like this to donors; cultural barriers were still so great that it would be taboo for a male stranger to sit alone with any group of women here. But some, such as Dr Mohammed Bidri Abu Hadia of the Abu Hadia Society for Women and Community Development, or the Canada-based Mr Ali El Ashi of the Charity Fund would impress even the most diehard feminist: Abu Hadia had over the past decade sponsored 159 girls to attend secondary school and university and was one of the most highly regarded organizations on women in the entire country, even though it was run by a Beja man.

13

LEAVING KHARTOUM

GETTING OUT OF KHARTOUM WAS NEVER EASY. You needed first a travel permit, which, depending on your intended destination, could take weeks to obtain (at the very least several days), and, if you wanted to visit one of the archaeological sites, you needed yet another permit. You could not simply show up at, say, the pyramids of Meroe, pay for a ticket, and go in. Travel permits were demanded at city exits by surly plainclothes youths in sunglasses; although you might then go several days on your route without being stopped. The need to jump through these bureaucratic hoops made the idea of just going for a drive on a Friday or Saturday a discouraging prospect.

While the potholed, dusty, and hot streets of Khartoum were not conducive to recreational walking there was one almost secret location where, ten minutes' drive from our home in Amarat, Jenny and I could be walking in green pastures by the Nile, with not a car in sight. Tuti Island is an asymmetrical tear-shaped tract of land, 4 x 2 km, formed where the Blue Nile divides into two, just before it joins the White. Every August, when the twin rivers are in flood, a little land is carved off one side and added to another, and some portions may go completely underwater. Composed of rich silt from the Ethiopian highlands, Tuti is prime agricultural land and as such it has been inhabited far longer than Khartoum itself.

The island is reached by small ferry boats that leave every few minutes from a muddy bank in front of the Friendship Hall conference centre on Nile Avenue. The place is easily spotted because dozens of poorly parked and – even for Khartoum – exceptionally battered old cars jam most of the road; these are the mainland cars kept here by island dwellers for their forays into Khartoum. The fare is ten dinars – about four cents – and the passengers on the five-minute ride over include sheep and goats, island shopkeepers, and perhaps one of the scions of the old, traditional, and very wealthy families who control most of the land holdings on the island. Over the ferry landing looms what looks from a distance like a water tower but, on closer examination, turns out to be an enormous cylindrical advertising hoarding: a mockup of a Nile Power flashlight battery.

A straggling mud-walled village occupies the centre of the island, a five-minute walk from the ferry landing. Children stop their playing in the dust to eye you curiously, but with no hostility; they don't seem to get many strangers here. The old men sitting on the stoops of mysterious and apparently vacant mansions smile and mutter a "Salaam Aleikum."

The eastern end of the island is given over to intensive cultivation of maize, sorghum, and a kind of clover that is the staple donkey fodder. Fellaheen labour in the fields; a yoke of oxen plods back and forth imperturbably, pulling a homemade wooden plough as a djellabiya-clad old man desultorily exhorts them with guttural commands. In a grove of wild lime trees, some small girls gathering fruit giggle as you pass them.

Tuti is not always bucolic. On one walk, an aubergine farmer stopped us for a chat. One day twenty years ago, exactly where we were standing, his eye had been caught by a young man swimming across the Blue Nile from Khartoum. The man kept disappearing underwater, and our friend Yussuf realized he was shouting in increasing panic as he struggled to keep his head above water. There was some violent splashing, then nothing; Yussuf realized a crocodile – "at least nine metres long" – had taken the man. A hunter was sent for and, though he hit the crocodile on his first attempt, the shots appeared to have no effect; next day he had to return and do the job with what Yussuf described as "an elephant gun." The crocodile was dissected at the zoo, and a fresh human leg was found inside it.

More recently, just two years ago, there had been great excitement when islanders had surrounded a confused hippo who had gotten into the habit of feeding nocturnally in the island's rich vegetable patches. Again a hunter was sent for, this time to fire a tranquilizing dart so, hopefully, the poor animal could be transferred to the zoo. But they miscalculated the dose and the hippo died, to be eaten that night in a huge feast.

You can just make out a distant hum that must be the traffic of Khartoum, but the dominant sound is the chug-chug of the old Indian-made Lister diesel pumps that feed the irrigation channels. If it's winter and the wind is in the northeast, there's the pungent peaty smell of the improvised brick kilns that spring up all along the banks of the Blue once the annual flood waters have receded.

DIPLOMATIC LIFE FOLLOWS the seasons, too. First, every autumn, there is a wave of credential ceremonies. The presentation of credentials by an ambassador (and the simultaneous delivery of a formal letter of recall for their predecessor) is both the symbolic and the real moment at which the representative of one country may begin their work in another. Although the original purpose of the ceremony – proving to the receiving state that the bearer is indeed who they claim to be by means of a personally signed letter from the head of the sending state – has long ago been surpassed, in most countries the convention is still strictly observed; prior to this ceremony, the new ambassador may undertake no substantive meetings or hold any social event.

In mid-2002, Canada appointed Rosaline Murray to succeed John Schram as the Canadian ambassador to Sudan, resident in Addis Ababa, and for several months I pursued the Foreign Ministry so as to set up a date for her credentials ceremony. There were long, unexplained delays. In a not unusual machiavellian ploy, Sudan was simultaneously requesting from Ottawa permission to post an ambassador rather than a lower-status chargé d'affaires to the Canadian capital; news of Ms Murray's date came through to me just a few hours after the Sudanese request had been accepted.

There was a further glitch: a couple of days before the scheduled ceremony, all diplomatic missions received a note stating that, in formal communications, President Bashir was no longer – as had been the previous custom – to be addressed by his military title (lieutenant general); this was presumably a gesture meant to convince us all that Sudan was now truly a democracy. Our problem was that our formal letters of credence and recall had been signed long ago by "Your Good Friend" the governor general of Canada and used Bashir's military rank. There would be no time to have a new version signed, sent, and received. With some trepidation, we decided to go ahead anyway. There were six new ambassadors on the roster that morning: Canada, Pakistan, who was resident in Khartoum, and four others resident in Cairo: Ireland, Australia, Croatia, and the Czech Republic.

Promptly at nine, black limousines, all with carefully shrouded national flags on their little flagstaffs, rolled up. We were all marshaled into the correct cars; flunkies followed in a more motley flotilla, and the whole expedition was led by siren-blaring motorcycles. At the doorway of the Republican Palace, overlooking the Blue Nile, a pair of turban-clad dervishes saluted and came sharply to attention as we mounted the red-carpeted stairs, then walked between a pair of elephant tusks and, more menacingly, two brightly polished Maxim machine guns rescued from the gunboat *Melik*. After being ushered into a brightly decorated yellow and gold reception room, we all made small talk and sipped the inevitable Pepsi while, presumably, the Presidential Guard organized itself.

At the appointed moment, Ms Murray and the Canadian delegation were ushered out again, this time to the steps at the rear of the building that overlook the Palace gardens. Drawn up before us, no doubt sweating profusely in their heavy dark blue serge as they stood to attention in forty-degree sunshine, was the one-hundred-strong Guard and on their right, in red, the presidential band. "O Canada" was performed quite respectably, followed by the lively Sudanese national anthem. Then, accompanied by a military man of obscure rank and delegation, Ms Murray inspected the guard. Having found them to be satisfactory, she was escorted up the left hand of the two curving staircases that lead to the upper floor – reputedly the approximate location where Gordon was speared to death by the Mahdist mob in 1885 – and into a large pale blue-and-white hallway, where the president, in a turban and brown and gold robes, stood waiting expectantly.

There was a short exchange of formalities, the letters of credence and recall were handed over, and then, while we junior officials were led to high-backed gilt chairs on one side to whisper among ourselves, our new ambassador and the president exchanged pleasantries for ten minutes in their own set of chairs in the middle of the room. Nothing too controversial: a few good wishes for success in the peace process, to which the president responded agreeably and added a few slightly dissonant comments about Canada's expertise in agriculture. Then rapidly out of the front doors again and back into the limo – this time with the Canadian flag fluttering openly in the hot breeze. The band was by now, no doubt, already into the Irish anthem.

THERE ARE A NUMBER of Commonwealth countries represented in Khartoum. The 11 November Remembrance Day ceremony, organized by the British Embassy, is another of the year's milestones. As early as August, a letter comes around from the British Embassy, listing the various versions of wreaths that can be bought through the embassy and the Earl Haig Fund, and then in October comes the gilt-edged invitation to the ceremonies, which are held in the Commonwealth War Cemetery, in the residential quarter known as Khartoum 2.

The cemetery is a quiet, leafy, and green oasis of calmness, with perfectly manicured lawns and row upon row of those uniform, pale yellow sandstone grave markers that can be found in every such cemetery around the world (the British Embassy stocks a few spare markers in its basement). At about half past ten, on what is invariably a hot morning, diplomats and stalwarts of the British community assemble in a hushed, dark-suited group at the cemetery gates, and Geoff, the British security officer who is former Army, explains to the rookies their role in the ceremonies.

A short but moving service is held, and the standing congregation, shifting almost imperceptibly to follow the shade of the great oak trees, mumbles the responses: "We shall remember them." The choir from the Episcopal Church concludes with "The Lord Is My Shepherd." We move over to the cenotaph itself, and in groups of four the assembled diplomats lay their wreaths. The French then have their own little ceremony by the graves of the five or six French servicemen: their military attachés, crisply dressed in ceremonial whites, march briskly back and forth and bark out salutes. When it's over, everyone stands to attention and faces the cenotaph again. A Sudanese Army band plays a ragged "Last Post," followed by the reveille; the bugler wavers and bubbles at the crucial moment, but it doesn't seem to matter. Afterwards, everyone is invited for a buffet lunch and a cold beer in the gardens of the British Residence.

NATIONAL DAY RECEPTIONS serve as further landmarks. These are invariably held in the evening – due to the daytime heat – and usually in the gardens of the residence of the ambassador. Because the months of May to August are especially hot and prone to both rain and dust storms, some embassies shift their National Days to more salubrious periods.

The routine is always the same. A fortnight before the day in question, the obligatory gilt-edged card arrives, invariably addressed to Mr and Mrs (unlike in some more austere capitals, where only "principals" are likely to be invited). There are only a few caterers in town – the Hilton, the Meridien, the Acropole – and veterans on the diplomatic scene will know which embassy uses which caterer, an important factor to be taken into account when deciding to have dinner that night or not. Dress is relatively formal: full suits and ties for the men, which can make for uncomfortable evenings. If you arrive punctually, there is a short reception line, to whose members it is appropriate to mumble "congratulations."

Waiters then appear. But they carry only soft drinks. Once again, local knowledge is at a premium; if this is a Western do, there will invariably be a liquor bar, too; but you have to know where to find it (usually tucked away discreetly behind the bougainvillea). To begin with, there are only Westerners huddled around the bar: diplomats, United Nations staffers, members of international aid organizations. But after about an hour, a few traditionally dressed Sudanese amble over and, after checking that there are no Cabinet Ministers in sight, place their order, too; a few of the more bashful may, in an embarrassed way, ask a Westerner to get a drink for them, rather than run the risk of being spotted by some fundamentalist ideologue. There are almost never speeches, unless it's a farewell party, but at the larger events, such as Bastille Day, a band plays the national anthem (which most people ignore).

National Days are surprisingly well-attended. This may be partly because it is only at these events that non-diplomatic foreigners and distinguished Sudanese can have easy access to alcohol, and partly because – with no cinemas or bars in town – there is not much else to do. In an information-starved society such as this, National Day receptions are good places to do some catching up on news, opinions, rumours, and gossip; most Sudanese love to talk politics even in ordinary circumstances, and with a glass of whisky in their hands they become positively voluble, even indiscreet.

Ottawa tended not to see things this way, though, and we were effectively prohibited from holding large events of this kind at the taxpayers' expense, the argument being that they were not directly in the interests of Canada. True enough, in that, for example, the French ambassador, on Bastille Day, certainly was not able to gather sufficient information in the national interest to justify the expenditure of several thousand dollars. But, as I saw it, it was a question of paying your dues: certainly Canada gained from the networking I was able to do and the contacts I established at such events throughout the year, and it seemed a little cheap to attend everyone else's events and not do one ourselves. The Canadian community invariably grumbled at this, too, for they would see all French nationals being invited to Bastille Day, all Dutch to the Dutch national day, and so on.

I told them they wouldn't get free parties in Canada on 1 July (although this was not strictly true – in Ottawa the government-sponsored celebrations are usually quite lavish). But in an attempt to placate the Canadians, I twice offered up my garden space; with the cooperation of community-minded compatriots, we organized potluck evenings for the expatriate community on a cost-sharing basis. These were greatly enjoyed and were a great deal more informal than the traditional National Day receptions; jackets and ties were banned. We were lucky enough that the manager of the Hilton Hotel, Pieter, was part Canadian, so he would arrange to have tableloads of salads brought and, on one memorable occasion, a huge 1 m² cake in the colours of the Canadian flag; Talisman, meanwhile, provided meat and a barbecue chef plus a few mysteriously obtained cases of beer (although we had to be careful not thus to give the company any free publicity; there were Canadians in the development world who would refuse to attend if they thought the party was in any way sponsored by the oil company). A friendly Polish priest laid on a disco, complete with Leonard Cohen tapes.

The mix we obtained at these parties was an interesting one. There were of course the oil company folks, the UN, and aid workers. But there were also a surprising number of Sudanese-born Canadians. Some of these had immigrated to Canada many years ago and were perhaps on a brief visit back home; others had left, obtained Canadian passports, but then returned home definitively. They weren't always too familiar with Canadian traditions; it took me fifteen minutes to explain to one woman the idea of a potluck barbecue, and I think she was still left with the impression that I was irredeemably mean to expect people to bring their own food to a party.

Some embassies also put on cultural events of various kinds; although I often attended and enjoyed these, their main beneficiaries seemed to be the expatriate community members, which was perhaps rather counter-productive. Valery, the long-serving and very genial (if rather cynical) Russian ambassador periodically held Russian Film Festivals. One of these, which I attended, was a hilarious set of films about a group of lugu-brious and generally very Russian friends who meet ostensibly to go hunt-ing and fishing, but really so that they can hold massive vodka-drinking binges that end in comic disaster; entertaining viewing in a city where the only filmic alternative is the occasional cut and censored Hindi love story dubbed into Arabic. But the few Sudanese who attended seemed a little bemused – as well they might in this dry society – by the spectacle of Russians getting horribly drunk presented as a positive image of new Russia. The French played things more safely: modern classic French films such as *Le Fabuleux destin d'Amélie Poulin* on the ambassador's tennis court by moonlight and once, memorably, ballads in French by blind but exquisitely talented Sudanese singer Amal el Nour.

Sudan's own national day was the anniversary of independence (1 Janu-ary 1956). Usually there were parades in the capital, but in 2003, in recog-nition of growing talk of peace, celebrations were moved symbolically to the Southern city of Malakal.

Sudan Airways' entire domestic jet fleet (two 737s) was requisitioned to fly down diplomats and other officials (pity the airline's clients who had planned to be travelling somewhere else that day ...), a fleet of buses had been pre-positioned by barge, and what seemed to be the whole pop-ulation of Upper Nile State was rousted out to line the dusty dirt streets and greet the visitors. At the football grounds where the ceremonies took place, it was like one of the great battle scenes from *War and Peace*. Thou-sands of persons, many in traditional dress with huge leather shields and brandishing spears, swept back and forth at a trot and in great waves while a much-stressed MC attempted to impose some order; everywhere flags and banners flew and snapped smartly in the sunshine and the strong north wind; trumpets competed with great bass drums. President Bashir wore a military uniform, which initially prompted speculation that we were in for exhortations to jihad, but he soon donned a more peaceful-looking white toga, which is the garb of Shillook Kings. It was a colourful day.

There was a further annual celebration which the Ministry of Foreign Affairs was always at great pains to have the diplomatic corps attend. This was on 29 and 30 June and was rather misleadingly called the Anniversary of the National Salvation Revolution; the so-called Revolution was in fact the NIF's 1989 military coup that signalled the end of Sadiq el-Mahdi's fragile democracy. In light of this, representatives of the Western embassies usually found themselves "too busy" to attend.

2003 was an exception in this regard also. The night in question, a keynote speech by the president, to be delivered in the gardens of the Republican Palace, had been announced. After some soul-searching, a consensus was reached among the diplomats that we would indeed attend, in the hope that some breakthrough in the peace process might be signalled. We need not have bothered. There were two hours of speeches in Arabic, with no translation or interpretation, but which, even with my minimal linguistic capabilities, I could deduce consisted largely of a recital of kilometres of road built and pupils enrolled in school. Next day, with the exception of the French ambassador, we all declined when the road show moved down to Juba aboard the Sudan Airways fleet. I could not imagine Southerners being enthused at the prospect of celebrating the coup.

GENERALLY, WITH THE EXCEPTION of small invitation-only events, concerts were unheard of. But in June 2002, Coca Cola (recently returned to Sudan to an enormous welcome from the soda-addicted Sudanese) launched its first major attack on the hitherto dominant Pepsi in the unlikely form of a seventy-year-old balladeer unknown in the West. Mohammed Wardi, known as The Golden Throat in the Arab world and as the Grandfather of Sudanese Funk to the few Western cognoscenti, had his first hit – in his native Nubian – in 1960. While many of his songs were romantic evocations of rural life on the Nile, he joined the Communist Party at an early age and never hesitated to bring politics into his music. He was a bitter opponent of Dictator/President Jaafar Nimeiri and served eighteen months in jail for supporting an abortive coup against him in 1971. In 1990, fearing arrest again, this time by the new National Islamic Front administration of Hassan al-Turabi and Omar Bashir, he fled to Egypt, and later to the USA.

Wardi's arrival at Khartoum airport led to crowd scenes that had not been witnessed in Sudan for fifteen years – one commentator said (perhaps hyperbolically) it was "like when the Beatles first flew to New York." Coke revelled in the publicity. Wardi's week-long series of concerts was a total sellout; ticket promotions based on collecting Coke bottletops led to riot scenes in the streets.

The last of the concerts was held on a Thursday, and it was the grandest. On a hot night and under a crescent moon on the south bank of the Blue Nile, Wardi sang to twenty thousand of his entranced and adoring fans. By Western standards, he was an unlikely looking star. Sporting a yellow shirt and an elegant jacket and tie, backed by a thirty-piece orchestra and choir (including Amal el Nour), he performed with a gentle smile and a casual, expansive manner for nearly four hours: one lilting fifteen-minute ballad after another, interrupted only by jarring Coke promos. Giant screens fed his video image to the thousands who had been unable to get in, and it took two hours for the traffic jam at the end of the concert to break up.

Wardi's style was wistful – a kind of Arab John Lennon, in "Imagine" mode. A few of his songs had bite, and even non-Arabic speakers such as myself could sense tremors running through the crowd at the opening bars of some of his more polemical songs. There was "October": a eulogy to the students who died in the failed October 1971 coup against Nimeiri led by Hashem al'Ata. And "North and South": a paeon to the diversity of Sudan and a call for an end to war. And, most moving and stirringly, the utopian "When Morning Comes," with its call for an end to military rule, beatings, and torture.

Throughout, uniformed riot police armed with two-metre sticks looked on impassively. Even Wardi's comment, at the 11:00 p.m. curfew – "We'll go on for a while yet; we're not singing against the government, so why would they close us down?" – brought only cheers from the good-natured crowd, and no reaction from the police. While a spectacular closing fire-work performance was apparently unauthorized and provoked a worried call from the first vice-president, who was later said to have feared a coup was beginning, there were no consequences.

Wardi was undecided as to whether or not he would now remain in Sudan. He said he had no intention of compromising on his political beliefs. After a meeting with President Bashir, he stated his opposition to the government: "I am a human being, and every human being is against dictatorship. I will continue to denounce it." However, he suffered from kidney failure, and thought that the need for dialysis might drive him back to the USA, quite apart from political considerations.

It is sometimes difficult, so close to the action, to determine what is a historic development, and what will turn out with the benefit of hindsight to have been irrelevant, a red herring. But it's my guess that in years to come historians of Sudan might just point to the hot June nights when Wardi sang again in Khartoum, to the adoring crowds that welcomed him back, and to the passivity of the authorities as some kind of sign. Perhaps things were now not quite as dark as they once had been.

IF THE DIPLOMATIC SOCIAL SCENE waxed and waned according to the climate, for the Sudanese the peak of the social season was always Ramadan. The month-long Muslim period of fasting comes ten days earlier each year, but I was lucky in that during my time in Sudan it coincided with the relatively cool months of November and December.

It was not a good idea to arrange for incoming delegations in this period, or indeed to try to hold substantive meetings: in the daytime the Sudanese were generally irritable, uncooperative, and worked even shorter hours than usual. But once the sun started to dip towards the horizon, everyone would head feverishly towards wherever that evening's fattur might happen to be; the statistics for traffic accidents would go up dramatically.

It was perfectly acceptable, even smiled upon approvingly, to crash organized fatturs; the more mouths a host fed, the greater his credit in heaven. Several times driving home along Cemetery Road or Airport Road at Ramadan, with darkness coming on, I was energetically flagged down by complete strangers on the side of the road and enjoined earnestly to partake in their fuul; they were offended if I attempted to make excuses and drove on.

Notable personalities would also organize especially grand fatturs. Normally, women were not expected to come to such events (or, if they did, they would be shunted off to eat with the other women and talk of inconsequential things such as cooking and babies, while the men gossiped about politics), but for diplomats exceptions were made. Thus Sadiq al-Mahdi's fatturs, held in the beautiful grounds of his faded residence, would welcome Marianne, Switzerland's chargée, and Rita, the US deputy chargée.

The grandest event of all was the presidential fattur. Formal invitations from the president went out to over a thousand people. We would all gather at about 6:00 p.m. in the gardens behind the Republican Palace, and then at about 6:15 the signal was given to move over to two or three hundred small tables set with bottled water, dates, pineapple, and peanuts. Everyone would nibble delicately at these for a moment or two, then the Muslims (who made up 95 percent of those attending) moved once again, to a set of long red carpets set out in five or six parallel rows, oriented towards Mecca. As dusk settled, an imam led them in prayers and obeisances, while the Westerners murmured inconsequentially in a small group to one side.

Once prayers were over, we moved to yet another set of tables, this time laden down with a full meal. For the first few minutes there would be a concentrated silence, while everyone made up for a long day's fasting, but then conversation would begin flowing. From a sound stage, Koran readings were intoned to music. It was all very atmospheric and quite impressive, but as soon as the president got up to leave, which was quite quickly, everyone else was expected to go as well; I would arrive home still hungry.

ALSO PUNCTUATING THE CALENDAR would be Sudanese weddings. In my first two or three weeks in Khartoum, I was invited to several. I thought people were just being very polite and welcoming and that they did not really expect me to attend, but I soon realized this was not so. The larger the wedding party, the more successful the event was usually judged to have been, and parties of 1,500 guests or more were not uncommon.

A typical wedding would last three or four nights, with various discrete components. There was, for example, the henna party. After days or weeks of being deliberately fattened up (it was considered desirable for a bride at the wedding ceremonies to be seen to be bursting from her dress) and – in the most traditional of families – "smoked" over a sandalwood fire clad only a blanket, the bride would be clucked over and ornately painted in black henna by her most intimate female friends.

And then there was the bridal dance. This was a women's only event, the only exceptions being made for the groom himself and brothers (who were required to face outwards and keep curious male onlookers away). The centrepiece of this evening was a long ritualized dance performed by the bride, laden down with all her gold and her traditional headdress complete with false hair, before the embarrassed-looking groom. I only ever saw the dance on the video of a friend's wedding, but it was – for Sudan – surprisingly frank, even erotic; I was told that in olden days brides would actually perform naked. The key moment was when the bride had to pretend to faint and fall: the groom was supposed to catch her before she fell; if he failed, this was a bad omen and the marriage could be called off. The evening would be punctuated by the high-pitched female ululations that are so characteristic of all Sudanese celebrations.

The final night would consist of the formal presentation of the bride and groom, usually clad in Western wedding outfits, to a thousand or so of their family and friends. Families would often rent one of Khartoum's large clubs – the Coptic Club or the Syrian Club – for the event, which would start at 8:00 p.m. Full dinner was served to all, and the bride and groom would process in and sit on an elevated platform. There would be an odd mix of live traditional music (sometimes, to the ire of conservative clerics, top stars would be flown in from Egypt or Lebanon) and canned Western music: Céline Dion's theme song from *Titanic* and "The Power of Love" were great favourites, to such an extent that they could be heard booming over Amarat most Friday evenings.

AN IMPORTANT PLANK in Khartoum's strategy to emerge from a decade of isolation was to offer to host as many international gatherings as possible – each one sending progressively more reassuring messages to the world and to the Sudanese public that Sudan was no longer a pariah, that it was accepted and respected, that world leaders had no qualms in travelling here. Most of these gatherings were strong on style, weak on substance. Perhaps the grandest I had the opportunity to witness was in June 2002: the twenty-ninth Foreign Ministers' Summit of the Organization of the Islamic Conference (OIC).

Khartoum was spruced up like never before for this event. Roads that had not been swept for decades and that most people assumed to be sand tracks, were revealed to be tarmac; the route from the airport was planted lavishly with geraniums and festooned with flags and high-sounding slogans in French, Arabic, and sometimes quaint English ("Honourable Friends: Good Stay!"); grand moonlit banquets were laid on in the grounds of the Republican Palace. Representatives from all fifty-seven members of the OIC flooded in – most at ministerial level – although a number were spotted leaving well before the proceedings were over. Between speeches at the long opening session, an imam chanted verses from the Koran and flattered the participants with those flowery metaphors in which Arabic seems so rich but which suffer in translation. It was the biggest event ever staged by the sorely stretched Foreign Ministry – and as such something of a triumph for this country that was still considered in some Western quarters as a camp follower of the so-called "Axis of Evil."

For observers, the key point of interest was whether, at this first ordinary session of the OIC since 9/11, terrorism or Israel/Palestine would top the agenda. The Middle East won out, no doubt partly because the event began only hours after President Bush made his latest big speech on the USA's Middle East policy. There was of course unanimous support for the Palestinian cause, although delegates stopped short of explicit justification of suicide bombings, and expressions of solidarity with Yasser Arafat were generally couched carefully in terms of "the elected leader of the Palestinian authority." Only Ibrahim Fall, representing the UN secretary general, actually condemned suicide bombings; he was met with a stony silence (but at least was not booed).

Palestinian quasi-Foreign Minister Farouq Kadumi was given third place on the list of speakers to the plenary, following Bashir and the Foreign Minister of Guinea (speaking on behalf of the African group). Although his was the most eagerly awaited presentation, it was short and relatively non-controversial. From Bashir's opening remarks, he picked up in particular on Sudan's experience in "throwing off colonialism" and then astutely shifted to what was to this gathering the single most appealing and unimpeachable feature of the Palestinian struggle: its insistence on the holy place of Al-Quds as capital of the Palestinian state. "The enemies of Islam," he concluded darkly, "are attempting to encircle us and maintain us in servility."

On terrorism, the subject on which all of us Western diplomats were hoping to hear a clear, moral stand by the Arab states, the conference was notable for the lack of an explicit condemnation of 9/11 and of al-Qaeda taking the name of Islam in vain. Rather, there was repeated bitter complaint that 9/11 had "marred the image of Islam" and the Palestinian cause, and it was suggested by several that it gave anti-Islamic elements in the West an excuse they had long been waiting for to launch a campaign against Muslims worldwide. The word "conspiracy" was mentioned more than once.

The common note throughout was that Islam was in trouble. OIC Secretary General Abdel Aziz Balgez recognized that "for many Islam is synonymous with terrorism" and worried that ordinary law-abiding Muslims might begin to lose confidence in their faith. President Bashir suggested "we are at a decisive moment ... the Islamic peoples are face to face with their destiny." He went on to wax nostalgic about the glory days of Muslim Andalusia (Granada and the Alhambra ...), while another speaker reminisced that "we were masters of the world when we were masters of thought and science."

The suggested responses all seemed to be about solidarity and spin, not substance. There was not a single mention of the role of women in Islam and no mention of the Koranic schools that were widely identified as breeding grounds for fanaticism. The word "democracy" was heard only when the secretary general of the organization admitted "we are accused of being anti-modern, anti-democratic," while President Bashir allowed it might be a good idea to "stay in touch with our masses" (if only for self-preservation, seemed to be the subtext). The international president of Islamic Daawa noted to much tut-tutting that two-thirds of the world's refugees were Muslim, but it seemed to occur to no-one that most of those unfortunates were refugees from their own Islamic governments, whether due to poverty, repression, corruption, and/or human rights abuse.

No doubt in deference to the host country and in spite of the fact that one analysis of Sudan's civil war put it in the context of the millennium-old forced Islamization of a resistant Africa, there was only one substantive reference in formal statements to Sudan when the head of Islamic Daawa absurdly described it as a "model of peace and cohesion." If any indication were needed of the unreality of some of these proceedings, one needed look no further.

These events invariably culminated, as did this one, in a grand banquet on the gardens of the Republican Palace. The setting was lush: dozens of tables scattered across the lawns, the floodlit southern facade of the palace, waiters who processed out with theatrical military precision, fairy lights in the trees. There were even plastic fluorescent palm trees, but they could not compete with the huge, magnificent (and real) royal palms that dated from the colonial era. On summer nights, huge fans were brought in and hooked up to a network of hoses that crisscrossed the lawns and over which everyone tripped. The hoses fed a fine spray of water into the air just in front of each fan: large clouds of vapour wafted around in the flood-lighting rather eerily and left your shoulders damp.

After we had all stood around waiting for an hour or so, the band signalled the arrival of the president and his guests of honour with a brisk rendition of the national anthem, and we took our seats. A politically correct "folkloric" show of Southern dancers and singers was amplified to such a degree that all conversation was impossible, but, after we had been kept waiting for so long, the food was then served at breakneck speed.

Almost invariably the weather cooperated, and the scene under the moon and stars could be quite romantic. But Kofi Annan's visit came in the middle of the season at which fierce haboubs – sudden dust and rain storms – can come out of nowhere. A dish of cold Nile Perch was being served when I noticed that within the last couple of minutes the stars had become obscured and even the floodlights on the perimeter of the garden were starting to fade into a dusty brown fog. With an audible *whoomp* a wave of combined wind and dust hit: plastic chairs and tables blew over, table cloths flew into the trees, women held on frantically to their dresses, and people began to rub their eyes as stinging dust blew everywhere (including onto the fish). Unusually, that night there were speeches, but the sound system immediately failed: Annan and Bashir silently mouthed politesses at each other for a few minutes, while the president's robes flew up. We all tried to pretend nothing unusual was happening. My black suit turned brown. As quickly as the haboub had arrived, it left. The waiters discreetly righted tables and picked up plates, menus, and pieces of fish. On we went. The evening came to an abrupt end when the president decided he had had enough – well before dessert had been served.

ALSO AIMED LARGELY AT conveying to outsiders an impression of normalcy was the regular holding of party conventions by the National Congress Party. The July 2001 opening of the convention, held in the grounds of the party's headquarters at the former Catholic Club, where I several times met with Professor Omer, was a particularly grand affair, with 4,500 delegates in attendance from all over the country. A huge polished granite podium adorned with fluorescent electric palm trees had been erected specially for the occasion in a hangar-size building, and there were lavish refreshments over a period of several days.

Delegates sat by state, with the women's and youth claques separate. Diplomats were half-buried in huge soft leather armchairs at the front, along with most of the Cabinet (this was clearly a command performance for all of them). Speeches were punctuated by the customary "Allahu Akhbar"s and waving of traditional walking sticks, but rather less usual were some politically correct "Alleluia"s, apparently orchestrated to demon-

FAR IN THE WASTE SUDAN

strate the party's pluralism. There was also a performance by a choir of some Christian denomination, dressed in red-and-white Crusader smocks that, given the political climate in the region at this time, seemed more than a touch bizarre. President Bashir's keynote speech ended in him being mobbed by enthusiastic djellabiya-clad party elders, who gathered below the podium several hundred strong, waving their sticks or a single finger in the air, chanting rhythmically. As one diplomatic colleague commented "All it needs now is for them to start singing "We Are the Champions."

Unsurprisingly, the party's inner council of four hundred (the Shura) re-elected President Bashir as president of the party, and Ali Osman Tahaa and Moses Macar as deputy presidents; not coincidentally, the latter two were – respectively – already first and second vice-presidents of Sudan. A little more interesting was the election for secretary general – the de facto chief ideologue of the party. Professor Ibrahim Ahmed Omer had some months ago indicated his desire to retire, and there had been speculation that this influential position might now be taken by Ghazi Salah al-Dien; but Omer was "persuaded" to stay on. In a word, no change at the top.

The event reminded me of the several party conventions I had attended of Mexico's then-ruling Institutional Revolutionary Party (PRI): over-whelming in its lavishness and organization, and entirely devoid of self-doubt. As such, the "no change" signal it sent was at odds with the highly visible rapprochement that had taken place with the USA that year, especially post-9/11. I hoped that the National Congress Party would not match the PRI's world record of holding power uninterrupted for seventy-one years.

JUST AROUND THE CORNER from the World Food Programme, off Airport Road, was the block of flats formerly inhabited by Ilich Ramirez Sanchez, more commonly known as Carlos the Jackal. My good friend Jake Hamm, a Manitoba farmer volunteering with the Fellowship for African Relief, lived for a while in one of these apartments.

Linked to the attempted 1973 murder of British millionaire Edward Sieff (of Marks & Spencers), the subsequent takeover of the French Embassy in The Hague, the killing of two French intelligence agents, and the 1976 kidnapping of the OPEC Oil Ministers in Vienna, Carlos had disappeared from sight in the late 1980s. For exactly how long he lived in Sudan is not known, but by 1994 both Egyptian and French intelligence had caught up with him in Khartoum. The Egyptians even videotaped him carousing at a private wedding party in Amarat.

The French Government put the screws to Hassan al-Turabi: on the one hand he was presented with evidence that Carlos was anything but the morally upright and puritanical pro-Palestinian freedom fighter he posed as, and on the other (reportedly ...) was promised that French influence would be used at the International Monetary Fund to secure some critical loans for Sudan. In August 1994, with Turabi's reluctant acquiescence, the trap was set.

On 13 August – so runs the official account – Carlos was admitted to the Ibn Khaldoon Hospital (near the current Canadian Embassy Office) for a minor surgical operation to correct his low sperm count. As he was recovering, Sudanese intelligence officials informed him that a plot on his life had been uncovered and that he must immediately move to a safe location they had secured for him, a villa in Taif, near Turabi's own home. Carlos acquiesced.

At 3:00 a.m. on 14 August, masked men broke into his bedroom, injected him with a tranquilizing drug, cuffed him, put a hood over his head, bundled him into a sack, and rushed him to an executive jet at the airport. A six-and-a-half-hour flight took him to Villacoublay Military Airfield, near Paris, where he was delivered to a judge and immediately charged with the 1975 Rue Touillier murder of the two French agents. He remains in prison to this day, notwithstanding various appeals his lawyers have made against the illegal manner of his arrest.

A racier but perhaps less credible version of the story has a Mata Hari from Sudanese intelligence seducing a reluctant Carlos into marriage, but requiring him to convert to Islam first. He dithers but finally agrees. A condition, of course, is that he must be circumcised. He goes to the same hospital, undergoes a general anaesthetic ... and wakes up in his French prison cell (with or without his foreskin, we do not know).

VARIOUS LOCATIONS ASSOCIATED WITH the more recent iteration of the war on terrorism saw an upsurge of visitors following 9/11. These included the suburban house in the Riyadh district that had been inhabited by Osama bin-Laden for several years; his cook enjoyed at least fifteen minutes of fame in late 2001: he told breathless reporters from all over the world how bin-Laden liked his rice done and how good he was with small children. On McNimer Street was the Al Safina pharmacy that had served as bin-Laden's office.

The favourite war tourism site was in Khartoum North, just north of the diplomatic quarter of El Kafouri. In August 1998, late-night news on CNN showed live footage from this suburb – a medicine factory in flames – while reporting that the USA had struck a decisive blow against terrorism. Seven cruise missiles, launched from US warships in the Gulf, had landed on the al-Shifa plant, destroying it totally. "Only" one nightwatchman was killed, and the adjoining World Food Programme warehouse was left untouched: a compliment to the precision of US weaponry. Although some Sudanese later claimed they had seen the missiles racing up the Blue Nile, going under the Burri bridge, then turning sharp left over the Papal Nuncio's residence and up the road to the factory, and others swore they had heard a B-52 overhead, the attack was a huge surprise to almost everyone.

The al-Shifa site is now the responsibility of the same Department of Antiquities that is the custodian of the three-thousand-year-old Pyramids at Meroe and the priceless if dusty and largely ignored collection at the National Archeological Museum. A tall and dignified man in flowing robes let me in, first showing me a few parts of missile motor rescued from the devastation, then letting me wander freely around the site. Most unusually for Khartoum, he gestured that I was welcome to take photographs. There were some two hectares of ruins, left exactly as they were found the morning after the attack; thousands of brown glass medicine bottles lay littered around, some of them fused by the heat of the missiles' impact, and medicine labels blew around in the hot afternoon wind. Children played in the concrete debris, and some youths dug around for interesting scraps.

It was by now widely accepted that al-Shifa was exactly what its aggrieved owners and the Government of Sudan said it was: a medicine factory, whose prime client was the United Nations Children's Fund. If proof were needed, the US Government was reported to have made a USD $60 million out-of-court settlement with the factory's owner, and in the months following the attack vetoed a call by Khartoum that the United Nations send specialist inspectors to verify the US allegations that this was a bin-Laden installation producing nerve gas.

The al-Shifa fiasco was more than a footnote, the factory more than an offbeat and macabre tourist attraction. For the average Sudanese, who had and continued to have little time for the Islamist regime in Khartoum, al-Shifa was a demonstration that the world's foremost superpower was capable of gross mistakes of judgement and tactics and that the United States could not even be expected to apologize after the fact.

It was not lost on world-aware Sudanese that al-Shifa and the parallel attack on Afghanistan came just as the US presidency was undergoing a particularly embarrassing moment: the Monica Lewinsky affair. Sudan, it had now become apparent, was not for the USA exactly a foe to be opposed (that, educated Sudanese could have understood and even sympathized with) but rather a worthless place that could safely be bombed when a distraction was urgently needed at home. That realization hurt, especially to those Sudanese who had actually considered the USA a friend to be counted upon in the common cause against the despised NIF regime.

In the medium term and in the most obvious sense, al-Shifa and the prospect that the bombing could be repeated at any time and with even less of an excuse probably brought the USA some security dividends; post-9/11, certainly, Khartoum cooperated in delivering intelligence material as fast as it could, no doubt fearing more Cruises. The unseen effect of al-Shifa was that, while it increased fear of the USA in Sudan, it greatly decreased the considerable respect in which the United States had hitherto been held: thenceforth, the USA was a bully to be feared and obeyed whose moral standing was now hardly any higher than that of the other school-yard bullies. Cooperation – compliance, even – went up with al-Shifa, but so did resentment and a bitter sense of injustice.

As I stood in the al-Shifa ruins one day in early 2003, with war in the Gulf in the offing and the TV news full of Hans Blix and his United Nations weapons inspectors, I found myself studying a half-burnt label for what looked like some kind of cow medicine. My quiet but articulate guide looked at what I was studying, shrugged, and said: "I just hope they find more than this in Baghdad ..."

LATE IN 2002 my hosts at the British Embassy had advised me that, with a peace agreement possibly in the offing, they planned to expand and would accordingly need all of their office space back; I had until the end of April 2003 to find a new place. The saga of finding and moving into a new property was fraught not only with all the problems one might expect in Sudan – the fact that there is no advertised property market, that realtors operate on an entirely informal and cutthroat basis, and that professional construction contractors do not exist – but, more seriously, with a high level of incoherence, inattention, and indecision on Ottawa's part.

My first instructions were to "Find a modest place that would allow for some expansion, maybe from three to five staff," which evolved into "No, go the whole hog and get a big place that will eventually allow us to expand to full embassy status," then – once a lease had been signed on a large property – devolved back to "Actually, we've cut our original budget by 90 percent, and you'll have to make do with fitting up less space than you have now; and by the way, you'll have to stick with that antiquated communications platform, even though no-one here knows how to fix it anymore ..."

Things always get done, somehow, in Sudan. So by late July and the third anniversary of my arrival in Khartoum, the Canadian Office was independent of the British, occupying one corner of a large yellow villa on Airport Road; the remainder of the house was to serve as the residence for my successor. Ottawa had scrimped outrageously on basics such as air conditioning, squeezed our two support staff together into one small room, dismissed the idea of fixing up the villa's small swimming pool as "an extravagance," and studiously (or carelessly?) maintained the frustratingly vague and limiting title of Head of Office for my successor. But we were open, with our own identity and apparently committed to a few more years at least, notwithstanding Talisman's departure from Sudan (which cynics had said would signal our own departure).

WHEN "SHOCK AND AWE" hit Baghdad in early April 2003, the reaction on the streets of Khartoum was disbelief and outrage: the sourness lingering from al-Shifa was suddenly sharpened. Over the ensuing three weeks there were seventeen major demonstrations in the Sudanese capital, two of which turned uncharacteristically violent, resulting in the deaths of several students at the hands of panicky riot police. For the first time in living memory, Westerners were briefly targeted, with all hawaijas paying the price for the British- and American-led war against Iraq: gasoline was thrown over a United Nations vehicle, and only by miracle did it fail to ignite; the car of a teacher at Unity School was surrounded and rocked; a few Westerners were spat at. New crash barriers were erected outside the British Embassy, and several times when demonstrations seemed to be coming near, staff were sent home, out of harm's way. I made sure that

I had a tiny Canadian flag clearly visible in my corner office window that looked out onto the dusty street where any hostile crowd would likely materialize; the joke among our British hosts was that I was their human shield (Canada's stance on the war in Iraq providing some measure of immunity). Briefly, foreigners stopped going to each other's parties: it was sensed that scenes of apparent rejoicing, however innocent and unrelated to the conflict in Iraq, might be provocative.

The talk on the street every morning was of the latest scenes shown on Al Jazeera, especially of the women and children killed in bombing runs. The US public's horror at the treatment of their country's prisoners of war was met with derision, and the perceived hypocrisy of Western TV channels (notably the BBC, which had only the previous evening showed hooded and kneeling Iraqi prisoners quaking with fear) was lampooned. The tank round that killed an Al Jazeera reporter was cast in Sudan as deliberate targeting and a blatant breach of the Geneva Conventions. Every day that went by with no revelations of weapons of mass destruction reinforced the perception that WMDs would never be found in Iraq, or that, if they were, they would turn out to have been planted. One newspaper echoed the mood: "If the Americans wanted to find an evil man with weapons of mass destruction, they need have looked no further than Tel Aviv."

The government stayed mum, an attitude that for a brief period inflamed demonstrators further. Why the silence? Overly energetic and public condemnation of the Americans might jeopardize everything so hard won over the past two to three years of the charm offensive and could also cause the USA to call off its mediation of the peace deal that pragmatists within government now recognized as their best hope for political survival. Meanwhile, if the mood on the street persisted, it could become dangerous for the government, and the peace process could be threatened from another direction. Witnesses of the most violent demonstrations said that intermingled with the predictable cries of "USA out" were a few of "NIF out" and "Bashir out"; the notion that by remaining silent on Iraq Khartoum was selling Islam down the river – "just like it is at the talks in Kenya" – was thought to be gaining some currency among hardliners within administration who were always looking for excuses to slow down, even pull out of, the talks.

This mood, while temporarily dangerous, might well pass, but I recalled that it was in a comparably sulky and anti-Western climate that in the early 1990s Osama bin-Laden put roots down in Khartoum and started to build up al-Qaeda. The vein he tapped was then one of resentment and perceived injustice mainly on the part of the government vis-à-vis the West. Now it was the people who were resentful – not the Sudanese Government – but if the ruling party felt it must for whatever reason follow the people we might then have a problem.

Eighteen months previously, you could not find a single sane or well-educated person in Sudan who had a good word for al-Qaeda or the 9/11 atrocities in the United States. But a Sudanese friend asked me in April 2003, "What do you think the reaction would be today, to another al-Qaeda attack in New York?" He didn't wait for an answer.

EPILOGUE
SUNSET OVER FASHODA

IN MAY 2003, I'm back in Malakal for one of my last field trips in Sudan. I'm welcomed off the Sudan Airways Antonov flight by William, a heavily built Nuer man from Leer, Western Upper Nile, who works for the Irish aid organization GOAL. William lives with his two wives, miscellaneous uncles, and children in a mud-walled house in the quarter known as Malakiya. For four days, he is my guide.

Under William's guidance, I keenly inspect the two supplementary feeding clinics that GOAL runs at Bem and Malakiya and its therapeutic feeding station (for severely malnourished children) in the town centre of Malakal. I'm pleased to see the warehouse stocked with Canadian-donated soya oil, and the nurses are handing out blue Canadian-donated vitamin A capsules.

William has me over for Friday fattur at his home, and afterwards, with his six year old son Emmanuel clinging to his hand, we watch a football game in which one of the two Army battalions stationed in Malakal takes on the other. The level of skill is atrocious, but the ground is rock-hard baked earth and the football doesn't bounce as it's supposed to: the players have an excuse. At half time, instead of cheerleaders, there's a tug-o-war between the two battalions, executed with much showy military discipline and panache. The large crowd (there isn't too much else to do) loves it, and the resident lunatic is ecstatic with the excitement of it all. In the second half, the game becomes a little less dull as some scoring occurs. With every goal, trumpets are played and fans race around the perimeter on Phoenix bicycles with regimental flags; the players hug and kiss each other self-consciously. A nattily dressed linesman signals officiously and overemphatically the off-sides and throw-ins with his little square flag; a group of cheeky little boys starts to imitate him.

Most of the life in town is down at the waterfront. For about 2 km, the steep right bank of the Nile is largely covered with enormous bundles of yellow reeds and straw, which have just been harvested after the long dry season and before the rains send more crops shooting up. Donkey carts are loading patiently and will transport new roofs and walls to homes in Malakal, but mostly these bundles will be placed on barges and sent north to Kosti, even to Khartoum.

Small boys have what look like neatly arranged piles of earth for sale; in fact, these are carefully scrounged remnants of builders' sand brought in from the north and gathered a handful at a time from the steel decks of the barges after unloading. Old women are sifting through other piles of sand with fine sieves: they are separating out, a few grains at a time, spherical grains of sorghum that, similarly, have spilled in loading, and will sell them on again. By the football field, a black hose snakes up from the river, gushing muddy water; donkeys and their drivers, almost exclusively small boys, are lining up to fill up while an overseer notes down their names and each two-barrel load they take. This is Malakal's municipal water supply.

Sitting against a fence, two old men are laboriously picking at an old automobile tire and reducing it to bundles of metre-long rubber ties; these they will sell as shoelaces or as ties for house construction. There are the ubiquitous tea ladies with their small square charcoal braziers; an array of jam jars containing sugar, tea, ground coffee and dark red hibiscus leaves; and tiny metal tables painted in pale blue. A glass of scorching hot tea, served on a small silver tray, costs ten cents. The Shillook women, unlike their Northern counterparts, wear their tobes knotted over one shoulder and go bareheaded.

At the water's edge long and narrow canoes made of sheet steel – for there isn't much suitable wood around here for boat-building – will take you across to Riverside, which, as far as I can see, consists of another enormous pile of straw and reeds, plus a few trucks. Here, lately, you can actually catch a truck up to Khartoum; it's a four- or five-day ride. William and I try to go over for half an hour to look around, but it seems you can never quite escape the long hand of state security, even here in Malakal. As we're just pushing off, an officious man in a white shirt shouts and beckons to us from a distance. When we wearily go over to see him, he demands my permit to cross the river (which, of course, I don't have).

Malakal smells of cow shit and urine – human or animal, I cannot tell – and there's only one more-or-less acceptable place to eat, which serves only goat bones in a spicy sauce at all times of day, but the fresh bread is good and there are cold Pepsis on hand. A dreamy cashier nurses a boombox from which soulful ballads in Arabic waft out sadly as an overhead fan keeps the flies circulating.

There's only one regular flight in and out of Malakal each week. I have resolved – after many prior long telephone conversations from Khartoum to Kosti and Mr Fareed of the River Transport Corporation – to get a barge back from Malakal north to Kosti, and then continue onwards to Khartoum by road, rather than wait an entire seven days for the next flight out. It has not been easy to get the necessary permits in Khartoum, and I've been warned that the barge schedules are at the very best approximate.

In Malakal, there's more tedious and largely inexplicable bureaucracy; I while away the gaps between visits to sundry elusive officials, including no less than five calls on the Army base, by reading an enormous three-volume history of the British Empire by James Morris within the quiet confines of the United Nations guesthouse. A 7:30 p.m. curfew ensures that even if there were any nightlife (and I strongly suspect there is not much) I would not be able to take advantage of it.

It has only been recently that, after twenty years of war, passenger steamer services on this stretch of the White Nile have tentatively resumed. The reach, 520 km in length, runs through the very heart of Sudan – joining North and South – and since Burton and Speke discovered the source of the White Nile in the nineteenth century it has been the principal route of communication from Arab and Muslim-dominated Northern Africa to sub-Saharan Africa. The grand old steamers that used to run all the way from Khartoum to Juba – a spectacular voyage of 1,500 km that typically took ten days – are still tied up, derelict, at the dockyard in Khartoum. Services have been interrupted because the Nile here is bordered on the right bank by territory under SPLM/A (Dinka) control, and on the left by the government-aligned Shillook Kingdom, whose king still reigns. Since October 2002 a truce has held, and five or six steamer runs have now been made in both directions. The World Food Programme has also taken advantage of the ceasefire to ship in relief supplies that it would otherwise have had to fly in at enormous expense.

The word "steamer" is misleading. A diesel-powered "pusher" typically assembles four or five enormous flat-topped steel barges before it, which are (rather haphazardly) lashed together and which serve as a kind of floating city for the miscellaneous cargo and populace that wish to make the trip – three to four days downstream, five to six up.

On my voyage, which begins at noon three days later than scheduled, there are about six hundred people on board the flotilla, plus a hundred goats and fifty or sixty long-horned Dinka cattle, all moving downstream at a stately walking pace. All life is here: there is an informal barber shop in one corner of the barge, cooking fires everywhere, a shisha pipe corner, a bible study class, tinny music coming from radios; even a (human) baby is born, on the second day out. After three days the goats, who have long since exhausted their fodder, are munching on the wooden hatches.

Water is taken straight from the Nile (probably not recommended), and sanitary facilities are predictably Dickensian. As the first hawaija to ride the *Wad Nijoomi* (named after a Mahdist general who inflicted a major defeat on the British in 1883) in twenty years, I inevitably attract a good degree of attention. The positive (if somewhat embarrassing) side of this is that there is no question that I should occupy anything less than the captain's cabin, which actually has a fan. I'm also deferentially presented with the only chair on board, a purple plastic lawn chair, which I place by the port rail. At night I can make out the Southern Cross low on the horizon, dead astern, and the Great Bear much higher and ahead.

Although the security situation is much improved, the government military are clearly not entirely confident. A squad of about thirty infantry travels with the pusher; on the top deck they mount two machine guns, and at the bows of the leading barge a heavy mortar – all pointing starboard (the SPLM/A side of the river). Their metal ammunition box has the date 1942 stamped on it. However, it is a measure of the new degree of relaxation that we stop at several villages flying the SPLM/A flag and that at one the Army goes ashore, without their weapons, to buy sacks of charcoal for onward resale in Kosti (the Sudanese Army seems sometimes to subsist largely on the trading capacities of its men).

As almost everywhere in Sudan, there is also perceptible ethnic tension along this route, exacerbated by competition for scarce resources. The nomadic Salim people, who normally confine themselves to the Shillook Kingdom on the left side of the bank (moving to the river in the dry season, inland in the wet season) are finding grazing increasingly scarce and are starting, with their distinctively coloured cattle, to cross to the Dinka side – with new conflicts resulting.

Along the river we stop at twenty or so communities, each greeted with a blast on the truck horn mounted on the pusher's bridge. There is not one single secondary school within reach, and only a handful of bush primary schools. In fairness to the government, this area has never been developed – for which the British colonial masters (until 1956) must take heavy blame. An old Shillook man who travels with me recalls independence day and asks me rhetorically: "Do you know how many university graduates there were in South Sudan on that day? Three. And how many secondary schools? One."

North of Monja, on the left bank, we pass the stranded and rusting hulk of an old steamer. "The Anuak," my friend goes on. "It was on its way north some time in the early 1960s, carrying away sacred artefacts of our people. There was a great storm, it was struck by lightning and burned down to the waterline. We're right on the northern limit of the Shillook Kingdom now."

Approaching Kosti, three days out from Malakal, we start to make out in the far distance clouds of smoke from the enormous Kenana sugar plantation, irrigated by massive canals and pumping stations that have literally turned the desert to shimmering green. Kenana may be an all-too-rare example of a commercially successful Sudanese agricultural scheme, but my companion again sadly remarks: "That scheme was supposed to have been built 400 km south of here at Melut; it was Nimeiri who decided we Southerners didn't deserve it ..." Melut is in the news again these days because of a reported oil strike; we will see if this brings any more prosperity to the South than Kenana or the conflictive oilfields to the west.

Oil is only the most recent strategic interest hereabouts. I ask about the ancient and rusting hulks I had seen littering the waterfront at Malakal, all with the acronym EID. There was a huge rusting diesel engine on its side

Another northbound barge overtakes the *Wad Nijoomi*

(made in Ashton Under Lyne) and a three-ton crane of Lanarkshire steel (made by Butters of Glasgow). Further inland there were crumbling villas with the same legend; they looked as though they had not been inhabited for thirty years. There was even an empty swimming pool, its white tiles cracked and stained, its bottom obscured by dead leaves and old junk.

These, I am told, are the assets and installations of the Egyptian Irrigation Department, which has had a significant presence in Malakal since 1927. But this is no development program by Egypt for impoverished Southerners and now gone to seed. Rather, the Egyptians have been here all this time (they are still here, but with a very low profile) for one purpose only: to measure the flow of the Nile.

Due to its location at the Nile's exit from the Sudd, Malakal is a key location for predicting the amount of water that each year, with the rains, will reach Egypt and the Aswan High Dam; it is an interesting measure of how

FAR IN THE WASTE SUDAN

obsessed Egypt is with the security of the Nile waters that it would maintain this distant outpost for so long and at such expense (I was reminded of visits I had made to the various ancient Nilometres in Upper Egypt, which five thousand years ago were anxiously consulted in the same way and which were used to predict crops and thus calculate taxation rates).

One stop on our voyage is the small village of Kodok, on the left bank, formerly known as Fashoda. Here, flush from his devastating victory at Omdurman, Kitchener of Khartoum appeared one day in 1898 at the head of a flotilla of gunboats. One of his captains was David Beatty, who would later attain glory at Jutland.

Kitchener came to face down an impudent young French captain called Marchand, who had the temerity to raise the French flag here and claim all of Equatorial Sudan, thus securing for France an axis across Africa (and blocking Britain's longed-for Cape to Cairo route). For a few days, it looked as though the scramble for Africa could result in an all-out war between France and Britain. But Marchand, who commanded at best twenty men, understandably blinked in the face of Kitchener's fleet and packed his bags. Gunboat diplomacy in its heyday.

There is nothing to recall Marchand. I am told that there used to be a monument to him at Kaka, a few more kilometres down river, but that some overzealous Muslim governor – "one of Turabi's people," said my Shillook friend – had it destroyed, only a few years back.

Theodore Roosevelt, twenty-sixth president of the United States, was another notable traveller on this stretch of the Nile a century ago (in 1910). "One night," he wrote in his journals, "we sat on deck and watched the stars and the dark, lonely river. The swimming crocodiles and plunging hippos made whirls and wakes of feeble light that glimmered for a moment against the black water. The unseen birds of the marsh and the night called to one another in strange voices. Often there were grass fires, burning, leaping lines of red, the lurid glare in the sky above them making even more sombre the surrounding gloom." Kodok today is a gathering of fifty or so straw tukuls – but still evocative as the sun sets, the hippos begin to grunt, the cattle egrets and Marabou storks fly home, and wood-fire smoke settles over the darkening waters of the great river.

These are days of hope for Sudan. As the *Wad Nijoomi* advances through what as recently as six months ago had been a Heart of Darkness, leaving a pall of oily diesel smoke to drift away in the heat over the Sudd, I can sense in the vibrancy of life onboard a cheering optimism.

These are enterprising and resilient people: survivors. But they are living in a place that has these past two decades receded far back into history. In many ways this land had been more developed and accessible in the time of Kitchener than it is now. For all its remoteness, opaque external interests still cast long shadows over this distant reach of the Nile.

ACKNOWLEDGMENTS

The author acknowledges with gratitude the permission of the Hon. Roy MacLaren to draw upon and quote from his *Canadians on the Nile* (UBC Press, 1978), the authoritative work on a little-known period of Canadian military history. He also wishes to thank Foreign Affairs Canada for posting him to Khartoum, and friends, colleagues, and superiors within Foreign Affairs for encouraging him, without fear of reprimand, to travel extensively within Sudan and report freely thereon. Most especially, he would like to thank the multitude of Sudanese and of expatriate aid and development workers who made him at home wherever he went and who are still working tirelessly and selflessly for a better Sudan.

All royalties from the sale of this volume will be donated to the Canadian non-governmental organization, the Fellowship for African Relief (FAR).

CHRONOLOGY OF MODERN
SUDANESE HISTORY

1955   Disorder breaks out in the South on the eve of Sudan's independence from Britain and Egypt; a Southern independence movement known as Anyanya ("poison") emerges.

1956   Sudan becomes independent.

1958   General Ibrahim Abboud leads a military coup against the civilian government elected earlier in the year.

1964   The "October Revolution" overthrows Abboud, and a national government is established.

1969   Jaafar Nimeiri leads the "May Revolution" military coup.

1972   The Addis Ababa peace agreement ends the first civil war: the South becomes a self-governing region.

1978   Oil is discovered by Chevron near Bentiu in Southern Sudan.

1983	Nimeiri divides the South into three regions. Islamic sharia is imposed in the North. Civil war breaks out again in the South, opposing government forces and the Sudan People's Liberation Movement/Army (SPLM/A), led by John Garang.
1984	Thee Chevron workers are killed by the SPLA.
1985	While out of the country, Nimeiri is deposed in a bloodless military coup.
1986	A coalition government is formed after general elections, with Sadiq al-Mahdi as prime minister.
1989	Operation Lifeline Sudan is established.
	Sadiq al-Mahdi is deposed in a military coup led by Brigadier (later Lieutenant) General Omar Hassan al-Bashir; Hassan al-Turabi is thought to be the mastermind. The National Islamic Front (NIF) administration is established – it later changes its name to the National Congress (NC).
	The Lord's Resistance Army (LRA) is created in Uganda.
1990	Twenty-eight military officers are executed in Khartoum for their role in an attempted counter-coup.
	Chevron withdraws from Sudan.
1992	Concorp International acquires Chevron's properties, resells them to State Petroleum, which in turn flips them to Arakis Energy Corporation of Canada.
1993	The USA adds Sudan to its list of State Sponsors of Terrorism.
1994	The Inter-Governmental Authority on Drought and Desertification (IGADD), later to become the Intergovernmental Authority on Development (IGAD) establishes a Standing Committee on Peace in Sudan and presents the warring parties with a draft Declaration of Principles (DOP).
1995	Egyptian President Hosni Mubarak accuses Sudan of being involved in an attempt to assassinate him in Addis Ababa.

1996	The Greater Nile Petroleum Corporation (GNPOC) is formed, comprised of Arakis, CNPC (China), Petronas (Malaysia), and Sudapet (Sudan).
	Sadiq al-Mahdi flees Sudan.
1997	The Sudanese Government accepts the IGAD Declaration of Principles and agrees to discuss self-determination for the South.
	The government, the South Sudan Independence Movement of Riek Machar, and Lam Akol's SPLA-United Movement sign the Khartoum Peace Agreement (April) and the Fashoda Agreement (September). Mainstream SPLM/A continues to fight.
	The USA imposes full economic sanctions on Sudan.
1998	Construction of the oil pipeline to the Red Sea begins.
	Talisman Energy of Calgary purchases Arakis.
	The USA launches a cruise missile attack on the Al-Shifa pharmaceutical plant in Khartoum.
1999	President Bashir dissolves the National Assembly and declares a state of emergency following a power struggle with Parliamentary Speaker Hassan al-Turabi.
	Sudan begins to export oil.
2000	(January) John Harker publishes his report on oil exploration and slavery in Southern Sudan.
	(August) The Canadian Office in Khartoum is opened.
	(October) IGAD talks start again at Lake Bogoria, Kenya.
	(November) Sadiq al-Mahdi returns to Sudan.
2001	(January) SPLA forces under Peter Gadiet attack the Tamur drilling rig.

(February) Hassan al-Turabi arrested and placed under house arrest a day after his party, the Popular National Congress (PNC), signs a memorandum of understanding with the SPLM/A.

(July) The joint Egyptian-Libyan Initiative (ELI) establishes a parallel peace process.

(August) The SPLA launches another attack on the oil installations at Heglig.

(September) The UN Security Council lifts largely symbolic sanctions against Sudan; USA economic sanctions remain.

(October) US President George W. Bush names Senator John Danforth as peace envoy.

2002   (January) The government and the SPLM/A sign the Burgenstock (Switzerland) agreement, providing for a six-month renewable ceasefire in the Nuba Mountains region of south-central Sudan.

(January) Riek Machar realigns with the SPLM/A.

(March) The Khartoum Agreement expires.

(July) The government and the SPLM/A sign the Machakos Protocol, covering self-determination for the South and separation of state and religion, signalling that the end of the nineteen-year civil war is in sight. Under the agreement, Southern Sudan will hold an independence referendum after a six-and-a-half-year power-sharing transition period, while the North is allowed to keep sharia law. A Cessation of Hostilities is agreed upon; further details still to be negotiated.

(October) Talisman Energy announces sale of its share in GNPOC, for USD $750 million.

2003   (February) A new rebel group calling itself the Darfur Liberation Movement (or Front) is launched. Justice and Equality Movement (JEM) rebels also emerge.

(March) Darfur Liberation Movement adopts new name: Sudan Liberation Movement/Army (SLM/A).

(April) – SLM launches concerted attacks on El Fasher and Nyala. Crisis in Darfur begins to deteriorate with widespread displacement, refugees fleeing into Chad, killing, and burning down of villages by government-allied militias (Janjaweed).

(September) Government and SPLM/A sign a security deal, clearing a major stumbling block to peace talks. Government and the SLM/A sign a ceasefire agreement, brokered by Chad, to pave the way for peace talks on Darfur.

(October) Government releases Hassan al-Turabi.

(October) Lam Akol leaves Khartoum for South Sudan and merges his SPLM/A-United faction with the SPLM/A.

(December) Government and SPLM/A negotiators agree in principle on sharing oil revenues.

2004   (January) Government and SPLM/A sign an accord on sharing the country's wealth during the six-and-a-half-year transitional period to follow the signing of a peace deal.

(February) President Bashir formally declares victory over rebel groups in Darfur. The rebel SLM/A and Justice and Equality Movement (JEM) dismiss government claims of victory and launch a new offensive.

(August) With the crisis in Darfur acquiring an ever-higher profile, the United Nations Security Council gives Khartoum thirty days to disarm the Janjaweed militia or face consequences.

(August) Hassan al-Turabi is rearrested on suspicion of involvement with the Darfur insurgency.

2005   (January) Nairobi, Kenya: signature by John Garang and Vice-President Ali Osman Tahaa of a Comprehensive Ceasefire Agreement, ending the North-South civil war.

ACRONYMS

ACF	Action contre la faim: France-based international aid organization
AFEX	Kenya-based catering company
BP	British Petroleum
CARE	An international development and relief agency
CEAWC	Committee to Eradicate the Abduction of Women and Children
CNPC	Chinese National Petroleum Company; one of the four partners in the GNPOC
DC	District commissioner; a senior rank in the British Colonial Service
DLF	Darfur Liberation Front: a rebel movement in western Sudan that emerged in early 2003; the immediate predecessor to the SLM/A
DOP	Declaration of Principles: a 1994 agreement between the Government of Sudan and the rebel SPLM/A, negotiated under the auspices of IGAD
DSO	Distinguished Service Order; a military decoration

DUP	Democratic Unionist Party: an opposition political party that prior to Sudan's independence had favoured union with Egypt
DZ	Drop zone
EDF	Equatoria Defense Force: a pro-government Southern militia, part of the South Sudan Defense Force
EID	Egyptian Irrigation Department
ELI	Egyptian-Libyan Initiative: a peace initiative launched jointly by Egypt and Libya; it made no allowance for the possibility of eventual independence for Southern Sudan
FAO	Food and Agriculture Organization: an agency of the United Nations
FAR	Fellowship for African Relief: a Canadian-based aid organization headquartered in Khartoum
FONM	Friends of the Nuba Mountains: a coalition of mainly Western countries supporting peace and development initiatives in the Nuba Mountains region of Sudan
GIAD	The name of a large industrial complex close to Khartoum, where automobiles and other heavy equipment (including tanks) are manufactured
GNPOC	Greater Nile Petroleum Operating Company: a four-company consortium formed to exploit oil resources in the Heglig region of Sudan; members initially included CNPC of China, Petronas of Malaysia, Sudapet of Sudan, and Talisman of Canada
GOAL	An Ireland-based aid and development organization
HAF	Humanitarian Aid Forum: a forum in Khartoum for interaction between Western donor countries, the United Nations, and non-governmental aid agencies
HMS	Her Majesty's Ship
IDEAS	Institute of Development, Environment and Agricultural Studies
IDP	Internally displaced person
IGAD	Intergovernmental Authority on Development: an East African organization with a mandate for regional integration; headquartered in Djibouti, it comprises the governments of Djibouti, Eritrea, Ethiopia, Kenya, Somalia, Uganda, and Sudan
INGO	International non-governmental organization

IPF	IGAD Partners's Forum: a group of mainly Western countries, including Canada, established to support financially the initiatives of IGAD
IRC	International Rescue Committee: an aid and development organization from the United States
JEM	Justice and Equality Movement: a rebel movement active in western Sudan
JMC	Joint Military Commission: a term used almost interchangeably with JMM (Joint Military Mission); a body, comprising representatives of the Government of Sudan, the rebel SPLM/A, and the international community, charged with overseeing a regional ceasefire in the Nuba Mountains and with running the JMM
JMM	The totality of the multi-agency and multinational mission in the Nuba Mountains
LRA	Lord's Resistance Army: a messianic and cult-like army founded in 1989 in Northern Uganda
MSF	Médecins sans frontières (Doctors without Borders): a now-international aid organization with various national branches (MSF/France, MSF/Holland, etc.)
NAFTA	North American Free Trade Agreement
NC	National Congress Party: the ruling party in Northern Sudan; successor of the NIF
NCO	Non-commissioned officer
NDA	National Democratic Alliance: a coalition of Sudanese opposition parties including the SPLM , the SLM, and the DUP (but not Umma)
NIDs	National immunization days
NIF	National Islamic Front: the coalition of Islamists that seized power in Sudan in a 1989 coup; later renamed the National Congress Party
NMPACT	Nuba Mountains Programme Advancing Conflict Transformation: a program including UN agencies and non-governmental aid organizations
NRRDO	Nuba Relief, Rehabilitation and Development Organization; the aid and development arm of the rebel forces in the Nuba Mountains
OIC	Organization of the Islamic Conference: a grouping of Islamic countries

OLS	Operation Lifeline Sudan
ONGC	India's national Oil and Natural Gas Company
OPEC	Organization of Petroleum Exporting Countries
Oxfam	UK-based aid and development organization
PACTA	Programme for Advancing Conflict Transformation in Abyei: a program including UN agencies and non-governmental aid organizations
PDF	Popular Defense Forces: a government-loyal militia group; sometimes also known as "mujahadeen"
PNCP	Popular National Congress Party: a breakaway Islamist party led by Hassan al-Turabi
PRI	Partido Revolucionario Institucional: a major political party in Mexico
RASS	Relief Association of South Sudan: initially the relief arm of the SPDF, now merged with the SRRA to form the SRRC
RFI	Radio France International
RM	Royal Marines
SEMA	Special Economic Measures Act: an Act of the Canadian parliament
SLM/A	Sudan Liberation Movement/Army (political and military wings, respectively); not to be confused with the SPLM/A
SPDF	Sudan People's Defense Force: a South-based army, traditionally Nuer-dominated, formed by Riak Machar in 2000 when he left the government; the SPDF later merged with the SPLM/A
SPLM/A	Sudanese People's Liberation Movement/Army (political and military wings, respectively); the principal rebel grouping in South Sudan
SRRA	Sudan Relief and Rehabilitation Agency: the aid and development arm of the SPLM/A, later known as the SRRC
SRRC	Sudan Relief and Rehabilitation Commission: successor to the SRRA, following the latter's merger with RASS
SSCC	Southern States Coordination Council: a shadow cabinet for South Sudan, based in Khartoum and with the support of the Government of Sudan
SSDF	South Sudan Defense Force: headquartered in Juba, the government-loyal armed wing of the SSCC; commanded by Paulino Matiep
SSIM	South Sudan Independence Movement: Nuer-dominated militia, initially led by Riak Machar, who split from the SPLM/A in 1991 to

form the SPLM/A-Nasir/United; in 1994 Riak became leader of the SSIM/A, and Lam Akol took the name of SPLM/A-United for his faction in west-central Upper Nile; in 1995 Riak and Garang signed a ceasefire and agreed to reintegrate their forces, but in April 1996 Riak signed a deal with the government and in 1997 the SSIM/A merged with those rebel factions who signed the April 1997 Khartoum peace accord to become the government-loyal SSDF; some SPLM/A aligned factions of the SSIM remained "out"

SSUM   South Sudan Unity Movement: Nuer-dominated government-loyal militia formed in 1998 by Paulino Matiep, incorporating forces from Anyana II with Nuer from SSDF, based around Bentiu and Mankien in Western Upper Nile/Unity State

STAR   Sudan Transitional Assistance for Rehabilitation (US Government aid program)

UNDP   United Nations Development Programme: a UN agency; in Sudan it was in most respects the "lead" UN agency

UNEOG   United Nations Emergency Operations Group

UNICEF   United Nations Children's Fund

UNITA   Angolan rebel movement formerly led by Jonas Savimbi

USAID   United States Agency for International Development

UXO   Unexploded ordnance

WFP   World Food Programme: an agency of the United Nations

INDEX

Alier, Abel, 86, 203–8, 217
Ambrose, Rev. Adi, 77
Amnesty International, 30, 89
Annan, Kofi, 73, 220, 304
Antonov bombers, 38, 64, 148, 159, 165, 166
Anzara, 178
Arakis Energy Corporation, 26–7, 37, 100, 324, 325
archeology, 20, 188–9, 194–7
Arkoweit, 280–2
army of Sudan, 37–8, 41, 47, 49, 53–4, 99, 119, 145, 204–5, 230, 235, 240; and child soldiers, 41–2, 45, 52; in Darfur, 260–3; and forced displacement, 164–7; and LRA, 76, 79
Atbara, 189, 192–3
Awiel, 133, 137, 148, 149, 150, 169
Axworthy, Foreign Minister Lloyd, 5, 31, 33–4, 35, 55
Azhari, President Ismael Ali, 23
Aziz, Abdul, 228, 237, 243–4

Babanusa, 131, 254
Bashir, President/General Omar, 26, 97–8, 101, 103, 112, 113, 115, 117, 171, 195, 267, 291–3, 296–8, 302–5; and coup, 96, 251, 324, 325; and human rights, 96
Beatty, David, 179, 319
Belloc, Hilaire, 192
Bentiu, 25, 39, 41, 45, 51–2, 159, 166, 176, 215, 254, 323
Biel, Tito, 53
bin-Laden, Osama, 9,13, 28, 95, 101, 104, 107, 194, 256, 274, 306–7, 310–11
Bol, Nhial, 93–4
Bolad, Dawood Yahya, 261
bombing. See Antonov bombers
British Embassy, 16,17, 50, 236, 293–4, 308; closure 29

Bruce, James, 196
Buckee, Dr James, 34, 36, 56–7
Burckhardt, John Lewis, 194–5
Burgenstock agreement, 229, 235, 326
Bush, President George W., 302, 326
Bushra, Maj. Gen. Ibrahim, 262
Butler, Capt. William, 191

Cailliaud, Frédéric, 197
Canada, and aid, 92, 125, 128, 135, 154, 214, 216, 222, 226, 230, 237–8, 241, 244, 247, 255–6, 266, 268, 277, 286–7, 313; and business ethics, 44, 57; Canadians at Heglig, 37, 46, 48; government policy and relations towards/with Sudan, 5, 17, 28, 31–3, 38, 55, 71, 100, 102; and LRA, 76–8; and national day festivities, 295; and Nile Basin Initiative, 116; opens/moves office in Khartoum, 35, 308–9, 325; and peace process, 36, 110, 114, 158, 172, 208; pilots, 30; and Turabi, 100; voyageurs with Wolseley, 189–91
Canadian Embassy (Addis Ababa), 17, 35, 291
Capeling, Ralph, 56
CARE, 45–6, 52, 135–6, 138
Carlos ("the Jackal"), 28, 305–306
Carter Centre, 76, 79, 80
CEAWC, 253–4
Chevron Oil, 25–6, 27, 205, 254, 323
child soldiers, 41–2, 150–1, 172–3
Christian Aid, 30
Christian Solidarity International, 29
Churchill, Winston 8, 12, 192
CIDA, 165, 176, 216, 230, 238, 277
CNPC, 26, 54–5, 58, 325
colonial history, 3–4, 7–8, 20, 21–3, 179, 189–92, 198–200, 317–19
Concorp International, 26, 324

MacLaren, Hon. Roy, 191
Magaya, Maj. Gen. Alison Manani, 208
Mahdi, Qutbi al-, 105–7, 119
Mahdi, Sadiq al-, 6, 26, 28, 95, 98, 112–20, 206, 299, 324, 325; and OLS, 60; overthrow, 27, 209, 297, 324, 325
Mahdi, the (Muhammad Ahmad) 3, 4, 8, 62, 112, 190, 192, 200, 260, 282–3
Malakal, 127, 128–31, 215, 296–7, 313–15
Malen Gok, 150
Malok, Elijah, 163, 171
Malual Arop, Martin, 208–11
Malualkon, 169, 174
Malwal, Bona 106, 116
Malwal, Joseph, 208
Mankien, 51–2
Maper, 166, 176
Marchand, Capt., 319
Matiep, Paulino, 39, 42, 45, 49, 53, 211–13
Maygoma, 91–2
Mayom, 39–40, 43, 45
Médecins sans frontières, 46, 129, 135, 143, 144, 164, 175, 177
Meiram, 251–6
Melik, HMS, 179–81, 292
Meroe, 194, 195–7, 198, 201, 289, 307
Merowe, 22, 186, 194
Metemmeh, 190, 198
Mirghani, Ahmed al-, 99, 121–2
Mirghani, Osman al-, 88, 99, 121
Miri Hills, 229, 244
Mokhtar, Mohammed, 39, 41
Morris, James, 20, 315
Mubarak, President Hosni, 28, 101, 324
Muglad, 51, 253
Murrahaleen, 29, 54, 133, 137, 149, 252, 254
Murray, Ambassador Rosaline, 291–2
Musawwarat, 200–2
Museveni, President Yoweri, 74, 78,

Mustafa Ismael, Foreign Minister, 109, 119, 262

Nafie, Nafie al-, 105, 171
Naga, 200–2
National Congress Party, 95, 102–3, 108, 113, 209, 304–5, 324
National Islamic Front (NIF), 26, 27, 95–6, 119, 204, 297, 324
NDA, 85–7, 88–9, 105, 114
Neretiti, 259, 260
Nimeiri, President Jaafar, 25, 28, 95, 96, 220, 297–8, 317, 323, 324
Northern Mountain Helicopters, 37, 49
Norway, government of, 7, 36, 163, 172, 234, 237
Norwegian Church Aid, 138
Norwegian People's Aid, 30, 69
NRRDO, 168
Nuba Mountains, 65, 71–2, 89, 110, 147, 159, 162, 167–8, 171, 173, 208, 220, 227–46, 326
Nubia, 227
Nugdallah, Sara, 119
Nur, Abdel Wahid Mohamed, 262
Nurri, 188
Nyala, 257, 260, 263, 265

OIC, 301–3
oil, development of industry, 5, 25–7, 30, 221; import levels, 26; production, 36; revenues, 100, 106, 110, 134, 157, 205, 327; strategic importance to USA, 115
Okello, Joseph, 85
Okerruk, Martin, 162
Okomo, John Baptist, 77
OLS, 59–74, 154, 324
Omdurman, 16, 18, 21, 112, 184–6, 215; battle, 8, 179–80, 192, 319
Omer, Dr Ibrahim Ahmed, 101–5, 262, 304–5

ONGC, 54–5
Oxfam, 147, 259, 286, 287

Palace, Republican (Khartoum), 20–1, 292–3, 299–300
Parr, Peter, 49, 159, 165–6
Pearson Peacekeeping Centre, 230, 237
Petronas, 26, 54–5, 58, 209, 325
Pharyang, 43–4, 46, 55
Pickwick Club, 17, 33
PNCP, 85, 96–8, 105, 206, 326
poliomyelitis, 267–9
Port Sudan, 11, 26, 36, 42, 62, 142, 189, 276, 281, 284–7
Presbyterian Church of Sudan, 34, 58

Raga, 137, 147, 155, 172
RASS, 146, 176
Reeves, Dr Eric, 30, 54
Renk, 123–8, 138
Rice, USA Undersecretary Susan, 85, 97, 114
Riefenstahl, Leni, 228,
Roseires dam, 123, 220
Rubkona, 41, 45, 49
Rumbek, 147, 153, 155, 157, 161, 163, 164, 165, 170, 172, 175, 176, 177

Sadiq. *See* Mahdi, Sadiq al-
Salah al-Dien, Dr Ghazi, 101, 105, 107–11, 119, 171, 210, 225, 305
Samaritan's Purse, 147, 150–1, 167
sanctions. *See* USA; SEMA
Save the Children, 77, 147, 149, 154, 250, 253
Scroggins, Deborah, 70
SEMA (Special Economic Measures Act), 32
Sennar, 272–3
sharia (customary Islamic law), 5, 28, 96, 98–9, 109, 115, 120, 326

Shendi, 195–6, 198
Sheng el-Tobar, 266
Sheppard, Jackie, 56
Shifa, al-. *See* al-Shifa
Short, Minister Clare, 170
Sim-Sim, 277–80
Slatin Pasah, 260
slavery, 29–30, 250, 253, 254. *See also* abduction; CEAWC
SLM, 262–3, 265, 326, 327
SPDF, 146, 149, 158, 159, 165, 167, 176
SPLM/A, 16, 42, 100–1, 104, 112, 114, 120, 126, 128, 133, 135–6, 137, 144, 147, 150, 159, 166–7, 177, 203, 207, 213, 224; attacks on oilfields, 26, 31, 46,48–9, 50–1, 69, 106, 110–11, 157, 252, 316, 325; and Canada, 35, 38, 55, 150; and child soldiers, 150–1, 172–3; and Christianity, 158, 216; and currency, 157; emergence of 5, 324; and governance, 71, 146–7, 152–3, 156, 160–2, 170, 217; and justice, 160–2, 170; in Nuba, 74 167–8, 228–46; and OLS, 5–60, 65; and peace process, 162–4, 169–70, 214–15; popularity in the USA, 29, 114, 122; and women, 151–2, 216
SRRA, 151, 153, 162, 166, 176, 238
SRRC, 176, 178
SSCC, 211–12
SSDF, 211, 213–14
SSIM, 53, 212
SSUM, 53
State Petroleum, 26, 324
Suakin, 189, 282–4
Sudan Peace Act, 34
Sudapet, 26, 58, 325
Suleiman, Ghazi, 87–9, 107
Suleiman, Lt Gen. Ibrahim , 264
Switzerland, government of, 86, 234, 237, 299